Media and Crime in the U.S.

Sara Miller McCune founded SAGE Publishing in 1965 to support the dissemination of usable knowledge and educate a global community. SAGE publishes more than 1000 journals and over 800 new books each year, spanning a wide range of subject areas. Our growing selection of library products includes archives, data, case studies and video. SAGE remains majority owned by our founder and after her lifetime will become owned by a charitable trust that secures the company's continued independence.

Los Angeles | London | New Delhi | Singapore | Washington DC | Melbourne

Media and Crime in the U.S.

Yvonne Jewkes
University of Brighton

Travis Linnemann
Eastern Kentucky University

Los Angeles | London | New Delhi
Singapore | Washington DC | Melbourne

FOR INFORMATION:

SAGE Publications, Inc.
2455 Teller Road
Thousand Oaks, California 91320
E-mail: order@sagepub.com

SAGE Publications Ltd.
1 Oliver's Yard
55 City Road
London EC1Y 1SP
United Kingdom

SAGE Publications India Pvt. Ltd.
B 1/I 1 Mohan Cooperative Industrial Area
Mathura Road, New Delhi 110 044
India

SAGE Publications Asia-Pacific Pte. Ltd.
3 Church Street
#10-04 Samsung Hub
Singapore 049483

Acquisitions Editor: Jessica Miller
Editorial Assistant: Jennifer Rubio
Content Development Editor: Laura Kirkhuff
Marketing Manager: Amy Lammers
Copy Editor: Rachel Keith
Typesetter: C&M Digitals (P) Ltd.
Proofreader: Dennis W. Webb
Indexer: Jean Casalegno
Cover Designer: Scott Van Atta

Printed in the United States of America

Library of Congress Cataloging-in-Publication Data

Names: Jewkes, Yvonne, author. | Linnemann, Travis, author.

Title: Media and crime in the U.S. / Yvonne Jewkes, University of Brighton, Travis Linnemann, Eastern Kentucky University.

Description: Thousand Oaks : Sage, [2018] | Includes bibliographical references and index.

Identifiers: LCCN 2017009813 | ISBN 9781483373904 (pbk. : alk. paper)

Subjects: LCSH: Mass media and crime—United States. | Mass media and criminal justice—United States. | Crime in mass media.

Classification: LCC P96.C742 U639 2018 | DDC 364.0973—dc23
LC record available at https://lccn.loc.gov/2017009813

This book is printed on acid-free paper.

17 18 19 20 21 10 9 8 7 6 5 4 3 2 1

Brief Contents

Detailed Contents

Acknowledgments

SAGE would like to thank the following reviewers whose input helped shape this book:

Bond Benton, State University of New York at Fredonia

Kevin Drakulich, Northeastern University

Brooke Gialopsos, Mount St. Joseph University

Caryn Horwitz, Miami Dade College

Reginia Judge, Montclair State University

Stephanie Karas, University of Houston–Downtown

Larry Karson, University of Houston–Downtown

Kristin Kenneavy, Ramapo College of New Jersey

Emily Lenning, Fayetteville State University

Jaimee Limmer, Northern Arizona University

Andrew C. Michaud, California State University, Sacramento

Brooke Miller, University of North Texas

Kasey Carmile Ragan, University of California, Irvine

Richard P. Wiebe, Fitchburg State University

Richard Wormser, University of New Haven, Fordham University

James L. Wright, Dalton State College

Introduction

As in so many other areas of social, economic, and political life, it may be true that the United States is exceptional when it comes to the ways in which it communicates about crime, violence, and disorder. A relentless fascination with serial killers, monstrous women, and youth gone mad is enacted across an expansive cultural register. But despite a long, dubious history, crime and media in the U.S. context arguably came into its own with a car chase broadcast live on national television on Friday, June 17, 1994. That morning, Los Angeles Police Department detectives contacted an elite Hollywood attorney named Robert Shapiro to advise him that one of his clients, O. J. Simpson, was wanted for questioning in the murders of his wife, Nicole Brown Simpson, and her friend Ronald Goldman. Later that day, when Simpson failed to surrender to police as arranged by Shapiro, a manhunt ensued. By 5 p.m., local news stations were live-broadcasting the parade of highway patrol vehicles tailing Simpson's white Ford Bronco down stretches of California highway as crowds of onlookers gathered on roadsides and overpasses.

The now-infamous chase served as the opening scene in a spectacular trial that unfolded over the next year and a half, captivating spectators worldwide and laying bare the many limitations of American criminal justice. Billed by many as the "trial of the century," the criminal prosecution and eventual exoneration of the former NFL star undoubtedly served as a blueprint for the many televised criminal trials and crime infotainment programs that have followed. However, we should be careful to note that while the Simpson case unfolded on television in a unique, perhaps unheralded fashion, the American public has long been captivated by the lurid mysteries of violent crime. Even the moniker "trial of the century" predates broadcast television by nearly five decades. From the case of two narcissistic socialites, Nathan Leopold and Richard Loeb, who aimed to commit and get away with the "perfect murder," to the trials of two Italian-born anarchists, Nicola Sacco and Bartolomeo Vanzetti, who were executed in 1927 for the supposedly politically inspired murders

PHOTO I.1
The chase for OJ Simpson and his infamous white Ford Bronco.

of two company guards, the American cultural landscape has long been scarred by high-profile crimes and their attendant courtroom spectacles.

Today, when surveying the U.S. media landscape, it is as though one horrific crime bleeds into the next. In this way, we might say that representations of crime in the U.S. take the shape of what the late cultural theorist Raymond Williams called flow. In a continuous stream of mundane and spectacular crime stories—from newspaper accounts of local arrests, nightly news broadcasts of the day's "top stories," police procedurals "ripped from the headlines," and big-budget Hollywood films to social media feeds and stories shared between friends—crime and its mediated representations perpetually circulate in the whirring background of everyday life. Even today we can trace the cultural reverberations of the Simpson case in the FX miniseries *The People v. OJ Simpson: An American Crime Story* and a multipart installment of the popular ESPN documentary film series *30 for 30* focusing on the intersection of celebrity, sport, and crime. In fact, if we consider that Robert Kardashian gained national prominence as Simpson's attorney, we might say that his daughters' considerable fame flows directly from the notorious trial.

While always in the background, the flow of mediated crime stories also has power to engage the public in new, exciting, and sometimes terrifying ways. For instance, the two bombs that exploded near the finish line of the Boston Marathon on April 15, 2013, exposed the American public's relationship with crime and the media in many of the same ways the chase of O. J. Simpson's Bronco had nearly two decades before. Yet the Boston Marathon also starkly revealed how user-generated content and social media have altered the ways in which crime stories are communicated. The pressure cooker bombs, loaded with gunpowder, nails, and ball bearings and placed in nylon backpacks, were left on the street near the end of the 23-mile route amidst the large crowds of onlookers there to cheer on some 23,000 runners. Claiming the lives of three innocent bystanders and wounding nearly 200 people in total, the explosions set off a spectacular manhunt that stretched across Boston's streets and social media for weeks and a criminal trial that would not conclude for another two years (in 2016, all of this reemerged in the form of a big-budget Hollywood film starring Mark Wahlberg). The following day, with no group claiming responsibility, FBI investigators announced that they were considering a wide range of suspects. So far, regrettably, so familiar.

But as news emerged of CCTV (closed-circuit television) footage taken from a department store located near the scene of the second blast, showing a potential suspect carrying and possibly dropping a black backpack, a brigade of amateur Internet detectives helped to **crowdsource** the investigation. While police had the benefit of sophisticated facial recognition technology, members of the public relied largely upon instinct and perhaps a misplaced sense of civic duty. One group posted a 57-picture array on the website imgur.com focusing on people wearing black backpacks. Likewise, on the social media site Reddit, users created more than 100 threads to host images captured by CCTV or on mobile phones and a dedicated subreddit, r/findbostonbombers, to assist the manhunt. As a Boston police commissioner announced that, at the time of the bombings, "this was probably one of the most photographed areas in the entire country," the police and hundreds of **vigilante viewers** were simultaneously combing through vast numbers of photos and video clips of the bomb scene, before and after the explosions.

Three days after the bombings, the FBI held a press conference showing photographs and security images of two suspects watching the marathon, each wearing a large, dark-colored backpack. Perhaps even more damning, still and video footage showed that the suspects, rather than fleeing after the blasts like the rest of the terrified bystanders, remained at the scene to survey the carnage before calmly walking away. In response to the news conference, additional photographs and video from mobile phones were provided by the public, and a wounded victim who lost both of his legs in the bombings gave a detailed description of one of the bombers to investigators, stating that he saw him place a backpack beside him approximately two and a half minutes prior to the explosion. The suspects were soon identified as Chechen-born brothers Dzhokhar Tsarnaev, aged 19, and Tamerlan Tsarnaev, aged 26. Amidst feverish speculation, more details emerged of the events following the explosions. Shortly after the young men walked away from the scene of their destruction, they killed an MIT policeman, carjacked an SUV, and initiated an exchange of gunfire with the police, during which an officer was injured but survived with severe blood loss. Tamerlan was shot several times in the crossfire, and his brother subsequently ran him over with the stolen SUV as he escaped. He was pronounced dead at the scene. Four days after the bombing on April 19, police found Dzhokhar hiding inside a boat in a backyard in nearby Watertown. Despite his being wounded and unarmed, the police opened fire on the figure beneath the boat's tarpaulin cover, only ceasing fire when ordered to do so by a senior officer. At this point, a crowd had gathered and were snapping photos and taking video footage of the scene. As Dzhokhar climbed out of the boat and was arrested, a police photographer took several images, which he subsequently offered to *Boston* magazine. His motive was reported to be that he wanted to show the real story of what happened and to counter the "fluffed and buffed" rock star image used of Dzhokhar on the cover of *Rolling Stone* magazine (http://www.bostonmagazine.com/news/blog/2013/07/18/tsarnaev/). Of course, images are endlessly interpretable, and many felt that the police officer's photographs showed Dzhokhar in an equally positive light—vulnerable and heroic. The photographer was subsequently suspended from the police and ordered not to talk to the media.

The Boston Marathon bombing raises many points of interest from a criminological and legal perspective, not least being whether the federal death penalty would be applied. Thirty charges were brought against Dzhokhar Tsarnaev (including using a weapon of mass destruction), more than half of which carry the death penalty. The case also raised the question of where execution would be administered, given that Massachusetts had abolished the death penalty in 1984. But from a media-criminology perspective, it is an especially interesting case because of the open access afforded journalists. First, there was the excited amateur sleuthing that took place on social networking sites and then was faithfully reported in the world's media. This quickly tipped over into more dangerous territory with several "suspects" being incorrectly identified and libeled online and in the traditional media. One of the early misidentifications was of a 22-year-old student who had gone missing a month before, having suspending his studies while suffering from severe depression. Users of social media pinpointed this individual as the "stand-out suspect," a claim that was proved wrong—but only after the young man's family had endured several distressing days of speculation and accusation. On April 23, four days after Dzhokhar's capture, the missing student's body was found in a nearby river and identified through dental records. Although the cause of death wasn't immediately known, foul play was not suspected.

Once the brothers had been correctly identified from very clear security camera footage taken the day of the race, there simply was not enough time for the police to control the public's access to their final confrontation with the Tsarnaevs. Social media quickly became inundated with news of developments as they were happening, as the *Chicago Tribune* reported on April 19, 2013:

> It was all happening in a small town near Boston on Friday evening, but social media was the place to be as police in Watertown, Mass., closed in on and then arrested Boston Marathon bombing suspect Dzhokhar Tsarnaev.
>
> @BostonGlobe: Dzhokhar Tsarnaev IN CUSTODY!
>
> @mayortommenino: "We got him"
>
> @SeanKellyTV: Loud applause at end of Franklin Street as SWAT walks out to crowd . . .
>
> UPDATE: Boston Police are asking social media users not to post information they hear on police frequencies/scanner channels.

Boston Police Dept. ✔
@bostonpolice

👤 Follow ∨

Suspect in custody. Officers sweeping the area. Stand by for further info.

RETWEETS 66,928   LIKES 17,707

5:45 PM - 19 Apr 2013

↩ 6.9K   ↻ 67K   ♥ 18K

PHOTO I.2
Boston Police Department uses Twitter to alert residents of the search for the Tsarnaevs.

With the older Tsarnaev dead and the other in custody, police turned toward the brothers' online identities—Facebook and vKontakte (a Russian version of Facebook) pages, Twitter accounts, and YouTube histories—which revealed much about their personalities, histories, and motivations for such a terrible crime. The fact that 19-year-old Dzhokhar seemed fairly ordinary in relation to his older, radicalized brother did little to dampen the furor of public outrage and condemnation. Controversies continued to rage after Dzhokhar was captured, from the FBI's denial of his Miranda rights during questioning to debates about whether, despite being an American citizen, he should be tried as an unlawful enemy combatant, preventing him from any legal counsel. In the end, he was granted a defense attorney, but special administrative measures were imposed, leaving him isolated from communication with his family and lawyers despite there being no evidence to suggest his credibility as a threat in the future (the measures, which were illegal and could have jeopardized the prosecution, were lifted in October 2013).

In the end, the seemingly average young man who, on April 14, 2013, was a college student, part-time lifeguard, and avid skateboarder who hoped to become a dentist, is incarcerated alongside members of al-Qaeda and domestic terrorists such as the "Unabomber" and Timothy McVeigh's co-conspirator, Terry Nichols, while awaiting his eventual execution. Meanwhile, inevitably, conspiracy theories proliferate. Readers' comments in online newspapers, magazines, and blogs tend to articulate conservative, anti-Islam views in various shades of vitriol, but many sites are devoted to alternative versions of events, including troubling theories that the bombing was a "false flag" staged by the U.S. government. This discourse continues to circulate online in forums such as the "Dzhokhar Tsarnaev Is Innocent" Facebook page and throughout social media with easily disseminated memes.

Dzhokar Tsarnaev
INNOCENT

FBI via Getty Images

PHOTO I.3
A social media group alleges the Tsarnaevs' innocence.

THE VOLUME

For media-criminologists, the relationship between crime and mobile/social media is arguably the most important development to have occurred over the last decade—not just in terms of the way news about crime is reported and circulated, but in the ways in which it is produced and gathered too. Recently, we have learned about the lengths to which both journalists and governments will go to gain "secret" information about us. Social media forums have come and gone (MySpace, Bebo), and even the once ubiquitous Facebook and Twitter are being challenged by more instant, personal, time-limited image-and-messaging/blogging sites (Instagram, Snapchat, Tumblr, Flickr, WhatsApp, Pinterest, and the like). No doubt, by the time this book is published, more newcomers will have come onto the scene.

But while means of communication change, the "message" seems remarkably similar. The theoretical frameworks that help us to understand media influence, the contested terrain of moral panics, the media's polarized approach to children as victims and as perpetrators of crime, the frequently misogynistic portrayals of women who offend (and those who are crime victims), the preferred meanings with which the police imbue reporting of crime, the insidious surveillance culture within which most of us live, and the news values that determine which events are considered worthy of being brought to our attention all broadly remain constant. The rise of mobile and social media means that everyday crime news is now more immediate, more visual, and more democratic in terms of its production than at any time previously.

The ubiquity of social/mobile media also means that the stakes have been raised considerably in terms of the level of sensationalism required to gain mainstream media attention. As social media campaigns of the Islamic State (ISIS or ISIL) show, governments' ability to starve "terrorists" of the oxygen of publicity, as British prime minister (1979–1990) Margaret Thatcher once famously put it, has disappeared, at least prior to arrest and conviction. While the Islamic State (or claimed as such) terrorist attacks on Paris, Brussels, Nice, and Berlin in 2015 and 2016 may seem a long way (geographically and conceptually) from the United States, the release in 2014/2015 by ISIS of videos (instantaneously circulated on Twitter and picked up by global media outlets) showing the brutal executions of Western hostages, including two American journalists, brought their "cause" to a shocked U.S. audience. But as this tragic series of events also illustrates, while "Jihadi John" (as the press dubbed one of the chief executioners) and his ISIS comrades are portrayed as caricatured monsters or cartoon villains, it is still the case that the lives of some victims are regarded as more worthy than others. A good-looking, "all-American" hero who "just loved people" and was "afflicted by a chronic need to help" (as he was described in *Rolling Stone;* Ehrlich, 2016), photojournalist James Wright Foley might be said to be an "ideal" victim; certainly his name is now well known in countries around the world. Other executed hostages, including Israeli-American journalist Steven Sotloff, received less attention (despite footage of their murders also going viral on social media) and are consequently less known even in the U.S. Meanwhile, other "Western" victims (among them British humanitarian aid workers David Haines and Alan Henning, Japanese security contractor Haruna Yukawa and journalist Kenji Goto, and French mountaineering guide Hervé Gourdel), may be almost entirely unheard of in the United States.

Such ethnocentric concerns must be addressed head-on at this point, because *Media and Crime in the U.S.* has a particular mission, which we do not want to be misunderstood. Americans—including American media producers and consumers—are frequently accused by scholars elsewhere of parochialism and self-interest. This is not without foundation, but it is also entirely unsurprising: As a rule, the larger and more self-sufficient a country, the more locally focused its media (as well as its economy, its education system, and so forth). The American media simply cannot cover foreign affairs to the extent that they are covered in, say, Holland, the UK, or Italy, when they have so much domestic news to air that is (or is perceived to be) of more immediate importance and direct relevance to the home audience. Meanwhile, with Donald Trump—a former reality TV star and prolific communicator of controversial views on Twitter—taking office as U.S. president as this volume goes to press, it feels as if the world's media is watching America with unprecedented scrutiny. But, as *Media and Crime in the U.S.* is written for students in higher education who, we anticipate, will have inquiring minds, expansive imaginations, and a thirst for knowledge (as well, perhaps, as being well traveled), we believe that a comparative approach is valuable and so, despite its title, this volume will not focus *exclusively* on cases from the United States.

The book is written by two authors, one British (Yvonne Jewkes, from the University of Brighton) and the other American (Travis Linnemann, from Eastern Kentucky University), and it is born out of the success of its original version, *Media and Crime* (first published in 2004 and now in its third edition, 2014, and sole-authored by Jewkes). Despite being primarily focused on criminal cases and their media representations in the United Kingdom, *Media and Crime* found an appreciative audience in the United States, leading its publisher, SAGE, to propose a new version that combines issues, cases, and approaches from the U.S. *and* UK (as well as many other countries, at least tangentially). The aim of this new volume, then, is to engage the reader with case studies that illustrate the similarities and differences between media constructions of crime and justice in two nations that share many aspects of their history, language, culture, and mediascape and yet have significant points of divergence as well. We believe that students of media and crime in the U.S. not only should engage with *global* debates about the power of *global* media, but that they will learn more about their own nation's responses to criminal behavior by understanding it in the context of comparative analysis from the country whose scholarly tradition in the field of media and crime is so intertwined with its own.

Like its preceding UK-based editions, this book includes a number of pedagogic features (overviews, key terms that are highlighted at their first relevant appearance in the chapter, summaries, study questions, suggestions for further reading, and a glossary) which, it is hoped, will make it engaging and accessible—as well as stimulating and intellectually challenging—to students and instructors. But, like other books in the Key Approaches to Criminology series, *Media and Crime in the U.S.* is intended to be much more than an overview of the literature or a teaching text. In addition to going over necessary but well-trodden paths, it is hoped that the book will move key debates forward, develop existing knowledge, and offer new and innovative ways of thinking about the relationship between media and crime (and, indeed, media studies and criminology). The first two chapters provide the foundation for what follows, and many of the themes and debates introduced here are then picked up and developed in relation to specific subjects and case studies in the remainder of the volume. Chapter 1 brings together theoretical analysis from criminology, sociology, media studies, and cultural studies to provide a critical understanding of the relationships between these areas of academic study and to synthesize their contributions to our understanding of the relationship between media and crime. Chapter 2 then discusses the "manufacture" of crime news and considers why crime has always been, and remains, so eminently "newsworthy." The chapter introduces a set of "news values" that shape the selection and presentation of stories involving crime, deviance, and punishment in contemporary news production. Although the chapter concentrates solely on news, these criteria—which alert us to the subtle biases that inform public perceptions of crime—extend beyond the newsroom and underpin much of our mediated picture of crime in the United States.

The next four chapters of the book illustrate the extent to which crime and justice are constructed according to prevailing cultural assumptions and ideologies by examining a number of different issues that have gained significant media attention. Although they are divergent in terms of subject, the overriding theme of the book is that contemporary media deal only in binary oppositions, polarizing public responses to criminals and victims of crime, perpetuating psychically held notions of "self" and "other," and contributing to the formation of identities based on "insider" and "outsider" status. The book thus argues that the media, in all its forms, is one of the primary sites of social inclusion and exclusion, a theme that is explored in Chapter 3 in relation to "moral panics." So influential has Stanley Cohen's *Folk Devils and Moral Panics* been that a book about media and crime could not have omitted the concept he made famous. The moral panic thesis is therefore discussed, but in such a way as to move beyond the faithful rewriting of Cohen's famous study of mods and rockers that is favored by many commentators and to problematize moral panics as they have traditionally been conceived.

Chapter 4 develops the previous chapter's examination of moral panics over youth by considering the degree to which, in today's media landscape, children and young people are viewed both as folk devils and as the victims of folk devils—notably pedophiles. The chapter discusses the extent to which mediated constructions of children in the 21st century are still seen through the lens of 19th-century, idealized images of childhood as a time of innocence—a (mis)representation that only serves to fuel public hysteria when children commit very serious offenses or are themselves the victims of such crimes.

Chapter 5 is also concerned with constructions of offenders that remain curiously embedded in a previous age, only here the focus is on deviant women, especially those who murder and commit serious sexual crimes. Using psychoanalytical and feminist theories, this chapter introduces a psychosocial perspective to argue that the media reinforce misogynist images of females who fail to conform to deeply held cultural beliefs about "ideal" womanhood. For such women, their construction as "others" renders them subject to hostile censure, and their crimes can come to occupy a peculiarly symbolic place in the collective psyche.

Chapter 6 begins by considering how victims, offenders, and the police are constructed through police television crime dramas. The chapter concludes that, in the main, crime narratives are constructed around female victims (usually either very young or elderly) and male offenders (often black, usually strangers), either in the victim's home (increasing the impression of personal violation and female vulnerability) or in public places ("the streets," where we are all at risk), and are investigated and brought to a successful and "just" conclusion by the benevolence of police power. The chapter also discusses some of the incidents that have recently damaged public confidence in the police and looks at their attempts to manage their reputation or control their image through social media networks, including Facebook and Twitter. For the police, new media platforms are a double-edged sword: On the one hand, they permit officers to engage in "open" dialogue with the public; on the other, they can be used to create and circulate ordinary citizens' footage of police misconduct.

Chapter 7 takes up the theme of what representations in films have to tell about the social and political contexts of real policing and changing social attitudes toward crime. Given the many thousands of films that could possibly have been discussed in this chapter, it is of necessity highly selective and rather personal in its scope and content. However, the analysis of the appeal of movies about crime and prisons, the focus on ideal masculine types in these films, the reflections on the potential power of documentaries to influence public opinion about offenders, and the discussion of what cinematic "remakes" have to tell us about changing cultural fears and anxieties are all intended to resonate with themes raised elsewhere in this volume.

Chapter 8 returns to the theme of demonized "others" in its examination of the extent to which surveillance technologies are employed as repressive forms of regulation and social control. The chapter suggests that, despite recent accusations that we are all under constant surveillance in all aspects of our lives, the surveillant gaze falls disproportionately on some sections of society. The representation of surveillance as panoptic is ultimately challenged because, not only does surveillance raise important questions about social exclusion and "otherness" (which are especially meaningful given the preponderance of surveillance images on television and in popular culture), but it also may be regarded as something that is desirable and fun. The numerous references to Facebook and other social media that appear in this volume testify to the fact that we have become a society that likes to be watched.

Much of Chapter 8 inevitably discusses the kinds of surveillance facilitated by the Internet and social media, and Chapter 9 develops this theme with an examination of "cybercrime." The subject of mixed and contested opinion regarding its importance and profile in the broader picture of offending behavior, cybercrime sometimes seems at best intangible to many people. Optimists see computer-mediated technologies as a potential source of democratization, and this chapter discusses examples of the "people power" that has come with mass ownership of computers. However, not only is access to the Internet unevenly distributed across the globe, but it has also become something of an ideological battleground between states and citizens, as the case study of China discussed here illustrates. Furthermore, when we recall some of the arguments made in Chapter 8 and consider the surveillant opportunities that cyberspace brings, we may have mixed feelings about our growing dependence on the World Wide Web.

Chapter 10 attempts to round things off by offering some thoughts and words of caution about conducting research in the field of media-criminology and also by reviewing and reflecting on the key themes and issues that have emerged from the previous chapters. It contends that the media's stigmatization—not only of offenders, but also of those who simply look "different"—is a necessary counterpoint to their sentimentalization and even sanctification of certain victims of the most serious crimes and their families. Without "others," "outsiders," "strangers," and "enemies within," the media would not succeed in constructing the moral consensus required to sell newspapers, gain audiences, and, most importantly, maintain a world at one with itself.

KEY TERMS

- Crowdsource 2

- Vigilante viewers 2

Theorizing Media and Crime

OVERVIEW

Chapter 1 provides:

- An overview of the theoretical contours that have shaped the academic fields of criminology and media studies during the modern period.

- A discussion of the "media effects" debate; its origins, its epistemological value, and its influence on contemporary debates about media, crime, and violence.

- An analysis of the theories—both individual (behaviorism, positivism) and social (anomie, dominant ideology)—that have dominated debates about the relationship between media and crime within the academy.

- An analysis of the theories (pluralism, left realism) that have emerged from within the academy but have explicitly addressed the implications of theory for practitioners and policymakers.

- An exploration of new, emerging theories, which can broadly be called "postmodern," including cultural criminology.

KEY TERMS

- anomie 20
- behaviorism 13
- crime 12
- criminalization 22
- critical criminology 22
- cultural criminology 33
- deviance 12
- effects research 13
- folk devils 19
- hegemony 21
- hypodermic syringe model 17

- ideological 22
- late modernity 30
- left realism 29
- Marxism 21
- mass media 12
- mass society 13
- mediated 28
- paradigm 21
- pluralism 27
- political economy 22
- positivism 15
- postmodernism 30
- psychoanalysis 15
- reception analysis 29
- stereotyping 28

Why are we so fascinated by **crime** and **deviance**? If the media can so successfully engage the public's fascination, can they equally tap into—and increase—people's fears about crime? Is the media's interest in—some would say, obsession with—crime *harmful?* What exactly *is* the relationship between the **mass media** and crime? Students and researchers of both criminology and media studies have sought to understand the connections between media and crime for well over a century. It's interesting to note that, although criminologists and media theorists rarely work together, striking parallels can be found between their efforts to understand and "unpack" the relationships between crime, deviance, and criminal justice on the one hand and media and popular culture on the other. Indeed, it is not just at the inter-face between crime and media that we find similarities between the two disciplines. Parallels between criminology and media studies are evident even when we consider some of the most fundamental questions that have concerned academics in each field, such as "What *makes* a criminal?" and "Why do the mass media *matter?*"

The reason for this is that as criminology and media studies have developed as areas of interest, they have been shaped by a number of different theoretical and empirical perspectives that have, in turn, been heavily influenced by developments in related fields, notably sociology and psychology, but also other disciplines across the arts, sciences, and social sciences. Equally, academic research is almost always shaped by external forces and events from the social, political, economic, and cultural worlds. Consequently, we can look back through history and note how major episodes and developments—for example, Freud's "discovery" of the unconscious, or the exile of Jewish intellectuals to America at the time of Nazi ascendancy in Germany—have influenced the intellectual contours of both criminology and media studies in ways that, at times, have synthesized the concerns of each. In addition, the interdisciplinary nature of both subject areas and their shared origins in the social sciences has meant that, since the 1960s when they were introduced as degree studies at universities, a number of key figures working at the nexus between criminology and media/cultural studies have succeeded in bringing their work to readerships in both subject areas—Stanley Cohen, Richard Ericson, Stuart Hall, Jock Young, Jack Katz, Mark Fishman, and Gray Cavender, to name a few.

The purpose of this first chapter is to introduce some of this cross-disciplinary scholarship and to develop a theoretical context for what follows in the remainder of the book. The chapter is not intended to provide a comprehensive overview of all the theoretical perspectives that have shaped media research and criminology in the modern era—an endeavor that could fill at least an entire book on its own. Instead, it will draw from each tradition a few of the major theoretical "pegs" upon which we can hang our consideration of the relationship between media and crime. These approaches are presented in an analogous fashion with an emphasis on the points of similarity and convergence between the two fields of study (but remember that, in the main, scholars in media studies have worked entirely independently of those in criminology and vice versa). In addition, the theoretical perspectives discussed in this chapter are presented in the broadly chronological order in which they were developed, although it is important to stress that theories do not simply appear and then, at some later date, disappear, to be replaced by something altogether more sophisticated and enlightening. While we can take an overview of the development of an academic discipline and detect some degree of linearity insofar as we can see fundamental shifts in critical thinking, this linearity does not mean that there were always decisive breaks in opinion as each theoretical phase came and went. In fact, there is a great deal of overlap in the approaches that follow, with many points of correspondence as well as conflict. Nor does it necessarily indicate a coherence of opinion within each theoretical position or even any real sense of progress in our understanding and knowledge of certain issues. As John Tierney puts it

> There is always a danger of oversimplification when trying to paint in some historical background, of ending up with such broad brushstrokes that the past becomes a caricature of itself, smoothed out and shed of all those irksome details that confound an apparent coherence and elegant simplicity. (1996, p. 49)

Notwithstanding that what follows is of necessity selective, condensed, and painted with a very broad brush, this chapter seeks to locate the last 50 years of university-taught media studies and criminology—across two continents—within over 100 years of intellectual discourse about the theoretical and empirical connections between media and crime. Our discussion begins with one of the most enduring questions in the field, that of media "effects."

MEDIA "EFFECTS"

One of the most persistent debates in academic and lay circles concerning the mass media is the extent to which media can be said to cause antisocial, deviant, or criminal behavior: In other words, to what extent do the media "make us do things?" The academic study of this phenomenon—effects research, as it has come to be known—developed from two main sources: mass society theory and behaviorism. Although deriving from different disciplines—sociology and psychology, respectively—these two approaches find compatibility in their essentially pessimistic view of society and their belief that human nature is unstable and susceptible to external influences. This section explores how mass society theory and psychological behaviorism gave rise to the notion that media images are responsible for eroding moral standards, subverting consensual codes of behavior and corrupting young minds.

Since the advent of the modern media industry, it is often taken as an unassailable fact that society has become more violent. The arrival and growth of film, television, computer technologies, and social media have served to intensify public anxieties, but there are few crime waves that are genuinely new phenomena despite the media's efforts

FIGURE 1.1

Is there more crime in the U.S. now than there was a year ago? (1989–2011)

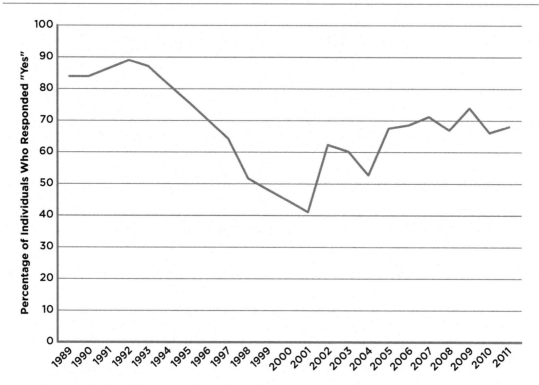

Source: Based on data from Gallup, Inc. and University at Albany Sourcebook of Criminal Justice Statistics.

to present them as such. For many observers, it is a matter of "common sense" that society has become increasingly characterized by crime—especially violent crime—since the advent of the mass media, even though crime surveys show declining rates of offending in many jurisdictions. For instance, the Uniform Crime Reports published annually by the Federal Bureau of Investigation have shown a fairly consistent reduction in rates of violent crime since a peak in 1993 (747.1 per 100,000 in 1993 compared to 386.9 in 2012). Yet, as an annual nationally representative opinion survey shows (Figure 1.1), a large segment of the U.S. public consistently reports that crime is getting worse, not better.

In other words, despite the well-publicized "crime drop," a fairly sizable portion of the American public still believe rates of violent crime to be on the rise, a mythology often blamed on an insufficiently regulated media. Yet, as Pearson (1983) illustrates, the history of respectable fears goes back several hundred years, and public outrage at perceived crime waves has become more intensely focused with the introduction of each new media innovation. From theatrical productions in the 18th century, to the birth of commercial cinema and the emergence of cheap, crime tabloids known as "penny dreadfuls" at the end of the 19th century, to jazz and "pulp fiction" in the early 20th century, popular fears about the influence of text and visual images on vulnerable minds have been well rehearsed. As significant advancements were made throughout the 20th century in photography, cinema, the popular press, television, and, latterly, mobile communication technologies and the Internet, it became common for writers and thinkers to mourn the passing of a literate culture, which was believed to require a degree of critical thinking, and bemoan its replacement, a visual popular culture that was believed to plug directly into the mind of the masses without need for rational thought or interpretation.

Mass Society Theory

Emerging in the latter years of the 19th century and early 20th century, "mass society" became firmly established as a sociological theory after the Second World War. The term usually carries negative connotations, referring to the masses or the "common people," who are characterized by their lack of individuality, their alienation from the moral and ethical values to be gained from work and religion, their political apathy, and their taste for "low" culture. In most versions of the theory, individuals are seen as uneducated, ignorant, potentially unruly, and prone to violence. The late 19th and early 20th centuries marked a period of tremendous turbulence and uncertainty, and mass society theorists held that social upheavals associated with industrialization, urbanization, and the Great War in Europe had made people feel increasingly vulnerable. Within this atomized society, two important strands of thought can be detected. First, it was believed that as communities fragmented and traditional social ties were dismantled, society became a mass of isolated individuals cut adrift from kinship and organic ties and lacking moral cohesion. An increase in crime and antisocial behavior seemed inevitable, and as mass society took hold—in all its complex, overbureaucratized incomprehensibility—citizens turned away from the authorities, who were seen as remote, indifferent, and incompetent. Instead, they sought solutions to crime at a personal, community-orientated, "micro" level, which included vigilantism, personal security devices, and, in some countries, guns. The second significant development that emerged from conceptualizations of mass society was that the media were seen as both an aid to people's well-being under difficult circumstances and a powerful force for controlling people's thoughts and diverting them from political action.

Behaviorism and Positivism

In addition to mass society theory, models of media effects have been strongly influenced by behaviorism, an empiricist approach pioneered by American psychologist J. B. Watson in the first decade of the 20th century. Deriving from a philosophy known as **positivism**, which emerged from the natural sciences and regards the world as fixed and quantifiable, behaviorism represented a major challenge to the more dominant perspective of **psychoanalysis**. Shifting the research focus away from the realm of the mind with its emphasis on introspection and individual interpretation, behavioral psychologists argued that an individual's identity was shaped by their responses to the external environment, which formed stable and recognizable patterns of behavior that could be publicly observed. In addition to emulating the scientific examination of relations between organisms in the natural world, Watson was inspired by Russian physiologist Ivan Pavlov, who was famously conducting experiments with dogs, producing "conditioned responses" (salivating) to external stimuli (a bell ringing). The impact of these developments led to a belief that the complex structures and systems that make up human behavior could be observed and measured and predictions of future behavior made. In addition to stimulus–response experiments in psychology and the natural sciences, developments were occurring elsewhere that took a similar view of human behavior; for example, the modern education system was being established with learning being seen as something to be tested and examined.

Meanwhile, in criminology, the search for objective knowledge through the positive application of science was also having a significant impact. The endeavor to observe and measure the relationship between "cause and effect" led to a belief that criminality is not a matter of free will but caused by a biological, psychological, or social disposition over which the offender has little or no control. Through gaining knowledge about how behavior is determined by such conditions—be they genetic deficiencies or disadvantages associated with their social environments—it was believed that problems such as crime and deviance could be examined and treated. The most famous name in positivist criminology is Cesare Lombroso, an Italian physician who studied the bodies of executed criminals and concluded that lawbreakers were physically different from nonoffenders. He claimed that criminals were atavistic throwbacks to an earlier stage of biological development and could be identified by physical abnormalities such as prominent jaws, strong canine teeth, sloping foreheads, unusual ear size, and so on. Although in more recent years, positivist forms of criminology have become theoretically more sophisticated, Lombroso's rather crude approach to biological criminology is still evident today, particularly in popular media discourses about women and children who commit serious and violent crime (see Chapters 4 and 5).

While criminologists in the early decades of the 20th century were concerning themselves with isolating the variables most likely to be found in criminals as distinct from noncriminals, media researchers were also developing new theories based on positivist assumptions and behaviorist methods. The notion that all human action is modeled on the conditioned reflex, so that one's action is precipitated by responses to stimuli in one's environment rather than being a matter of individual agency, made the new media of mass communication an obvious candidate for concern. Amid rising levels of affluence, advertisers were to become regarded as "hidden persuaders" who could influence people to purchase consumer goods almost against their better judgment. Additionally, experiments were conducted under laboratory conditions to try to establish a direct causal link between media images and resultant changes in behavior, notably an inclination among research participants to demonstrate markedly agitated or aggressive tendencies.

One of the most famous series of experiments was conducted by Albert Bandura and colleagues at Stanford University, California, in the 1950s and 1960s, in which children were shown a film or cartoon depicting some kind of violent act and were then given "Bobo" dolls to play with (these were large inflatable dolls with weighted bases to ensure that they wobbled but did not stay down when struck). Their behavior toward the dolls was used as a measure of the program's effect, and when the children were observed behaving aggressively (compared to a control group who did not watch the violent content), it was taken as evidence that a direct relationship existed between "screen violence" and juvenile aggression. Although these studies were undoubtedly influential and indeed have attained a certain notoriety, they are hugely problematic and have been rejected by most contemporary media scholars on the grounds of their many flaws and inconsistencies. Bandura and his colleagues have been widely discredited for, among other things, failing to replicate a "real-life" media environment; reducing complex patterns of human behavior to a single factor among a wide network of mediating influences and therefore treating children as unsophisticated "lab rats"; being able to measure only immediate responses to media content and having nothing to say about the long-term, cumulative effects of exposure to violent material; using dolls that were designed to frustrate; praising or rewarding children when they behaved as "expected"; and overlooking the fact that children who had not been shown any film stimulus were nevertheless found to behave aggressively toward the Bobo doll if left with it—especially if they felt it was expected of them by the experimenter.

Effects research is sometimes called the **hypodermic syringe model** because the relationship between media and audiences is conceptualized as a mechanistic and unsophisticated process by which the media "inject" values, ideas, and information directly into the passive receiver, producing direct and unmediated "effects" that, in turn, have a negative influence on thoughts and actions. Anxieties about media effects have traditionally taken one of three forms. The first is a moral or religious anxiety that exposure to the popular media encourages lewd behavior and corrupts established norms of decency and moral certitude. A second anxiety, from the intellectual right, is that the mass media undermine the civilizing influence of high culture (great literature, art, and so on) and debase tastes. A third concern, which has traditionally been associated with the intellectual left, was that the mass media represent the ruling elite and manipulate mass consciousness in their interests. This view was given a particular impetus by the emergence of fascist and totalitarian governments across Europe in the 1920s and 1930s, which used propaganda to great effect in winning the hearts and minds of the people. The belief that the new media of mass communications were among the most powerful weapons of these political regimes was given academic attention by members of the Frankfurt School—a group of predominantly Jewish scholars who themselves fled Hitler's Germany for America.

A famous example that appears to support mass society theory's belief in an omnipresent and potentially harmful media and behaviorism's assumptions about the observable reactions of a susceptible audience concerns the radio transmission of H. G. Wells's *War of the Worlds,* which aired on the Columbia Broadcasting System (CBS) on Halloween Night in October 1938. The broadcast was a fictitious drama concerning the invasion of aliens from Mars, but many believed they were listening to a *real* report of a Martian attack. While the broadcast was on air, panic broke out. People all over the U.S. prayed, cried, fled their homes, and telephoned loved ones to say emotional farewells (Cantril, 1940, as cited in O'Sullivan & Jewkes, 1997). One in six listeners were said to have been very frightened by the broadcast, a fear that was exacerbated by the stature of the narrator, Orson Welles, and by the cast of "experts" giving orders for evacuation and attack. As one listener said: "I believed the broadcast as soon as I heard the professor from Princeton and the officials in Washington" (p. 9). This case provides a powerfully resonant metaphor for the belief that the modern media are capable of exerting harmful influences, of triggering mass outbreaks of negative social consequence, and of causing damaging psychological effects. However, to characterize the episode as "proof" of the hypodermic syringe effect of the media would be very misleading. The relationship between stimulus and response was not simple or direct because the panic experienced by some listeners was not without context. It was the time of the Depression, and American citizens were experiencing a prolonged period of economic unrest and widespread unemployment and were looking to their leaders for reassurance and direction. War was breaking out in Europe, and many believed that an attack by a foreign power was imminent. It is of little surprise, then, that the realistic quality of the broadcast—played out as an extended news report in which the radio announcer appeared to be actually witnessing terrible events unfolding before him—powerfully tapped into the feelings of insecurity, change, and loss being experienced by many American people to produce panic.

The Legacy of Effects Research

Scholars in the UK have strongly resisted attempts to assert a direct, causal link between media images and deviant behavior. The same cannot be said for those here in the United States, as researchers and various activist groups continue to search for links between things like video games or music and antisocial behaviors. Still, for many, the idea of isolating television, film, or any other medium as a variable and ignoring all the other factors that might influence a person's behavior is considered too crude and reductive an idea to be of any epistemological value. Much effects research cannot adequately address the subtleties of media meanings, the polysemy of media texts (that is, their being open to multiple interpretations), the unique characteristics and identity of the audience member, or the social and cultural context within which the encounter between media text and audience member occurs. It mistakenly assumes that we all have the same ideas about what constitutes "aggression," "violence," and "deviance" and that those who are susceptible to harmful portrayals can be affected by a "one-off" media incident, regardless of the wider context of a lifetime of meaning-making. Media effects research also tends to ignore the possibility that influence flows in both directions—which is to say that the characteristics, interests, and concerns of the audience may actually hold some sway over what the media produce.

But despite obvious flaws, behaviorist assumptions about the power of the media to influence criminal and antisocial behavior persist, especially—and somewhat ironically—in discussions within the popular media, which are frequently intended to bring pressure on governments and other authorities to tighten up controls on other elements of the media. Of particular salience in the public imagination is the notion that media content may lead to copycat acts of violence. This view is prominently aired when spree killings occur, especially those on school and college campuses perpetrated by disaffected students, and when new films and computer games are released that are clearly aimed at consumers younger than the official age classification awarded them. Assumptions about harmful media effects draw on Lombrosian ideas about the kinds of individuals most likely to be affected. In addition, they dovetail neatly with mass society theorists' fears that institutions such as the family and religion are losing their power to shape young minds and that socialization happens instead via external forces, notably the media. Whether assessing the effects of advertising, measuring the usefulness of political campaigns in predicting voting behavior, deciding film and video game classifications, or introducing software to aid parents in controlling their children's exposure to certain forms of Internet content, much policy in these areas is underpinned by mediacentric, message-specific, micro-orientated, positivist, authoritarian, short-term assumptions of human behavior.

The ongoing political debate about censorship and control of the media tends to periodically reach an apotheosis when serious, high-profile crimes occur, especially those perpetrated by children or young people. There can arguably be no better example of this than the tragic death of a two-year-old child at the hands of two older boys in Liverpool, UK, in February 1993, which continues to have repercussions in political, legal, cultural, and media spheres more than 20 years later (and which will be discussed further in Chapter 4). There was a great deal of speculation in the popular press at the time of the offense that the young murderers (who were age 10) had watched and imitated *Child's Play 3,* a mildly violent American film about a psychopathic doll. Despite there being no evidence that the boys ever saw the film and consistent denials from the police that there was a connection, the insidious features of *Child's Play 3* were soon ingrained in the public consciousness:

> Our gut tells us they must have seen the evil doll Chucky. They must have loved the film. And they must have seen it over and over again, because some of the things they did are almost exact copies of the screenplay . . . We all know that violence begets violence. (*Daily Mirror,* December 1, 1993, quoted in Petley, 1997, p. 188)

Despite the highly questionable evidence for the potentially harmful effects of media content, the proposition that media portrayals of crime and violence desensitize the viewer to "real" pain and suffering, and may excite or arouse some people to commit similar acts, persists in the popular imagination, where it is rarely applied universally but tends to be tinged with a distinct class-edged bias. Echoes of both mass society theory and criminological positivism can be detected in the lingering notion of a threatening "underclass" who pose the greatest threat to society. This view, appealing to commonsense notions of "intelligent people" versus the dark shapeless mass that forms the residue of society, also has a gendered bias. The contemporary culture of blame is frequently directed at the "monstrous offspring" of "bad mothers," a construction that combines two contemporary folk devils and taps into cultural fears of the "other," which will be explored further in Chapters 4 and 5. Consequently, when particularly horrific crimes come to light, the knee-jerk reaction of a society unwilling to concede that depravity and cruelty reside within its midst is frequently to attribute blame to the familiar scapegoat of the mass media.

Another element of the sentiment expressed in the British newspaper quoted above, which also has its roots in mass society theory, concerns a broader preoccupation with the globalization of cultural forms and products and, in particular, the American origin of much popular global culture. Television, film, video, and the Internet have been targets for criticism *outside* the U.S. by those who view anything American in origin as intrinsically cheap and trashy—or worse. In the UK, fears dating back more than a century have become crystallized in the view that the popular media are slowly corrupting the "British" way of life by importing values that are altogether more vulgar from the other side of the Atlantic. The concerns of Frankfurt School theorists Theodor Adorno and Max Horkheimer about the debasement of "high" culture by "low" popular cultural forms found synthesis in the UK with elitist concerns about an American-inspired youth culture in postwar Britain. In a fairly consistent fashion, moral panics have appeared in the UK only months after their appearance in the United States, and a wide range of phenomena— rock-and-roll music, mugging, dangerous dogs, carjacking, satanic child abuse, gun crime, gang warfare, and crystal meth addiction—have been characterized by media as essentially "un-British"—an unwelcome and alien crime wave of American origin (see Chapter 3).

STRAIN THEORY AND ANOMIE

By the 1960s, academic scholars were turning their backs on positivist, behaviorist research, believing that it attributed too much power to the media and underestimated the importance of the social contexts of media consumption, the social structures that mediate the relationship between the state and the individual, and the sophistication and diversity of the audience. Similarly, positivist approaches to explaining crime in terms of its individual, biological roots were giving way to more sociologically informed approaches, which originated in the work of the Chicago School in the 1920s and 1930s. The overriding concern of Chicago School sociology was to understand the role of social environment and social interaction on deviant and criminal behavior. In other words, it was recognized that where people grow up and who they associate with is closely linked to their likelihood of involvement in crime and antisocial behavior.

Limitations of space preclude a full discussion of sociological approaches to crime here, but one important early theory that has a bearing on the present discussion of the relationship between media and crime is Robert Merton's (1938) strain theory, or anomie. Like mass society theory, strain theory takes as its starting point a decline of community and social order and its replacement by alienation and disorder. Whole sections of society are cut adrift, unable to conform to the norms that traditionally bind communities together. Yet, within this state of normlessness, society as a whole remains more or less intact. Social cohesion may be partly accounted for by the pursuit of common objectives, and anomie draws attention to the goals that people are encouraged to aspire to, such as a comfortable level of wealth or status, and their means of attaining those goals; for example, hard work. Through socialization, most come to accept both the goals *and* the legitimate means of achieving them, a process summed up in the notion of the "American Dream." But anomie describes a situation where a society places strong emphasis on a particular goal but far less emphasis on the appropriate means of achieving it. It is this imbalance that can lead some individuals, whom Merton terms "innovators," to pursue nonconformist or illegal paths to achieve the culturally sanctioned goals of success and wealth and is one of the key factors involved in the internalization of cultural goals is the media that, it might be argued, instill in people needs and desires that may not be gratifiable by means other than criminal. The anomic drive might thus be less concerned with feelings of desperation and have more to do with conspicuous consumption and the desire for peer approval. Some researchers even suggest that strain theory may help to explain serial killing, arguing that the growth of the American economy since the 1960s has resulted in a commensurate rise in the numbers of serial killings. Inevitably, some sections of the population will be excluded from the general rise in living standards, which, in a culture that glorifies violence, may lead some disaffected individuals to a (usually misdirected) desire for revenge (Coleman & Norris, 2000).

Anomie has fallen in and out of favor with remarkable fluidity over the years, but from its nadir in the 1970s, when Rock and McIntosh referred to the "exhaustion of the anomie tradition" (Downes & Rock, 1988, p. 110), it has recently enjoyed something of a revival thanks to two diverse phenomena. The first is the emergence of interest within cultural criminology in transgressive forms of excitement, ranging from extreme sports to violent crime, as a means of combating the routinized alienation that besets contemporary life. The second is the growth of the Internet and social media, which seem to offer a solution to the problems of dislocation by fostering a sense of community across time and space. In the world of virtual reality, anomie is both "a condition and a pleasure" (Osborne, 2002, p. 29).

MARXISM, CRITICAL CRIMINOLOGY, AND THE "DOMINANT IDEOLOGY" APPROACH

It is clear from the discussion so far that the mid-20th century saw a change in focus from the individual to society. This **paradigm** shift led to the predominance of Marxist-inspired models of media power and, in particular, to the writings of Karl Marx (1818–1883) and Antonio Gramsci (1891–1937). Their theories of social structure led to the development of an approach known as the "dominant ideology" model, which was taken up enthusiastically by both criminologists and media researchers in the 1960s and dominated academic discussions of media power for over 20 years.

Marxism proposes that the media—like all other capitalist institutions—are owned by the ruling bourgeois elite and operate in the interests of that class, denying access to oppositional or alternative views. Although the media were far from being the mass phenomena in Marx's lifetime that they are today, their position as a key capitalist industry, and their power to widely disseminate messages that affirm the validity and legitimacy of a stratified society, made his theories seem very relevant at a later time when the mass media were going through a combined process of expansion, deregulation, and concentration of ownership and control. Gramsci developed Marx's theories to incorporate the concept of **hegemony**, which has played a central role in theorizing about the media's portrayal of crime, deviance, and law and order. In brief, hegemony refers to the process by which the ruling classes win approval for their actions by consent rather than by coercion. This is largely achieved through social and cultural institutions such as the law, the family, the education system, and of course, the media. All such institutions reproduce everyday representations and meanings in such a way as to render the class interests of those in power apparently natural and inevitable. The media thus play a crucial role in the winning of consent for a social system, its values, and its dominant interests, or in the rejection of them. This is an important refinement of Marx's original formulation, for Gramsci dispensed with the idea that people passively take on, in toto, the ideas of the ruling elite (a position usually termed "false consciousness"), and instead established a model of power in which different cultural elements are subtly articulated together to appeal to the widest possible spectrum of opinion.

The writings of Marx and Gramsci inform the theoretical organization of much of the most important and influential work that emerged within the social sciences in the 1970s and 1980s. For example, although Marx himself had little to say about crime, the rediscovery of his theories of social structure gave impetus to a new "radical" criminology that sought to expose the significance of the impact of structural inequalities upon crime and, crucially, upon **criminalization**. Also drawing heavily on labeling theory, which posits that crime and deviance are not the product of either a "sick individual" or a "sick society" but that "deviant behavior is behavior that people so label" (Becker, 1963, p. 8), were a new generation of radical criminologists such as British scholars Ian Taylor, Paul Walton, and Jock Young, who in their hugely influential *The New Criminology* (1973) took this proposition and gave it a Marxist edge, arguing that the power to label people as deviants or criminals and prosecute and punish them accordingly was a function of the state. In other words, acts are defined as criminal because it is in the interests of the ruling class to define them as such, and while the powerful will violate laws with impunity, working-class crimes will be punished.

Inspired by the "new criminology," a number of further "radical" studies emerged that drew attention to the criminogenic function of the state and the role of the media in orchestrating public panics about crime and deflecting concerns away from the social problems that emanate from capitalism. This work became known as **critical criminology**, and of particular importance are Stuart Hall, Chas Critcher, Tony Jefferson, John Clarke, and Brian Roberts and their book *Policing the Crisis: Mugging, the State and Law and Order* (1978/2013). Again emerging from the UK, *Policing the Crisis* remains one of the most important texts on the **ideological** role of the media in defining and reporting crime and deviance. In media research, the work of the Glasgow University Media Group (GUMG) is also of note. The GUMG produced a series of "Bad News" studies based on empirical and semiotic analysis, looking at bias in television news coverage of industrial conflicts, political disputes, and acts of war. The central finding in these studies is that television news represses the diversity of opinions in any given situation, reproduces a dominant ideology (based on, for example, middle-class, anti-dissent, and pro-family views), and silences contradictory voices.

Another important perspective that influenced studies of media power throughout the 1980s and beyond was the **political economy** approach, which claims that the undisputed fact of increasing concentration of media ownership in recent years makes Marx's analysis all the more relevant to contemporary debates about the power of the media.

Political economy focuses on relations between media and other economic and political institutions and argues that, since the mass media are largely privately owned, the drive for profit will shape their output and political position. Concentration of ownership, it is suggested, leads to a decline in the material available (although there are more channels in which to communicate), a preoccupation with ratings at the expense of quality and choice, and a preference for previously successful formulae over innovation and risk-taking. The net result of these processes is that the material offered is reduced to the commercially viable, popular, easily understood, and largely unchallenging.

Some writers go as far as to suggest that the "dumbing down" of culture is part of a wider manipulative strategy on the part of the military-industrial complex to prevent people from engaging in serious political thought or activity. For example, Noam Chomsky's "propaganda model" demonstrates how certain stories are underrepresented in the media because of powerful military-industrial interests. In a content analysis of the *New York Times,* he shows how atrocities committed by Indonesia in East Timor received a fraction of the coverage devoted to the Khmer Rouge killings in Cambodia. Chomsky claims that the reason for this imbalanced coverage is that the weaponry used to slaughter the people of East Timor was supplied by America, Britain, and Holland (Herman & Chomsky, 1992).

There are countless other examples that could be drawn on to make the point that, when it comes to global power structures, the media are highly selective in what they report. On the other hand, it is sometimes the case that journalists go where politicians fear to tread. The diplomatic protocols surrounding East–West relations, and the shifts in global power that have taken place over the last two decades, have resulted in a situation where leaders in the West have become cautious about criticizing other nations' human rights records. The news that then-president Barack Obama canceled a visit by the Dalai Lama to "keep China happy" (Spillius, 2009) was treated with scorn by many news outlets, who recalled that 18 months earlier, Obama had lobbied his predecessor, George W. Bush, to boycott the Beijing Olympics opening ceremony in protest of the bloody repression of a popular uprising in Tibet. Time will tell the extent to which Donald Trump is allowed to continue tweeting in a personal capacity his vociferous criticism of China, but his outburst at the end of 2016 criticizing China's military and economic policies, while he was still president elect, suggests that the rift between America and China might be widening—though Marxists might say that Trump has his own ideological agenda and that his use of social media illustrates that he puts protecting his business interests and celebrity status above the potential diplomatic and trade interests of the nation.

Although not without their critics, the Marxist-inspired works discussed in this section were among the first to systematically and rigorously interrogate the role of the media in shaping our understanding, not only of crime and deviance but also of the processes of criminalization. The common theme in all these studies is that information flows from the top down, with the media representing the views of political leaders, military leaders, police chiefs, judges, prominent intellectuals, advertisers and big business, newspaper owners, and vocal opinion leaders. At the same time, they reduce the viewer, reader, or listener to the role of passive receiver, overshadowing his or her opinions, concerns, and beliefs. Thus, a hierarchy of credibility is established in which the opinions and definitions of powerful members of society are privileged while the "ordinary" viewer or reader is prevented by lack of comparative material from engaging in critical or comparative thinking (Ericson, Baranek, & Chan, 1987).

This structured relationship between the media and its "powerful" sources has important consequences for the representation of crime, criminals, and criminal justice, particularly with respect to those whose lifestyle or behavior deviates from the norms established by a white, male, heterosexual, educationally privileged elite. For example, in *Policing the Crisis* (1978/2013), Hall and his colleagues demonstrate how the press significantly overreacted to the perceived threat of violent crime in English cities in the early 1970s and created a moral panic about "mugging," but only *after* there had been an intensification of police mobilization against black offenders. The net result of these forces—public fear and hostility fueled by sensationalized media reporting and heavy-handed treatment of black people by the police—combined to produce a situation where more black people were arrested and sentenced, which in turn set the spiral for continuing media attention. But as Hall and his colleagues explain, this episode can be set against a backdrop of economic and structural crisis in 1970s Britain, whereby the disintegration of traditional, regulated forms of life led to a displaced reaction onto black and Asian immigrants and their descendants. The central thesis of the book is that by the 1970s, the consent that might previously have been won by the ruling classes was being severely undermined and the state was struggling to retain power. The birth of the "law and order" society, evidenced in the development of a preemptive escalation of social control directed at a minority population, served to divert public attention from the looming economic and structural crisis, crystallize public fears in the figure of the black mugger, create a coherent popular discourse that sanctioned harsher criminal punishments, and ultimately justify the drift toward ideological repression. All these developments were disclosed, supported, and made acceptable by a media that had become one of the most important instruments in maintaining hegemonic power. Of course, the conditions identified by Hall and colleagues parallel developments in the U.S., where deindustrialization, job loss, and rising inequality were conflated with, if not positioned oddly, as the effects of the mid 1980s "crack epidemic" (Reinarman & Levine, 1997).

Critics of the Marxist approach suggest that it overstates the *intent* of powerful institutions to deceive the public; that it is not the case that media industries maintain a policy of *deliberately* ignoring or marginalizing significant portions of their audience. Rather, the apparent deception may be attributed to an underlying frame of mind that characterizes news organizations (Halloran, 1970). In other words, journalists are like those who work within any organization or institution in that they are gradually socialized into the ways and ethos of that environment and come to recognize the appropriate ways of responding to the subtle pressures that are always there but rarely become overtly apparent. In a news room, these "ways of responding" range from the individual reporter's intuitive "hunch" through perceptions about what constitutes a "good story" and "giving the public what it wants" to more structured ideological biases that predispose the media to focus on certain events and turn them into "news." But those who support the idea of hegemony maintain that alternative definitions of any given situation may not get aired simply because there is no longer the spread of sources that there once was. The ownership and control of the mass media is concentrated in the hands of fewer and fewer individuals, and editors rely on a relatively limited pool of expert and readily available sources. Presently, the vast majority of television, newspapers, radio, and film in the U.S. is controlled by a handful of companies. These official sources and accredited "experts," together with the journalists themselves, thus become the "primary definers" of much news and information—a kind of deviance-defining elite (Ericson et al., 1987). Consequently, according to proponents of the "dominant ideology" approach, there is an increasing risk that culturally dominant groups impose patterns of belief and behavior that conflict with those of ethnic, cultural, and religious minorities. Feminists have argued that gender inequalities in society are also reproduced ideologically by a patriarchal media industry, an issue that will be examined further in Chapter 5.

The Legacy of Marxism: Critical Criminology and Corporate Crime

As we have seen, the dominant ideology approach has successfully highlighted the extent to which those in power manipulate the media agenda to harness support for policies that criminalize those with the least power in society. But Marxist-inspired criminologies have also been useful in raising awareness of the crimes of the powerful themselves; in other words, the offenses committed by corporations, businesspeople, politicians, governments, and states. Critical criminologists whose intellectual roots lie in Marxism have noted that the media rarely cover "white-collar" or "corporate" crime unless it has a "big-bang" element and contains several features considered conventionally newsworthy (see Chapter 2). Their reluctance to portray corporate wrongs contrasts with the manufacturing of "street" crime waves and reflects a pervasive bias in the labeling of criminals. Although this inclination extends beyond the media and arguably constitutes a collective ignorance toward corporate crime on the part of all social institutions, there is little doubt that the media are among the most guilty in perpetuating very narrow definitions of crime. In fact, the media might be said to be doubly culpable: first for portraying affluence as the ultimate anomic goal and glamorizing images of offending and, second, for pandering to public tastes for drama and immediacy over complexity. To paraphrase Steven Box, the public more easily understands what it means for an old lady to have five dollars snatched from her purse than it grasps the financial significance of corporate crime (1983, p. 31).

Criminologists have sought to redress this imbalance and to expose the crimes of governments and corporations. For example, Steve Tombs and Dave Whyte (2007) have estimated that 2 million people are killed at work each year. With the exception of high-profile cases, such as the gas leak at Bhopal, India, in 1984 or the collapse of the eight-story Rana Plaza clothing factory building near Dhaka, Bangladesh, in 2013, both of which killed thousands of people, crimes that have occurred as a result of corporate negligence fail to attract a great deal of interest. Even the reported deaths of more than 1,000 migrant workers on Qatar building sites, as the Gulf state prepares to host the FIFA World Cup in 2022, has received a fraction of the media coverage devoted to other issues, including the heat in which the qualifying soccer teams will be expected to play in. Like allegations of corruption and bribery, claims that migrant slave labor is being used to build the infrastructure for this global sporting event may become prominent in the news only if the decision to hold the event in Qatar is reversed—and it would still be unlikely to make much of a splash in the U.S., where soccer is still a relatively minor sport.

But as Chapter 2 will demonstrate, crime is by and large portrayed by the media as a matter of individual pathology and moral failings, which militates against the investigation and reporting of wrongdoings in a large organization. On the whole, corporate crimes are not the stuff of catchy headlines and tend to be reported, if at all, in such a way as to reinforce impressions of their exceptional nature and distinction from "ordinary" crime. The underdeveloped vocabulary of corporate crime compounds the difficulty of regarding it as an offense. Words such as "accident" and "disaster" appear in contexts where "crime" and "negligence" might be more accurate. Where they succeed in making the news agenda, corporate crimes are frequently treated not as offenses but as "scandals" or "abuses of power," terminology that implies "sexy upper-world intrigue" (Punch, 1996). Alternatively, they may be presented as "acts of God," thus reinforcing the notion that modern life is beset by risks and that actions that result in casualties and/or fatalities are random or preordained, depending on your religious convictions. The choice of this kind of language not only serves the purposes of a commercial media steeped in circulation and ratings wars but also suits corporations themselves, who are able to secure powerful political allies and carefully control and manage information about damning incidents (Herman & Chomsky, 1992). So, while a few journalists uphold the investigative tradition and are prepared to act as whistleblowers when they uncover corporate offenses, the vast majority of media institutions—according to radical crime and media theorists—either ignore the crimes of the powerful or misrepresent them. As a consequence, news reporting remains coupled with state definitions of crime and criminal law.

A related area that does not attract much media attention, although it is a burgeoning field of critical criminology, is "green" crime. A new generation of scholars are examining notions of environmental harm and justice following the publication of a special issue of *Theoretical Criminology* on "green criminology" in 1998. Since then, debates about the meaning of "green" as related to criminology have resulted in a wealth of scholarship that has taken the discipline into new and imaginative areas of concern, including climate change, air and water pollution, genetically modified food, and animal abuse (South & Brisman, 2013; Walters, 2010; White, 2013). Some green criminologists have made dramatic, even apocalyptic, claims about the impacts of environmental harm; for example, predicting that climate change will become one of the major forces driving *all* crime over the course of this century (Agnew, 2012, p. 21). However, like corporate crime more generally, ecological and environmental offenses can be difficult to communicate succinctly, attempts to attribute blame can appear tenuous, and audiences may simply fail to connect with stories about issues that do not necessarily seem to affect them obviously, directly, and immediately.

PLURALISM, COMPETITION, AND IDEOLOGICAL STRUGGLE

The theoretical models outlined so far share a belief in the omnipresence of the media and hold assumptions about a passive and stratified audience, with those at the bottom of the socioeconomic strata being the most vulnerable to media influences, whether they be "effects" caused by media content or discrimination at the hands of a powerful elite that uses the mass media as its mouthpiece. By contrast, the "competitive" or "pluralist" paradigm that emerged during the 1980s and 1990s tends to be a more positive reading of the mass media as an embodiment of intellectual freedom and diversity offered to a knowledgeable and skeptical audience. Given this favorable characterization of the media industry, it is unsurprising that, while the "dominant ideology" perspective has been influential within the academy, pluralism has been championed by practitioners and policymakers.

Pluralists argue that the processes of deregulation, privatization, and technological advancement that have gone on over the last three decades have succeeded in removing the media from state regulation and censorship, encouraged open competition between media institutions, and given media users more individual power. Advocates of these processes have heralded a new age of freedom in which the greatly increased number of television and radio channels, magazine titles, and, particularly, Internet-based networking services have offered a previously unimaginable extension of public choice in a media market of plurality and openness. The result has been that, in addition to the primary definers already mentioned—politicians, police chiefs, and so on—there also exist "counterdefiners," people with views and ideas that conflict with those of official commentators and that are given voice by through various media channels. Consequently, it is suggested that while we can still identify a dominant economic class in an abstract, materialistic sense, it rarely acts as a coherent political force and is consistently challenged by individuals and organizations campaigning for policy changes in areas such as criminal justice. Furthermore, traditional ideological inequalities formed along lines of class, gender, and race no longer inhabit the static positions suggested by those who favor the dominant ideology approach outlined previously. Thanks to higher education, social mobility, the Internet, and the rise of "celebrity culture," the contemporary "ruling class" is more culturally diverse than at any time previously, and the modern media has been at the forefront of the erosion of traditional elitist values (McNair, 1998).

The expansion and proliferation of media channels and the Internet have certainly made more accessible the views and ideas of a greater diversity of people. In the past, the pluralist perspective might have been said to be limited by its sheer idealism because it does not take account of the many vested interests in media ownership and control, or of the fact that, for all the proliferation of new channels, media industries are still predominantly owned and controlled by a small handful of white, wealthy, middle-class men (or corporations started by such men). However, even though the media still may be regarded as a potential site of ideological struggle, proponents of the competitive, pluralist paradigm believe that *all* minority interests can be served by the plurality of channels of communication available. In particular, social media are said to have democratized contemporary cultural life, with Twitter and blogs providing powerful channels of influence and offering a form of public participation to those who traditionally may not have had access to it.

However, social media have also joined competition and deregulation in being said to pose a serious threat to informed media commentary and analysis. Following accusations that in a commercial marketplace, competition for audience share leads to "soundbite" journalism, in which there is little room for background, explanation, or context, those who have not embraced social media despair at the idea of communicating anything meaningfully in 140 characters! Further, it is argued, while there may be greater public engagement with shocking or visually dramatic events, there is little evidence of extensive public participation in the issues of policy, politics, and reform that underlie such stories, or of a media willing to communicate such a context to the public (Barak, 1994; Manning, 2001). Public participation in **mediated** discourse may *appear* to be more inclusive; after all, more people can air their views on the serious issues of the day—not just on Twitter but also via talk radio, television audience shows, newspapers' reader comments, and other online forums. In fact, texting and social media have broadened traditional channels of communication to the extent that television news broadcasts now encourage viewers to send in their thoughts and opinions to be transmitted almost instantaneously on air. But the 20- or 30-second viewer contribution has arguably been introduced at the expense of complex analysis or detailed critique, and *media* pluralism—that is, many channels—does not necessarily result in *message* pluralism—diversity of content (Barak, 1994).

Critics argue that the mainstream media continue to provide homogenized versions of reality that avoid controversy and preserve the status quo. Consequently, ignorance among audiences is perpetuated, and the labeling, **stereotyping**, and criminalization of certain groups (often along lines of class, race, and gender) persists. We might view the resilience of the *National Enquirer* as evidence of homogenized and stereotyping news output. Described by one critic as an "impeccable source for space-alien abductions," the supermarket tabloid is nevertheless nearing its ninth decade of providing American consumers with salacious headlines and dubious information about all facets of social life, including crime (Grochowski, 2002). Political economists would argue that the increasingly commercialized character of media groups like the *National Enquirer* and *E!* results in tried and tested formulae—a focus on entertainment, gossip, and celebrity (much of it misogynistically directed at women's bodies) with a good measure of terrifying stories, frequently involving violent and atypical crimes, thrown in.

The tendency to play it safe by offering the shocking, the sensational, and the "real" is also evident in TV schedules where mainstream programming is dominated by seemingly endless and increasingly stale imitations of once-innovative ideas. Even 24-hour rolling news services are restricted by the news values to which they have to conform (see Chapter 2) and by the pressures of having to succeed in a commercial environment. As Jay Blumler (1991) suggests, while American broadcast news media may have a tradition of professional political journalism, it can nonetheless be the case that "heightened competition tempts national network news . . . to avoid complexity and hit only those highlights that will gain and keep viewers' attention" (p. 207). These "highlights" will rarely involve in-depth political commentary or sustained analysis. Instead, viewers are fed a diet of "infotainment" that may have a strong "human interest" angle, a particularly dramatic or violent element, or a visually arresting component. This trend—often described by its critics as the "dumbing down" of news and current affairs media—privileges audience ratings over analysis and debate and results in "a flawed process of public accountability, with few forums in which issues can be regularly explored from multiple perspectives" (p. 207). Crime is a subject that is especially limited and constrained by a media agenda on an endless quest for populist, profitable programming. One of the few strands of "documentary" filmmaking that has survived the wave of deregulation celebrated by pluralists is the "true crime" genre, where a serious criminal case is reexamined via a predictable formula, starting with a dramatized reconstruction of the crime itself and then a smug-with-hindsight examination of the sometimes bungled, frequently tortuous police investigation before the dramatic denouement when the culprit is captured and convicted. Such programs—which are commonly concerned with highly unusual yet prominent cases involving rapists and serial killers—pander to the thrill-seeking, voyeuristic element of the audience while at the same time quenching their thirst for retribution.

While pluralism has traditionally been viewed as an expression of how things *could* be rather than how things *are,* there is no disputing that Internet-based forums are democratizing communication and allowing more freedom of expression. However, skeptics would argue that the apparent openness that social media afford to their users must be squared with a recognition that dominant groups still enjoy structural advantages and that there are ongoing contested processes both inside social institutions and within the media themselves.

REALISM AND RECEPTION ANALYSIS

Throughout the 1980s, established theories were being challenged by new approaches that turned on their heads some previously held assumptions and altered the focus of scholars in both criminology and media studies. In criminology, a new perspective called **left realism** emerged as both a product of and reaction to what it saw as the idealistic stance of the left, represented in works like *Policing the Crisis* (Hall, Critcher, Jefferson, Clarke, & Roberts, 1978/2013). Accusing writers on the left of adopting reductionist arguments about crime and romanticizing working-class offenders, left realists claimed that the political arena had been left open to conservative campaigns on law and order that chose to overlook the fact that most crime is not interclass (that is, perpetrated by working-class people on middle-class victims) but *intra*class (perpetrated on members of one's own class and community). In the UK, influential writers John Lea and Jock Young (1984) urged criminologists to "get real" about crime, to focus on the seriousness of its effects—especially for women and ethnic minorities—and to make the experiences of victims of crime a focus of their analyses. After all, if there was no rational core to the proposition that crime is a serious problem, the media would have no power of leverage over the public consciousness, and the numerous attempts to theorize the relationship between media and crime discussed in this chapter would simply never have materialized.

Meanwhile, in media and cultural studies, a form of audience research called **reception analysis**, pioneered by David Morley, dominated the agenda throughout the 1980s and 1990s. Researchers reconceptualized media influence, seeing it no longer as a force beyond an individual's control but as a resource that is consciously *used* by people. In the modern communications environment where there is a proliferation of media and the omniscience of any single medium or channel has diminished, most audience members will select images and meanings that relate to their sense of self-identity or to their wider experiences of work, family, and social relationships. Furthermore, in an age of democratic, interactive, technology-driven communications, it is argued that media and popular culture are made from "within" and "below," not imposed from without and above as has been traditionally conceptualized (Fiske, 1989). By the mid-1990s, researchers had dismissed concerns about what the media *do* to people and turned the question around, asking instead, "What do people do *with* the media?"

An example of criminological research using this approach is *Captive Audience* (Jewkes, 2002). Here the aim was to examine the media's role in the exercise of power relations and the construction of masculine identities in prisons. At the time, most prisoners in England had access to television, although for some it was in communal TV areas and for others it was within their own rooms ("in-cell TV" was just being rolled out across the prison estate). The study found that communal TV viewing in prison replicates many of Morley's findings concerning TV within the family. "We discuss what we want to watch and the biggest wins. That's me. I'm the biggest" is a typical comment from a male respondent in Morley's 1986 study that had resonance in the prison context. In this prison study, solitary viewing (and reading and listening) revealed a range of motivations and identity constructions, some of which were familiar to all media consumers (passing time, becoming informed, chilling out) and some of which had a particular salience (enhancing one's credentials as a violent man, "tuning out" the aggressive prison culture) or poignancy (escapism, evoking memories of loved ones) in the context of the prison.

LATE MODERNITY AND POSTMODERNISM

There is a clear trajectory that links the theories discussed so far, even if development has come from antagonism as well as agreement between different schools of thought. Postmodernism is a paradigm shift that impacted a range of academic disciplines including criminology, becoming a ubiquitous and unavoidable term throughout the 1990s. Postmodernism is frequently presented as an emphatic and decisive break with all that went before, with large-scale theories like Marxism being rejected for their all-embracing claims to knowledge and "truth." Most commentators now prefer to describe the current epoch in terms of late modernity, to indicate that, while there have been radical changes in patterns of global cultural, political, and economic life, they have not entirely *replaced* the structural characteristics associated with "modern" society: class structure, capitalism, industrialism, militarism, the nation state, and so on.

However, traces of earlier theories can be found in postmodern accounts. Like reception analysts, postmodernist writers view audiences as active and creative meaning-makers. In common with realists, they share a concern for fear of crime and victimization and make problematic concepts such as "crime" and "deviance," just as labeling theorists did in an earlier period. Furthermore, like advocates of the pluralist approach, postmodernists suggest that the media market has been deregulated, leading to an explosion of programs, titles, and formats to choose from. All tastes and interests are now catered to, and it is the consumer who ultimately has the power to choose what he or she watches, listens to, reads, and engages with, but equally what he or she ignores, rejects, or subverts. In this glossy, interactive media marketplace, anything goes—so long as it doesn't strain an attention span of three minutes and is packaged as "entertainment." Postmodernism, then, is concerned with the excesses of information and entertainment now available, and it emphasizes the style and packaging of media output in addition to the actual substance of its content. This is the "society of the spectacle" (Debord, 1967/1997), a "hyperreality" in which media domination suffuses to such an extent that the distinction between image and reality no longer exists (Baudrillard, 1981, 1983). Mass media and the collapse of meaning have produced a culture centered on immediate consumption and sensationalized impact but with little depth of analysis or contextualization (Osborne, 2002). It is the fragmentary, ephemeral, and ambiguous that are observed, and pleasure, spectacle, pastiche, parody, and irony are the staples of postmodern media output. The media's responsibility is to entertain, and audience gratification is the only impact worth striving for.

This abandonment of a distinction between information and entertainment raises two problems, however. The first is the threat to meaningful debate that postmodernism seems to imply. A media marketplace based on a pluralist model of ideological struggle may suffice as a forum for debate, but it relies on the public's ability to discriminate between what is true and what is not, between fact and interpretation. In an early critique of postmodernism, Dick Hebdige warns:

> The idea of a verifiable information order, however precarious and shifting, however subject to negotiation and contestation by competing ideologies, does not survive the transition to this version of new times . . . today aliens from Mars kidnap joggers, yesterday Auschwitz didn't happen, tomorrow who cares what happens? Here the so-called "depthlessness" of the postmodern era extends beyond . . . the tendency of the media to feed more and more greedily off each other, to affect the function and status of information itself. (1989, p. 51)

The second difficulty with postmodernism lies in how we define "entertainment." As Hall et al. (1978/2013) suggest, violence—including violent crime—is often regarded as intrinsically entertaining to an audience who, it is argued, have become more emotionally detached and desensitized to the vast array of visual images bombarding them from every corner of the world. Many see this as an escalating problem and highlight that it has become necessary to accelerate the drama of each successive action to maintain the same level of coverage (Mander, 1980).

It is usually organizations that fall outside mainstream consensus politics that best understand this theory of acceleration. Groups with a radical political agenda are well practiced in the art of manipulating the media and will frequently "create" a story through the use of controversial but stage-managed techniques, knowing that it will make "good copy." Greenpeace, the Animal Liberation Front, Fathers 4 Justice, and anti-globalization, anti-capitalism movements are examples of pressure groups that have been extremely successful in garnering media attention and ensuring attention-grabbing headlines. Even the police have adopted the techniques of heightened drama and suspense to produce spectacular, even voyeuristic television, with stage-managed press conferences involving "victims" of serious crimes whom they suspect of foul play, and dramatic raids on the homes of suspected burglars and drug dealers in which police officers are accompanied by television cameras. But it is arguably terrorists who have taken the lesson of sensationalized impact to heart to the greatest and most devastating effect:

> The spectacularly violent acts of terrorists can be viewed as performances for the benefit of a journalistic culture addicted to high drama . . . the terrorist act is the ultimate "pseudo-event"—a politically and militarily meaningless act unless it receives recognition and coverage in the news media. (McNair, 1998, p. 142)

However, the desire to "play up to the cameras" may be no less true of state aggressors as it is of terrorists and dissidents. For example, military campaigns may also be planned as media episodes, as was witnessed in the 2003 Allied War on Iraq when journalists were "embedded" with military personnel and were allowed unprecedented access to troops and operations. Similarly:

> When President Reagan bombed Libya [in 1986], he didn't do it at the most effective time of day, from a military point of view. The timing of the raid was principally determined by the timing of the American television news; it was planned in such a way as to maximize its television impact. It was timed to enable Reagan to announce on the main evening news that it had "just happened"—it was planned as a television event. (Morley, 1992, p. 63–64)

But the most compelling example to date of a postmodern media "performance" occurred September 11, 2001. The terrorist attacks on the World Trade Center took place when millions of Americans would be tuned in to the breakfast news programs on television. The timing of the actions ensured that viewers across the world who missed the terrifying aftermath of the first attack on the north tower would tune in to see "live" pictures of the second hijacked aircraft being flown into the south tower 16 minutes later. The television pictures from that day—transmitted immediately around the globe—have arguably become the most visually arresting and memorable news images ever seen, evoking countless cinematic representations from *The Towering Inferno* to *Independence Day*. The "event that shook the world" had such an overwhelming impact because of the immediacy and dramatic potency of its image on screen; it was truly a postmodern spectacle. Terrorist attacks on "innocent" civilians chime with the postmodern idea that we are all potential victims. Postmodern analyses reject traditional criminological concerns with the causes and consequences of crime, pointing instead to the fragmentation of societies, the fear that paralyzes many communities, the random violence that seems to erupt at all levels of society, and the apparent inability of governments to do anything about these problems. This concern with a lurking, unpredictable danger is fortified by an omnipresent media. Postmodernist critic Richard Osborne suggests that the ubiquity of mediated crime reinforces our sense of being victims: "Media discourses about crime now constitute all viewers as equally subject to the fragmented and random danger of criminality, and in so doing provide the preconditions for endless narratives of criminality that rehearse this ever-present danger" (Osborne, 1995, p. 27). Perversely, then, the media's inclination to make all audience members equal in their potential "victimness" lies at the core of the postmodern fascination with crime. For Osborne, there is "something obsessive in the media's, and the viewer's, love of such narratives, an hysterical replaying of the possibility of being a victim and staving it off" (p. 29).

Another aspect of the hysteria that surrounds criminal cases, fusing the fear of becoming a victim with the postmodern imperative for entertaining the audience, is the media's inability, or unwillingness, to separate the ordinary from the extraordinary. The audience is bombarded in both factual media and in fictional representations by crimes that are very rare, such as serial killings and abductions of children by strangers. The presentation of the atypical as typical serves to exacerbate public anxiety and deflect attention from much more commonplace offenses such as street crime, corporate crime, and abuse of children within the family. Reporting of the "ever-present danger" of the predatory pedophile or young thug who is prepared to kill with little provocation are the stock-in-trade of a media industry that understands that shock, outrage, and fear sell newspapers. In recent years, interest has turned to the collective outpouring of grief that has been witnessed in relation to certain violent and/or criminal acts, which has resulted in them occupying a particular symbolic place in the popular imagination. It has been suggested that the "coming together" of individuals to express collective anguish and to gaze upon the scene of crimes in a gesture of empathy and solidarity with those who have been victimized is a sign of the desire for community, a hearkening back to pre-mass-society collectivity or an assertion of "people power" (Blackman & Walkerdine, 2001, p. 2). But equally, it might be regarded as a voyeuristic desire to be part of the hyperreal, to take part in a globally mediated event and say "I was there."

CULTURAL CRIMINOLOGY

The populist, entertainment imperative of the postmodernist approach is central to the developing perspective known as **cultural criminology** most commonly associated with the work of its American originator, Jeff Ferrell, and with the criminology department at the University of Kent in the UK (e.g., Ferrell, Hayward, & Young, 2015; Hayward & Presdee, 2010). This approach seeks to understand both the public's mediated fascination with violence and crime and also the enactment of violence and crime *as* pleasure or spectacle. Its debt to earlier work by Stuart Hall, Stanley Cohen, Phil Cohen, and Jock Young (who was himself part of the cultural criminology vanguard) is evident in its proposition that all crime is grounded in culture and that cultural practices are embedded in dominant processes of power. It therefore supports the early Marxist-influenced, critical criminological view that criminal acts are acts of resistance to authority. But unlike earlier accounts that conceptualized resistance as something that was internalized and expressed through personal and subcultural style, cultural criminologists also emphasize the externalization of excitement and ecstasy derived from transgression and resistance. Here, cultural criminology is indebted to the work of sociologist Jack Katz, who argues in *Seductions of Crime* (1990) that crime is not simply driven by acquisition, materialism, or economic need but also the enactment of power, identity, presence, status, and the cultivation of "sneaky thrills." Many criminal activities involve risk-taking and danger, but may in fact represent an attempt to break free of one's demeaning and restraining circumstances, to exercise control and take responsibility for one's own destiny. In a social world where individuals find themselves overcontrolled and yet without control, crime offers some the possibility of excitement *and* control. The consistently high levels of lethal violence among young people who live in marginalized neighborhoods in Chicago, for instance, might be understood as individual acts of violent self-expression—an attempt by those with little self-determination to articulate their will—which, somewhat ironically, makes the individuals involved feel alive.

For some cultural criminologists, crime is a participatory and transgressive performance, a "carnival," and the streets its theatre. Some commentators have found this a refreshing antidote to Marxist-inspired studies such as *Policing the Crisis* insofar as cultural criminology avoids the condescension of criminal-as-victim (of disadvantageous circumstances; Jefferson, 2002). Mike Presdee provided some of the most compelling examples from Britain of the carnival of crime. Describing the large-scale ritualized joyriding (automobile theft) that he observed in marginalized neighborhoods in the 1990s, Presdee comments:

> Their joyriding became a celebration of a particular form of car culture that was carnivalesque in nature, performance centred and criminal. The sport of joyriding went something like this: a team of local youths would spot a hot hatch (the car of choice) and steal it (or arrange with others to have it stolen). It would be delivered to another team who would do it up, delivering it finally to the drivers. In the evenings, the cars were raced round the estate, not aimlessly but in a way designed to show off skill. Furthermore, two competing groups (teams) attempted to outdo the other. These displays were watched by certain residents of the estate who, the story goes, were charged a pound for the pleasure, sitting in picnic chairs at the sides of the road. Often after these races the cars were burned on deserted land. (2000, p. 49)

Similarly, in an exploration of the ways in which fire setting is, for some, an act of rebelliousness, resistance, defiance, and destruction, Presdee explains the primeval attraction of arson via stories from the U.S. and UK:

> On Monday 6 December 2004 in Indian Head, Washington, USA, unknown arsonists put a complete new up-market housing development to the "torch," burning 26 houses in one spectacular conflagration! It was a five million pound bonfire that was deliberate, and organized, changing both the landscape and society in one swift and totally destructive act . . . [Meanwhile in a field in Gloucester on Bonfire night]:

they got wooden boards and placed those over the fire and as the flames rekindled the fire dance began again. They faced each other bouncing on the bridges of burning boards, jousting with each other with burning sticks as the howling wind made the flames more dangerous. Like mediaeval knights they fought in the fire and the watching crowd feasted on this spectacle of fire. (Presdee, 2011, pp. 120, 124)

Riots, protests, and other outbreaks of disorder can also be viewed in this way. It is not the case that all carnivalesque performances involve crime, but it can be said with some certainty that participation in them can lead to criminalization. It is therefore not just the cultural significance of crime but the criminalization of certain cultural practices that cultural criminologists are interested in.

While cultural criminology is not without its critics (P. Mason, 2006, archly refers to it as "ghettoized '70s retro chic"), it is undeniable that it has had a significant impact on the ways in which connections between crime, media, and culture are made. Cultural criminology celebrates postmodern notions of difference, discontinuity, and diversity and breaks down restrictive and negative stereotypes. What were formerly regarded as unconventional interest groups or simply public nuisances have been embraced amid a renewed verve for ethnographic enquiry and a fascination for the power of the image. For example, in *Crimes of Style* (1996), Ferrell explores the meaning and practice of graffiti: the building up of the "tagging" experience, the mastery of the art, the aesthetic attention to detail, the thrill of getting away with it (or getting caught); and the network of friendships built up with fellow artists, all of which take shape and meaning within the immediate contingencies of boredom, disaffection, and alienation. The comment of a graffiti artist in the celebrated documentary *Style Wars* sums up the feeling of transcendence experienced:

> I think it's something you can never recapture again once you experience it . . . even the smell you get, like when you first smell trains, it's a good smell too, like, a dedicated graffiti writer . . . you're there in the midst of all the metal and, like, you're here to produce something. (Chalfant & Silver, 1983)

Once viewed exclusively in terms of teenage delinquency and mindless vandalism, graffiti is one of the many "underground" subcultural practices that has been appropriated by corporations and repackaged for mass consumption (see Snyder, 2011). It has even been featured on the U.S. version of *The Apprentice* (NBC) in an episode that required the two competing teams to create a graffiti advertisement on a 20-foot wall in Harlem, New York, for the Sony PlayStation game *Gran Turismo 4*. The show's star, Donald Trump, announced, without a trace of irony, that there is a "new form of urban advertising—it's called graffiti," before going on to exclaim, "I'm not thrilled with graffiti. I don't like graffiti, but some of it is truly amazing." The sums of money demanded for works by British street artist Banksy (some of which have been illegally removed from the buildings on which they were painted) provide further evidence of the transition of graffiti from underground to the mainstream.

The emergence of cultural criminology can be characterized as a challenge to "crime science" and to the lingering influence of positivism, which, it is suggested, has led to a vacuum in so-called "expert" knowledge surrounding the pursuit of pleasure. The over-riding concern with reason and scientific rationality means that traditional criminology has been unable to account for "feelings" such as rage, excitement, pleasure, and desire. The activities described by Katz, Ferrell, Presdee, Hayward, and others certainly convey the sense of excitement and desire that are at the heart of many criminalized behaviors, but they also hint at the possibility that such pleasures can be transmuted into something darker and more distorted. They recognize that postmodern media—*Big Brother*, *Here Comes Honey Boo Boo*, and *The Voice* being prime(time) examples—merge "fun" and "hate," "cruelty" and "playfulness," "celebrity" and "nobody," "inclusive" and "exploitative," "accessible" and "extremist." In this respect they share many qualities with the Internet, which celebrates a world of entertainment, spectacle, performance, and fetish. When it comes to privatized pleasure and public displays of narcissism, cyberspace is arguably the cardinal site of the carnival of crime (see Chapter 9).

SUMMARY

While of necessity a distillation of the historical development of two fields of inquiry (in addition to noting the importance of the broader terrain of sociology), this chapter has traced the origins and development of the major theories that have shaped the contours of both criminology and media studies and attempted to provide a broad overview of points of convergence and conflict between the two across two continents (America and Europe). In so doing, it has established that there is no body of relatively consistent, agreed-upon, and formalized assertions that can readily be termed "media theory" or "criminological theory." Although such phrases are widely used, neither field has been unified by the development of a standard set of concepts, an inter-related body of hypotheses, or an overall explanatory framework. However, it has proposed that a sense of progressive development is nevertheless evident in ideas concerning media and crime. Despite their obvious etiological and methodological differences, the theoretical approaches discussed in this chapter have clear points of convergence that have enabled us to locate them in the wider context of social, cultural, political, and economic developments that were concomitantly taking place. In summary, the

theoretical "pegs" upon which our analysis has been hung are as follows:

- **Media effects:** Early theories connecting media and crime were characterized by an overwhelmingly negative view of both the role of the media and the susceptibility of the audience. Like Martians with their ray guns, the new media of mass communications were perceived through early-20th-century eyes as alien invaders injecting their messages directly into the minds of a captive audience. Although some academic researchers have strongly resisted attempts to assert the existence of a causal link between media and crime, rendering the debate all but redundant in media scholarship, notions of a potentially harmful media capable of eliciting negative or antisocial consequences remain at the heart of popular or mainstream discourses, including those that have been incorporated into policy.

- **Strain theory and anomie:** Merton's development of anomie helps us to understand the strain caused by a disjuncture between the cultural goals of wealth and status and legitimate means of achieving those goals. For those with few means of attaining success through normal, legal channels, the media might be said to place incalculable pressure, creating a huge ungratified well of desire with little opportunity of fulfilment. It is in such circumstances that some individuals pursue the culturally desirable objectives of success and material wealth via illegitimate paths. Recent commentators on anomie have suggested that disaffected individuals overcome feelings of isolation and normlessness by forming communities based on shared tastes and opinions and that social media and the Internet have, for some, countered the sense of dislocation that gaps in wealth and status inevitably produce.

- **Dominant ideology:** With the rediscovery of Marx's writings on social structure, scholars in the 1960s and 1970s focused their attentions on the extent to which consent is "manufactured" by the powerful along ideological lines. According to the dominant ideology approach, the power to criminalize and decriminalize certain groups and behaviors lies with the ruling elite, who—in a process known as "hegemony"—win popular approval for their actions via social institutions, including the media. In short, powerful groups achieve public consensus on definitions of crime and deviance and gain mass support for increasingly draconian measures of control and containment, not by force or coercion but by using the media to subtly construct a web of meaning from a number of ideological threads, which are then articulated into a coherent popular discourse.

- **Pluralism:** This perspective emerged as a challenge to hegemonic models of media power. Pluralism emphasizes the diversity and plurality of media channels available, thus countering the notion that any ideology can be dominant for any length of time if it does not reflect what people experience to be true. Although there is undoubtedly a firm alliance between most

politicians and sections of the journalistic media, pluralists argue that the media's tendency to ignore, ridicule, or demonize those whose politics and lifestyle lie beyond the consensual norm is changing, precisely because public sentiments have changed. There is growing antipathy for the apparatus of political communication, and people's responses to crime will always be much more complex and diverse than any headline or soundbite might suggest. In addition, it might be argued that the quantity and rapidity of contemporary news-making undermines the notion of elite power and ensures that governments are accountable and responsive to their electorate.

- **Postmodernism:** As far as we can state that there are "defining characteristics" of postmodernism, they include the end of any belief in an overarching scientific rationality, the abandonment of empiricist theories of truth, and an emphasis on the fragmentation of experience and the diversification of viewpoints. The postmodernist rejection of claims to truth proposed by the "grand theories" of the past challenges us to accept that we live in a world of contradictions and inconsistencies that are not amenable to objective modes of thought. Within criminology, postmodernism implies an abandonment of the concept of crime and the construction of a new language and mode of thought to define processes of criminalization and censure. It is often suggested that, for postmodernists, there are no valid questions worth asking, and Henry and Milovanovic (1996) insist that crime will stop being a problem only when the justice system, media, and criminologists stop focusing attention on it.

- **Cultural criminology:** Media and culture are central to this form of criminological analysis; style is substance, and meaning resides in representation. Consequently, crime and crime control can only be understood as an ongoing spiral of intertextual, image-driven media loops (Ferrell, 2001). Cultural criminology embraces postmodern ideas and underpins them with some more "radical" yet established concerns, borrowing especially from the classic Chicago School tradition of ethnography as well as the work of British scholars in the 1970s on subcultures and mediated forms of social control. And, in a decisive break with traditional, "positivist" criminologies that have been unconcerned with "feeling" and "pleasure," cultural criminology also draws attention to the fact that crime can have a carnivalesque quality; it is exhilarating, performative, and dangerous.

STUDY QUESTIONS

1. Choose one of the theories discussed in this chapter and discuss the contribution it has made to our understanding of the relationship between media and crime.

2. As the *War of the Worlds* radio broadcast demonstrates, concerns about media effects frequently reflect or crystallize deeper anxieties in periods of social upheaval. What examples of contemporary concerns about the effects of the media can you think of, and in what ways might they be attributed to wider anxieties about social change?

3. Conduct an analysis of a week's news. What evidence can you find for the proposition that news is ideology and that the mass media are effectively assimilated into the goals of government policy on crime, law, and order?

4. In a challenge to Marxist-inspired critiques, some cultural theorists (e.g., Fiske, 1989) argue that all popular culture is the "people's culture" and emerges from "below" rather than being imposed from "above." It is thus seen to be independent of, and resistant to, the dominant hegemonic norms. What implications does this have for those who hold deviant or oppositional viewpoints? Can "popular" culture really be described as nonhierarchical when it celebrates power and violence for men and sexual availability and victimization among women and children?

5. At the heart of postmodern analyses lies the thorny question of why crime is threatening and frightening yet at the same time popular and "entertaining." How would you attempt to answer this question?

FURTHER READING

- A good place to start is the collection of readings with annotations brought together by Chris Greer: *Crime and Media: A Reader* (Routledge, 2009).

- Your university library may hold the three-volume set *Crime and Media*, by Y. Jewkes (SAGE, 2009), which is part of the SAGE Library of Criminology and is also a collection of readings with original commentaries.

- *Crime, Culture and the Media*, by E. Carrabine (Polity, 2008), is a challenging but rewarding resource.

- In addition, there are now numerous good introductions to criminological theory. The best of them, especially from a media/crime perspective, is *Criminology: A Sociological Introduction* (third edition), by E. Carrabine et al. (Routledge, 2014), which covers all the theories discussed here and also devotes a specific chapter to the relationship between crime and media.

- Covering many of the theories discussed in this chapter and anticipating the discussion of news in Chapter 2 is the classic *Power Without*

Responsibility: Press, Broadcasting and the Internet in Britain, by J. Curran and J. Seaton (Routledge, 2010), now in its seventh edition.

- For a fun take on media criminology, which manages to combine theoretical sophistication with its application to cinema, *Criminology Goes to the Movies: Crime Theory and Popular Culture*, by N. Rafter and M. Brown (New York University Press, 2011), is highly recommended.

- Several works that come under the rubric "cultural criminology" are immensely readable, and some have consequently found a readership beyond university scholars. Examples include Jeff Ferrell's exploits as a dumpster diver in *Empire of Scrounge* (New York University Press, 2005) and Alison Young's homage to street art and graffiti, *Street Art World* (Reaktion, 2016).

- Finally, *Crime, Media, Culture: An International Journal* (http://cmc.sagepub.com) is devoted to cross-disciplinary work that promotes understanding of the relationship between crime, criminal justice, media, and culture.

Student Study Site

WANT A BETTER GRADE?

Get the tools you need to sharpen your study skills. Access practice quizzes, eFlashcards, SAGE journal articles, and more at study.sagepub.com/jewkesus.

The Construction of Crime News

2

OVERVIEW

Chapter 2 provides:

- An analysis of how crime news is "manufactured" along ideological lines.

- An understanding of the ways in which the demands and constraints of news production intertwine with the perceived interests of the target audience to produce a set of organizational "news values."

- An overview of 12 key news values that are prominent in the construction

of crime news at the beginning of the 21st century.

- Discussion of the ways in which the construction of news sets the agenda for public and political debate.

- Two case studies of archetypal newsworthy stories.

- An examination of how new technologies are changing the ways in which news is produced and consumed.

KEY TERMS

The diversity of theoretical approaches discussed in the previous chapter will have alerted you to the fact that the influence of the media can be conceptualized both negatively and positively, depending on the perspective adopted. Those who have attempted to demonstrate a link between media content and crime or deviance have taken a variety of theoretical positions to establish alternative, and frequently opposi- tional, views, ranging from the idea that the media industry is responsible for much of the crime that blights our society to the idea that media perform a public service in edu- cating us about crime and crime prevention. Some have even argued that media are rede- fining and making obsolete traditional notions of crime and deviance. It is clear from these divergent viewpoints that the media's role in representing reality is highly contested and subject to interpretation. Although accounts of criminal activities in film, television drama, music lyrics, computer games, and websites are arguably of greatest salience in discussions of media influence, the reporting of crime news is also of importance and is no less shaped by the mission to entertain. Indeed, while it might be expected that the news simply reports the "facts" of an event and is an accurate representation of the overall picture of crime, this is not the case. Even the most cursory investigation of crime reporting demonstrates that crime news follows markedly different patterns from both the "reality" of crime and its representation in official statistics. Thus, despite often being described as a "window on the world" or a mirror reflecting "real life," the media might be more accurately thought of, borrowing Ferrell, Hayward, and Young's (2015) imagery, as a carnivalesque "Hall of Mirrors," bending and distorting the viewer's perception of the world. And with the advent of fake news, it might even be a whole lot more confusing—and dangerous—than that, as we will discuss below.

Whether we adhere to the "effects" theory of media influence, the hegemonic under- standing of media power as an expression of elite interests, the pluralist idea of an open media marketplace, or notions of a postmodernist mediascape, we have to conclude that media images are *not* reality; they are a *version* of reality that is culturally determined and dependent on two related factors. First, the mediated picture of "reality" is shaped by the production processes of news organizations and the structural determinants of news-making, any or all of which may influence the image of crime, criminals, and the criminal justice system in the minds of the public. These factors include the overreporting of crimes that have been "solved" and resulted in a conviction; the deployment of reporters at institutional settings, such as courts and police precincts, where they are likely to come across interesting stories; the need to produce stories that fit the time schedules of news production; the concentration on specific crimes at the expense of causal explanations; the consideration of personal safety, which results in camera operators covering incidents of public disorder from behind police lines; and an overreliance on "official," accredited sources for information. The second factor that shapes news production concerns the assumptions media professionals make about their audience. TV news producers, journalists, bloggers, and writers of all kinds sift through and select news items and—in a process known as agenda-setting—will prioritize some stories over others. Then they edit words, adopt a particular tone (some stories will be treated seriously; others might get a humorous or ironic treatment), and decide on the visual images that will accompany the story, all of which constitutes the framing of a story. It is in these ways that those who work in the media select a handful of events from the unfathomable number of possibilities that occur around the world every day and turn them into stories that convey meanings, offer solutions, associate certain groups of people with particular kinds of behavior, and provide "pictures of the world" that help to structure our frames of reference.

Far from being a random or personal process, editors and journalists select, produce, and present news according to a range of professional criteria that are used as benchmarks to determine a story's newsworthiness. This is not to say that alternative definitions do not exist or that other nonmediated influences are at least as important. But if a story does not contain at least some of the characteristics deemed newsworthy, it will not appear on the news agenda. News values, then, are the value judgments journalists and editors make about the public appeal of a story as well as whether it is in the public interest. The former can be measured quantitatively: Put simply, lack of public appeal will be reflected in poor sales figures or ratings and is frequently used to justify the growing dependence on stories with a dramatic, sensationalist, or celebrity component. The issue of public interest is rather more complicated and may involve external interference, such as corporate or, more commonly, political pressures. In the UK, for example, the main public service channel, the BBC, is subject to a range of restrictions that are framed by notions of "impartiality." The press, however, is hampered by very few limitations regarding what it may print and, in the U.S., neither television nor newspapers face such restrictions.

However, in any country's news organizations, pressure might be so abstrusely exerted as to appear as self-censorship on the part of editors and producers. The news values that set the media agenda rarely amount to a journalistic conspiracy—they are much subtler than that. Nowhere in a newsroom will you find a list pinned to the wall reminding reporters and editors what their "angle" on a story should be. Rather, the commercial, legislative, and technical pressures that characterize journalism, together with a range of occupational conventions—which are often expressed in terms of "having a good nose for a story," but which actually have more to do with journalists sharing the same ideological values as the majority of their audience—results in a normalization of particular interests and values (Wykes, 2001). This shared ethos enables those who work in news organizations to systematically sort, grade, and select potential news stories and discard those that are of no perceived interest or relevance to the audience.

While agenda-setting is usually guided by pragmatic concerns, framing is an ideological process. As journalist Scott London has described, the informational content of a news report is less important than the interpretive commentary that attends it:

> This is especially evident in television news which is replete with metaphors, catch-phrases, and other symbolic devices that provide a shorthand way of suggesting the

underlying storyline. These devices provide the rhetorical bridge by which discrete bits of information are given a context and relationship to one another . . . The frames for a given story are seldom conscientiously chosen but represent instead the effort of the journalist or sponsor to convey a story in a direct and meaningful way. As such, news frames are frequently drawn from, and reflective of, shared cultural narratives and myths and resonate with the larger social themes to which journalists tend to be acutely sensitive. (London, n.d.)

Arguably even more important than metaphor, catchphrases and other linguistic forms of framing are the visual images that accompany news reports (in the press as well as on television), which will be discussed below.

The first people to attempt to systematically identify and categorize the news values that commonly determine and structure reported events were Johan Galtung and Mari Ruge (1965/1973). Their concern was with news reporting generally rather than crime news per se, and they studied only a limited range of publications (broadcast news was still in its infancy) from the perspective of Norwegian academics writing for the *Journal of International Peace Studies*. Nevertheless, their findings that incidents and events were more likely to be reported if they were, for example, unexpected, close to home, of a significant threshold in terms of dramatic impact, and negative in essence, clearly made them relevant to crime reporting, and their research continues to be a touchstone for students of crime news today. However, the contemporary landscape of crime and punishment in the U.S. is considerably different from that of 1960s Norway! Most obviously, the United States committed itself to mass imprisonment, the largest project of penal expansion since the Soviet Gulags and perhaps in recorded human history. To reckon the scale of American mass imprisonment, consider that in 1958 there were 26,938 full-time correctional workers, managing a population of just over 160,000 state and federal prisoners (Schnur, 1958). Fifty years later, American prisons employ more than a half million workers, who oversee a population of 2.3 million prisoners and another 4.7 million people governed by probation and parole. It should also be noted that this massive expansion cannot be explained by a proportional rise in either crime or the U.S. population as a whole.

As mind-boggling as the scale of American punishment is, its scope is just as astounding. In the present context, new categories of crime and hence criminals are born perpetually, evidenced by nightly news reports referencing road rage, air rage, identity theft, online grooming, trolling, suicide bombing, revenge porn—crimes that were virtually unheard of 25 years ago. Indeed, one needs only consider the advent of the Internet and its adjoined prefix "cyber"—homicide, suicide, sex crimes—to reckon the manner in which new types of crimes and criminals proliferate. Even the now ubiquitous "serial killer" did not exist in its current cultural form until properly named by Federal Bureau of Investigations (FBI) agent Robert Ressler and subsequently codified by the political work of the FBI's Behavioral Sciences Unit (Jenkins, 1994).

Of course, all of this is inseparably entwined with crime's representation. As the U.S. media landscape changed in the postwar years, so did the cultural complexion of crime. Moving from a few channels broadcast in black and white to 24-hour cable news networks and television sets in every home, crime-focused reality TV programming, and ubiquitous police procedurals, crime moved from a topic of lurid impolite conversation to the center of American social and cultural life in less than a half century. As Robert McChesney has shown, between 1990 and 1996, television crime news coverage nearly tripled even as crime began to drop precipitously (McChesney, 1999). Innumerable programs, from sensational ambush shows like NBC's *To Catch a Predator* and truTV's *Bait Car;* to the ever-popular "profiling" genre and its prime-time cable juggernauts *Law and Order* and *Criminal Minds;* to MSNBC's *Locked Up* and its many spinoffs, *Raw, World Tour, Extended Stay, Special Investigation,* and *Life After,* which voyeuristically take up punishment, dominate American television markets. Even a trip to a neighborhood convenience store or gas station is sure to confront consumers with the "true crimes" of supermarket tabloids and the sordid images of mugshot magazines like *The Slammer* and *Just Busted.*

While images and imagery of crime abound, some critics argue that the pressure on those who work in television and news media to produce the ordinary as extraordinary shades into the postmodern, and that what was historically described as news-gathering has, in the new millennium, begun to take on the same constructed–for–(social) media quality that postmodernists refer to as "simulation" (Osborne, 2002, p. 131). Never has simulation seemed more evident than with the rise of "fake news" in 2016, which some commentators have said was instrumental in two seismic moments in Anglo-American history: the British exit from the European Union ("Brexit") and the election of Republican Donald Trump over his Democrat rival Hillary Clinton in the 2016 presidential elections. Fake news is usually propagandist, occasionally simply entertaining, and invariably circulated via social media. But in these two watershed political events, it may have had serious consequences for democracy. Headlines proclaiming that the queen had threatened to abdicate if Britain left Europe and that the pope endorsed Trump's bid for leadership have led politicians in Europe and America to call for inquiries into how and where fake new is generated and to demand that sites such as Facebook verify news content before allowing it online. The time seems right, then, for a reassessment of the criteria that structure the news that we read, hear, watch, and browse online at the beginning of the 21st century. So what constitutes "newsworthiness" in 2018?

Of course, some of the criteria identified by Galtung and Ruge in 1973 (which were developed further by British sociologist Steve Chibnall in 1977) still apply and will be drawn on in the analysis that follows. It is also important to remember that different values may determine the selection and presentation of events by different news media (and, for that matter, by different or competing organizations), and that the broadcast media tend to follow the news agenda of the press in deciding which stories are newsworthy. Of course, the news values of the *New York Times* are likely to be different from those of the *Wall Street Journal* and different again from those of MSNBC—not to mention *The Guardian, Canberra Times,* or *Ming Pao.* Even among news organizations that appear to be very similar, such as the tabloid press, there may be differences in news reporting that are largely accounted for by the house style of the publication in question. For example, some stress the "human interest" angle of a crime story (with firsthand accounts from victims and witnesses; an emphasis on tragedy, sentimentality, and so on) and may be primarily designed to appeal to a female readership, while others sensationalize crime news, emphasizing sex and sleaze but simultaneously adopting a scandalized and prurient tone.

News values are also subject to subtle changes over time, and a story does not have to conform to all the criteria to make the news—although events that score highly on the newsworthiness scale (that is, conform to several of the news values) are more likely to be reported. Newsworthiness criteria vary across different countries and cultures, and it should be noted that the list that follows has been devised primarily with Western audiences and American and British media in mind. Readers in, or with knowledge of, other countries might like to consider how notions of newsworthiness differ across geographical boundaries and perhaps construct their own list of news values pertinent to the area they are most familiar with. The list that follows is, then, by no means exhaustive, but it considers a total of 12 features that are evident in the output of most contemporary media institutions and are of particular significance when examining the reporting of crime.

One other point that should be borne in mind is that while "crime" could in itself be classified as a news value, it goes without saying that in a study of crime news, all the news values outlined in this chapter pertain explicitly to *crime*. It is also taken for granted that the vast majority of crime stories are *negative* in essence, and that news must contain an element of "newness" or *novelty;* the news has to tell us things we did not already know (McNair, 1998). Crime, negativity, and novelty do not therefore appear in the list below as discrete news values but are themes that underpin all the criteria discussed. It is understood that *any* crime has the potential to be a news story, that it will contain negative features (even if the outcome is positive and it is presented as an essentially "good news" story), and that it will contain new or novel elements (even if it has been composed with other, similar stories to reinforce a particular agenda or to create the impression of a "crime wave"). This list of news values is concerned, therefore, with how previously unreported, negative stories about crime—already potentially of interest—are determined even more newsworthy by their interplay with other features of news reporting.

NEWS VALUES FOR A NEW MILLENNIUM

The 12 news structures and news values that shape crime news listed below are discussed in the rest of this chapter:

- Threshold
- Predictability
- Simplification
- Individualism

- Risk
- Sex
- Celebrity or high-status persons
- Proximity

- Violence or conflict
- Visual spectacle or graphic imagery
- Children
- Conservative ideology and political diversion

Threshold

Events have to meet a certain level of perceived importance or drama to be considered newsworthy. The threshold of a potential story varies according to whether the news reporters and editors in question work within a local, national, or global medium. In other words, petty crimes such as vandalism and street robberies are likely to feature in the local press (and will probably be front-page news in rural or low-crime areas), but it takes offenses of a greater magnitude to meet the threshold of national or international media. In addition, once a story has reached the required threshold to make the news, it may then have to meet further criteria to stay on the news agenda, and the media frequently keep a crime wave or particular crime story alive by creating new thresholds.

For instance, a perennial staple of American crime news reporting is the assumed link between drugs and violent crime. Although this link is complicated and contested, it is reaffirmed and refreshed by each "new" drug that enters the public's imagination. For instance, in 2011, the American news media began to report on the growing "epidemic" of synthetic cathinones, known colloquially as "bath salts." One of the many high-profile commentators to take up the issue was celebrity physician Dr. Mehmet Oz. In May of that year, "Dr. Oz" wrote an article for *Time Magazine* titled "Bath Salts: Evil Lurking in Your Corner Store" (Oz, 2011). Describing the drug as a "supercharged instrument of suffering" and a "pharmacological hell," Dr. Oz linked "bath salts" directly to violent behavior and suicide. In concert with such thinking, state and federal governments moved quickly to pass legislation to criminalize its use. Then, in early 2012, a series of unrelated violent crimes escalated the language of epidemic and emergency. The most fantastic of these was the case of Miami man Rudy Eugene, who was shot to death by police during a gruesome, daytime attack on a homeless man on a deserted highway overpass. Because of the bizarre circumstances of the attack—Eugene was naked and tore large chunks of flesh from his victim's face with his mouth—the speculation of local police that bath salts were the cause was widely accepted as fact by media and the public alike. For several weeks, the American news media eagerly followed suit, linking similar violent crimes together under the edifice of drug-induced "cannibalism" and, even more spectacularly, a "zombie apocalypse." Even after toxicology reports found no bath salts in Rudy Eugene's system, local police still publicly insisted that drugs were the cause, helping to reaffirm newsworthiness of the "bath salts epidemic."

To the casual observer, all of this might appear novel and funny, or dire, depending on your outlook. However, in the context of the history of illegal drugs, the links to violence and the language of epidemic are well worn; it is only the drugs that change. This is not to suggest that there is absolutely no association between drugs and violence, or that new drugs and their attendant difficulties do not spring up from time to time. Rather, the point is that the underlying assumption that drugs *cause* violence remains

THE ZOMBIE MURDERERS

A new generation of drug users is committing horrifying crimes

By RONALD KOTULAK

CHICAGO — (Special) — When a ...

PHOTO 2.1
Early 1980s
report of
drug induced
zombification.

relatively unchanged and that new stories emerge because of the incessant need for journalists to produce "fresh" content. This might simply involve an escalation of the level of drama attached to the story, or it might require the implementation of other news structures and news values to sustain the life of the story. These additional thresholds may, then, take many forms (we might add to the above list any number of other factors including the "whimsical," the "humorous," the "bizarre," the "grotesque," the "nostalgic," the "sentimental," and so on; see Hall, Critcher, Jefferson, Clarke, & Roberts, 1978/2013; Roshier, 1973). As the recent bout with bath salts reveals, even the seemingly absurd "drug zombie" trope is, in fact, not a recent development. In February 1980, news media reported an alarming outbreak of spectacular violence in Chicago committed by "zombies" high on PCP. One report warned, "Zombie murders committed by heavy drug users were rare in the 60s but now appear to be increasing sharply" (Kotulak, 1980).

Predictability

As the introduction to this chapter suggested, an event that is rare, extraordinary, or unexpected will be considered newsworthy. Like the thresholds outlined above, unpredictability gives a story novelty value. In particular, the media's "discovery" of a "new" crime is often sufficient to give it prominence. But equally, a story that is *predictable* may be deemed newsworthy because news organizations can plan their coverage in advance and deploy their resources (e.g., reporters and photographers) accordingly. Crime itself is frequently spontaneous and sporadic, but news media will know in advance if a government official is to announce a new initiative to combat crime or the FBI is due to release its annual crime statistics and will plan their coverage before the event actually occurs. In the case of the FBI's Uniform Crime Reports, articles proclaiming the "most dangerous" cities in America soon follow. This is also true of criminal trials, which can contain an element of predictability. Media organizations can estimate the time that a criminal case will remain in court and, having deployed personnel and equipment, are likely to retain those resources there until the end of the trial. Hence, a degree of continuity of coverage is also ensured.

Another aspect of predictability is that, for the most part, the media agenda is structured in an ordered and predictable fashion. Having set the moral framework of a debate, those who work in the media will rarely do a U-turn and refashion it according to a different set of principles. Put simply, if the media expect something to happen, it will happen, and journalists will usually have determined the angle from which they will report a story before they even arrive at the scene. One of the first examples of this tendency was the media coverage of anti–Vietnam War demonstrations in London in 1968 (Halloran, Elliott, & Murdock, 1970). The media anticipated violence and were going to report the event as a violent occasion, whatever the reality on the day. Consequently, one isolated incident of anti-police violence dominated coverage of the demonstration and deflected attention from its general peacefulness and, indeed, its antiwar message. In recent years, anti-capitalism and anti-globalization demonstrations around the world (most notably at the annual summit meetings of government leaders) have received similar treatment, leading many to conclude that the media tend to report events in the ways they have previously reported them. The rise of the Occupy Wall Street (OWS) movement in late 2011 was followed by claims of protester violence, which hold true to the patterns of reporting established during the student protests of 1968. Citing two alleged crimes, Sean O'Rourke (2011), writing for Fox News, blasted the National Organization of Women (NOW) for its supposed silence on an "epidemic of reported rapes and sexual assault against women" that had "plagued the Occupy Wall Street movement." Similarly, the website of the late conservative blogger Andrew Breitbart published a "rap sheet" that documented over 200 offenses supposedly perpetrated by OWS protesters. With reports of "crimes" ranging from protesters "harassing police with fake reports" to singing "F*** the USA," the "rap sheet" sought to expose how "the MSM [mainstream media] is willfully covering up the violence, vandalism, and anti-Semitism that truly does define this movement."

Simplification

Events do not have to be simple to make the news (although it helps), but they must be reducible to a minimum number of parts or themes. This process of simplification has several aspects. First, news reporting is marked by brevity so as not to strain the attention span of the audience. Second, the range of possible meanings inherent in the story must be restricted. Unlike other textual discourses—novels, poems, films, and so on—where the capacity of a story to generate multiple and diverse meanings is celebrated, news discourse is generally not open to interpretation and audiences are invited to come to consensual conclusions about a story (Galtung & Ruge, 1965/1973). Immediate or sudden events, such as the discovery of a body or an armed robbery, are likely to be reported because their "meaning" can be arrived at very quickly, but crime trends, which are more complex and may take a long time to unfold, are difficult to report unless they can be marked by means of devices such as the release of a report or official statistics. In other words, a "hook" is required on which to hang such stories so that they fit with the daily or hourly time span of most media.

Not only does news reporting privilege brevity, clarity, and unambiguity in its presentation, but it encourages the reader, viewer, and listener to suspend their skills of critical interpretation and respond in unanimous accord. As far as crime news is concerned, this usually amounts to moral indignation and censure directed at anyone who transgresses the legal or moral codes of society. In the aftermath of high-profile criminal and terrorism cases, notions of potential "dangerousness" have come to be applied indiscriminately to whole sections of society. In this oversimplified worldview of popular journalism, sufferers of mental illness can be portrayed as potential murderers; asylum seekers as potential terrorists; gun club members become potential spree killers; and, most insidiously, children and young people come to be seen as "evil monsters" with no hope of rehabilitation.

For instance, in the earliest days of mass incarceration, then-president Reagan, spurred on by his neoconservative advisers, pushed for hardline criminal justice reform focusing on the specter of so-called "career criminals." In a radio address to the nation in late 1982, Reagan made the case for emergency and a plan to deal with it:

My fellow Americans:

Today I want to talk with you about a subject that's been very much on my mind, even as we've been busy with budgets, interest rates, and legislation. It's a subject I know you've been thinking about too—crime in our society.

Many of you have written to me how afraid you are to walk the streets alone at night. We must make America safe again, especially for women and elderly who face so many moments of fear. You have every right to be concerned. We live in the midst of a crime epidemic that took the lives of more than 22,000 people last year and has touched nearly one-third of American households, costing them about $8.8 billion per year in financial losses.

During the past decade alone, violent crime rose by nearly 60 percent. Study after study shows that most serious crimes are the work of a relatively small group of hardened criminals. Let me give you an example—subway crime in New York City. Transit police there estimate that only 500 habitual criminal offenders are responsible for nearly half the crimes in New York's subways last year.

It's time to get these hardened criminals off the street and into jail . . . (Reagan, 1982)

This sort of address advances a very simple understanding of the dynamics of crime and victimization and an even simpler policy solution. For Reagan, the only recourse to deal with the "hardened criminals" who stalk the night, terrifying "women" and the "elderly," was incarceration. It is precisely this sort of paternalistic logic that helped to build the largest prison population the world has ever known.

Simplification of news can boil down to partiality; an accusation sometimes leveled at broadcasters in the UK and U.S. is that they are pro-Israeli in their coverage of the conflict in the Gaza Strip. At other times, simplification takes the form of an unquestioning patriotism, particularly in relation to acts of terrorism. American journalist–turned–media critic Danny Schechter (2003) has observed a sudden early change of focus in news reporting in the aftermath of 9/11. He describes what he sees as a manipulation by the U.S. government (perpetuated faithfully by the mainstream media) to turn around the initial introspective and disbelieving tone of coverage to an emphatically robust style of nationalism. This easily transmutes into a situation where anyone who opposes the "War on Terror" is regarded as "unpatriotic" or treacherously "anti-American." This sort of thinking was most famously articulated by former president George W. Bush when, in September 2001, during an address to Congress and the American people, he announced, "Every nation, in every region, now has a decision to make. Either you are with us, or you are with the terrorists. From this day forward, any nation that continues to harbor or support terrorism will be regarded by the United States as a hostile regime." The address reveals in plain language how the United States' enemies are constructed as pure evil and stripped of their histories and motivations. Mythen and Walklate (2006) similarly argue that, following terrorist attacks in New York, Washington, Madrid, and London by groups claiming allegiance to al-Qaeda, the creation of common enemies in these countries and their allies has resulted in a simplification of complex issues and personalities and a separation of cause and effect, both of which add to the public's perceptions of the terrorist as an irrational "other" whose motivations are greed or fanaticism rather than socioeconomic or geopolitical.

The experiences of marginalization that such individuals commonly experience are underplayed by politicians and the media, who continue to discuss individual moral responsibility as if it exists in a vacuum, somehow detached from the circumstances in which people find themselves. As Mythen and Walklate argue, this arrangement leaves little room for rational attempts to understand the values, objectives, and grievances of these individuals and instead reduces them to simplified inhuman objects of hate. The power and importance of simplification becomes even more evident when a government official fails to invoke such divisive language. Following the May 2012 attacks on the U.S. embassy at Benghazi, Libya, which left four Americans dead, President Obama came under fire for not immediately and definitively denouncing it as an act of terrorism. At a press conference more than a year later, Obama was still defending his initial statements, arguing, "The day after it happened, I acknowledged that this was an act of terrorism."

The discussion about simplification of news alerts us to the fact the mass media are inclined to deal in **binary oppositions**. Thus, stories involving crime and criminals, including terrorists, are frequently presented within a context that emphasizes good versus evil, folk heroes and folk devils, black against white, guilty or innocent, "normal" as opposed to "sick," "deviant," or "dangerous," and so on. Such polarized frameworks of understanding result in the construction of mutually exclusive categories; for example, parents cannot also be pedophiles; individuals driven to carry out suicide bombings and other terrorist acts are entirely evil and have no "good" qualities to redeem them. All of these processes of simplification add up to a mediated vision of crime in which shades of gray are absent and a complex reality is substituted for a simple, incontestable, and preferably bite-sized message.

Individualism

The news value individualism connects *simplification* and *risk* (see below). Individual definitions of crime, and rationalizations that highlight individual responses to crime, are preferred to more complex cultural and political explanations. The media engage in a process of personalization to simplify stories and give them a "human interest" appeal, which results in events being viewed as the actions and reactions of people. Consequently, social, political, and economic issues tend to be reported only as the conflict of interests between individuals (the president and the Speaker of the House, for example), while the complex interrelationship between political ideology and policy may be embodied in a single figure, such as the "drug czar" (director of the Office of National Drug Control Policy). The effect of this is that "the social origins of events are lost, and individual motivation is assumed to be the origin of all action" (Fiske, 1987, p. 294).

Both offenders and those who are *potentially offended against* are constructed within an individualist framework. Put simply, the criminal is usually described as being "impulsive, a loner, maladjusted, irrational, animal-like, aggressive and violent" (Blackman & Walkerdine, 2001, p. 6)—all qualities that allude to the offender's autonomous status and lack of normative social ties. The media coverage of "lone wolf" Anders Breivik, who murdered 77 people in Norway in 2011 and is discussed below, was framed in this way, despite his terrorist attacks clearly being inspired by well-known and long-standing right-wing political ideologies (Berntzen & Sandberg, 2014) and by other mass shootings (Sandberg, Oksanen, Berntzen, & Kiilakoski, 2014). Furthermore, news reporting frequently encourages the public to see themselves as vigilantes and positions those who are offended against (or who fear being the victims of crime) as vulnerable and isolated, let down by an ineffective social system and at risk from dangerous predators. Those who try to protect themselves from victimization are frequently portrayed as "have-a-go-heroes" and, when killed in the commission of an offense, are constructed as "tragic innocents." Meanwhile, as discussed in the previous chapter, institutions, corporations, and governments may be literally getting away with murder. Even when an offense that occurs within a large organization actually makes the news, it may once again be explained by recourse to individual pathology.

For instance, a case that garnered considerable media attention in 2009 was a fraudulent investment scheme operated by high-profile financier Bernard Madoff, which paid investors from money contributed by other investors rather than from real profits to the tune of $65 billion. The victims Madoff ensnared in his massive Ponzi scheme ranged from A-list celebrities like Steven Spielberg to charities like JEHT Foundation, which rather ironically was dedicated to reform of the criminal justice system. Perhaps because of the scale of these crimes, media coverage focused on Madoff, who—unusually for a white-collar criminal—was described by his trial judge as "extraordinarily evil." More recently, two Pennsylvania criminal court judges, Mark Ciavarella and Michael Conahan, were sentenced to 28 years and 18 months, respectively, for their parts in the so-called "kids for cash" scam. The pair pleaded guilty to a host of charges, which included accepting more than $2.6 million in kickbacks from a local developer, Robert K. Mericle. Ciavaralla and Conahan used their connections and political influence to secure approval to build two for-profit youth detention facilities, steering the contracts toward Mericle and then, most ghastly of all, sentencing children, in many instances for minor crimes, to the facilities in order to further benefit Mericle. At his sentencing, the ever-defiant Ciavaralla lashed out at prosecutors for attacking his character and ruining his reputation: "Those three words [kids for cash] made me the personification of evil . . . They made me toxic and caused a public uproar the likes of which this community has never seen." In the eyes of many, jailing children to line your pockets is as "evil" it gets. Yet, public outcry that focuses only on the moral failings of individuals often fails to critique the systematic dysfunction and utter lack of oversight that enabled such swindling, let alone the broader culture of materialism that made pilfering charities and sentencing children to jail for money rational business decisions in the minds of a few men.

For Robert Reiner and his colleagues (Reiner, Livingstone, & Allen, 2001), individualism is a consequence of the increasing tendency to view society as being obsessed with "risk" and all its attendant notions, including risk assessment, risk management, and risk avoidance (see "Risk" below). The new vocabulary surrounding this "foxy but evocative term" (Leacock & Sparks, 2002, p. 199) highlights a shift in perceptions of how risk should best be dealt with. As social problems have come to be seen as the product of chance or of individual action and solutions are sought at the level of individual self-help strategies—such as insurance or personal protection—a "winner–loser" casino culture is created (Reiner et al., 2001, p. 177). Individuals are held responsible for their fates, and the media devalue any styles of life other than spectacular consumerism (Reiner et al., 2001, p. 178). The outcome of individualism in criminal justice is that deviants are defined in terms of their "difference" and isolated socially and physically through practices of containment, incapacitation, and surveillance. Popularly conceived as a "breed apart," many offenders are judged within a moral framework, which constructs them as morally deficient malcontents who must be dealt with punitively and taught the lesson of individual responsibility (Surette, 1994).

Risk

Given that the notion of modern life being characterized by risk has become such a widespread and taken-for-granted assumption, it is surprising to find that the media devote little attention to crime avoidance, crime prevention, or personal safety. The exception to this is if a message about prevention can be incorporated into an ongoing narrative about a serious offender "at large," in which case the story will be imbued with a sense of urgency and drama (Greer, 2003). The vast majority of serious violent crimes, including murder and rape, are committed by people known to the victim. There are also clearly discernible patterns of victimization in certain socioeconomic groups and geographical locations. Yet the news media persist in presenting a picture of serious crime as random, meaningless, unpredictable, and ready to strike anyone at any time (Chermak, 1994, p. 125). Such discourse as exists in the media regarding prevention and personal safety invariably relates to offenses committed by strangers, thus implicitly promoting stereotypes of dangerous criminals prepared to strike indiscriminately (Greer, 2003; Soothill & Walby, 1991; see also Chapter 6).

The idea that we are all potential victims is a relatively new phenomenon. After the Second World War, news stories encouraged compassion for offenders by providing details designed to elicit sympathy for their circumstances, thus endorsing the rehabilitative ideal that dominated penal policy at that time (Reiner, 2001). In today's more risk-obsessed and retributive times, crime stories have become increasingly victim-centered. Perceived vulnerability is emphasized over actual victimization such that fear of crime might be more accurately conceived of as a fear for personal safety. Sometimes the media exploit public concerns by exaggerating potential risks in order to play into people's wider fears and anxieties. A week after the September 11, 2001, attacks, letters containing anthrax were delivered to several prominent Washington politicians and members of the news media, claiming five lives and sickening many more. So began the so-called "Amerithrax" investigation, which spanned nearly a decade. And though the FBI closed its investigation in late 2010, finding biodefense scientist Bruce Edward Ivins wholly responsible, questions of coconspirators or even his involvement remain. Even though the sender of the letter targeted very specific victims, in the wake of the attacks, coverage of the Amerithrax case no doubt contributed to and reflected a generalized sense of social anxiety, if not an opportunistic form of what Pat Carlen (2008) calls "risk-crazed" governance. Yet it must be remembered that audiences are not passive or undiscriminating. Many crime scares and moral panics simply never get off the ground (Jenkins, 2009), and while it might be argued that the media fail to provide the public with the resources to independently construct alternative definitions and frameworks, people's sense of personal risk will usually correspond to their past personal experiences and a realistic assessment of the likelihood of future victimization above and beyond anything they see or hear in the media.

Sex

One of the most salient news values—especially in the tabloid press—is that of sex. Several studies of the press (see, e.g., Ditton & Duffy, 1983; Greer, 2003; S. J. Smith, 1984) reveal that newspapers overreport crimes of a sexual nature, thus distorting the overall picture of crime that the public receives and instilling exaggerated fears among women regarding their likelihood of being victims of such crimes. Jason Ditton and James Duffy (1983) found that when reporting assaults against women, the press frequently relates sex and violence so that the two become virtually indistinguishable. Furthermore, the overreporting of such crimes has been so significant that, for example, in the early 1980s, crimes involving sex and violence reported in one English newspaper accounted for only 2.4% of recorded incidents yet occupied 45.8% of newspaper coverage. So interlinked are the themes of sex and violence, and so powerfully do they combine to illustrate the value of "risk," that the prime example of newsworthiness is arguably the figure of the compulsive male lone hunter, driven by a sexual desire that finds its outlet in the murder of "innocent" victims (Cameron & Frazer, 1987). As such, sexually motivated murders by someone unknown to the victim invariably receive substantial, often sensational, attention. On the other hand, sexual crimes against women where violence is not an overriding component of the story (bluntly, sex crimes that are nonfatal) and sexual assaults by someone known or related to the victim are generally regarded as routine and "pedestrian" and may garner only limited analysis (Carter, 1998; Naylor, 2001). Moreover, sexually motivated murders of prostitutes—who do not conform to media constructions of "innocent" victims—also invariably receive considerably less coverage than those of other women.

Bronwyn Naylor (2001) argues that the frequency with which articles appear about apparently random stranger violence against "ordinary" women and girls not only indicates that such stories fulfill key news values but also that they permit highly sexualized, even pornographic representations of women. At the same time, these narratives tend to be highly individualized so that offenses involving females—whether as victims or as perpetrators—are rarely reported by the popular media without reference, often sustained and explicit, to their sexualities and sexual histories. Victims are frequently eroticized; for example, in the Arizona murder trial of Jodi Arias, media coverage focused on the sex life of Arias and her boyfriend/victim Travis Alexander. Providing descriptions of Arias as a "sultry temptress" and "Femme Fatale," the pair's sex life, and Alexander's brutal death, it elaborated lurid motives for the crime and the sexuality of both the murderer and murdered. Even if their crimes have no sexual element, female offenders are often portrayed as sexual predators (see Chapter 5). As it did in the Arias case, sexuality clearly came to bear in the Italian murder trial of American student Amanda Knox—dubbed "Foxy Knoxy" by members of the media. This narrative is so widely used that it leads Naylor to question the purpose of such stories and how readers consume them:

> These stories draw on narratives about particular kinds of masculinity and about violent pornography, reiterating a discourse about masculine violence as a "natural force," both random and inevitable. They normalize this violence, drawing on and repeating the narrative that all men are potentially violent and that all women are potentially and "naturally" victims of male violence. (Naylor, 2001, p. 186)

She goes on to suggest that not only does the media's obsession with "stranger-danger" give a (statistically false) impression that the public sphere is unsafe and the private sphere is safe, but also that it influences government decisions about the prioritization of resources, resulting in the allocation of funding toward very visible preventative measures (such as street lighting and closed-circuit television [CCTV] cameras) and away from refuges, "or indeed from any broader structural analysis of violence" (Naylor, 2001, p. 186).

Celebrity or High-Status Persons

The obsession with celebrity is evident everywhere in the media, and a story is always more likely to make the news if it has a well-known name attached to it. Put simply, the level of deviance required to attract media attention is significantly lower than for offenses committed by "ordinary" citizens because a certain threshold of meaningfulness has already been achieved. As such, a "personality" will frequently be the recipient of media attention even if involved in a fairly mundane or routine crime that would not be deemed newsworthy if it concerned an "ordinary" member of the public. Whether they are victims or perpetrators of crime, celebrities, their lives, and their experiences are deemed intrinsically interesting to the audience. Even otherwise underrepresented categories of crime such as libel, perjury, and embezzlement are guaranteed widespread media attention if they have a "name" associated with them. However, it is sexual deviance that dominates the news agenda of the tabloids, and a celebrity or high-status person who unexpectedly takes personal and professional risks by engaging in a sexually deviant act is an enduring feature of news in the postmodern mediascape, providing a titillating juxtaposition of high life and low life for an audience who, it is assumed, lead conventional and law-abiding "mid lives" (Barak, 1994).

So elevated has celebrity status become that it even blinds the populace to crimes that may have been taking place quite publicly over several decades or been covered up by numerous individuals and institutions who could have intervened. For example, two highly newsworthy cases came to light in 2012 that, in hindsight, were seemingly obvious to many observers. In the U.S., the doping scandal involving cyclist Lance Armstrong, seven-time winner of the Tour de France, challenged widespread beliefs about the nature of sport and spirit of fair play. Armstrong, who dominated professional cycling like no other before him, was publicly shamed, lost millions of dollars in endorsements, and was ultimately stripped of his titles for using banned performance-enhancing techniques. Yet when it was finally proven that he had cheated the rules for nearly the balance of his career, the public response was largely incredulous. Perhaps, however, it was not so much that the public could not consider that its hero might be a fraud—indeed, Armstrong's utter dominance should have piqued the skepticism of even his most ardent supporter— but that many simply *chose* not to because doing so would force them to confront the fragility of broader systems of social worth and value. This is a point Armstrong himself has made: "That reality that the world has seen now is uncomfortable for many people" (B. Miller, 2013). That is, in the wake of the Armstrong scandal, the public was forced to confront its values and the very nature of celebrity.

The second example comes from the UK and involves a popular TV and radio personality, Jimmy Savile. After his death in late 2011 at age 84, evidence gradually came to light suggesting that Savile, an adored public figure, had sexually abused an unprecedented number of young people over a period of decades. For the British public, the case remains one of the most shocking in living memory. Early allegations led to a major criminal inquiry involving 28 police forces, three internal BBC inquiries, and the resignation of a BBC director general. The Savile case has been described by the Metropolitan Police as a watershed moment in child abuse investigations. While the media have, for several years, reported other prolific sexual predators and alleged high-level cover-ups by institutions including schools, care homes, and the Catholic church, it seems that it was Savile's celebrity status that allowed him to abuse on a massive scale—police estimate that he may actually have abused well over 1,000 victims, most of whom were children and young people.

The star's fall from grace was all the more dramatic for the fact that it was a very long drop from the elevated position he had occupied for five decades. Jimmy Savile wasn't any ordinary celebrity. He was a cultural icon from the earliest days of popular radio and television, part of the cultural fabric of British life. The BBC show *Top of the Pops,* which he presented from the very first edition in 1964, was, in its heyday, watched by 15 million viewers, and his other main vehicle, the BBC TV show *Jim'll Fix It,* broadcast between 1975 and 1994, was watched by up to 20 million people. To grasp the gravity of the Savile scandal, imagine if beloved TV personality Dick Clark, who hosted *American Bandstand* and Times Square New Year's Eve specials for more than 50 years, had been embroiled in such a controversy. Indeed, like Armstrong in the U.S., the fall of Savile shook the foundations of British cultural life.

Like Dick Clark, Jimmy Savile rose to fame at a time when there were only three (and latterly four) TV channels, and his programs were points of commonality and connection among people of a certain generation (or generations, because they ran for so long). On top of this, he had a high-profile career as a charity fund-raiser, helping to contribute millions to good causes. He was awarded a knighthood as well as a papal knighthood and counted members of the royal family among his friends. He even reportedly acted as some kind of broker in Prince Charles and Princess Diana's failing marriage. Many of Savile's crimes were carried out in places he had privileged physical access to (it has been reported that staff, including senior managers, at Broadmoor Hospital called him "Doctor" and afforded him free access to the entire site). Meanwhile, Britain's tabloids and TV executives promoted him as a "secular saint" (Cross, 2014; Furedi, 2013). When rumors of his offenses first started to circulate, it was hard to imagine just how far the star would descend. Two years into the police investigation, Operation Yewtree, over 500 victims had come forward and, every time we, the audience, thought that the story had reached new depths, it just got worse, with reports that Savile had abused paralyzed children in spine injury wards—children who were wheelchair bound and had no speech—and even reports that he was a necrophiliac who enjoyed access to hospital mortuaries. Underlining the widespread belief that Savile's celebrity status made him "untouchable," fellow BBC presenter Jeremy Paxman (whose program *Newsnight* canceled a documentary investigating allegations about Savile's behavior, much to Paxman's chagrin) asked, "What was the BBC doing promoting . . . this absurd and malign figure? They have never felt comfortable with popular culture and they have therefore given those who claim to perpetrate it too much license" (as quoted in Plunkett, 2013).

Convicted criminals can also become media "celebrities" by virtue of the notoriety of their crimes. Sometimes criminals are cast as folk devils by the media, and they are deemed newsworthy long after their convictions because the mass media take a moral stance, promoting public distaste and revulsion toward their crimes. One such example is Charles Manson, who through his accomplices, the so-called Manson Family, orchestrated the murders of at least seven people across southern California in the late 1960s. Arrested shortly after the murders and incarcerated since, Manson has nevertheless remained on the media's radar and is periodically the subject of news media, documentary, and cinematic productions half a century later.

Occupying a similarly significant symbolic space in the American social imaginary are serial killers David Berkowitz (Son of Sam), Jeffery Dahmer, and John Wayne Gacy; mafiosi like John Gotti; school shooters like Adam Lanza; and politically motivated killers such as Ted Kaczynski and Timothy McVeigh. All these figures have become iconic, cultural reference points of their particular crimes and identities. In fact, within the ghoulish subculture of **murderabilia** collectors, we can say that killers like Manson, Berkowitz, and Bundy operate in many of the ways that Beyoncé and Bieber do in the broader consumer culture. That is, they are idols, and nearly every part of their identities is commodified for consumption. For instance, the menacing black-and-white booking photo of Charles Manson that first appeared publicly on the cover of *Life* magazine in 1969, coupled with the now-famous line "Charlie don't surf" from Francis Ford Coppola's brilliant *Apocalypse Now,* has been a favorite T-shirt of edgy musicians for decades. In fact, until recently, today's Manson enthusiast could still purchase the shirt, for $20, directly from www.charlesmansonfanclub.com (also see https://www.pinterest

.com/pin/155374255864754250). Just as the ubiquitous Che Guevara T-shirt is worn to represent a particular radical countercultural aesthetic, it is safe to say that the iconic "Charlie don't surf" T-shirt offers the wearer a similar sort of commodified transgression drawing directly upon crime and violence.

Arguably the most notorious figure in the history of the British criminal justice system is Myra Hindley (the "Moors murderess"), who, with her partner, Ian Brady, was convicted in 1966 of her part in the abduction, torture, and murder of five children. Until her death in November 2002, Hindley was Britain's longest-serving prisoner and was a regular figure in the pages of the popular press, which waged a systematic and profoundly retributive campaign that culminated with front-page copy on the day after her death announcing that the "devil" had gone to hell "where she belonged" (see Chapter 5). So successful was the campaign to keep her in prison that it became all but impossible for penal authorities to even publicly contemplate the release of Hindley. Like that of Charles Manson, Hindley's booking photo has come to signify both the savagery of her crimes and the perverse celebrity that followed. As Alexa Wright argues, "this striking well-composed black-and-white photo could almost be a studio portrait. There is something glamorous about Hindley's seemingly provocative gaze, bleached and backcombed hair and fashionable clothing which, combined with the narratives of deviance that surround her, renders that particular picture simultaneously intriguing and monstrous" (Wright, 2013, p. 137; see Photo 5.2, p. 136, in Chapter 5). A painting produced in 1997 in which the artist, Marcus Harvey, used thousands of children's handprints to reproduce Hindley's infamous police photo, and a screen print by Russell Young of model Kate Moss in the same iconic image of Hindley, are among artistic works that further demonstrate her ongoing relevance as an enduring and recognizable "icon of evil" in UK popular culture. There have also been numerous films and TV series about the case, including *Myra: The Untold Story*, transmitted in 2013, a full 50 years after Hindley and Brady embarked on their murder spree (Hindley's partner, Ian Brady, has had a tiny fraction of the coverage afforded Myra; see Chapter 5).

It is not just those who represent show business and notorious crime who are elevated to visibility in the news. High-status individuals in "ordinary" life (businesspeople, politicians, professionals, the clergy, and so on) are also deemed newsworthy and are frequently used to give a "personal" angle to stories that otherwise might not make the news. This is especially germane when such individuals are defined as deviants; the more clearly and unambiguously the deviant personality can be defined (thus reducing uncertainty and reflecting the underlying news judgment of "simplification"), the more intrinsically newsworthy the story is assumed to be, especially if it intersects with other news values. This is equally true of local media that report the deviant activities of people from the community they serve. Here, the value of "proximity" comes into play (see below), but the recipient of news attention will normally be of high status within the community; for example, a teacher, priest, or doctor. Paradoxically, then, despite the media's general tendency to portray crime as a menace wrought by a disaffected underclass on ordinary, respectable folk, it is the middle-class, high-status, or celebrity offender who is deemed most newsworthy and will have the greatest number of column inches or hours of airtime devoted to his or her deviant activities.

Proximity

Proximity has both spatial and cultural dynamics. Spatial proximity refers to the geographical "nearness" of an event, while cultural proximity refers to the "relevance" of an event to an audience. These factors often intertwine so that it is those news stories that are perceived to reflect recipients' existing framework of values, beliefs, and interests and occur within geographical proximity to them that are most likely to be reported. Proximity obviously varies between local and national news. For example, a relatively "ordinary" crime like mugging or arson may be reported in local media but might not make the national news agenda unless it conforms to other news values; for example, perhaps it was especially violent or involved a celebrity. The converse of this trend is that events that occur in regions remote from the centralized bases of news organization or in countries that are not explicitly linked (in alliance or in opposition) to the U.S. rarely make national news. Indeed, there are some areas of the world that are unlikely to be prominent on the news agendas of the U.S., UK, and other industrialized nations, however high a threshold is reached by potential news stories. The United States is particularly prone to accusations of **ethnocentrism** for its tendency to look inward for its news coverage. However, while the American news media—and we, the American public, for that matter—frequently come in for criticism for our perceived lack of interest in world affairs, it is with some justification that we focus on events that occur within our own boundaries. For example, the extended global coverage of two hijacked passenger jets slamming into the twin towers of the New York World Trade Center on September 11, 2001, like earlier footage taken in Dallas in November 1963 of the assassination of President John F. Kennedy, illustrates the degree to which America is regarded as a world superpower. The news of the United States is world news in a truly global sense, and both of these crimes cast a long shadow in the collective memory of people with no connection to the events of those days. But as others have pointed out, for those not of the "First World," there have been other "September 11ths" that have received little, if any, media coverage in the West (Carrington & Hogg, 2002).

Cultural proximity also changes according to the political climate and cultural mood of the times, and there may be a domestication of foreign news, whereby events in other areas of the world will receive media attention if they are perceived to impinge on the home culture of the reporter and her or his audience. If there is no discernible relevance to the target audience, a story has to be commensurately bigger and more dramatic to be regarded as newsworthy. British novelist Michael Frayn comments facetiously:

> The crash survey showed that people were not interested in reading about road crashes unless there were at least 10 dead. A road crash with 10 dead, the majority felt, was slightly less interesting than a rail crash with one dead . . . Even a rail crash on the Continent made the grade provided there were at least 5 dead. If it was in the United States the minimum number of dead rose to 20; in South America 100; in Africa 200; in China 500. But people really preferred an air crash . . . backed up with a story about a middle-aged housewife who had been booked to fly aboard the plane but who had changed her mind at the last moment. (Frayn, 1965, p. 60)

Cultural proximity also pertains to the individual actors in any crime story that receives global coverage. When individuals from different nations are involved, any country's media can appear to "take sides" to a degree that might, at best, be classified as patriotism and, at worst, xenophobia. Again, in the case of American student Amanda Knox, convicted by an Italian court of the murder of her British housemate, Meredith Kercher, in Perugia in November 2007, it is interesting to observe the different tones adopted by the U.S., UK, and Italian media in their reporting of Knox throughout her long court trial (Gies & Bortoluzzi, 2016). While American media (relying to a large degree on her affluent, middle-class, "respectable" parents as sources) portrayed her as a wholesome, all-American girl-next-door, the British press and many Internet sites have persistently concentrated on the sexual proclivities of "Foxy Knoxy" and portrayed her in an altogether more sinister light. They also made much of pictures she had posted on social networking sites of her posing with a machine gun, and fantasy stories she had composed involving drugs and rape. But Knox's fellow students at the University of Washington argue that there appears to be a thinly disguised vendetta against Knox in some of the international media simply because she is American—or, rather, "a pot-smoking, unstable, sex-crazed American" (http://www.com.washington.edu/commIR/v012/editionOne).

When a person goes missing (whether or not foul play is immediately suspected), the likelihood of the national media lending their weight behind a campaign to find the missing person depends on several interrelated factors. If the individual in question is young, female, white, middle class, and conventionally attractive, the media are more likely to cover the case than if the missing person is, say, a working-class boy or an older woman. Even in cases where abduction and/or murder is immediately suspected, the likelihood of media interest will vary in accordance with the background of the victim. If the victim is male, working class, of African-American or Asian descent, or a persistent runaway; has been incarcerated; has drug problems; or is a prostitute (or any combination of these factors), reporters perceive that their audience is less likely to relate to, or empathize with, the victim, and the case gets commensurately lower publicity. The compliance of the victim's family in giving repeated press conferences and making themselves a central part of the story is also a crucial factor in determining its newsworthiness, as is their willingness to part with photographs and home video footage of their missing child.

The cases are too many to list. Elizabeth Smart, Jessica Lunsford, Polly Klaas—all quickly became prime-time television spectacles, structured by the now-obligatory press conference and grieving parents pleading for their children's return. In the cases of Lunsford and Klaas, media attention no doubt helped win support for hardline criminal sentencing laws aimed at sex offenders and recidivists. Generally, though, all it takes to garner considerable media attention is a case involving an attractive, photogenic female child from a "respectable," middle-class home with parents who have quickly become media-savvy and are prepared to make repeated pleas for help on behalf of the police. When there are added dramatic elements—such as an unsolved murder case, a suspicion of family involvement and/or cover-up, a bungled police investigation, or something particularly visually appealing (to a salacious news outlet, that is) about the victim, a criminal event can almost take on a life of its own. Witness the coverage of six-year-old JonBenét Ramsey's murder in Boulder, Colorado, in December 1996. As a child beauty queen, JonBenét had multiple photos taken of her in her short life, usually heavily made up, frequently in rather sexualized costumes and poses. The fact that no one has ever been prosecuted for the murder, though suspicion has fallen on both parents and JonBenét's older brother at various times, has ensured that the case remains a perennial staple of tabloid newspapers and magazines in the U.S. and beyond even two decades later.

In contrast, cases involving poor and minority children often fail to generate interest nationally. Take, for instance, four-year-old African-American Jaquilla Scales, who, like JonBenét Ramsey, was abducted from her bedroom (in Wichita, Kansas, in 2001). While Ramsey, Smart, Lunsford, and Klaas have appeared on the front pages of newspapers, on the covers of magazines, on television and in documentary films, Jaquilla, who has never been found, barely made a blip on the public's register. Speaking to the apparent disinterest in Jaquilla's case, her grandmother, Mattie Mitchell, entreated, "But the thing about it, the ghetto mamas love their babies just like the rich people do. And they [news producers] need to recognize that." Critics have labeled this the "missing white girl syndrome," a condition in which the news media help position certain cases as deserving of attention and hence resources while helping to make the victimization of poor and minority children and families seem normal (Stillman, 2007, p. 491). There is some empirical support for existence of "the syndrome." For instance, Scripps Howard News Service studied 162 missing-children cases covered by the Associated Press and 43 covered by CNN between January 1, 2000, and December 31, 2004. The study found that stories about missing white children accounted for 67% of the AP's and 76% of CNN's coverage while accounting for only 53% of the missing-children cases at that time.

Responding to the study, Ernie Allen, then president of the National Center for Missing and Exploited Children, stated:

> I don't think this results from conscious or subconscious racism. But there's no question that if a case resonates, if it touches the heartstrings, if it makes people think, "That could be my child," then it's likely to pass the test to be considered newsworthy. Does that skew in favor of white kids? Yes, it probably does.

Sociologist David Finkelhor, director of the Crimes Against Children Research Center at the University of New Hampshire, added:

> I think there are explanations other than that black kids and Hispanic kids are not objects of concern or compassion ... Middle-class white families have good social networks and are able to mobilize people better, making it a matter of communitywide attention. But minority parents may not see the media as a likely source of help. (Scripps Howard News Service, 2005)

Likewise, CNN correspondent Tom Foreman (2006) argued that he had "never, not even once, seen a story spiked because the victim was not attractive enough or the wrong race." He had, however, simply seen

> plenty of stories fall by the wayside, pushed down and out of the show, because a consensus develops that says, "You know, I don't think our viewers are very interested in this case."

Is that racism or realism? We can't cover every murder, but ignoring them all or reporting just statistics seems irresponsible. So how should we decide whose life or loss is covered? (Foreman, 2006)

In many ways, all three attribute the disparity in missing-children cases to the will of the market (S. Cohen & Young, 1973). That is, the news media are simply pandering to what they see as a market for their product. Sociologist Eduardo Bonilla-Silva calls the willingness to entertain timing, geography, social networks, or even poverty as reasons for disparate coverage the "anything but racism" strategy. He points out that newsworthiness is simply determined. In Allen's words, if a story makes people think, "That could be my child," it is in fact a powerful admission that the media see only missing white children as sufficiently proximal to interest the general public (Bonilla-Silva, 2012). Considering this, is it any wonder that of the 47 children that went missing between July and December 2008 (according to the National Center for Missing and Exploited Children), it was the disappearance of Caylee Anthony, the daughter of a young attractive upper-class white woman from Florida, that came to dominate the news in the following months? Yet we should not assume that this is a wholly American phenomenon. For example, a short time after the disappearance of 14-year-old Milly Dowler from Surrey, England, in March 2002, the body of a teenage girl was recovered from a disused quarry. Before the body had even been identified, sections of the tabloid press were carrying headlines announcing that Milly had been found. But it turned out to be the corpse of another 14-year-old girl, Hannah Williams, who had disappeared a year earlier. Yet it was the hunt for Milly that continued to dominate the news for the weeks and months to follow. Almost as soon as she was found, Hannah was forgotten. Quite simply, unlike Milly, who was portrayed as the "ideal" middle-class teenager, Hannah's background made it difficult to build a campaign around her. She was working class and had run away before. Furthermore, her mother—a single parent on a low income—"wasn't really press-conference material" according to a police spokeswoman (Bright, 2002, p. 23).

Violence or Conflict

The news value arguably most common to all media is that of violence because it fulfills the media's desire to present dramatic events in the most graphic possible fashion. Even the most regulated media institutions are constantly pushing back the boundaries of acceptable reportage when it comes to depicting acts of violence because it represents a basic violation of the person and marks the distinction between those who are of society and those who are outside it. Only the state has the monopoly of legitimate violence, and this "violence" is used to safeguard society against "illegitimate" uses (Hall et al., 1978/2013). However, violence has become so ubiquitous that—although still considered newsworthy—it is frequently reported in a routine, mundane manner with little follow-up or analysis. Unless a story involving violence conforms to several other news values or provides a suitable threshold to keep alive an existing set of stories, even the most serious acts of violence may be used as "fillers" and consigned to the inside pages of a newspaper. Yet, whether treated sensationally or unsensationally, violence—including violent death—remains a staple of media reporting. For instance, researchers focusing on news media coverage of youth violence in Chicago found that despite a significant decline in youth homicides, a disproportionately large portion of local crime news pertaining to youth involved murders. This sort of overreporting, according to the researchers, led many Chicagoans to be ill informed about the state of youth crime in their community (Boulahanis & Heltsley, 2004). More generally, large nationally representative surveys of the American public report similar findings. As alluded to in the previous chapter, since 1989, the Gallup Poll has included the question "Is there more crime in the US than there was a year ago, or less?" in its (nearly) annual survey. Despite a well-documented decline in serious and violent crime over the last two decades, each year a large majority of those surveyed believed crime to be on the rise. In fact, on average, about 67% of those surveyed believed this to be the case.

Cultural criminologists argue that crime, violence, humiliation, and cruelty are objectified, commodified, and desired to the extent that they are widely distributed through all forms of media to be pleasurably consumed. Presdee offers numerous examples that he claims are evidence of the consumer's need for privately enjoyed, carnivalesque transgression. From "sports" that, having all but disappeared, are now enjoying a dramatic upturn in popularity (albeit underground), from dog-fighting to "reality TV" to gangsta rap, the evidence of our lust for pain and humiliation is all around us:

> The mass of society bare their souls to the media who, in turn, transform them into the commodity of entertainment. Confidentialities are turned against the subject, transforming them into the object of hurt and humiliation as their social being is commodified ready for consumption. (Presdee, 2000, p. 75)

Little wonder, then, that news has followed a similarly dramatic and vicarious path. With an increasing imperative to bring drama and immediacy to news production, the caveat "You may find some of the pictures that follow distressing" seems to preface an increasing number of television news reports. This leads us to consider the spectacle of violence as portrayed through graphic imagery.

Visual Spectacle and Graphic Imagery

Television news is generally given greater credence by the public than newspapers, partly because it is perceived to be less partisan than the press but also because it offers higher-quality (moving) images that are frequently held to demonstrate the "truth" of a story or to verify the particular angle from which the news team has chosen to cover it. Chris Greer has suggested that of all the changes in journalistic perceptions of news values over the last half century, it is the visual that most emphatically marks the difference between the criteria described by Galtung and Ruge in the 1960s (1965/1973) and the ones described here. For Greer (2009), the primacy of the visual has been hastened by technological developments (the exponential growth of mobile digital technologies, the Internet, etc.) and consolidated by the shift to a more explicitly visual culture; we all take it for granted that any news story will be accompanied by images—and increasingly, thanks to mobile phones/cameras, Facebook, and so forth, images that have not been approved for publication by the subject, as the earlier discussion of Amanda Knox highlighted (see also discussion below about "citizen journalism"). Quite simply, in the second decade of the 21st century, potential news stories are likely to make the news only if they can be portrayed in images as well as words, and the "availability of the right image can help elevate a crime victim or offender to iconic status" (Greer, 2009, p. 227; cf. Hayward & Presdee, 2010). Travis Linnemann and his colleagues (Linnemann, Hanson, & Williams, 2013) suggest that visual representation of the traumatic and grotesque is designed to tap into the same human tendency that compels people to gawk when passing the scene of an accident (see Chapter 10). In this way, we can say that the shocking, often violent image is a defining feature of spectatorship (see also Brown, 2009).

As described above, violence is a primary component of news selection. But there are many different types of violence, and it tends to be acts of violence that have a strong visual impact and can be graphically presented that are most likely to receive extensive media coverage. In August 2012, Jeffrey Johnson opened fire at New York City's Empire State Building, killing one person and wounding several others. The graphic photographs shot by stunned onlookers contributed directly to the story's national profile. For instance, when the Instagram user "mr mookie" posted a photo of one of the wounded bystanders bleeding and splayed out on a curb, representatives from various global news services—*The Guardian,* Reuters, *The Globe and Mail,* Blottr, Associated Press—clamored to be the first to obtain its rights. Another particularly graphic photo of the body of Steven Ercolino, the only person other than Johnson to die in the incident, elicited much discussion among news professionals and the public alike. The photo, which appeared on the front page of the August 24 *New York Times* online edition, showing Ercolino face down on the pavement with ribbons of almost cartoonish bright red blood streaming toward the gutter, led many to question the decorum of publishing such an image and call for its removal. Still, others in the media, such as Kenny Irby of the newsgroup Poynter, defended the utility of the image and the right of the *New York Times* to publish it. Irby reasoned, "The New York Times photo, while it is incredibly compelling and disturbing, what makes it graphic is the blood, the color . . . but blood is an inextricable part of a mortal wound." For this reporter, images, much like words, simply convey the facts of an incident, however disturbing. And while we may not necessarily agree on the supposed simplicity of photographic representation, the visual is an undeniable facet of a story's appeal.

In the UK, the very public murder, in May 2013, of off-duty soldier Lee Rigby on a busy London street by two Islamist extremists, captured on CCTV and on footage filmed on witnesses' mobile phones, is another prime example. A video of one of the perpetrators "justifying" the killing, while still covered in the victim's blood, was carried by ITN's website and visited so many times that the site crashed. However, while "spectacular" crimes get a lot of attention because they make good copy and are visually arresting on television, it seems that crimes that occur in private spheres, or that are not subject to public scrutiny, become even more marginalized, even more invisible. Hence, crimes like domestic violence, child abuse, elder abuse, accidents at work, pollution of the environment, much white-collar crime, corporate corruption, state violence, and governments' denial or abuse of human rights all receive comparatively little media attention despite their arguably greater cost to individuals and society. Similarly, long-term developments, which may be more important than immediate, dramatic incidents in terms of their effects, may not be covered because they cannot be accompanied by dramatic visual imagery. Furthermore, TV shows like *Big Brother*, which blur the line between entertainment and reality and call into question the extent to which people behave "normally" while being watched on television, might make us question whether court trials should be televised. In some countries, court trials have made celebrities out of lawyers and judges and led to accusations that they, too, are not immune to playing up for the cameras. In addition, "real" footage of the kind captured on CCTV or on phone cameras by witnesses and bystanders as a criminal event unfolds is increasingly being used in news broadcasts to visually highlight the event's immediacy and "authenticity." Such images have graphically and poignantly contributed to the spectacle of crime and violence in the postmodern era.

Many of the most shocking events that occurred in the last few years of the 20th century entered the collective consciousness with such horrifying impact precisely because news reports were accompanied by images of the victim at the time of, immediately prior to, or soon after a serious violent incident. The video footage of black motorist Rodney King being beaten by four white LA police officers, the live broadcast of the O. J. Simpson chase, and the ISIS propaganda footage of Western hostages being beheaded are well-known examples of graphic imagery being used to heighten the drama of already newsworthy stories. What's more, with the recent proliferation of body-worn cameras in policing, it is a certainty that the dire circumstances of violent confrontations will remain a staple of U.S. news productions. Combining the mundane ordinariness of everyday life with the grim inevitability of what is about to unfold, cellphone, body-cam, and CCTV footage—played out by the media on a seemingly endless loop—appeals to the voyeuristic elements in all of us while at the same time reinforcing our sense of horror, revulsion, and powerlessness. In fact, in the contemporary moment, where we have, in the words of Haggerty and Ericson (2000), witnessed the "disappearance of disappearance," those cases that do not have documentary footage might appear most unusual and suspicious (see Chapter 8 for further discussion of CCTV and surveillance).

Children

Writing in 1978, Stuart Hall and his colleagues (1978/2013) argued that any crime can be lifted into news visibility if violence becomes associated with it, but Philip Jenkins (1992) suggests that any crime can be lifted into news visibility if children are associated with it. This is true whether the children at the center of the story are victims or offenders, although Jenkins concentrates on child victims, who, he says, guarantee the newsworthiness of a story. We would argue that this is not necessarily the case. Sexual abuse within the family remains so low on the media's agenda as to render it virtually invisible, and as we shall see in later chapters, the mass media persist in preserving the image of the ideal family and underplaying or ignoring the fact that sexual violence exists—indeed, is endemic—in *all* communities, and that sexual abuse of children is more likely to occur within the family than at the hands of an "evil stranger."

However, it is undoubtedly true that a focus on children means that deviant behavior in the public sphere automatically crosses a higher threshold of victimization than would have been possible if adults alone had been involved. Jenkins says that children ensure the media's commitment to what might be called "morality campaigns." In the 1970s, those who wished to denounce and stigmatize homosexuality, the sale of pornography, or religious deviation (for example, satanism) found little support in the prevailing moral climate. But the inclusion of children in stories about these activities makes it impossible to condone them within any conventional moral or legal framework. Thus, we have witnessed over the last 50 years a process of escalation whereby morality campaigns are now directed "not against homosexuality but at pedophilia, not pornography but child pornography, not satanism but ritual child abuse" (Jenkins, 1992, p. 11).

Children who commit crimes have arguably become especially newsworthy. In the UK, the widely discussed murder of two-year-old James Bulger by two 10-year-olds was the first case for at least a generation in which the media constructed preteen children as "demons" rather than as "innocents." The case also proved a watershed in terms of criminal justice and crime prevention. The 10-year-olds were tried in an adult court, and the case was the impetus for a massive expansion of CCTV equipment in public spaces throughout the UK. But at a more fundamental level, it presented a dilemma for the mass media. Childhood is a social construction; in other words, it is subject to a continuous process of (re)invention and (re)definition and, even in the modern period, has gone through numerous incarnations from 18th-century romantic portrayals of childhood as a time of innocence to more recent conceptions of childhood as a potential site of psychological and psychiatric problems. But with the exception of a brief period in the early 19th century when children were viewed as inherently corrupt and in need of overt control and moral guidance (which coincided with a period when child labor was the norm among the working classes, before legislation took children out of factories, mills, and mines and relocated them in schools and reformatories), the notion of children being "evil" has not been prominent.

By and large, childhood has been seen as fundamentally separate from adulthood, and children have been regarded as requiring nurture and protection, whether by philanthropic reformers, educators, parents, welfare agencies, the medical profession, or the law. But with the murder of James Bulger by two older children, the UK public's notion of childhood innocence gave way to themes of childhood horror and evil. Outrage was fueled, in part, by sensational and vindictive press reporting that variously described the 10-year-olds as "brutes," "monsters," "animals," and "the spawn of Satan." The reasons why children and young people are the usual subjects of such moral panics will be explored in Chapters 3 and 4, but suffice it to say here that the young are frequently used as a kind of measuring stick or social barometer with which to test the health of society more generally. Children and adolescents represent the future, and if they engage in deviant behavior, it is often viewed as symptomatic of a society that is declining ever further into a moral morass. For the media, then, "deviant youth" is used as a shorthand ascription for a range of gloomy and fatalistic predictions about spiraling levels of crime and amoral behavior in society at large.

Conservative Ideology and Political Diversion

What all the news values discussed so far have in common is their reliance on a broadly right-wing consensus that, in many news channels (especially the tabloid press), is justified as encapsulating an "American way of life"—a sentiment successfully exploited by Trump in his presidential campaign slogan "Make America Great Again" (itself originating in Ronald Reagan's campaign of 1980). In matters of crime and deviance, this agenda emphasizes deterrence and repression and voices support for more police, more prisons, harsher policies on immigration and refugees, and a tougher criminal justice system. In addition, it appears that we now live in a society where political process and media discourse are indistinguishable and mutually constitutive. The symbiotic relationship between the mass media and politicians is illustrated by the support given by the former to the latter in matters of law and order. For decades now, "populist punitiveness" has characterized American penal policy. A particularly notorious example of this sort of conservative ideological rhetoric is the case of the so-called "superpredator." In an article that appeared in the conservative magazine *The Weekly Standard* on November 27, 1995, then–Princeton political scientist John Dilulio claimed that a combination of demographic and cultural changes were lining up to unleash untold levels of youth violence across America. He wrote:

> On the horizon, therefore, are tens of thousands of severely morally impoverished juvenile superpredators. They are perfectly capable of committing the most heinous acts of physical violence for the most trivial reasons (for example, a perception of slight disrespect or the accident of being in their path). (Dilulio, 1995, p. 27)

For Dilulio, youth violence and the impending crime wave are not attributable to decades of economic inequality, social isolation, and exclusion but rather moral poverty, rooted in "fatherless, godless and jobless" families. Later, Dilulio teamed up with two other highly-placed archconservatives, then–secretary of education William Bennett and "drug czar" John Walters, to advance the superpredator thesis further in *Body Count: Moral Poverty . . . and How to Win America's War Against Crime and Drugs* (1996). Of course, not only did the authors' predictions of impending waves of morally impoverished "fatherless, godless and jobless" children said to rise from inner-city slums prove incorrect, but they perfectly coincided with the beginning of precipitous drops in serious and violent crime. Nevertheless, because of the considerable power and influence held by the three, their alarmist warnings of the "coming of the superpredators" had, and perhaps continue to have, serious effects on criminal justice policy and public opinion nearly two decades later. Despite the lessons of the past, even today there seems little serious opposition from either major political party to directly challenge conservative crime control rhetoric supporting policies such as the notorious stop-and-frisk program of the New York City Police Department (NYPD), sentencing enhancements for "gang-related" crimes, or the general trend toward increasingly longer sentences for nonviolent crimes. All of these issues are most directly conveyed to the public at large by the mass media.

Despite newspapers' claiming to be the voice of the people, their criminalization of certain individuals and activities highlights the general perceived intolerance toward anyone or anything that transgresses an essentially conservative agenda. It is also a partial explanation for the vigorous policing and punishment of so-called "victimless crimes": recreational use of drugs; sexual permissiveness, especially among young people; public displays of homosexuality and lesbianism; antiestablishment demonstrators exercising their democratic right to protest and film the police. All are activities that are subject to continuous, and sometimes overblown, repression. At times, the generalized climate of hostility toward marginal groups and "unconventional" norms (to the dominant culture of journalists, at least) spills over into racism and xenophobia. As documented by Hall and his colleagues in *Policing the Crisis* (1978/2013), the moral concerns over mugging in the 1970s were focused on young men of African-Caribbean descent; the inner-city riots of the 1980s were frequently attributed entirely to black youths; and recent media coverage of the immigration into Britain of people from other countries frequently demonstrates a shocking disregard for others' human rights and the media's inability (or unwillingness) to differentiate between political refugees and illegal immigrants. Even people from ethnic and/or religious minorities born and raised in the U.S. (or the UK or Germany or France) may be subjected to overwhelmingly negative press. For example, people of Islamic faith or appearance have been consistently identified in negative contexts, even when cast as victims, since the terrorist attacks on the twin towers of the World Trade Center. This simplistic and unfavorable coverage of Muslims has only intensified with recent bombings in several major European cities and with the emergence of the Jihadist militant group Islamic State.

This jingoistic fervor has had very real consequences for the people on the business end of panicked media-enabled derision. Following the September 11 attacks, there were dozens of retaliatory hate crimes perpetrated against American citizens (with at least the appearance) of Middle Eastern ancestry. When, for instance, Balbir Singh Sodhi, a Sikh, was shot and killed at an Arizona gas station, the first words of the killer, Frank Roque, to police were reportedly, "I'm a patriot and an American. I'm American. I'm a damn American!" That Roque ignored differences between Sikh and Arab cultures, seeing both Sodhi and the 9/11 hijackers simply as "towel heads," is powerful evidence of the volatility of punitive, populist vitriol. More recently, revelations of an NYPD surveillance program that targeted American Muslims exposed how these stark binaries operate structurally. The program employed a variety of techniques to monitor and map the New York City neighborhoods of 28 or so "ancestries of interest," most of which linked to Islam. However, the NYPD purposefully excluded the activities of non-Muslims (Coptic Christian Egyptians, Iranian Jews) within those same neighborhoods and concentrated their efforts on infiltrating mosques at Muslim community centers.

The concentration of news media on the criminal and deviant activities of people from the lowest socioeconomic classes and from religious, ethnic, and cultural minorities serves to perpetuate a sense of a stratified, deeply divided, and mutually hostile population. Some politicians—not least President Trump—have been quick to galvanize the support of an anxious and fearful public and have undoubtedly contributed to negative reporting, which has agitated social tensions. By simultaneously focusing attention on hapless victims of serious crime and calling for tougher, more retributive punishment, politicians not only promote an essentially conservative agenda but also deflect attention from other serious social problems. Indeed, it could be argued that much of what makes up our newspapers is in fact a mere side-show, a diversionary tactic that removes attention from more serious problems in society, particularly those of a political nature. The media hysteria that has, in recent years, accompanied victims of HIV and AIDS, lone/unmarried parents, teenage and preteen mothers, child abusers, satanic ritual abusers, juvenile delinquents, joyriders, ravers, marijuana users, pedophiles, homosexual members of government (indeed, homosexuals generally), adulterous celebrities, and girl gangs might all be reasonably argued to constitute part of the overtly sanctimonious moral discourse directed at the institution of the family that has characterized the media and political agendas since the 1980s. From Barry Goldwater's notorious "violence in the streets" speech at the 1964 Republican National Convention and Richard Nixon's bold declaration of drugs and drug users as "public enemy number one" in 1971 to Ronald and Nancy Reagan's "Just Say No" campaign and Bill Clinton's dismantling of social welfare under the guise of "welfare to work" and "tough on crime" criminal justice expansion, successive political administrations have harnessed the mass media to criminalize certain groups of people and divert attention from the systemic social problems of their making: poverty, patriarchy, and an education system that is failing its pupils among them.

TWO EXAMPLES OF NEWSWORTHY STORIES PAR EXCELLENCE

The Murder of the Clutter Family and Truman Capote's *In Cold Blood*

In 1959, in Holcomb, a tiny farm town on the west Kansas wheat plains, two ex-convicts entered the home of Herbert and Bonnie Clutter in the dead of night with the intention of robbing the wealthy farmers. When the robbery went sour, the men murdered the couple and their two children, Nancy and Kenyon, "in cold blood." Sometime later and thousands of miles away in New York City, celebrated novelist Truman Capote came across an account of the murders in the *New York Times*. While provocative enough to draw national media attention, the crime was not necessarily unusual, the Clutters being just the latest of some 8,500 or so murders that year. Something clearly seized Capote's imagination, however. Perhaps it was the headline "Wealthy Farmer, 3 of Family Slain" and photo of Herb Clutter that drew Capote in. Maybe it was simply the shock of such a crime marring the serene and presumably safe landscapes of rural Kansas. It could be that a sheriff's speculation that the murders were the work of a "psychopathic killer" set Capote's wheels turning. However it happened, when he got up from reading that article, Capote is said to have had the subject of his next book decided.

The book, widely regarded as the first and perhaps most important of the modern true crime genre—*In Cold Blood: A True Account of a Multiple Murder and Its Consequences*—has haunted the minds of the public with the horrors of random crimes and senseless violence since its initial publication in 1965 (Capote, 1993). Hailed by many as a masterpiece even before its release, *In Cold Blood* has spawned numerous films, incessant writing, and vigorous debate since. The novel marks not only the birth of a genre but a change in the ways in which crime, law, and punishment appear in American popular culture. As Shulamit Almog writes:

Capote did more than describing the murky face of America; he also interpreted it and took an active part in the way it will be represented in the future. The book was a first swallow, signaling the future trend of public demand for succulent representations of appalling criminal events, and the possible means to satiate it. Capote turned the hideous murder not only into art, but also into entertainment that attracted and satisfied huge audiences. (2012, p. 365)

Almog rightly sees *In Cold Blood* as an important intersection of violence, art, and entertainment. Whereas other similarly celebrated novels of the day, such as *I Am a Fugitive From a Georgia Chain Gang!* and *To Kill a Mockingbird*, feature themes of hope, justice, and redemption, *In Cold Blood* focuses almost wholly on the spectacle of brutal and calculated violence. Narrated by Capote's disembodied voice, his "non-fiction" style forces his characters "into a spectacle that offers readers of the book vicarious participation in the slaughter of an entire family" (Hickman, 2005, p. 465).

An entire family murdered in their home by ghoulish intruders was certainly newsworthy in its own right. That their murders occurred in a tiny farm town, far out on the Bible Belt, no doubt met the required threshold of perceived interest for readers of the original *New York Times* article and Capote's subsequent "true crime" masterpiece.

Of course, the manhunt, capture, trial, and eventual execution of the killers, Richard Hickock and Perry Smith, offered certain predictability for the local reporters covering the story. Even mundane workings of Capote, a well-known celebrity, as he researched the crime, became steady and predictable fodder for local reporters. The motives of the two murderers were easily simplified, boiled down to greed and personal defect. Local news reports described one of the men, Richard Hickock, as a once-promising student and athlete from a decent hardworking Kansas farm family who somehow went terribly wrong. When commenting on speculation that a head injury was the cause of his murderous turn, Capote invoked a sort of Lombrosian stigmata, remarking that it was as though Hickock's "head had been halved like an apple, then put together a fraction off center" (Capote, 1993, p. 31). Offering another theory of the crime, others suggested that it was the friend he had made in prison, Perry Smith, who led Hickock astray. The older of the pair, Smith had moved all over the western half of the United States as his alcoholic father chased work. Local news speculated, as did Capote, that his chaotic and perhaps abusive upbringing nurtured murderous impulses. Like Hickock, Smith's appearance was striking. He stood just 5 feet 4 inches, and a motorcycle accident had left him with an obvious limp and his "chunky, dwarfish legs . . . pitifully scarred" (Capote, 1993, p. 31). Physical impairments, abusive childhoods, deviant friends—whatever it was, the story simply boiled down to the failings of two individuals, Richard Hickock and Perry Smith.

As first told by Hickock and Smith to investigators and later interpreted by Capote, the circumstances of the crime made the story all the more compelling. A fellow prisoner at Lansing Penitentiary, William Floyd Wells had worked the Clutter farm nearly a decade before the murders. Though he thought well of the Clutters, it was his jailhouse fib of a cash hoard that Herb kept on hand to pay his workers that charted Hickock and Smith's course. It was even Wells's directions that led the killers to the Clutters' farm.

That there was never any money, outside the few dollars robbed from Bonnie's purse, made the crimes seem all the more random and pointless, undergirding an understanding of social life as governed by chance and risk. Capote's embellished account of how Smith kept Hickock from raping 16-year-old Nancy Clutter marked the crimes with lurid sexually deviancy against children.

Then there were the Clutters. Representing the picture-perfect image of a wholesome all-American family, they were, as described by those who knew them, "the last people you'd ever murder." Herb was an "eminent Republican and church leader" (Capote, 1993, p. 34). Bonnie had clearly done her wifely duties, as evidenced by their beautiful home and well-mannered children. Nancy and Kenyon were popular and admired pictures of all-American wholesomeness. Industrious, conservative, white Protestant farmers, the Clutters seemed the perfect family. An anonymous resident quoted in *Life* put it this way:

> Feeling wouldn't run so high ... if that had happened to anyone except them. Anyone less admired. Prosperous. Secure. But that family represented everything people hereabouts really value and respect, and that such a thing could happen to them—well, it's like being told there is no God. (Avedon, 1966, p. 61)

If not geographically, this was as culturally proximate to the white American middle class as you could come. This wasn't the random murder of some unlucky farmer family—this was the murder of *the* American family. Graphic images of the Clutters' violent deaths described by the eminent talent of Truman Capote were enlivened by gruesome crime scene photographs leaked to the media, which can still be found on the Internet. All of this, of course, leads to and lends support to the harshest of retributive punishments. That Hickock and Smith met their fates on the end of a hangman's rope at the gallows of Lansing Penitentiary only advanced an understanding of social life where guilt is punished, innocence is avenged, and order is restored. In this way, both everyday media coverage and Capote's artistic retelling write the conservative ideology of police power and penal authority into the social imaginary (Linnemann, 2015).

Anders Behring Breivik and the Spree Killing of 77 People in Norway

On July 22, 2011, a bomb exploded in a vehicle outside a government building in central Oslo, killing eight people inside. As news of the blast was being broadcast around the world, the 32-year-old man who had planted the bomb, Anders Behring Breivik, dressed in a police uniform and boarded a ferry to the island of Utøya, 25 miles northwest of Oslo, where 564 young people were attending a summer camp organized by the youth wing of the Labour Party. Breivik went on an hour-and-a-half shooting spree, killing 69 people, mostly teenagers, before being arrested by police.

In the UK, the large number of victims and the capture of the gunman alive ensured that the story met the required threshold of interest. The publication of Breivik's propagandist websites, the discovery of explosives at his house, and his subsequent trial created further "mini" thresholds to keep the story fresh in public mind. A grim predictability was woven through the account of the crime via recourse to stories about terrorism (e.g., in London and Madrid) and reports suggesting that his actions bore many of the hallmarks of U.S. school shootings. Many elements of the story were simplified—he was a "Nazi"; his complex personality disorders were presented as psychosis or schizophrenia; the murders were constructed as individual and random—a cruel act of chance—suggesting once again that any of us (or our children) is at risk from similar kinds of attack; his crimes were partially explained by reference to sex—his sexual frustration, his lack of sexual experience, his claims that he'd seen the ravages of promiscuity and venereal disease within his own family. The attention given to mass murderers is such that Breivik has inevitably become a celebrity in his own right. The cultural proximity of Norway to other Western nations ensured its newsworthiness; in addition, the news media emphasized reported links to English far-right groups, and Foreign Secretary William Hague was reported as saying that the UK stood "shoulder to shoulder" with Norway. The violence of the events that day was reinforced by the circulation of graphic images of the victims' bodies and then again a month after the attacks when news media published images of Breivik reenacting the murders at Utøya for the benefit of police investigators. The fact that Breivik's victims were mostly young people from "respectable," middle-class backgrounds made the story even more newsworthy, and the press initially suggested that they were even younger than they were (many newspapers stated his crime as "gunning down children on a holiday island"). The presence of a moralistic conservative ideology was most evident in the early reporting as events were still unfolding; initial speculation centered on the possibility of homegrown fundamentalist Muslims being responsible, reflecting a global media preoccupation with the threat of a terrorist attack, a barely disguised "Islamophobia" within Western media, and a perception of an emerging threat from the extreme right in Europe. These fixations, which are frequently conflated, all contributed to a heightened sense of risk. However, once Breivik was captured, news media hastily sought to distance themselves from his brand of political extremism.

This brief analysis relates to UK media, but this terrible crime has been analyzed by Cere, Jewkes, and Ugelvik (2013), who use the case to highlight some of the subtle discrepancies underpinning crime news reporting in the UK, Norway, and Italy that reflect broader social, cultural, and political differences among the three countries. Among their findings is that in Italy, coverage of the Breivik case was rather subdued at the time of the events, perhaps due to awareness that his actions were politically motivated. Right-wing individuals and organizations have left an indelible mark on Italian political and media culture. Memories of bombings in Milan, Brescia, and Bologna and of other crimes, including the killing of two Senegalese immigrants in Florence in 2011 by a right-wing sympathizer, are always in the background of any discussion of right-wing violent actions, and hence the coverage was not only concerned with this particular individual but also with the broader international context of his dramatic actions. Unsurprisingly, Norwegian coverage of the case has been extensive, and many of the normal "rules" of reporting have been broken in this usually sober and ethically conscious nation. For example, while it is illegal to photograph or film defendants in a criminal case, an exception was made by the court in the case of Breivik, and Cere et al. (2013) argue that the opposite of simplification occurred in the reporting of the story. Rather, the news media exhausted every possible angle, producing a hugely complex and often confusing mélange of contrasting impressions—all of which must be seen within the wider cultural bricolage of stories about acts of terror. Analyzing the story from a cultural criminological standpoint, Sandberg et al. (2014) argue that Breivik's crimes followed a cultural script, formed and reformed down years of reporting of campus killings in the U.S. In a media-saturated world, Breivik's actions on July 22, 2011, constitute an edited and reedited performance, combining violence, fame-seeking, and an extreme form of masculinity. The fact that the attacks were unprecedented in their extent and brutality for a country with little experience of political violence—a low crime rate and just under 35 murders a year on average—made the story all the more shocking, both within Norway and outside it (Berntzen & Sandberg, 2014; Mathiesen, 2013).

NEWS PRODUCTION AND CONSUMPTION IN A DIGITAL GLOBAL MARKETPLACE: THE RISE OF THE CITIZEN JOURNALIST

Finally, in our analysis of crime news, it is worth mentioning the impact of new media (although in advanced, industrialized nations, satellite and digital media can hardly be called "new" any more). One of the most profound changes of recent years is that many of us now consume much of our news online, and the democratic nature of Internet communication, together with its global penetration and immediacy, have given rise to the citizen journalist. "User-generated content," or UGC, as it is known in the media industries, encompasses images taken on mobile phone cameras, texts and emails sent by audience members to media outlets, and contributions to Internet sites such as Twitter and YouTube.

Twitter has particularly captured the imaginations of mainstream journalists (see Chapter 9). BBC journalist Rory Cellan-Jones describes the microblogging service as being "like a very fast, but not entirely reliable news agency" that he uses to gain immediate notice of breaking stories and file his reports before many of his competitors (http://www.bbc.co.uk/blogs/technology/). Although now frequently associated with the celebrities who use it, Twitter first came to many people's attention when pictures were posted of a US Airways plane making a forced landing into New York's Hudson River in January 2009. Although not a story about crime, it met most of the news criteria outlined in this chapter and was notable for the novelty of a major air incident in which every one of the 155 people on board survived. The story has been made into a movie, *Sully,* starring Tom Hanks, recalling the incredible images at the time of an Airbus A320 submerged in the freezing river with its passengers standing along its wings, underlining the drama and spectacle of this event. A passenger on a passing ferry took a photo of the stricken airplane on his mobile phone and posted it on Twitter. By the following day, over 97,000 people had viewed the image and its owner was doing interviews with many of the major global news organizations.

Personal, mobile communication technologies have not only added a new dimension to the manufacture of news but, in a few cases, have had far-reaching consequences for democracy. In May 2008, it was reported that the Chinese government had responded to the devastation caused by an earthquake in the Sichuan province, in which tens of thousands of people perished, by moderating its control of the Internet. This meant that those affected by the tragedy could use video-sharing sites, blogs, chat rooms, instant messaging services, and the like to circulate graphic pictures and accounts of their experiences. For these new citizen journalists, the Chinese government's relaxation of its generally tough stance on Internet content brought an unprecedented level of freedom (see Chapter 9). Another example of an event brought to the attention of a global audience by a citizen journalist was the killing of a young Iranian woman, Neda Agha-Soltan, who was shot during an anti-government protest in Tehran on June 20, 2009. A university student, Neda was a bystander watching the protests when she was shot by a man believed to be a member of the pro-government militia (later "identified" when photographs of his ID card were posted on the Internet and then published by newspapers). With journalists forced to stay in their hotel rooms, these amateur recordings quickly became the only means of getting uncensored news about the protests and the murder of Neda out of Tehran. Within hours of Neda's death, graphic scenes captured by an unknown eyewitness showing her bleeding to death on the street had been posted online and were being published and broadcast in newspapers and bulletins around the world. Commenting on the immediacy and power of this sort of street-level journalism, Justin Turner argues that the mainstream American news media used the footage of Neda's death to add "enmity to the ever-growing grammar of racist and xenophobic rhetoric directed at Iran, the Middle East and Arab culture," while alternative "accounts which might explain her death in more complex, which is to say less neocolonial or Orientalist ways, failed to gain significant traction" (Turner, 2015, p. 86). The shaky video footage even received a Polk Award, one of the highest honors in journalism, representing the first time such a prize had been awarded to an anonymous individual.

Of course, what these illustrations from China and Iran also demonstrate is that, although it is undoubtedly true that major crimes or disasters now generate more material from ordinary eyewitnesses, the extent to which news production and consumption has fundamentally changed can be overemphasized. As Rory Cellan-Jones suggests, technologically savvy journalists are learning how to access that content and turn it into mainstream media fodder. Furthermore, the relationship between citizen journalism and mainstream media outlets is symbiotic; many of the contributions to Twitter and YouTube are simply regurgitating reports from 24-hour news stations, and, while they provide instant information about anything that is happening in the world and are a brilliantly effective way of sharing information, they cannot be relied on to be entirely accurate or impartial. For journalists like Cellan-Jones, that makes the work of mainstream media outlets and professional reporters all the more relevant.

Presenting more of a dilemma for traditional media companies are the forums that encourage the public to express opinions about events in the news. For example, the assassination of Pakistan's opposition leader, Benazir Bhutto, in 2007 resulted in several contributions to news websites that were anti-Islam and prompted discussions about whether online comments should be temporarily withdrawn. The issue was not just that the comments might be deemed offensive by some visitors to the site; they also raised questions about their editorial value and how far they should influence the coverage more widely. In a lecture at Leeds University in the UK in January 2008, the director of BBC World Service, Peter Horrocks, explained the process of sifting through the vast amount of opinion expressed by ordinary people:

> The top 20 or 30 recommended posts all had variations on the theme, attacking Islam in comprehensive terms. Most of them weren't making distinctions between different aspects of Islam, they were simply damning the religion as a whole. To be honest it was pretty boring wading through them and wouldn't have added much to anyone's understanding of the causes or consequences of the assassination. Buried amongst the comments however . . . were insights from those who had met Benazir or knew her. And there were valuable eyewitness comments from people who were at the scene in Rawalpindi. Our team that deals with user content sifted through the chaff to find some excellent wheat. (Horrocks, 2008)

The right to freedom of speech—even if it prompts views based on some form of hatred—is always going to prove controversial, and all media organizations must tread a careful line. It is arguable that forums that encourage audience participation promote a particularly emotive brand of **populism** whereby the views of a small minority who get sufficiently outraged to bother texting or emailing a news organization, radio station, or Internet forum come to represent the editorial line taken by those media outlets. While Horrocks is generally positive about it, saying "there is no doubt that the stronger voice of the audience is having a beneficial effect on the range of stories and perspectives that journalists cover," he also admits that the average 10,000 emails or posts the BBC receives on its "Have Your Say" site each day represent fewer than 1% of its users, and he asks rhetorically, "What organization—a political party, a business, a trades union—would allow its stance to be totally driven by such a small minority?" (Horrocks, 2008).

This discussion highlights that the proliferation of new media—far from encouraging a plurality of news channels—may simply have augmented the dominance of traditional media and forced them to become more competitive. As a senior manager within the BBC, Horrocks gives fascinating insight into the way news production has changed since the advent of digital mobile communication technologies. Not only does the BBC have a dedicated UGC unit working alongside their conventional journalistic resources, dealing solely with information and opinion from the audience—and coping with "spikes" in such material when a particularly newsworthy event occurs (Horrocks gives the example of a high school shooting)—but the corporation has also invested in personal social media in locations that are difficult to report from:

> In northern Nigeria, for example, we are using mobile phones which we provided to villages. In each village there is one person who is known as "the keeper of the mobile." This was a way we learnt about a government confrontation

with a village about land rights. We looked into that story, and used BBC journalistic rigours to cover that story. (Bunz, 2010)

It would appear, then, that far from being the anarchic, decentralized "countercultural" space we might assume it to be, the Internet replicates the dominance of established media organizations (Curran, 2010). This may not be surprising, given the steep costs of establishing, maintaining, and promoting high-profile sites. However, John Pratt (2007) suggests that, despite established news organizations being the primary news sources online, their drive to be more attractive to audiences and advertisers has resulted in the picture of crime becoming even more skewed as they feed audiences an escalating diet of serious, violent, unusual offenses and trivia involving celebrities and scandals. In some sense, then, while we might be broadly optimistic about the role of new information technologies in giving ordinary citizens a voice and bringing news from remote corners of the world, we should exercise caution because of the types of crime most likely to be regarded by journalists, editors, and directors as newsworthy.

NEWS VALUES AND CRIME NEWS PRODUCTION: SOME CONCLUDING THOUGHTS

While the possibility of a direct causal relationship between media consumption and behavioral response (for example, between violent screen images and real-life violence) is downplayed by most critical media scholars, it is nonetheless widely accepted that those who work in the media do have some degree of influence in terms of what potential stories they select and how they then organize them, defining or amplifying some issues over others. The time and space available for news is not infinite and journalism is, of necessity, a selective account of reality. No story can be told without judgments being made about the viability of sending costly resources to film, photograph, and report it, or without implicit suppositions being made about the beliefs and values of the people who will be reading, viewing, or listening to it.

The desire to accommodate public tastes and interests has prompted some critics to accuse the media of pandering to what one production staffer called the "lowest common denominator" of the audience. In the age of reality television, this criticism has only intensified, and both broadcast and print media have been accused of "dumbing down" their news coverage and measuring newsworthiness by the degree of amusement or revulsion a story provokes in the audience. The news values that have been discussed in this chapter seem to support this view. They illustrate that the news media do not cover systemically all forms and expressions of crime and victimization and that they pander to the most voyeuristic desires of the audience by exaggerating and dramatizing relatively unusual crimes while ignoring or downplaying the crimes that are most likely to happen to the "average" person. At the same time, they sympathize with some victims while blaming others.

SUMMARY

- News values are the combined outcome of two different but interrelated factors that together determine the selection and presentation of news. First, news values are shaped by a range of technological, political, and economic forces that structure and constrain the form and content of any reported event at the point of news-gathering. Second, news values cater to the perceived interests of the audience and capture the public mood, a factor usually summed up by news editors as "giving the public what it wants."

- Drawing on "classic" studies that analyzed news production in the mid-20th century, this chapter has developed a set of 12 news values appropriate to the new millennium. While faithful to certain news fundamentals that were highlighted in these works, the chapter has suggested that as society has evolved, so too have the cultural and psychological triggers that condition audience responses and, correspondingly, influence the construction of media narratives.

- In addition to the news values discussed in detail, it is taken for granted that crime is inherently highly newsworthy and is usually "novel" and "negative" in essence. News values not only shape the production of crime news in the 21st century but also aid our understanding of why public perceptions about crime are frequently inaccurate despite media audiences being more sophisticated and better equipped to see through "spin" than ever before.

- The emergence of mobile digital forms of communication and the proliferation of Internet sites that permit various forms of "citizen journalism" have democratized news production, but the news received by the vast majority of audiences still comes from traditional media organizations, who are becoming increasingly adept at weaving user-generated content (UGC) into conventional sources and traditional styles of reporting. The cardinal news values discussed here are as relevant to "new" media as they are to traditional press and broadcasting.

- The 12 news values discussed in this chapter will be drawn on throughout the remainder of this book to demonstrate how types of crime and specific criminal cases are selected and presented according to prevailing cultural assumptions and ideologies.

STUDY QUESTIONS

1. How have news values changed over the last 50 years? Which of the news values identified in this chapter would you say have become most prominent recently? What do these variations tell us about the changing nature of society?

2. As the discussion of Anders Breivik's act of mass murder illustrated, news values, while broadly similar across "Western," industrialized nations, do nonetheless differ in subtle ways, reflecting the particular socioeconomic, political, and cultural contours of any given country. Reflect on how news values might differ across cultural contexts and, particularly, how news values in the U.S. differ from those elsewhere in the world.

3. This chapter has focused mainly on the news values used to set the national news agenda. What news values are most evident in crime reports in your local newspaper or on your local radio or television news program? How do they differ from those in the national and international media?

4. Using international news services accessed via "new" media technologies, conduct a content

analysis of the major crime news stories covered and draw up a list of the news values prioritized.

5. "The availability of an image may determine whether or not a story is run. The availability of the right image can help elevate a crime victim or offender to iconic status" (Greer, 2009, p. 227). What examples can you think of (or find) that bear out this statement?

6. Donald Trump's victory in the 2016 presidential election has been dogged by claims that fake news stories—including that Hillary Clinton sold weapons to ISIS and that the pope had endorsed Trump—altered the outcome. A Stanford University study, however, suggests that such reports were important but not dominant (Allcott & Gentzkow, 2017). Fake news aside, what reasons would you pinpoint as being decisive factors in the mediatized versions of Trump and Clinton that voters received? How would the theoretical perspectives outlined in Chapter 1 explain Trump's victory?

FURTHER READING

- It is still worth returning to the seminal study of press news values produced by J. Galtung and M. Ruge, originally published in 1965 but most easily accessed in *The Manufacture of News,* edited by S. Cohen and J. Young (Constable, 1973).

- *Law and Order News,* by S. Chibnall (Tavistock, 1977), also still deserves close attention.

- Other resources of interest include *When Crime Waves,* by V. F. Sacco (SAGE, 2005), and *Constructing Crime: Perspectives on Making News and Social Problems,* by G. Potter and V. E. Kappeler (Waveland, 2006).

- For an analysis of different countries' treatment of the same (or similar) crime stories, see *When Children Kill Children: Penal Populism and Political Culture,* by D. A. Green (Oxford University Press, 2008); "Media and Crime: A Comparative Analysis of Crime News in the UK, Norway and Italy," by R. Cere, Y. Jewkes, and T. Ugelvik, T., in *The Routledge Handbook of European Criminology,* edited by S. Body-Gendrot, M. Hough, K. Kerezsi, R. Lévy, and S. Snacken (Routledge, 2013); and *Transmedia Crime Stories: The Trial of Amanda Knox and Raffaele Sollecito in the Globalised Media Sphere,* edited by L. Gies and M. Bortoluzzi (Palgrave, 2016).

- If you are interested in how "fake news" may or may not have affected the outcome of the 2016 presidential race, read "Social Media and Fake News in the 2016 Election," by H. Allcott and M. Gentzkow (https://web.stanford.edu/~gentzkow/research/fakenews.pdf; 2017).

Student Study Site

WANT A BETTER GRADE?

Get the tools you need to sharpen your study skills. Access practice quizzes, eFlashcards, SAGE journal articles, and more at study.sagepub.com/jewkesus.

Media and Moral Panics

3

OVERVIEW

Chapter 3 provides:

- An overview of the well-known but often misinterpreted and misrepresented concept of "moral panics."

- An analysis of the pros and cons of the moral panic model as a conceptual tool for understanding public responses to mediated crime and deviance.

- An examination of the five defining features that identify moral panics as they have traditionally been conceived.

- A discussion of "deviancy amplification" and the extent to which attempts by authorities to control deviant behavior actually lead to its increase.

- A brief exploration of the status of pedophilia as a moral panic.

KEY TERMS

- consensus 85
- demonization 86
- deviancy amplification spiral 85
- labeling 80

- mega-cases 80
- moral majority 94
- moral panic 80
- risk 87
- signal crime 80

- social reaction 85
- stigmatizing 91
- subculture 81
- youth 88

"Moral panic" is a familiar term in academic studies of crime, deviance, and the media. It refers to public and political reactions to minority or marginalized individuals and groups who appear to be some kind of threat to consensual values and interests. The media—usually led by the press—will define a group or act as "deviant" and focus on it to the exclusion of almost everything else. The concept of moral panic originated in British sociology in the 1970s with the publication of Stanley Cohen's (1972/2002) *Folk Devils and Moral Panics: The Creation of the Mods and Rockers.* Although not the first scholar to explore the role of the mass media in labeling nonconformist groups and manufacturing crime waves (that was Jock Young in 1971), Cohen has been credited as providing the first *systematic* empirical study of the media amplification of deviancy and subsequent public responses. Since then, the concept of moral panics has been applied, developed, lauded, and criticized in equal measure (Critcher, 2003; Goode & Ben-Yehuda, 1994; Hall, Critcher, Jefferson, Clarke, & Roberts, 1978/2013; Jenkins, 1992; Thomson, 1998; Waddington, 1986; Watney, 1987). In fact, so enshrined is the notion that it is not only found in criminology textbooks but has also entered the public consciousness and is regularly referred to within the popular media, who have uncritically employed it to describe public reactions to numerous social phenomena from sex offenders and "swine flu" to refugees and predatory bankers.

Yet the field out of which the moral panic thesis emerged and was made famous—sociology—all but abandoned the term within 10 years of its inception, and it usually warrants only the briefest of mentions in the best-selling textbooks in the discipline. Further, despite the fact that an understanding of moral panics relies on a working knowledge of the production practices of the media, few university degree courses in media studies give more than a glancing acknowledgment of the media's alleged power to define and amplify deviance to the level where society experiences a sense of collective panic akin to a disaster mentality. By contrast, the concept was considered to still have sufficient currency within criminology to warrant special issues of *Crime, Media, Culture* in December 2011 and the *British Journal of Criminology* in January 2009. It has also spawned a number of related criminological concepts, including signal crimes, which posits that media coverage engenders fear of crime, causing long-term modifications in people's behavior (Innes, 2003, 2004), and mega-cases, which notes that newspapers engage readers in stories by encouraging them to become "mediated witnesses" and identify with victims of crime (Peelo, 2006).

This chapter aims to account for the divergences between different disciplines within the social sciences and to consider the pros and cons of the moral panic thesis as a conceptual tool for criminologists. Certainly, in its early formation, the concept of moral panic lent itself to amalgamation with American criminology, which was highly influential in the UK. It is relatively easy to comprehend how the conceptualization of moral panics by Stanley Cohen, Jock Young, Stuart Hall, and others found intellectual and empirical compatibility with American sociology, particularly with Edwin Lemert's (1951) study of social pathology, Howard Becker's (1963) analysis of the labeling of "outsiders," and David Matza's (1964) study of delinquency and drift. Moreover, it is no coincidence that the emergence of a distinctive British school of subcultural theory accompanied a succession of youth subcultures in the UK, starting with the teddy boys in the 1950s, followed by mods and rockers and hippies in the 1960s and skinheads, punks, and African-Caribbean groups such as rude boys and Rastafarians in the 1970s. Since that time, criminologists have continued to test the validity of the moral panic model, and it has recently enjoyed a particularly strong revival in relation to the media reporting of child abusers and pedophiles (Critcher, 2003; Jenkins, 1992, 2001, 2009; Silverman & Wilson, 2002; see also Chapter 4).

With this evolution in mind, this chapter considers the background and defining features of the moral panic model as it has traditionally been conceived. The discussion pays particularly close attention to moral panics directed at deviant youth, a theme that will be developed in the following chapter, which explores the confusion and paradoxes that surround contemporary attitudes toward children.

THE BACKGROUND OF THE MORAL PANIC MODEL

Cohen opens his book with this much-quoted passage:

> Societies appear to be subject, every now and then, to periods of moral panic. A condition, episode, person or group of persons emerges to become defined as a threat to societal values and interests; its nature is presented in a stylised and stereotypical fashion by the mass media; the moral barricades are manned by editors, bishops, politicians and other right-thinking people; socially accredited experts pronounce their diagnoses and solutions; ways of coping are evolved or (more often) resorted to; the condition then disappears, submerges or deteriorates and becomes more visible. Sometimes the object of the panic is quite novel and at other times it is something which has been in existence long enough, but suddenly appears in the limelight. Sometimes the panic passes over and is forgotten, except in folklore and collective memory; at other times it has more serious and long-lasting repercussions and might produce such changes as those in legal and social policy or even in the way the society conceives itself. (1972/2002, p. 9)

As Cohen intimates in this extract, threats to societal values and interests are not *always* personalized. However, when we think of subculture membership, there are, broadly speaking, five types of people who may be the targets of moral outrage: (a) those who commit criminal and antisocial acts (invariably young, working-class men—and, increasingly, women; see, for instance, "slut shaming"); (b) individuals who commit very serious offenses, including sexual offenses against children, violent offenses against strangers, and murder; (c) those whose behavior strays from organizational procedures or who break conventional codes of conduct in the workplace, such as those who take part in industrial actions and strikes; (d) those who simply adopt patterns of behavior, styles of dress, or ways of presenting themselves that are different from the "norm," such as mods, rockers, punks, goths, Emos, hippies, skinheads, and urban gang members; and (e) the miscellaneous groups of people who fail to conform to consensual, conservative ideals, especially concerning the traditional institution of the family. These might include people with AIDS (which, throughout the early 1980s, was coined the "gay plague" by sections of the popular press), lone mothers, drug users, and "welfare cheats."

Although these groups are immensely diverse, five distinct but interconnected factors have conventionally been identified in most moral panics (listed below and then discussed in greater detail). However, this chapter will argue that the five defining features of moral panics highlighted in traditional conceptualizations are inadequately theorized and that the relationship between them is more complex than is often suggested. Integral to the discussion, then, will be a consideration of the deficiencies of the moral panic model and the problems with its application, which have caused some to argue that it has no validity. P. J. Waddington (1986) is one such critic. He argues that the notion of moral panics is riddled with value-laden terminology, and he has gone so far as to suggest that the concept should be abandoned altogether. The discussion that follows will attempt to represent both pros and cons of the moral panic model as a conceptual tool and will assess the extent to which it aids our understanding of public responses to mediated events.

The five defining features of the model are:

1. Moral panics occur when the mass media take a reasonably ordinary event and present it as an extraordinary occurrence.

2. The media set in motion a "deviancy amplification spiral" in which a moral discourse is established by journalists and various other authorities, opinion leaders, and moral entrepreneurs, who collectively demonize the perceived wrongdoers as a source of moral decline and social disintegration.

3. Moral panics clarify the moral boundaries of the society in which they occur, creating consensus and concern.

4. Moral panics occur during periods of rapid social change and can be said to locate and crystallize wider social anxieties about risk.

5. It is usually young people who are targeted, as they are a metaphor for the future and their behavior is regarded as a barometer with which to test the health or sickness of a society.

How the Mass Media Turn the Ordinary Into the Extraordinary

The banality and sheer "ordinariness" of the events that gave rise to a moral panic in an English seaside town in 1964 are beautifully captured by Cohen:

> Easter 1964 was worse than usual. It was cold and wet, and in fact Easter Sunday was the coldest for 80 years. The shopkeepers and stall owners were

irritated by the lack of business and the young people had their own boredom and irritation fanned by rumours of café owners and barmen refusing to serve some of them. A few groups started scuffling on the pavements and throwing stones at each other. The Mods and Rockers factions—a division initially based on clothing and life styles, later rigidified, but at that time not fully established—started separating out. Those on bikes and scooters roared up and down, windows were broken, some beach huts were wrecked and one boy fired a starting pistol in the air. (1972/2002, p. 29)

Although Cohen admits that these two days were "unpleasant, oppressive and sometimes frightening" (1972/2002, p. 29), the levels of actual intimidation, conflict, and violence in the coastal town of Clacton (and in Brighton, where similar incidents occurred during the same period) were relatively low. The media, however, carried headlines such as "Day of Terror by Scooter Gangs" (*Daily Telegraph*) and "Youngsters Beat Up Town" (*Daily Express*), and they routinely used phrases such as "riot," "orgy of destruction," "battle," "siege," and "screaming mob" to convey an impression of an embattled town from which innocent holidaymakers were fleeing from a rampaging mob. Indeed, the term "riot" has since become a stock phrase used by journalists to cover *any* emotionally charged incident involving three or more people (Knopf, 1970).

Like any other newsworthy event, the media construct moral panics according to their criteria of "news values." Exaggeration and distortion are thus key elements in the meeting of the required *threshold* to turn a potential news event into an actual story. Moral panics will also frequently involve the news value *predictability* in the sense of media prognoses that what has happened will inevitably happen again. Even when it does not, a story will be constructed to that effect through the reporting of nonevents that appear to confirm their predictions. *Simplification* occurs through a process of symbolization whereby names can be made to signify complex ideas and emotions. A word ("mod" or "youth") becomes symbolic of a status ("deviant"), and objects (a particular hairstyle, form of clothing, type of motorbike, or even pet dog) come to signify that status and the negative emotions attached to it. The cumulative effect is that the term ("mod" or "youth") becomes disassociated with any previously neutral connotations it had and acquires wholly negative meanings. When it comes to political and public responses to these processes, one of Cohen's key findings was that, while the media frequently associate certain minority groups with deviance and condemn their use of *violence,* they nonetheless accept that violence is a legitimate way for the police to deal with problems and is sometimes a necessary form of retaliation. The media-constructed definitions of the situation are therefore reinforced, and all sides behave as "expected" (S. Cohen & Young, 1973).

The Role of the Authorities in the Deviancy Amplification Process

It has been suggested that moral panics have their origins in moral crusades such as the Prohibition Movement of 1900–1920 and, before that, the European witch hunts of the 16th and 17th centuries and later Salem, Massachusetts (Goode & Ben-Yehuda,

1994). The moral crusaders of contemporary society are journalists, newspaper editors, politicians, the police, and pressure groups, who combine to set in motion a spiral of events in which the attention given to the deviants leads to their criminalization and marginalization. One version of the moral panic model thus suggests that it is those with vested interests who use the media as a conduit to make a moral statement about a particular individual, group, or behavior (although the question of source is by no means straightforward or universally agreed upon, as we shall see shortly). It is argued that those in power label minority groups as subversive, with a view to exploiting public fears, and then step in to provide a "popular" solution to the problem which, in the current rhetoric of populist punitiveness, usually amounts to getting tougher on crime. But not only does increased attention appear to validate the media's initial concern; it may also result in the target group feeling increasingly alienated, particularly when—as often happens—politicians and other "opinion leaders" enter the fray, demanding tougher action to control and punish the "deviants" and warning of the possible dangers to society if their activities are not held in check. Such widespread condemnation may lead the group to feel more persecuted and marginalized, resulting in an increase in their deviant activity so

FIGURE 3.1

Deviancy amplification spiral: The reporting of deviance within a framework of exaggeration, distortion, prediction, and symbolization sets into motion a series of interrelated responses.

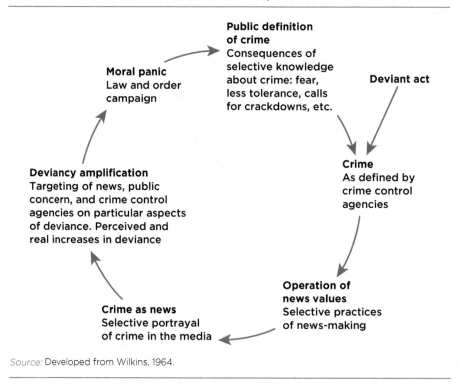

Source: Developed from Wilkins, 1964.

that they appear to become more like the creatures originally created by the media. The continuing deviancy results in greater police attention, more arrests, and further media coverage. Thus, a "**deviancy amplification spiral**" (Wilkins, 1964) is set in motion (see Figure 3.1). Although a conservative analysis would posit that the spiral demonstrates the media's justification in responding to public interest and rising crime, a more radical account would argue that the hysteria generated in this process is an effective way for governments to control their citizens, dissuade people from adopting unconventional lifestyles and coerce them into conforming to society's mores.

The deviancy amplification spiral thus describes what happens when a society outlaws a particular group. As negative **social reaction** escalates and the "deviants" become increasingly isolated, they become more and more criminally oriented. The spiral of deviancy may go on for weeks or even months, but it never spirals out of control for a number of reasons. Media interest will eventually wane and move on to other issues, and, after a period of time, the "folk devil" will become familiar and therefore be perceived as less of a threat. Ways of coping with the perceived threat are developed, either as a result of new legislation introduced to minimize or eliminate the problem or more mundane strategies evolved by the people most affected. Finally, in the case of youth subcultures, the deviant may eventually stop being deviant, grow up, and move on.

Defining Moral Boundaries and Creating Consensus

In the identification of a group responsible for a perceived threat, a division quickly becomes apparent between "us"—decent, respectable, and moral—and "them"—deviant, undesirable outsiders. The perception that the threat is real, serious, and caused by an identifiable minority does not have to constitute a universal belief or even be held by a majority, but the national press will report it in such a way as to imply that their condemnation of the threatening behavior represents a **consensus**. In addressing an imagined national community, newspapers will frequently appeal to a nostalgic conservative ideology, a desire for retribution, and a much-vaunted opinion that "common sense" should prevail. What these three combined factors amount to is a popular ideological perception that "thing's aren't what they used to be." In an echo of mass society theory a century ago (see Chapter 1), many have argued that society is rapidly and inexorably deteriorating due to a decline in religious morality, a growing lack of respect for authority, the disintegration of the traditional nuclear family, the media as provider of role models for the nation's children, and—in very recent years—the existence of perverts who prey on our children via the Internet. Moreover, there is widespread acceptance among politicians and the media that the appropriate response to this sorry state of affairs is to call for tougher action on the part of the police, the courts, and the prisons. Take this letter written in the 1950s by a "family doctor" in regard to one youth subculture:

> Teddy boys . . . are all of unsound mind in the sense that they are all suffering from a form of psychosis. Apart from the birch or the rope, depending on the gravity of their crimes, what they need is rehabilitation in a psychopathic institution. (Brake, 1980, p. 11)

In the ensuing half century, it arguably is not the sentiment that has changed, but the age at which young people are pathologized, diminishing to the level where elementary school–aged children are seen to be at risk of turning "bad." In addition, the notion of "troublesome youth" has been emphatically enshrined in political rhetoric and law with a range of policies that demonize and criminalize children. One needs only to consider the range of curfew laws, "stay out" orders, and even the criminalization of youth style, most notably hoodies and saggy pants, to reckon the degree to which youth are a focus of such moralizations (cities in Illinois, Florida, and Louisiana have passed ordinances to punish "saggy pants" with fines, community service, and jail time). Campaigns such as these give the impression that youth deviance is an entirely new phenomenon—a perception that is surely open to challenge from anyone who can remember their own childhood! With the introduction of more and more legislation that seeks to privatize childhood, clearing the streets of young people and criminalizing behavior that once seemed like "normal" experiences in adolescence (everything from skateboarding to mild sexual experimentation), it is no wonder that childhood appears to be in crisis. These moves seem to indicate what Phil Scraton calls the "sharp end of a continuum of child rejection; a sharp end most accurately described as child-hate, in the same vein as race-hate, misogyny or homophobia" (2002, p. 15).

However, as we can see from the deviancy amplification spiral in Figure 3.1, it may be that some politicians and opinion leaders are simply seeking to gain political favor by voicing opposition to those whom the media has labeled "deviant." With politicians competing to come up with the best soundbite on morality ("moral vacuum," "moral crisis," etc.), a moral *panic* is virtually guaranteed, and in condemning the actions of a minority and being seen to be "tough on crime," politicians are assured of favorable coverage in the majority of the mainstream press. For instance, it is useful to recall the case of an Arkansas man, Ricky Ray Rector. In 1981, after killing a man in a barroom dispute, Rector agreed to surrender to police, specifically requesting that a childhood friend, Conway, Arkansas, police officer Robert Martin, take him into custody. Instead of surrendering, Rector shot and killed Martin and then turned the gun on himself. His suicide attempt failed, however, leaving Rector effectively "lobotomized" and with an IQ under 70. Courts found Rector fit to stand trial and subsequently levied a sentence of death. Bill Clinton, who was Arkansas governor at the time, refused Rector's final appeals for clemency and suspended his presidential campaign to return to Arkansas and personally preside over the execution. Critics panned the liberal politician, arguing that Rector, who was so profoundly impaired that he famously asked guards to save his pecan pie so that he could eat it after he was executed, provided the perfect opportunity for Clinton to prove he was "tough on crime" (Newburn & Jones, 2005).

The combined assault of lawmakers, law enforcers, and the newspapers, which purport to reflect the views of their readership, serves to widen the chasm between the activities of a few, isolated deviants and the rest of society, and in marginalizing those who are already on the periphery, they give an inner strength to the core. Thus, it might be suggested that not only do moral panics draw together communities in a sense of collective outrage, but they actually make the core feel more complacent in the affirmation of their own morality; when we have defined what is "evil," we know by implication what is "good." Consequently, conventional accounts of moral panics emphasize that they demonstrate that there are limits to how much diversity can be tolerated in a society and confirm the authority of those who make such judgments (Durkheim, 1895/1964).

Rapid Social Change—Risk

As we saw in our discussion of news values in the previous chapter, over recent years a number of commentators have characterized contemporary Western society as a "risk" society in which awareness of potential dangers to individual, group, and global concerns has overshadowed traditional, more mundane matters. For advocates of the moral panic thesis, they constitute one of the most salient examples of a culture attuned to the possibility of disaster, and the overriding features of a moral panic concerning a deviant group are, in many cases, said to be strikingly similar to those that characterize a natural disaster such as an earthquake or hurricane or a manmade disaster such as a bombing. In addition to following a sequence of warning-impact-reaction, the concept of moral panics might be said to have further parallels with disaster models in its capacity to expose to the public domain behavior, attitudes, and emotions that are usually confined to the private sphere. But the moral panic thesis has been criticized for its apparent inability to establish a link between the scale of the disaster and the scale of response to it. Not only does it fail to accurately determine public levels of concern and whether people are motivated by the media to the exclusion of all other influences, but it also makes it impossible to gauge whether the problem is a real one or not. For Goode and Ben-Yehuda (1994), this problem of proportionality is easily solved. Quite simply, problems become the subject of moral panics when they are familiar, close at hand, and appear to directly impinge on individuals' lives. Accordingly, future-oriented threats, such as the potentially catastrophic effects of the shrinking ozone layer, a rogue meteorite hitting earth, the risk of nuclear war, or even terrorist threats, are unlikely to become the subjects of moral panic. But even this seems too simplistic. Few folk devils have had a direct impact on the lives of more than a handful of people and, as described in Chapter 1, in times of political and social turbulence, even an invasion by Martians can seem a plausible occurrence.

The reasons why a society appears especially susceptible at certain times is debatable. A number of writers have pointed to the transition from a period of modernity to one of postmodernity as explanation for the apparent destabilization of many established aspects of social life. As with any transition from one kind of social order to another, traditional processes and values have been weakened and displaced. Liberal ideologies emphasizing individual choice have combined with advances in technology to produce a greater cultural pluralism and an increasing awareness of the possibilities of constructing new identities. At the same time, however, the blurring of public and private boundaries has extended to society's institutions, which have sought to regulate social life in ways previously unimaginable (see Chapters 8 and 9). Alternative visions and conflicting points of identification have been formed, which have led to what is often referred to as a "crisis of identity" whereby media-inspired and consumer-driven aspirations have started to merge and collide with traditional identifications (such as those based on class, race, gender, nationality), resulting in instability and ontological insecurity. The ambivalent and paradoxical nature of this period of late modernity is summed up by Berman:

> To be modern is to find ourselves in an environment that promises us adventure, power, joy, growth, transformation of ourselves and the world—and, at the same time, that threatens to destroy everything we have, everything we know, everything we are . . . modernity can be said to unite all mankind. But it is a paradoxical unity, a unity of disunity: it pours us all into a maelstrom of perpetual disintegration and renewal, of struggle and contradiction, of ambiguity and anguish. To be modern is to be part of a universe in which, as Marx said, "all that is solid melts into air." (1983, p. 1)

As described in Chapter 1, America was experiencing such a maelstrom of disintegration and renewal at the time of the 1938 *War of the Worlds* broadcast. But these processes can similarly be detected in the Britain of the mid-1950s: the time of the first modern, media-led moral panic, which was directed at teddy boys. At this time, a number of social trends were converging to challenge and decenter traditional norms and values. The "feel-good factor" still hung over Allied nations after victory against Hitler, but for Britons the celebrations were tempered by the trauma of the quarter of a million deaths and the destruction of homes and workplaces. The war had left the UK in a state of economic crisis, yet by the late 1950s a new spirit of optimism had emerged and the 1960s became a time of full employment. New social patterns were also radically altering the face of Britain: Family relationships changed as legislation was introduced to make divorce easier and more socially acceptable for women; new technologies and the emergence of the service and leisure industries were challenging traditional industrial practices, with semiprofessional and professional jobs being created at roughly the same pace as the number of manual workers declined; and migration of British citizens from New Commonwealth countries was taking place. All these factors combined to make many people feel very uncertain and anxious about their lives, and concerns about change, instability, and the displacement of what went before became consolidated in the group identities of the new youth subcultures.

Youth

The social construction of **youth** as a problem that had bubbled just beneath the surface of social and political life for many years exploded into the public consciousness in the late 1950s and almost immediately became the subject of sociological inquiry in both the U.S. and UK. It is often said that "youth" came into its own in both nations in the postwar era. Before the Second World War, young people tended to model themselves on their parents, and their clothes, manners, aspirations, and expectations were all characteristic of a previous era. But in the 1950s, led by American popular culture, young people became seen as a specific social category, distinct from other age groups, and the word "teenager" was coined for the first time. They rejected their parents' values and interests and became powerful citizens and consumers in their own right.

Traditional class boundaries were also broken down as the media and leisure industries homogenized teenagers into a vibrant, consumer group. Cafés, milk bars, soda shops, and dance halls sprang up in the United States and Britain, and a range of cultural products emerged that were explicitly aimed at a young audience. America exported film stars such as Marlon Brando and James Dean, rock-and-roll artists like Buddy Holly and Elvis, and television programs including *Ready, Steady, Go* and *American Bandstand* (all of which spawned their imitators in the UK), while pirate radio stations such as Caroline and Luxembourg and bands such as the Beatles were British phenomena that found American and worldwide audiences. All these new cultural and commercial "products" heightened the sense of excitement and freedom associated with being a teenager in the 1950s and 1960s. Teenagers were more affluent than they had ever been before and formed a larger section of society than other age groups because of the postwar "baby boom" years. They had significant purchasing power, and they represented vitality and social mobility to a degree that marked them out from other generations. More than at any time previously, youth represented the future in all its vibrant, urban modernity.

However, the combination of rapid social change with distinctive, unconventional, and often spectacular styles of physical appearance and behavior was a heady mixture. If "youth" represents the future, a future in the hands of these unconventional and unpredictable young people, who seemed to be actively resisting authority and rejecting everything that was traditional or conventional, was simply too frightening for many to contemplate. For all the unfettered fun attached to being a teenager in the late 1950s and early 1960s, there was a darker edge, a flip side to the apparently positive traits of youth. Modern life, the expansion of cities, and increased opportunities for leisure were the focus of growing disquiet. Young people represented vitality and social mobility to a degree that marked them out from previous generations, but "modern" equated to "brash," being cosmopolitan and classless were inextricably linked to having too much wealth and too little morality, and the homogeneity brought to young people by the growth in consumer industries aimed specifically at them made them thoughtless and selfish in the eyes of many older people. In the UK, many in the political establishment viewed the new American-influenced youth culture as inherently corrupt and vulgar, undermining British traditions and values—which only made it all the more attractive to British youth. As Cohen explains, this first generation of teenagers who eagerly consumed both the glamor and the danger that seemed to underpin much American media content symbolized the confused and paradoxical feelings that many held in this period of rapid social transformation:

> They touched the delicate and ambivalent nerves through which post-War social change in Britain was experienced. No one wanted depressions or austerity, but messages about "never having it so good" were ambivalent in that some people were having it too good and too quickly. (S. Cohen, 1972/2002, p. 192)

Young people were thus seen as both a catalyst for change and the guardians of future morality; they personified the desire to move forward, to innovate, to experiment, but were simultaneously the conduits of all the fears in society about change and the unknown. At one and the same time they represented all that was new, shiny, and modern and everything that was transitory, disposable, and tacky.

PROBLEMS WITH THE MORAL PANIC MODEL

The concept of "moral panics" has been widely criticized for its perceived limitations, yet it is a theory that just refuses to go away. A fundamental difficulty with moral panics is not the concept itself, but the way that it has been embraced by the generations of writers, researchers, journalists, and students since its inception in 1971, many of whom have created the impression of an outdated model that has outlived its usefulness. There are two common, flawed approaches. One is the failure to go beyond a faithful rewrite of the original text and a fawning, unreflective adherence to its theoretical premises. The other is a tendency to overextend the concept of moral panics, stretching it so much that it becomes a catchall term that encapsulates any public cause for concern, from economic crisis to immigration, but tells us nothing meaningful about the interrelationship among the media, social problems, social policy, and public opinion in the contemporary world (Hughes, Rohloff, David, & Petley, 2011). As Kidd-Hewitt and Osborne (1995) point out, media-criminology has become fixed within a pattern of inquiry that frequently relies on "ritualistic reproductions" or misrepresentations of Cohen's original conceptualization of the term, and *Folk Devils and Moral Panics* left "such significant and substantial foundation stones that they are constantly mistaken for the final edifice, instead of notable developments to be built upon" (Kidd-Hewitt & Osborne, 1995, p. 2). So what *are* the shortcomings of the moral panic thesis? Several points of possible ambiguity or contention have already been discussed, and it should already be clear that some aspects of the moral panic model are open to several different interpretations. But there remain some fundamental flaws in the idea of moral panics that have yet to be satisfactorily addressed, and it is to these that we now turn.

A Problem With "Deviance"

The deviancy amplification spiral is problematic on a number of counts. First, not all folk devils can be said to be vulnerable or *unfairly* maligned (pedophiles provide one such example; the bankers responsible for the recent economic crisis are arguably another), and the accelerating loss of credibility that is implied in the amplification process is not applicable to all groups. Furthermore, there has never been universal agreement about the length of time that public outrage has to be expressed for it to qualify as a moral panic. If we return to Cohen's formulation of the concept, we are bound to infer that moral panics are, by their very nature, short-term, sporadic episodes that explode with some volatility on the collective consciousness only to disappear a few weeks or months later. But the origins of some concerns—for example, juvenile delinquency—may go back a considerable length of time, and current anxieties about deviant youth have been well rehearsed in this country over several hundred years (G. Pearson, 1983). Even the current state of heightened anxiety over pedophiles has been sustained since the term was coined in 1996 (see Chapter 4). Further, McRobbie and Thornton (1995) argue that moral panics have ceased to be events that happen "every now and then" and instead have become the standard way of reporting news in an ever-increasing spiral of hyperbole and "ridiculous rhetoric" designed to grab our attention in a crowded media marketplace. In the current context of 24-hour rolling news and audience participation (via reality television, audience phone-ins, Internet blogs, talk radio, etc.), their observation seems persuasive. The deviancy amplification spiral has also been criticized for being too rigid and deterministic, grossly oversimplifying the notion of deviancy. There are different levels of what we call "deviancy," and a theory that accounts for public reactions to cannabis users may not be appropriate in accounting for public outrage over date rapists. Furthermore, the etiology of deviancy is rarely given the same consideration as the deviant action or behavior itself. Muncie, echoing Durkheim, comments:

> Moral Panics . . . form part of a sensitizing and legitimizing process for solidifying moral boundaries, identifying "enemies within," strengthening the powers of state control and enabling law and order to be promoted without cognisance of the social divisions and conflicts which produce deviance and political dissent. (Muncie, 2001, pp. 55–56)

In other words, moral panics define for society the moral parameters within which it is acceptable to behave, and marginalize and punish those groups who step outside those parameters, but rarely do they encourage examination of the reasons *why* the group is behaving in that way in the first place. All too often, "deviance" is simply used as a byword for "irrationality" (implying mental instability or even animality), "manipulability" (implying that those involved are passive dupes), or "unconventionality" (implying that they are weird, alien, uncontrollable). Thus, the causes of "deviance," which in some cases may be entirely legitimate, are seldom considered and are frequently overshadowed by scornful commentaries about the appearance and lifestyle of the groups involved. In addition, the media may resort to conjecture and exaggeration concerning violence or predictions of future violence, or by reference to any sporadic incidents of conflict that occur. As Hall says, "the tendency is . . . to deal with any problem, first by simplifying its causes, second by stigmatizing those involved, third by whipping up public feeling and fourth by stamping hard on it from above" (Hall, 1978, p. 34).

A Problem With "Morality"

A related difficulty with definition is that the "moral" element in moral panics has either been accepted unproblematically or otherwise glossed over with little concern for a particular episode's place within a wider structure of morality and in relation to changing forms of moral regulation (Thomson, 1998). In the following chapter, we will consider "morality" as it pertains to the sexualization of children and the age at which young people become sexually active. In brief, we might consider it somewhat hypocritical of society to impose legal sanctions on "underage" sex while at the same time tolerating the overt sexualization of much younger children in other cultural realms—fashion, music, advertising, and so on (Jewkes, 2010a). In Britain, the age of consent was set at 16 in an attempt to thwart the use of children as prostitutes in Victorian times. Prior to 1875, it had been 12. However, in the wake of several cases where 13- to 15-year-old girls have run away from home with their boyfriends, the debate about the age at which young people become sexually mature has been reignited. It is, however, a debate that is likely to become hijacked by moral crusaders, and it may prove impossible to discuss reasonably and rationally in a culture in which romanticized images of childhood as a time of winsome innocence prevail over a reality that includes child abuse, neglect, exploitation, and high teenage pregnancy rates.

Jock Young (1971, 1974) highlights a further aspect of the ambiguity inherent in definitions of morality, suggesting that many of the people who think of themselves as "moral" and take exception to the immorality of deviants actually have a grudging admiration—envy, even—for those who are seen to be "breaking the rules." According to Young (1971), if individuals live by a strict code of conduct that forbids certain pleasures and involves the deferring of gratification in certain areas, it is hardly surprising that they will react strongly against those whom they see to be taking "shortcuts." For Young, this ambivalence is a partial explanation of the vigorous repression of what might be termed "crimes without victims": homosexuality, prostitution, drug use, and—in the new moral climate—consensual sex among minors. But in many instances, moral panics appear to contain little or no moral element at all, and the term has become a shorthand description for *any* widespread concern, including, most prominently in recent years, health scares, especially those linking health problems to food and diet.

Problems With "Youth" and "Style"

In much of the moral panic literature, there is a presupposed assumption that the youth groups or other deviants involved are inevitably economically marginalized and turn to crime and deviance as an anomic means of combating the boredom and financial hardship associated with being out of work. Certainly, Cohen suggests that the mods and rockers were driven to violence as a result of feeling marginalized from the mass consumer culture directed at young people in the early 1960s. Yet an alternative reading might argue that the mods and rockers were the products of rising affluence and optimism, and far from being peripheral to the economic health of the country, they were largely responsible for making the 1960s swing! Since that time, youth fashions and subcultural affiliations have spawned multimillion-dollar industries, and today's young people have on offer a vast range of concurrent subcultures that may in some cases present the solutions to their subjective socioeconomic problems, but actually in most cases do little more than provide a temporary sense of "belonging," a statement of being independent of the parent culture and a form of conspicuous consumption.

Group identity is thus at least as likely to be a statement of style and status as it is to be an act of resistance through ritual. All youth cultures require a relatively high level of financial input, whether they are based on music, fashion, football, or some other "fanship," and as Cohen remarks in his introduction to the revised second edition of *Folk Devils and Moral Panics,* the delinquent quickly changed from "frustrated social climber" to "cultural innovator and critic" (Cohen, 1980, p. iv). Even the punks in the London of the 1970s, who are frequently characterized as a product of welfare despondency (Hebdige, 1979), were by no means all out of work and lacking economic means. Commitment to the punk movement was based on political disaffection, rebellion against the parent culture, enjoyment of the music, resistance to conventional codes of dress, and many other varied factors. But it was orchestrated by a music producer (Malcolm McLaren) and a fashion designer (Vivienne Westwood) and was essentially a commercial enterprise, put together in a fashion not unlike the "boy bands" of today. Entry into any youth subculture represents a part of the normal transition from childhood to adulthood that most young people in Western society pass through. But there are few, if any, youth cultures and styles that are not manufactured by one or more elements of the consumerist culture industry. Even the gang cultures of the impoverished inner-city ghettos of America and Britain have strong affiliations to particular designer labels.

Furthermore, "spectacular" youth subcultures—the stock-in-trade of moral panic promoters—are, arguably, not as evident as they once were. Moral panic theory tends to suggest that young people have restricted choices in their statements of style, personality, and consumption. However, for postmodernist critics, the subject has no fixed or permanent identity but assumes different identities at different times in an endless act of self-creation. Indeed, a postmodern critique would posit that identity is an "open slate . . . on which persons may inscribe, erase and rewrite" their histories and personalities at will (Gergen, 1991, p. 228), a phenomenon that has become positively celebrated with the expansion of the Internet. Even sexual identity is seen by some commentators as a reflexively organized endeavor involving an increasing number of choices and possibilities (Jewkes & Sharp, 2003). Thus, in today's multimedia society, young people are able to make the transition from childhood to adulthood via a vast and diverse range of coexistent subcultures, which they may move in and out of at will, thus making their attachments to particular groups only marginal and fleeting. As such, it might be suggested that the notion that moral panics define the limits of how much diversity a society can tolerate is simply not as compelling as it once was, although this is a contested issue. Some would argue that clothing and appearance can still be utilized as symbols of class conflict and social division, and that there remain subcultural styles that are not appropriated by mainstream consumer culture and are adopted by individuals and groups with the intention of making others feel ill at ease. Others would counter that in today's postmodern, technologically advanced, culturally fragmented, pastiche culture, diversity is not only tolerated but celebrated to the extent where "street" styles (that is, those emerging from the "bottom" or margins of society) are often very quickly absorbed into the mainstream fashion industry, a trend that makes the "deviant" cues of any one group appear less visible and less important in the wider context.

A further difficulty with the construction of youth as a social problem is that it might be suggested that youth now only exists in discourses about crime and deviance. "Youth" arguably no longer describes a generational category but instead encapsulates an attitude, a lifestyle not determined by age. The generation gap is shrinking, and unlike 70 years ago, when young people were more or less miniature versions of their parents, in contemporary society it is now very often adults who look to their children for style codes. Not only is it more likely that adolescents and their parents will share the same tastes in clothing, music, literature, and leisure pursuits than in any previous generation—a trend exemplified by the Harry Potter phenomenon and the widespread, intergenerational adoption of clothing like hoodies and sneakers—but increasingly young people are influencing the political agenda, especially in relation to issues such as animal rights and environmentalism. Collective concerns such as these not only transcend traditional class and ethnic distinctions but also demonstrate a "morality" and code of ethics that seem conservative in comparison with the youth subcultures of their parents' and grandparents' generations. Moreover, in a multimediated world where global media events vie for public attention, especially among the young, who use interpersonal forms of communication within small groups of friends, macro-level responses have declined in probability.

A Problem With "Risk"

Another weakness with the moral panic model is that the overstated reaction to youth cultures on the part of the "moral majority" is precipitated by a creeping sense of disorientation and bewilderment at the pace of change in modern life. This argument may underpin many parents' fears about their children's exposure to new and alternative media, including violent computer games and the Internet. But modernity has been a long project. Was there ever a generation that did not feel poised at the edge of something bigger, more exciting, and—for some—potentially more frightening? Frank Furedi (1997) has argued that we inhabit a "culture of fear" in which loss of optimism and a belief in our capacity to change the world for the better have given way to a crippling sense of vulnerability. In a similar vein, Eamonn Carrabine asserts that "few now dispute that we are living in times of high anxiety and that the mass media provide us with a daily diet of disasters from near and afar to continually remind us that we inhabit a world of crisis, danger and uncertainty" (2008, p. 162). But while "high anxiety" may be the goal of the media, in everyday practice it is ontologically unsustainable, and it seems overstated to characterize the current epoch as a universal, endlessly cyclical state of "panickyness" (Sparks, 1992, p. 65). Indeed, Stephen Farrall and David Gadd note that "few people fear crime frequently"; their research found that fewer than 1 in 10 people (8%) frequently experienced high levels of fear (2004, p. 127; see Chapter 6). Further, the inference in much writing on the subject that communities in our parents' and grandparents' day were tight-knit, self-policing, and prone to spontaneous organization of street parties, while today's media-addicted neighbors are frightened, atomized, and unknown to one another, is unproven and untenable. In the second, revised edition of *Folk Devils and Moral Panics,* Cohen himself surmises that the level and intensity of media activity is sometimes exaggerated by researchers and writers to "fit" their particular illustration of the moral panic thesis at work, and that the material selected as "proof" of the slide into crisis (newspaper editorials, in the main) does not amount to such monumental proportions (S. Cohen, 1980).

A Problem of "Source"

Although the panics over teddy boys in the 1950s and mods and rockers in the 1960s meet the criteria of the moral panic thesis in terms of being discrete, transitory incidents that appear to have emerged suddenly and explosively and disappeared equally abruptly sometime later, it has been left to other writers (McRobbie & Thornton, 1995; Watney, 1987) to point out that concerns about deviance are much more diffuse than is suggested in many accounts of panic. In other words, the disparate concerns over drugs, sexual permissiveness or perversion, liberal attitudes regarding marriage, the political reemergence of the far right, and youth violence are among the frequently conflicting issues that arise from a number of different sources and are dispersed throughout society. Meanwhile, specific moral panics, such as the periodic scares about gang-related knife and gun crime involving black youth, represent a generalized climate of hostility toward marginal groups and "unconventional" or untraditional norms. Far from happening out of the blue, as is sometimes suggested, moral panics may be viewed accordingly as part of the longer-term ideological struggles waged across society and within all fields of public representation (Watney, 1987). As such, the initial targeting of the deviants and the structured responses to them may be regarded as an integral part of the hegemonic function of the media, telling us far more about the nature of the media and their complex relationship with other social institutions than they do about the concerns of those in power.

The question of source also problematizes the idea that moral panics are the means by which elite interests become filtered down through society so that they appear to be to everyone's advantage. The term "moral panic" implies that public reaction is unjustified, and, in critical criminological accounts (e.g., Hall et al., 1978/2013), there is a suggestion that moral panics are essentially smokescreens put up by governments to cynically manipulate the media and public agendas. Some critics hang on to the belief that moral panics originate at a macro level and are engineered by a political and cultural elite as a deliberate and conscious effort to generate concern or fear that is actually misplaced. Others maintain that they originate at a more micro level with the general public, and that concerns expressed by the media, politicians, police, and so on are simply an expression or manifestation of wider, grassroots disquiet (a position more in line with Cohen's account and more credible in relation to the pedophile scare). A third model proposes that it is at a *meso* or middle level of society—with social agencies, pressure groups, lobbyists, and moral crusaders—that moral panics start. This theory is given credence by those who claim that it is interest groups who stand to gain the most from moral panics. We have already seen this view rehearsed in relation to panics over children viewing violence, where it is often asserted that it is pressure group leaders, academics, and politicians who seek to make a name for themselves by jumping on a populist bandwagon. A fourth view of the source of moral panics, and a variation on the meso-level explanation, is that it is journalists themselves who are primarily responsible for generating moral panics, simply as a way of increasing circulation or entertaining their audience (Young, 1974). Though we can no longer talk of the "mass" media in quite the same monolithic sense as we once did, the very existence of mug shot magazines that profit from the public humiliation of arrest might be seen as a powerful means of attracting readers and satisfying market demands while having scant regard for the political consequences of such action.

A Problem With "Audience"

The overriding problem with traditional characterizations of the moral panic model is that they presuppose that in finding consensus on certain issues, audiences are gullible and that they privilege mediated knowledge over direct experience, an assumption that is clearly not viable. In fact, more than any other factor, recent cultural and media theorists have resisted the moral panic thesis's implicit supposition that the public are naively trusting of media reports and cannot tell when they are being manipulated. In contrast to this assumption, research concerning the relationship between the media agenda and the public agenda (that is, what the public take from the media and think about or discuss among themselves) stresses that there are many examples of public indifference or resistance to issues that constitute political and/ or media crusades. Indeed, studies of advertising demonstrate that the least successful advertising campaigns are those commissioned by social agencies with the intention of changing people's behavior—for example, anti-drug campaigns and "safe-sex" messages—while the failure of the general public to take notice of issues deemed important by figures in power is evident in the falling numbers of couples who are marrying, despite the continuing efforts of political and church leaders. Furthermore, the 1992 Republican presidential campaign, with its overt moral agenda and "family values" crusade that openly attacked homosexuality, abortion, and divorce, fizzled out in a tide of public indifference (Goode & Ben-Yehuda, 1994). Quite simply, the demonization of those whose lifestyle and beliefs exist outside the political, social, or legal norm does not guarantee public—or even media—support. Official attempts to castigate, demonize, or ridicule "deviants" are often resisted, calling into question the notion of a gullible and docile public yielding to the interests of those in power.

There is also a problem in defining what constitutes a moral panic by guessing audience reaction. For example, while generally skeptical about the usefulness and validity of the moral panic model for understanding public responses to crime, many have argued (Jewkes, 2010a; Jewkes & Wykes, 2012; see Chapter 4) that pedophilia constitutes the moral panic of our age. That is, if we must use the term at all, then pedophilia would seem to fit the five criteria described earlier. The "deviancy amplification spiral" set in motion by journalists and various other authorities not only collectively demonizes the pedophile but also silences those who look for alternative explanations. Condemned as weak liberals seeking to make excuses for the worst examples of human depravity, those who seek to go beyond the commonsense notion that sexual dangerousness resides in strangers and "others" who are not like "us," and highlight the cultural hypocrisy of these attitudes within a society that otherwise fetishizes youthful bodies (Jewkes, 2010a), also risk moral censure. One of the many troubling aspects of the Jimmy Savile case in the UK was the ease with which he—as a popular cultural icon and pioneer of "youth TV"—managed to gain access to his young victims. It goes without saying that pedophilia marks the moral boundaries of today's society; it is the ultimate black-and-white issue with no shades of gray countenanced. Nonetheless, as the countless witnesses who covered up, excused, or turned a blind eye to Savile's assaults on children and young people proved, cultural tolerance toward sexual predators has changed over the last few decades. One mother who witnessed her teenage daughter being assaulted by Savile in the 1970s told a newspaper that, at the time, she felt proud that her little girl had been singled out for attention by the celebrity.

In more recent times, the very rapid spread of social media has also led to concerns about technologically proficient pedophiles "grooming" their young victims online—a doubly dangerous offense frequently held up as representing everything that is wrong with the Internet as well as the risks posed by adults who have a sexual preference for children. For example, in 2009 and 2010, Facebook became the subject of countless reports that appeared intended to instigate moral panic, culminating in calls in some quarters of the British popular press for the site to be closed down after a convicted sex offender was jailed for life for the kidnap, rape, and murder of a 17-year-old girl he "met" on the social networking site. For Yvonne Jewkes and Maggie Wykes (2012), one of the unfortunate outcomes of the media's focus on "cyber-peds" is that it has made "real-world" sexual crimes, especially those that occur within private and familial settings, even more invisible. The "mysterious, invisible, all-pervasive qualities of cyberspace enable all manner of mythologizing" and allow old behavior to be represented as "new, more significant threats" (p. 945). Countless stories have been reported in recent years involving young people and cyberbullying, "trolling," "sexting," or "revenge porn" that have, in many instances, had tragic outcomes for the persons involved.

So, it could indeed be argued that pedophilia constitutes an archetypal moral panic. It fits the model and has indisputably led to profound changes in behavior as childhood and adolescence have become increasingly privatized (see Chapters 4 and 9 for wider discussions of childhood and social retreat). But despite the hysterical tone adopted by a media that are happy to peddle overtly sexualized images of young people in other contexts, the issue of Internet-related sexual exploitation of children remains a somewhat hazy and intangible concept in the collective public conscience; we simply do not know what audiences make of it. Philip Jenkins—who once stated that the involvement of children *guarantees* news coverage of a story (see Chapter 2)—has more recently contradicted this statement by arguing that child pornography was a *potential* moral panic that "failed to launch" (Jenkins, 2009). As far as Jenkins is concerned, the public has failed to engage with an offense that would appear to have all the requisite components to detonate a panic. The reasons he gives boil down to the institutions that control "official" information on the subject (the police and, in the United States, the Federal Bureau of Investigation) and their poor grasp of technology (cf. Jewkes & Andrews, 2005), together with journalists' lack of access to the problem itself and the moral and legal embargoes on investigating crimes involving the sexual abuse of children. However, Jewkes and Wykes (2012) take issue with Jenkins's analysis, arguing that it is impossible to separate the real-world sexual interest in children from the "virtual" spaces that bring pedophiles together and gives them a highly effective means of producing and distributing pornographic images. Given the utter ubiquity of the Internet, then, the precise ways in which pedophilia, the Internet, and panic interact may be a subject that warrants future research (see Chapters 9 and 10). However, the fact that the pedophile's status as instigator of model panic remains contested may say as much about the usefulness, or otherwise, of the model than about public anxieties concerning pedophilia. Perhaps, then, we should accept that moral panic is merely a "polemical rather than an analytic concept" (Waddington, 1986, p. 258).

THE LONGEVITY AND LEGACY OF
THE MORAL PANIC MODEL: SOME
CONCLUDING THOUGHTS

Many of the criticisms leveled at moral panics in this chapter were confronted by Cohen himself in the introduction to the third edition of his famous book (1972/2002), published to celebrate the 30th anniversary of *Folk Devils and Moral Panics*. Here Cohen addressed some of the problems associated with the concept he popularized (notably, the problems of proportionality, volatility, and the value-laden aspect of the term). He also analyzed several "boundary marking" cases (including the Columbine High School massacre) and considers the extent to which they can be construed as "successful" moral panics (pp. ix ff.).

As indicated in the introduction to this chapter, it is difficult to explain why criminology—and its related fields—continue to place the moral panic at the heart of studies of deviance and disorder when both sociology and media studies have more or less ignored it for decades. Why the latter subject areas have neglected it for so long is perhaps easier to comprehend. British sociology moved from considerations of structural changes and class-based divisions in the 1970s to the rise of New Right economic policies and ideology in the 1980s. The moral panic thesis seemed less relevant because it appeared to focus on sporadic and discrete episodes making a sudden and dramatic impact rather than on the underlying political-economic trends and their relationship to discourse and ideology—a dilemma already apparent in Hall et al.'s (1978/2013) study of the moral panic over mugging. Media studies, on the other hand, which had wholeheartedly embraced sociological concerns in the 1960s and 1970s, had taken a cultural turn by the 1980s. New inquiries in the field emphasized the audience as active makers of meaning or postmodern critics who were well qualified to see through the ideological veils put up by journalists and reporters.

The moral panic thesis was thus regarded by the new vanguard as reactionary, paternalistic, and media-centric, and the fact that to a large extent it has been the mediated version of deviance and not the phenomenon itself that has been the focus of attention is highly problematic for many media researchers. It is for these kinds of reasons that McRobbie and Thornton (1995) have urged us to "rethink" moral panics in the context of a proliferating and fragmenting media. Following Simon Watney's (1987) study of media responses to HIV and AIDS in the 1980s, they call for a more sophisticated understanding of human motivations for marginalizing certain groups. Certainly, the genuine, deep-seated anxieties at the root of reaction, and the "outsiders" onto whom these anxieties are displaced, have become secondary concerns amidst all the rhetoric about the persuasive powers of the media. Meanwhile, "fear of crime" has become a phrase that is widely bandied about but seldom fully explained or understood (see Chapter 6), prompting Richard Sparks to observe that mediated lines of influence—or "effects"—are far more complicated and multidirectional than frequently characterized. His own research (conducted with Evi Girling and Ian Loader) into public perceptions of fear, risk, and crime illustrate the point. It may have become commonplace to regard the media as purveyors of highly emotive and punitive rhetoric exploited by opportunistic politicians to manipulate populist sentiment, but individuals will always make sense of global transitions and transformations, including crime and crime control, from within the context and contours of their local community, and mediated "fear of crime" becomes substantially more intelligible in the light of a deeper contextual understanding of time and place (Girling, Loader, & Sparks, 2000). As such, any recourse to the concept of moral panic must be tempered by a knowledge and understanding of blames attributed and solutions sought at a local level (though Sparks counsels against reiterating the usual standoff between moral panic and "realism"; that is, fear of crime is either falsely manufactured by the media *or* it is a genuine response based on realistic estimations of likely victimization). Focusing on the local does not mean that some crime stories do not exist on a global plane; some events will always transcend "crimes" and become representative of much larger social anxieties. But Sparks reminds us that the fact that such cases evoke universally emotional responses neither detracts from the locally constituted lens through which we view them nor makes the public necessarily gullible, reactionary, or punitive.

Above all, as mentioned in Chapter 1, contemporary media research is audience-centered, not media-centered, and the emphasis is very much on what people do *with* the media as opposed to what the media do *to* people. But whether the real causes of social problems are "closer to home" or simply much too complicated to understand (as I. Connell, 1985, argues), the concentration on symptoms, rather than causes or long-term effects, leads to a somewhat superficial analysis of crime and deviance and frequently negates the fact that those who commit crimes are not "others"—they are "us" and are of our making. Above all, the construction of crime and deviance as moral panic designed to sell newspapers signifies a shift from "hard" news toward the safe territory of sensationalized reporting and public entertainment. As Cohen himself notes, the increasingly desperate measures taken by media organizations to secure a significant audience share result in a hierarchy of newsworthiness whereby a celebrity athlete's ankle injury gains more media attention that a political massacre (1972/2002, p. xxxiii). Moral panics may thus alert us to the shifting sands of audience responses, ranging from significant social reaction at one extreme to disinterest and nonintervention (or even denial) at the other. Ultimately, perhaps, moral panics should be regarded in the way that Cohen intended—as a means of conceptualizing the lines of power in society and the ways in which "we are manipulated into taking some things too seriously and other things not seriously enough" (p. xxxv).

David Garland (2008) takes up this point, noting that there has been a shift away from moral panics as traditionally conceived, involving a vertical relation between society and a deviant group, toward "culture wars"—a more horizontal conflict between social groups. This not only implies a much more multifaceted and politically attuned approach to understanding the nature of power in society but also reminds us that, far from bowing under the weight of collective anxiety and endless, cyclical panickyness—a state that is ontologically unsustainable—there is some excitement and enjoyment to be had from passionate mass public outrage (cf. Sparks, 1992). Furthermore, strong reaction begets strong reaction. The emotiveness that frames moral panics may account for the amount of criminology students' research carried out on them as well as the fact that the journal

Crime, Media, Culture receives more articles submitted on some aspect or other of moral panic than on any other subject. As Cohen himself said, studying moral panics is "easy and a lot of fun" (1972/2002, p. xxxv). But implicit in his reflections 30 years on is the caveat that a faithful adherence to the original moral panic thesis may make it impossible to arrive at a balanced and reasonable estimation of the real role of media in people's lives and the true impact of crime on society.

SUMMARY

- Chapter 3 has interrogated the much-used but frequently misinterpreted concept of moral panics made famous by Stanley Cohen in 1972. It has discussed both strengths and weaknesses of the term and briefly considered why "moral panics" are at the heart of much criminological debate about political struggles and cultural reproduction yet barely feature in contemporary sociology and media studies texts on the subject.

- The discussion has centered on the five defining features of moral panics: the presentation of the ordinary as extraordinary; the amplifying role of authorities; definitions of morality; notions of risk associated with social change; and the salience of youth.

- The chapter has also examined the problems that these five features raise in the context of nearly 50 years of adaptation, adoption, expansion, and criticism, some of which came from Cohen himself (1972/2002, pp. vii ff.).

- We have considered the validity of the model in relation to pedophilia and reflected on whether it constitutes the moral panic of our age or a potential panic that never got off the ground.

- While it has been recognized that there are fundamental flaws in the way the term "moral panic" has been uncritically applied to issues ranging from asylum seekers to dangerous dogs, from health scares to the music of Marilyn Manson, it has not been suggested that the idea is invalid or unhelpful in conceptualizing social reactions to both immediate, short-term crises and long-term general reflections on the "state-of-our-times" (Cohen, 1972/2002, p. vii). As Cohen (1972/2002, pp. x–xi) points out, if we accept that moral panics may reflect genuine public anxieties rather than consisting only of media-generated froth, and that not all likely candidates for public outrage actually quite add up to a moral panic (Cohen highlights the example of the racist murder of Stephen Lawrence), then we have a sound conceptual basis for examining the ways in which morality and risk are perceived in postmodern society.

STUDY QUESTIONS

1. In your view, how convincing is the "moral panic" thesis in explaining media reporting of, and public responses to, minority and/or deviant groups?

2. Moral panics have traditionally been directed at male, working-class subcultures, and girls and women have been viewed as peripheral to the action. Can you think of any examples where girls or young women have been the recipients of moral outrage? How successful or otherwise has criminological theory been in offering explanations for female subcultural crime?

3. What recent examples of criminal or deviant behavior can you think of that might be

described as "moral panics"? What is the primary source of the labeling of "demons" in your chosen cases?

4. What kinds of crime are not the subjects of moral panics, and what effect does this have on public perceptions of crime?

FURTHER READING

- Although this chapter has focused on moral panics in the modern era, they are far from a new phenomenon. G. Pearson's *Hooligan: A History of Respectable Fears* (Macmillan, 1983) is the "classic" work on the moral panics that have shaped public anxieties about crime and delinquency through the centuries.

- It is worth paying close attention to *Folk Devils and Moral Panics*, by S. Cohen, S. (MacGibbon & Kee, 1972), especially the third edition with a revised and extended introduction (Routledge, 2002).

- Among the relatively recent books on media and crime, *Crime, Culture and the Media*, by E. Carrabine (Polity, 2008), takes a similar approach to that taken in this chapter insofar as it traces the origins of the moral panic thesis in sociology and highlights some of the problems successive generations of scholars have encountered while revising and reformulating it. Of the best attempts to "revisit" the concept, E. Goode and N. Ben-Yehuda's *Moral Panics: The Social Construction of Deviance* (Blackwell,

1994) remains one of the most interesting books on the subject.

- *Intimate Enemies: Moral Panics in Contemporary Great Britain*, by P. Jenkins (Aldine de Gruyter, 1992) is also excellent, especially on moral panics over juveniles.

- In January 2009, a special issue of the *British Journal of Criminology* was devoted to issues as diverse as the shaping of folk devils and moral panics about white-collar crimes, online pedophilia, prostitution, and organized crime policing ("Moral Panics—36 Years On," *BJC*, vol. 49, no. 1).

- Finally, in December 2011, a special issue of *Crime, Media, Culture: An International Journal* was published with the title "Moral Panics in the Contemporary World." Including some of the last articles written by the key progenitors of the moral panic concept, Stan Cohen and Jock Young, it illustrates how popular and influential the concept of moral panics continues to be but also how its utility may have been stretched to a point where it is no longer a helpful analytical tool.

Student Study Site

WANT A BETTER GRADE?

Get the tools you need to sharpen your study skills. Access practice quizzes, eFlashcards, SAGE journal articles, and more at study.sagepub.com/jewkesus.

Media Constructions of Children

"EVIL MONSTERS" AND "TRAGIC VICTIMS"

4

OVERVIEW

Chapter 4 provides:

- A discussion of the complex and frequently contradictory assumptions made about children.

- An analysis of public fears and anxieties surrounding childhood, using as a case study the murder of two-year-old James Bulger by two older children in the UK in 1993.

- A comparison of media representations of this crime and other reported incidents that portrayed children as "persistent offenders," "evil monsters," and so on, with alternative media accounts representing children as vulnerable innocents who must be protected, not from other children, but from adults who seek to harm and exploit them.

- Evidence that suggests that children killed by strangers are much more likely to receive media attention than those who are killed by close relatives in the home.

- Support for the suggestion (which, in a somewhat crude formulation, underpins the moral panic thesis) that high-profile crimes involving child victims draw people together and mobilize their feelings of loss and guilt to produce a sense of "imagined community."

KEY TERMS

- adultification 107
- children 104
- dangerousness 109
- doli incapax 107
- evil monsters 104
- imagined community 116
- infantilization 106
- pedophile 104
- precautionary principle 112
- stranger danger 110
- tragic victims 104

In the last chapter, we noted that some aspects of the behavior of contemporary youth that might once have been conceived as normal, natural, and an inevitable part of growing up are increasingly becoming subject to moral censure and viewed as symptomatic of a fractured society. Yet, alongside the manufacture of fears about young people and crime, there has been a homogenization of age brackets into aspirational lifestyle categories that has resulted in a blurring of the distinctions between youth and adulthood. It might be argued, then, that the hostility once directed at an age group who were fundamentally different in appearance and aspirations to their parents' generation has, more recently, transmuted into something more confused. Children and adolescents are still the subjects of moral panic and public outrage but, as we saw in our discussion of news values in Chapter 2, they are frequently also cast as tragic victims. In fact, never have society's attitudes toward young people been as polarized as they are currently. Alongside youth *as* folk devils, we now have children as *the victims of* folk devils. It is precisely this confusion that will be discussed in this chapter. First we will explore changing social constructions of childhood, then develop a more detailed critique concerning the paradoxical attitudes toward children and young people that emerged in the mid-1990s, when children became regarded both as evil monsters capable of committing the most depraved of acts and as impressionable innocents who must be safeguarded, especially from the new number-one demons—pedophiles.

CHILDREN AS "EVIL MONSTERS"

Since the teenage rebellions of the 1950s and 1960s, the age at which young people have been criminalized, if not demonized, has been in flux, and at least since the early 1990s there have been regular reports of preteenage children committing increasingly serious offenses ranging from burglary to rape. This trend has only served to reinforce the equivocal attitudes to youth noted by Cohen, to the extent where the precise boundaries of "youth" and "adolescence" are now unclear; no one seems to be sure exactly when childhood is left behind or when adulthood is achieved (Muncie, 2009). This problem is compounded by the fact that ideas about the onset of adolescence and the age at which children are deemed to understand the difference between right and wrong are not fixed but subject to contestation and change over time. Prior to the mid-19th century, when positivism emerged to challenge it, ideas about crime and punishment were dominated by a theoretical perspective known as "classicism." A central feature of this approach was that punishment should fit the crime, not the individual offender. As a result, children were seen as equally culpable as adults when they committed an offense and were liable to the same penalties, including incarceration in prisons and prison hulks and transportation to penal colonies. However, in the 19th century, a new conception of childhood emerged out of the dominant cultural, medical, and psychological discourses of the time. For the first time in modern history, childhood was thought of as a separate stage of development prior to the independence and responsibility that came with adulthood. Children were seen as requiring social and legal protections, and as such, it was during this period that compulsory schooling was introduced and laws were passed limiting the number of hours children could work and prohibiting them from working in certain industries.

FIGURE 4.1

Juvenile age of jurisdiction and transfer to adult court laws.

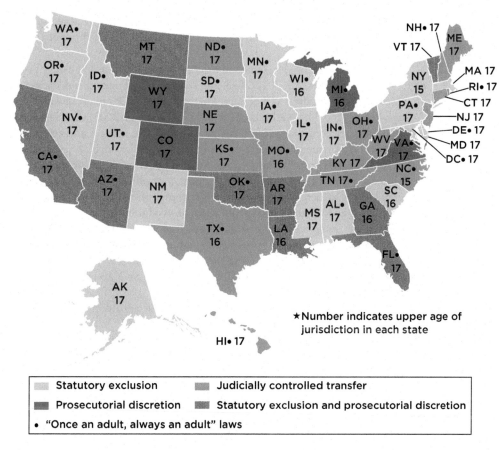

Source: Based on data from National Conference of State Legislatures (2017).

As criminologist Tony Platt (2009) has shown, the "Child Saver" movement of the early 1900s—supposedly founded on the altruistic desire of the wealthy to improve the conditions of poor children living in the ghettos of rapidly expanding American cities—was also driven by fear and the desire to control and contain future generations of the dangerous classes. And so, despite the benefits of compulsory schooling and labor protections, the social reality of childhood and particularly the culpability of youthful offenders remain fraught with complexity. For instance, with children winning the right to "divorce" their parents and young girls modeling the behavior of adult women and perhaps becoming overtly sexualized, some suggest we have seen the emergence of the *adultified* child. United States courts not only criminalize children at a much earlier age (see Figure 4.1) but also are by far more inclined to lock children up than other Western industrialized nations. In 2010, for instance, there were around 71,000 youth in residential treatment centers or incarcerated in secure facilities and another 1,800 youth under 18 who had been waived into the adult system and incarcerated in state prisons. And while the number of incarcerated youth has declined substantially over the last decade, rates of youth incarceration still far exceed those of the UK and other European nations.

By way of comparison, England and Wales maintained an average daily population of 1,544 youth in custody in 2012/2013, but, staggeringly, England and Wales incarcerate twice as many children as Belgium, Portugal, Spain, Denmark, Sweden, Finland, Austria, France, and The Netherlands combined (Goldson, 2003)! Yet, simultaneously, children are subjected to a greater degree of protective control and regulation that has led to a "major reorganization of the childhood experience . . . [whereby] roaming about with friends or walking to and from school are becoming increasingly rare experiences" (Furedi, 1997, p. 115). Furthermore, a combination of social, political, and economic forces, which includes increasingly competitive labor markets and housing costs, has resulted in many young people being forced to remain in a state of extended infantilization, living with their parents until they are well into their 20s or 30s. The so called "Boomerang Generation" of young adults (23 to 34) returning home to live with relatives has seen an uptick in recent decades, particularly since the 2008 recession, growing from about 11% in 1980 to around 22% in 2010 (Parker, 2012; see also Hayward, 2012b).

In the United States, contemporary debates over the culpability of youthful criminals probably have their roots in the 1924 murder of 14-year-old Robert Franks by two highly educated and wealthy young men, Nathan Leopold and Richard Loeb. Determined to plan and execute the "perfect crime," Leopold and Loeb murdered Franks, who was Loeb's second cousin, disposed of the body, and then orchestrated a kidnapping and ransom ruse in the attempt to cover their tracks. The two were quickly found out, however, after a unique pair of eyeglasses discovered with Franks's mutilated corpse was traced back to Leopold. The ensuing trial was elevated to spectacle when the boys' parents retained Clarence Darrow, the most prominent American jurist of the day. Since described as "the crime of the century," the senseless murder of Franks by two young "thrill killers" and the now-legendary defense launched by Darrow stand as a durable example of the contradictions raised by the crimes of the young.

These contradictions of course play out again and again, but nowhere more profoundly than they did in the case of the two preteen boys tried in an adult court for the murder of two-year-old James Bulger in the UK in 1993. We turn to this case now simply because, while it might not be well known in the U.S., this single case was a watershed in the history of British youth justice and in attitudes toward children there. Indeed, it is arguable that the moral panic generated by this case was so powerful that it led to a sentencing "arms race" between political parties vying to be strongest on law and order, with phrases like "Prison works" and "Tough on crime, tough on the causes of crime" underpinning a new punitiveness in sentencing policy and a dramatic rise in the prison population that has continued unchecked ever since.

In terms of its relevance for our discussion about paradoxical constructions of childhood, however, the conviction of two 10-year-olds for the murder of a toddler graphically illustrates how notions of childhood innocence and vulnerability coexist with images of mini-monsters, clearly delineating children as tragic victims and children as evil monsters. The *Daily Mail* of November 25, 1993, encapsulated this contradiction in its headline "The Evil and the Innocent," and, while the characterization of blond-haired, blue-eyed James as the epitome of an ideal child needed little reinforcement, the moral decrepitude of the 10-year-old murderers was achieved through interconnecting political, legal, and media discourses that sought to prove their guilt via a subtle process of adultification. As Terry Eagelton has remarked:

> We are ready to believe all kinds of sinister things about children, since they seem like a half-alien race in our midst. Since they do not work, it is not clear what they are for ... They have the uncanniness of things which resemble us in some ways but not in others. It is not hard to fantasise that they are collectively conspiring against us. (2010, p. 2)

As others have pointed out, in most European countries, evidence would have been heard that was deemed inadmissible in this case—evidence from the boys' "family backgrounds, their relationships with teachers and peers, their psycho-socio-sexual make-up" and so on (Morrison, 1997, p. 94). In fact, in most European countries, Venables and Thompson would have been considered too young to be tried at all, let alone tried in an adult court, and there would thus have been no question of guilt or innocence (Muncie, 1999). Under English law, however, children between the ages of 10 and 14 can be held accountable for a crime provided it can be established that they knew they were doing serious wrong rather than simply being "naughty," but they will—as a rule—be tried in a "youth court," which differs in style and approach to adult courts. In March 2010, children's commissioner Maggie Atkinson rekindled the debate about the ability of children to understand right from wrong (the legal doctrine known as *doli incapax*, meaning "incapable of wrong") when she called for the age of criminal responsibility to be raised to 12 and referred to the murder of James Bulger as "exceptionally unpleasant"—a phrase described by James's mother, Denise Fergus, as "twisted and insensitive." Illustrating the power and authority accorded to "victims," as discussed in Chapters 2, 6, and 10, Mrs. Fergus called for the commissioner to be fired and was given pages of press coverage to vent her displeasure. Atkinson was forced to apologize to Mrs. Fergus, publicly and privately, and government education minister Ed Balls felt moved to state publicly that, while he supported Atkinson, her comments that the age of criminal responsibility should be raised to 12 had been "ill-advised." This was despite the fact that there are few countries that set their age of criminal responsibility at or below this age, and most countries set it at 14 or above (16 in several countries including Spain and Japan; 18 in the case of Belgium and Luxembourg). This, then, may be an example of Britain's tendency to look toward America, rather than its near neighbors in Europe, in matters of law and punishment. Here in the United States, the pair would have been prosecuted by the juvenile court and, if adjudicated, incarcerated in facilities that for all outward appearances mirror adult prisons.

To return to the original trial in 1993, as Blake Morrison (1997) notes, expert witnesses were called to the court to give evidence about intellectual maturity, not mental disturbance, and when Venables and Thompson were convicted, it was deemed that they were old enough to understand the difference between right and wrong. Meanwhile, one of the defense attorneys showed the jury 247 press cuttings he had assembled that compared the boys to convicted child murderer Myra Hindley and deposed Iraqi despot Saddam Hussein, a move that probably only served to reinforce the judge's opinion that the murder was an act of "unparalleled evil and barbarity." Morrison contemplates the notion of Venables and Thompson being tried before a jury of 10-year-olds, since this would fulfill the role that juries are intended to serve—trial by one's peers. Of course, most people would regard such an idea as preposterous, not least because they would not trust the jurors' maturity, judgment, and intelligence. But, as Morrison concludes, these were the very qualities said to be present in the two boys when they killed James Bulger. They are also the kind of qualities that the then prime minister imbued them with when he appealed to the British public to condemn rather than understand, a sentiment echoed in his home secretary's blunt statement that no excuses could be made for "a section of the population who are essentially nasty pieces of work" (*The Times,* February 22, 1993). Meanwhile, the *Daily Star* vented feelings of vengeance and rage on behalf of the British public with their headline "How Do You Feel Now, You Little Bastards?" (November 25, 1993).

The hypocrisy of an adult society—given its own apparently insatiable appetite for violence, brutality, and war (Scraton, 2003)—heaping such ugly sentiments onto the heads of two 10-year-old murderers is an interesting phenomenon. In the aftermath of the Bulger case, the focus of public discourse was not on how two fairly ordinary lower-class families with many of the problems and difficulties that beset thousands of similar families across the country could implode to the degree where two children murder another child. As in the Leopold and Loeb case in the United States, the British public remained resolutely fixed on the idea that they were a couple of evil miscreants who came together and spurred each other on along a continuum of offenses, starting with skipping school and shoplifting and ending with the murder of a toddler they picked up in a shopping mall. As most certainly would have been the case in the United States, the unanimous cry from the British media was that these little boys should be locked up and the key thrown away, and, although now released from custody and granted lifetime anonymity, they remain prominent in the public consciousness thanks to the frequent iteration of the case in the press, where the boys' names are still evoked as justification for punitive sentencing. Yet in contrast, a similar case in Norway elicited a very different response from the media, politicians, and the public. There, the murder of a five-year-old by three children aged six, the year after the Bulger case, was reported as a tragic one-off accident and all four of the children involved were presented as victims, of whom those still alive should be reintegrated into society as swiftly as possible (Green, 2008a, 2008b). In another case in 2003, which had sad echoes of the Bulger murder, a 12-year-old boy in Japan was captured on CCTV leading a 4-year-old to his death. The older child could not be prosecuted under Japan's criminal code, which designates 16 as the age of criminal responsibility, and instead the boy was placed in a child welfare center while his needs—and those of his family—were assessed (http://news.bbc.co.uk).

Moreover, while the murder of James Bulger was reported as symptomatic of a wider problem of feckless youth, as Scraton (2003) observes, in the decade prior to

James Bulger's death, just one child under five had been killed per year by a stranger in the UK, and none by another child. By contrast, over 70 children under five had been murdered each year by a parent or an adult known to them. The media's unwillingness to report the extent of child abuse and murder within the home is further evidence of their obsession with the randomness of risk and their overwhelming tendency to locate **dangerousness** exclusively in the public realm. The net result of this emphasis is that it is pedophiles—including pedophiles who use the Internet to groom online and then commit contact offenses with children unrelated to them—who have come to be the recipients of moral outrage in the 21st century. In a tragic postscript to the Bulger case, a 27-year-old Jon Venables was recalled to prison in 2010 following reports that he had committed offenses related to child pornography. The Ministry of Justice refused to specify what the claims being made against him were, but not only did his arrest permit the broadcast and print media to replay and reanalyze the 1993 case all over again (with much the same hysteria and prejudice that accompanied the original coverage), but the nature of the allegations against him served to underline his characterization as an unredeemable and evil person incapable of being reintegrated.

CHILDREN AS "TRAGIC VICTIMS"

The term "pedophile" first rose to prominence in the 1980s and 1990s when the theme of "pedophile in the community" came to prominence (Kitzinger, 1999). In Europe there had been a significant increase in public awareness of cases being exposed that involved child sexual abuse in residential child care homes and other institutions where children were supposed to be protected. In Northern Ireland, several cases of Catholic priests accused of sexual offenses against children made headlines and fueled accusations of high-level cover-ups within the church (Greer, 2003). Anxiety escalated in the autumn of 1996 when a released pedophile was charged with a series of child murders in Belgium, and again there were accusations of a high-level cover-up, this time involving politicians, the police, and civil servants. In the U.S., changes in public discourse around such matters occurred alongside a number of similar high-profile cases. In the 1980s and 1990s, the McMartin preschool child abuse case and revelations of widespread exploitation of children by Catholic priests and "psychosexual serial killers" such as Ted Bundy, John Wayne Gacy, and Jeffery Dahmer received extensive coverage by American news media. In turn, pedophiles and sex offenders more generally moved to the forefront of the American public's frightened consciousness (Rafter, 2007).

America's concern over pedophilia is also entwined with a number of high-profile missing child and abduction cases. One of the best known is that of 12-year-old Johnny Gosch, who disappeared the morning of September 5, 1982, while delivering newspapers in his Des Moines, Iowa, neighborhood (it has long been speculated that sex abuse figured into Gosch's abduction). Frustrated by the seeming disinterest in her son's disappearance, Johnny's mother, Noreen Gosch, organized her own campaign, adeptly using news media, press conferences, and private investigators to draw attention to the case. Two years after Johnny's disappearance, the Gosch family partnered with the relatives of

PHOTO 4.1

The "Milk Carton Kids" campaign.

another (presumably) abducted Des Moines paperboy, Eugene Martin, to publicize their cases with photos printed on the sides of milk cartons produced by local dairies. The concept, first used in the 1979 disappearance of Etan Patz, continued for decades, placing the faces of thousands of missing children on an estimated 5 billion milk cartons and likewise as many breakfast tables and school lunches. While the "milk carton kids" campaign proved only marginally successful in helping to locate missing children (neither Patz nor Gosch nor Martin has been found) and was eventually abandoned as paper cartons were replaced by plastic jugs, the campaign did help raise awareness about child abduction, particularly **stranger danger** (see also Mokrzycki, 2015, and http://99percentinvisible.org/episode/milk-carton-kids/).

In the ensuing decades, a raft of pedophile- and sex offender–specific legislation followed similar cases. Named after Jacob Wetterling, an 11-year old boy abducted at gunpoint off a street near his Minnesota home, the 1994 Jacob Wetterling Crimes Against Children and Sexually Violent Offender Registration Act was the first federal legislation to require states to maintain a registry of those convicted of child abuse or sex offenses. A short time later, "Megan's Law" was created following the rape and murder, two years earlier, of seven-year-old Megan Kanka by a twice-convicted sex offender in her New Jersey neighborhood. These cases all tapped into existing concerns over the perceived lenient sentences being handed down to some convicted sex offenders. And though individual states were and still are free to develop and impose their own strategies to control sex offenders, in 2006 the Adam Walsh Child Protection and Safety Act mandated sex offender registration and reporting on a three-tiered system and allows for civil commitment (indefinite detention) of those offenders deemed most dangerous. Such laws are future-oriented and require police and supervision agencies to predict an individual's future behavior and make assessments based on the risks a person is thought to represent. In these cases, the usual civil liberties that would govern the treatment and punishment of suspected or past offenders are overridden, meaning that a person can be held indefinitely, even after their sentence has been served, if they are deemed a risk to reoffend (Ashenden, 2002).

Critics see civil commitment orders as highly problematic for a number of reasons (Cowburn & Dominelli, 2001). Not only has "risk assessment" been criticized for implicit bias, but the practice also raises expectations about protection of the vulnerable that cannot be fulfilled on the basis of professional knowledge about sex offenders as it presently stands and puts faith in the notion that community safety can be achieved by more sophisticated risk assessment methods and greater diligence on the part of workers within the criminal justice system. These views are at odds with the opinions of some professionals, who argue that putting the feelings of a community before the needs of individual offenders, or potential offenders, may result in community vigilantism and the driving of offenders underground. Second, future-oriented risk assessments pay little credence to the notion of rehabilitation for sex offenders, especially given the prevailing view that, where children are concerned, there is no risk worth taking. Third, it ignores yet again the much larger problem of women and children who are sexually abused within the private domain and perpetuates the myth of the home as a place of safety.

With the introduction of sex offender registries and community notification legislation such as "Megan's Law," politicians were given a powerful new focal point for their campaigns, all of which was aided by the work of an opportunistic media. For instance, conservative television personality Bill O'Reilly has made "Jessica's Law" a personal cause since late 2005. Invoking the names of children murdered by sex offenders, O'Reilly urges:

> These outrageous crimes could have been prevented . . . There is simply no question that Jessica's Law will save lives, and similar laws need to be instituted in every state. Which is why we at The Factor have been putting pressure on Governors. Now it's your turn. We have investigated all 50 states to determine which ones are tough on sexual predators and which ones treat these criminals with kid gloves. . . . If your state is soft or noncommittal, I urge you to write your Governor, who is paid by YOU. Please tell him or her, in your own words, how important this issue is to you—and remind the Governor that all politicians are ultimately accountable to you and your fellow voters. This is literally a life-and-death battle to save our youngest and most vulnerable citizens from abuse, torture, and murder. I hope you'll do your part. (http://www.billoreilly.com/jessicaslaw)

Nearly a decade later, O'Reilly is still campaigning for Jessica's Law, using his high-profile television program to praise politicians who support his agenda and publicly shame those who do not.

Another consequence of this sort of fear-drenched pandering is that the overriding image of the pedophile is still that of a monster who is not "one of us." The mediated image of the monstrous "stranger" is further entrenched by the everyday practices of criminal justice. For instance, in recent years, several states have enacted specific laws and practices intended to protect children from sex offenders on Halloween. Based on the misguided premise that children are at greater risk on this night than on any other, some states go as far as to prohibit convicted sex offenders from decorating their homes and require offenders to attend mandatory meetings with police or parole officials during peak "trick-or-treat" hours (Chaffin, Levenson, Letourneau, & Stern, 2009). In 2006, the New York State Division of Parole launched "Operation Halloween: Zero Tolerance," which it described as a "collaborative, multi-pronged containment strategy giving parents, caregivers, law enforcement and the community the assurance they need in knowing that our neighborhoods are safe." In addition to the "surveillance, unannounced home visits and curfew checks" of standard sex offender supervision, "Operation Halloween: Zero Tolerance" required that offenders return home at 3 p.m. or immediately following dismissal from work; remain in their residence until 6 a.m. the following morning; and be available by phone in their home should parole agents decide to call upon them.

Further, the program prohibited parolees from participating in any Halloween activity or wearing any costume. And as with similar measures in New Jersey, Virginia, Wisconsin, California, South Carolina, and North Carolina, "Operation Halloween" prohibits sex offenders from opening their door to any minors who are trick-or-treating. All of these laws and special supervision practices are of course based on the faulty premise that sex offenders prey on strangers and because of their uncontrollable impulsivity are highly likely to reoffend. Again, victimization surveys show that the vast majority of sexually abused children knew their attacker. Likewise, research also shows that a minority of convicted sex offenders are arrested for a second or subsequent sex offense. But as a Division of Parole spokesperson reasoned:

> There is nothing more frightening than the prospect of someone preying on a child. By implementing these special conditions, the Division of Parole will be doing everything in its power to make sure that all of New York's families can have a safe and enjoyable time while trick-or-treating. (New York State Division of Parole, 2006)

Clearly, programs such as these operate on the **precautionary principle**, which requires preparation for the worst case, however unlikely.

The precautionary logics that underpin "Operation Halloween" are not confined to the U.S. In the UK, the government falls back on a well-worn stereotype of the pedophile to illustrate how the orders might work, citing a man with a previous caution for indecent conduct toward a child "hanging around" outside a school, approaching departing children, and offering them sweets (Hough & Roberts, 1998; see "Education Ban"). As Ashenden notes, the presentation of an archetype of the pedophile has dual outcomes. First, it makes the topic less uncomfortable, as it feeds into a familiar stereotype and enables the public to disassociate themselves from the individual described, and second, it simultaneously maintains the horror of the unknown predator (Ashenden, 2002). Jewkes and Wykes (2012) further argue that stereotypes of sexual offenders (including "cyber-peds") divert attention from the fact that most child abuse takes place in the home, perpetrated by a family member or someone known to the victim. At one and the same time, then, the moral panic over pedophilia has perpetuated the notion that sexual dangerousness resides in strangers and that those strangers are not like "us." While "we" are "normal," morally decent, law-abiding citizens, "they" lurk at school gates and in playgrounds, preying on innocents in the pursuit of fulfilling their sexual depravities.

As described in the previous chapter, pedophilia seems to fit the criteria of a "moral panic." While it cannot be characterized as an "ordinary" crime, pedophilia is far from extraordinary. Yet the media persist in portraying it as a growing threat, a risk that could strike at random. Fears over pedophiles using the Internet to stalk or groom their victims may well be partially borne out of their parents' distrust of new computer and information technologies and their anxieties about the further fragmentation of the family. Other media technologies, from family home movies to CCTV, have made cases of child abduction by strangers especially fascinating, providing graphic imagery of the last movements of victims to a voyeuristic viewing public who already know their fate.

Moreover, like all moral panics, pedophilia has acquired a remarkable degree of consensus. There are few issues that have galvanized public reaction more fiercely than that of adults who have a sexual preference for children, and in response to those who act on their desires, procuring children in playgrounds and Internet chat rooms, there is striking unanimity in the condemnation expressed by the media, government officials, and local communities. It is easy to see, then, why the pedophile has been characterized as the folk devil par excellence in contemporary Western society. He (the kind of language and imagery used in popular discourses about pedophiles reinforce the presumption that sex offenders are male) is "*absolute* other" (Greer & Jewkes, 2005), an individual without *any* redeeming qualities, nearly always reduced to a set of subhuman, even bestial, thoughts and urges that are totally alien to right-minded people.

However, like many of the examples mentioned in the previous chapter, the pedophile crisis does not fit all the criteria traditionally associated with the moral panic model, the weaknesses of which should by now be clear. As discussed in Chapter 3, one of the fundamental discrepancies in accounts of moral panics is in explanations of their origins. In the case of pedophilia, the general view is that the process of demonization did not emanate from government (although it might be said that the new sex offender legislation and concomitant public debate had the effect of stigmatizing a large number of men, including those who had actually committed no offense). But most critics would argue on this point that the sex offender legislation was introduced in response to public fears rather than as a means of manufacturing them. Similarly, while it has been argued that public anxieties concerning youth crime generally, and the individual abduction cases outlined earlier in particular, were a manipulation on the part of governments to construct a "demonology of deviance" and advance a particular political agenda (Freeman, 1997), most commentators support the theory that the invocation of evil in these tragic cases was led by the judiciary and the media (Stokes, 2000). Having said that, we should not overlook the fact that a government does not have to manufacture a crisis in order to benefit from it, and that the construction of social problems as matters of individual wickedness rather than as failures of collective responsibility or social policy can work to the advantage of governments seeking to diffuse political responsibility (Freeman, 1997; Lacey, 1995).

The "outing" and persecution of known sex offenders might therefore best be viewed as a local or meso-level concern. Jenny Kitzinger argues that neighborhood pressure groups, disillusioned by the failure of authorities to prevent child abuse, were already taking direct action as early as the 1990s. Similar to the campaign led by Noreen Gosch that culminated in the "milk carton kids," protest groups, consisting mostly of mothers who were outraged at official impotence and scared for their children's safety, provided the impetus for extensive media reports about the sexual abuse of children. Philip Jenkins's (1992) study of the moral panic over satanic child abuse also supports the "meso" theory of source, albeit from a rather more cynical standpoint. He suggests that the "exposure" by social workers of a vast and unsuspected prevalence of child abuse fulfilled a number of ideological and professional needs, including providing much-needed extra funding for an underresourced service and much-sought-after credibility—initially, at least—for a relatively low-status profession.

The factors highlighted above reinforce the notion, proposed by left realists, that crime must be taken seriously and not regarded as mediated fabrication, but there is another pertinent point to be made, and it is one that is rarely discussed. By reducing serious crimes to moral panics, the media succeed in masking the collective sense of guilt that underpins traumatic events while at the same time pandering to the voyeur in all of us. In the case of James Bulger, a sense of shame and guilt extended beyond the immediate community (primarily the "Liverpool 38," as the press dubbed them; the people who saw James being dragged to the railway line where he met his death but who failed to intervene) and seeped into the conscience of the nation as a whole. Subsequent cases such as the abduction and murder of Polly Klaas and Megan Kanka have further shocked a society that effortlessly falls back on notions of "evil within our midst" while denying its own flaws and colluding in the demonization of offenders as "others." In his analysis of the Bulger trial, Morrison (1997) candidly reminds us that most of us experienced events in our youth of which we are now embarrassed or ashamed; after all, children can be cruel, selfish, and unconstrained. But at the same time as we recall, and recoil from, our own memories of ourselves as youths, we hang on to the ideal of children as precious innocents who must be protected from the sordid and the spoiled. No wonder that out of such incongruity, when children commit serious crimes, a deep and pervasive cultural unease is borne.

Our failure to protect youngsters from the "perverts" and "monsters" in our midst provokes a similar sense of collective anxiety and cultural unease. Yet, again, there are clear paradoxes in our cultural attitudes and legal responses to the sexualization and sexual victimization of young people. One particularly egregious case emerged in the early 2000s in Kansas, when a young man named Matthew Limon was convicted of criminal sodomy. Limon, who had just turned 18 at the time of the offense, admitted to having consensual oral sex with a 14-year-old boy, who like Limon, was a resident of a state-run school for "developmentally disabled youth." Even under the state's so-called "Romeo and Juliet" law, Limon would have been subject to the hefty penalty of 32 to 36 months in prison. But because that law excluded sexual contact between people of the same sex, Limon was sentenced to 206 months in prison. On October 21, 2005, after several appeals were denied by lower courts, the Kansas Supreme Court ruled that the state's law violated the equal protection clause of the U.S. Constitution and struck the "opposite sex" provision from its law. On November 4, 2005, after more than five years in prison, Matthew Limon was paroled.

In summary, the fervent, voyeuristic media coverage devoted to cases of abused, assaulted, missing, or murdered children gives them a superordinancy that lifts them above other, equally horrible, crimes. The decisions of those who work within media organizations to select certain stories and present them according to their professional codes and institutional news values can thus secure a powerful symbolic place in the public psyche while at the same time repressing the collective sense of guilt and denial that such cases provoke. They are directed at events that have sufficient cultural resonance to threaten the fundamental basis of the social order. Yet, in constructing an indefensible, demonized "other" against a backdrop of taken-for-granted normality, moral panics over children who kill and are killed avoid any real risk to the essential structures of society. Those who look for alternative explanations are silenced or condemned as "do-gooders" seeking to make excuses for the worst examples of human depravity (Stokes, 2000). Not only does this close down further etiological inquiry, but it also allows the community to remain emotionally and physically intact (cf. Aldridge, 2003; Barak, 1994).

MORAL PANICS AND THE REVIVAL OF "COMMUNITY": SOME CONCLUDING THOUGHTS

In the previous chapter, we reviewed the concept of moral panics that has traditionally united politics, media, and everyday life, and in this chapter we have focused on the fear and loathing that is directed at two modern folk devils, offending children and those who sexually victimize children, both of whom have been characterized as the "evil monsters in our midst." In Chapter 3, it was suggested that the moral panic model is unhelpful, and, certainly, it is problematic when applied to pedophilia because it suggests that genuine public fears about the sexual abuse and exploitation of children are unfounded or overstated. Quite simply, Cohen's thesis—or rather, its application by those who have adopted it—is open to the criticisms that it reduces serious problems to overblown media reporting, distorts the reality of crime that usually involves victims and often entails human suffering, and can only account for public, spectacular crimes, not the serious crimes that take place in private, hidden from the gaze of the media. The reduction of a widespread if largely hidden social problem to "accessible proportions" (Cowburn & Dominelli, 2001, p. 403) arguably makes the issues reviewed in this chapter something *other than* or *beyond* moral panic, a term that diminishes incidents such as the murder or sexual abuse of a child to mere media-generated hysteria, negating the very real and rational responses that such crimes provoke (Kitzinger, 1999).

However, there are elements of the moral panic thesis that are interesting to explore further in this context, not least the emphasis it places on the notion of "community." As noted in Chapter 3, the tendency to fall back on notions of "pure evil" are not that surprising; after all, once "evil" has been defined, the public knows by implication what "good" is. The labeling of pedophiles as "enemies within" thus gives the hub of the group (often referred to euphemistically as the "moral majority") a sense of their own cultural identity. This is especially apparent in the actions taken by communities in response to the releasing of convicted sex offenders in their towns:

[I] enjoyed walking up the street with a gang of women, all shouting to get the pedophile out. I can't help it but this is how I felt. Walking the streets with all the noise, I got a buzz out of it. I know it sounds really childish. But when I came back here and thought "what have I done" . . . Now, I think if we have been to innocent people's homes, then I am ashamed. I do think it has got a bit hysterical. And because of what's happened we have been made to look like riff-raff. (*Observer*, August 13, 2000, p. 4)

This statement recalls the 19th-century writings of Gustave Le Bon (1895/1960), who argued that crowds were the beast within, the absolute antithesis of rational citizens, and of Charles MacKay, who declared that people "go mad in herds, while they only recover their sense slowly, and one by one" (MacKay, 1841/1956, p. 5). Yet, is this coming together in unanimous condemnation of a perceived threat an act of madness, or is it, as Pratt (2002) suggests, a rational response to the state's failure to deal with sex offenders in ways that such groups think appropriate, a movement that speaks of resistance and empowerment? As society becomes more fragmented and entire groups of people are excluded on the basis of their appearance, their style, their behavior, and even on predictions concerning their potential behavior, people tend to congregate around those issues that offer them a sense of unity, some semblance of community. Through the perception of an identity held in common, each individual member of a group or crowd is able unconsciously to deny his or her feelings of powerlessness in a shared sense of power.

Despite their rarity, then, high-profile criminal cases involving child offenders or victims are used in much the same way as other cultural events that become part of a collective memory through mass media. Although late modernity is frequently said to be characterized by fragmentation, surveillance, regulation, dangerousness, and risk—all of which are said to mitigate against, if not make redundant, the notion of community—individual life histories are structured, shaped, and made sense of within frames of reference provided by the mass media. In fact, it may be precisely those "negative" characteristics of late modernity that fuel people's need for unity, and, in a context of uncertainty and insecurity, one of the primary means by which people are afforded a sense of social cohesion and connection with their communities may be via the media. It is therefore no longer only media personalities and celebrities who offer the illusion of intimacy (a phenomenon known in media studies as "parasocial interaction"; Horton & Wohl, 1956) but also the victims of violent crimes and their families whose circumstances guarantee sufficient "human interest" to bring people together in public outrage and mourning. It is, however, a climate of public mourning that—while instrumental to the creation and maintenance of an **imagined community** in otherwise fragmented and anonymous circumstances—is on "our" terms. People want contact and some form of interaction, but *not too much,* and that is why mediated experience can be so much more satisfying than lived experience. Public responses to crimes involving child victims (which range from "passive" responses such as memorial plaques, roadside shrines, and books of condolence to "active" expressions of violence and vigilantism) are a way of touching a stranger's life without having to endure one's own life being touched back by strangers in any palpable way—save from the fact that we feel better for having taken the time to send the message, sign the book, take part in "direct action." These expressions of grief and anger thus correspond with a particular imagination of proximity and closeness (the intimacy of a personal tribute, the primal pleasure of being part of a crowd bent on revenge), but it is an imagination that is largely faceless. Media-orchestrated, publicly articulated responses to serious and violent crime are thus basic components of imagined community, but it is a community that remains tangential and anonymous. Mediated expressions of fear and loathing are thus fundamentally in keeping with the nature of society in late modernity (see Chapter 10 for further discussion).

SUMMARY

- Part of the reason for the elasticity of "youth" as a concept is that adult society holds contradictory and conflicting views regarding the nature of youth. Views of childhood are paradoxically captured in notions of "innocence" and "evil" and are frequently enshrined in law and upheld daily by the popular media. One example of constructions of childhood "innocence" is encapsulated in the age at which individuals can legally consent to sexual intercourse, which varies considerably across different countries and U.S. states.

- The inconsistencies that lie at the heart of differing ages of criminal responsibility is key to the confusing ideas surrounding childhood in contemporary society. Moreover, such paradoxes play into the hands of a media that constructs events in terms of binary oppositions and stock stereotypes. The media can position child offenders and victims of crime along a continuum from "innocence" to "evil," individualizing their pathology or vulnerability, in order that deeper questions about social structures—the family, education, political institutions, and the media industries themselves—need never be asked.

- Children are viewed, somewhat paradoxically, as both "evil monsters" and "tragic victims." The murders of children by other children can be watersheds in public perceptions of childhood as well as in law. As Scraton (2003) argues, in the UK, James Bulger's death was exploited to the full, first by the Conservative party who, at their annual conference in 1993, whipped up fervor with demands for execution, castration, and flogging, and then by a Labour government which rushed through its wide-ranging Crime

and Disorder Act, 1998, and set about appearing tougher on crime than its Conservative predecessors. And throughout it all, the figures of Robert Thompson and Jon Venables, whose photographs were printed in every paper as soon as the guilty verdicts were reached, were a gift to a media that had squeezed every last drop out of stories about "persistent young offenders" and the "yob society" and were now given a new motif for evil with which to provoke respectable fears in the shape of two 10-year-old boys.

- At the same time, "our" children must be protected from "pedophiles," a social construction that reinforces public fear of stranger danger and provides the community with an identifiable hate figure onto whom they can project their anxiety and loathing. Such coverage has brought back to the fore notions of childhood innocence and vulnerability and emphasized the need to manage the threat posed by sex offenders via various "risk assessment" strategies while ignoring the reality of danger in the family and home. Mediated constructions of sex offenders and the public responses they shape thus not only present a partial image of the abuse and exploitation of children but also let the community, in its broadest sense, "off the hook" (Cowburn & Dominelli, 2001). The impression of random danger is perpetuated, but it is a risk that can be accommodated provided that it is contained within terms that emphasize community. Crimes involving young victims of older or adult offenders are therefore a primary vehicle for expressions of community "togetherness," ranging from vigilance to vigilantism and from public sorrow to public vengeance.

STUDY QUESTIONS

1. Why are children and young people frequently perceived to be not just *a* crime problem but *the* crime problem? What are the problems with this characterization?

2. How do the different theoretical perspectives reviewed in Chapter 1 view young people who commit crime?

3. This chapter has discussed the case of the abduction and murder of two-year-old James Bulger in the UK because it had such profound and far-reaching impacts on British criminal law, justice, public attitudes to children, and the organization of family life. What criminal cases in the U.S. can you think of that have had a similarly seismic impact on aspects of legal, social, and cultural experience?

4. To what extent, and in what ways, has recent media coverage of pedophilia skewed the picture of sexual abuse in the U.S.? How do media constructions of the "pedophile" differ from those of the "rapist" in an earlier age?

5. How is "childhood" constructed differently in other countries? Does the pedophile loom as large in the collective conscience of the U.S. and other nations as it does in the UK?

FURTHER READING

- Anthony Platt's (1969/2009) *The Child Savers: The Invention of Delinquency* remains a foundational text on youth crime.

- The murder of James Bulger has been reviewed extensively in both media studies and criminology. See, for example, B. Franklin and J. Petley's "Killing the Age of Innocence: Newspaper Reporting of the Death of James Bulger," in *Thatcher's Children? Politics, Childhood and Society in the 1980s and 1990s,* edited by J. Pilcher and S. Wagg (Falmer, 1996).

- More unusually, B. Morrison's *As If* (Granta, 1997) is a semiautobiographical analysis of the case by a journalist who attended the trial of Thompson and Venables and employed the case to reflect on his own experiences both as a child and as a parent.

- Keith Hayward's "Pantomime Justice: A Cultural Criminological Analysis of 'Life Stage Dissolution,'" in *Crime, Media, Culture, 8*(2), 213–229 (2012), offers an innovative analysis of life stage dissolution and youth culture.

- Finally, David Green has compared coverage of the Bulger murder with that of a very similar case in Norway and argued that the different cultural constructions of childhood that endure in each country have shaped the responses deemed appropriate for children who commit grave acts. See "Suitable Vehicles: Framing Blame and Justice When Children Kill a Child," in *Crime, Media, Culture: An International Journal, 4*(2), 197–220 (2008), and *When Children Kill Children: Penal Populism and Political Culture* (Oxford University Press, 2008), both by D. A. Green.

Student Study Site

WANT A BETTER GRADE?

Get the tools you need to sharpen your study skills. Access practice quizzes, eFlashcards, SAGE journal articles, and more at study.sagepub.com/jewkesus.

Media Misogyny
MONSTROUS WOMEN

OVERVIEW

Chapter 5 provides:

- An exploration—underpinned by psychosocial and feminist approaches—of mediated responses to very serious offending by women, concentrating mainly on women who kill and rape.

- A consideration of whether women are treated more harshly or more leniently by the criminal justice system.

- A discussion of whether women who commit violent crimes in partnership with a man are passive victims or active partners who kill through choice.

- An analysis of the standard stories, stereotypes, and stock motifs employed by the media to convey deviant women's "evilness."

- A consideration of women's "otherness" and why women who commit very serious crimes are much more newsworthy than men who similarly offend.

KEY TERMS

- agency 141
- carceral feminism 135
- difference 120
- essentialism 147
- familicide/family annihilation 144
- feminist 120
- filicide 138
- heteropatriarchy 127
- infanticide 138
- otherness 120
- psychosocial 120
- scopophilic 138
- spousal homicide 132
- unconscious 121

This chapter will consider the public's mediated responses to women who kill and commit other serious offenses. As we have already seen, the modern media are highly selective in their constructions of offenses, offenders, and victims. For a crime to be reported at all, let alone be the subject of the kind of persistent, frenzied coverage that might result in the construction of offenders as folk devils, the prevailing ideological climate must be especially hostile to the offense that has been committed. Something about the juxtaposition of time and place will result in a case standing out as extraordinary or exceptional even in a society where the most horrific of crimes may be presented, if at all, as run-of-the-mill episodes. Often, it is the existence of some kind of mediated representation such as graphic CCTV footage that jolts us out of our cozy stupor and forces us to recognize the reality of serious crime in places we least expect to see it. At the same time, the criminal act, its perpetrator(s), and/ or its victim(s) must conform to some of the key journalistic news values described in Chapter 2. The synthesis of these two contexts—ideological climate and journalistic assumptions—are instrumental in creating public consensus and in shaping the process by which some individuals are designated "others"—monsters in our midst. They also determine why some offenses cast a much longer shadow than other, more serious crimes. Following the line taken by many **feminist** critics, it will be argued in this chapter that the media tap into, and magnify, deep-seated public fears about deviant women while paying much less attention to equally serious male offenders whose profile does not meet the **psychosocial** criteria of "**otherness**." While many generalized points will be made about women's involvement in certain categories of offending (murder, manslaughter, infanticide and filicide, sexual assault, and rape) specific and, of necessity, selective—though highly newsworthy and notorious—cases will be referred to throughout the chapter as illustrations of media misogyny.

PSYCHOANALYTIC PERSPECTIVES

Contemporary media reflect other sociopolitical institutions in their attitudes toward marriage and the family, which remain curiously embedded in the Victorian age. Notions of the feminine as passive, maternal, married, and monogamous coexist with sentimental ideas about childhood innocence, resulting in any "other" identities—for example, single mothers and lesbian parents—being subjected to overt hostility (Wykes, 1998). When it comes to constructions of female offending (or, for that matter, female victimization), **difference** is readily constructed as deviance by causal association with crime. Despite the fact that women rarely stalk, kill strangers, or commit serial murder (in fact, in 2014, women were offenders in less than 12% of the murder cases where the offender was known), those who do so are highly newsworthy because of their novelty (Federal Bureau of Investigation, 2014). The media, then, are happy to acknowledge that violent or sexually deviant women are relatively uncommon but concede that they are all the more fascinating and diabolical as a result.

In a psychoanalytic interpretation, "difference" involves the denial of large parts of ourselves, or the projection of those parts of ourselves, that make us feel vulnerable to others. Stemming from Freud's conceptualization of the Oedipal conflict that arises when an infant begins to have sexual feelings and desires toward the opposite-sex parent and at the same time has accompanying feelings of resentment and jealousy toward the same-sex parent, this perspective helps to explain the persecution of the "other" throughout history. Put simply, in the case of the male child, he has previously seen himself as sharing an identity with his mother but is suddenly confronted with the reality of her sexual difference. This induces a fear of castration and a masculine identification with the father, not only physically but also as a source of cultural power and moral authority. In the context of this discovery, culture (that is, the Law of the Father) wins over individual desire, and the child "succumbs to a destructive unconscious solution" (Minsky, 1998, p. 83) in which he expels or externalizes the part of himself that he finds intolerable—in other words, the painful "victim" feelings of humiliation and vulnerability—and projects them onto his newly discovered "other," his mother. In this way, he is able to disown the harmful feelings that interfere with his newly discovered sense of power and project them onto "woman," who is now defined as "different and therefore bad" (p. 84). "Subsequently, women, femininity or passivity wherever it exists may be deemed contemptible and feared because it represents a despised, castrated part of the self" (p. 84). Symbolic cultural representations (e.g., those that reduce, repress, objectify, silence, humiliate, ridicule, or otherwise marginalize women and other "minorities") are intuitively adopted by individuals, identified with at a psychic level, and then played out within social relations, thus reinforcing and reproducing divisions and inequalities.

It is, then, the interplay between **unconscious** fears and culturally reinforced prejudices that defines who, at any given time, is designated "the scapegoat 'other'" against whom we bolster our own individual sense of identity (Minsky, 1998, p. 2), and the victimization of feminized "others" goes beyond gendered relationships and helps to explain not only sexism but also racism, nationalism, tribalism, terrorism, homophobia, and religious persecution. Implicit in all of these forms of intolerance is the notion of a despised "other" as the means to maintaining an idealized self. An understanding of "otherness" helps to explain why identities are often characterized by polarization and by the discursive marking of inclusion and exclusion within oppositional classificatory systems: "insiders" and "outsiders"; "us" and "them"; men and women; black and white; "normal" and "deviant"; and so on. Not surprisingly, then, notions of difference and otherness have been put forward as a theory of crime and victimization. As previously noted, media representations of immigrants, political refugees, and native-born black, Hispanic, and Asian people are frequently underpinned by powerful psychic notions of otherness that frequently find expression in a tendency to see crime perpetrated by nonwhite people as a product of their ethnicity, while crimes against nonwhites are all too frequently constructed in ways that are tantamount to blaming the victims.

The subject of this chapter, however, is the extent to which the relationship between unconscious fears and culturally constructed scapegoats can help to explain mediated responses to women who commit very serious crimes. Psychosocial and feminist theories will underpin the discussion and aid our understanding of the legal, criminological, and media discourses surrounding women who seriously offend. Unsurprisingly, given the parameters of this book, it is media rather than legal discourses that will be our focus. However, as Belinda Morrissey argues, the close relationship between legal and media institutions has meant that "the two function together and their representations ... mostly lend themselves to a single analysis, with dominant media depictions mirroring courtroom portrayals" (2003, p. 4). Both institutions have a vital role in maintaining notions of feminine wickedness in cases where women offend, just as they preserve ideas of feminine oppression in cases where women are portrayed as victims.

FEMINIST PERSPECTIVES

In brief, feminist criminological perspectives emerged in the 1970s to challenge the androcentrism (male-centeredness) of traditional criminology. The first feminist text to make a profound and sustained impact on criminology was Carol Smart's *Women, Crime and Criminology* (1977), which exposed the culturally biased assumptions about women that had underpinned traditional ideas about female criminality since the days of Lombroso over a century before. Smart's pioneering approach led to a number of other influential feminist studies (among them Chesney-Lind, 1997; Chesney-Lind & Pasko, 1997; Gelsthorpe & Morris, 1990; Heidensohn, 1985; Irwin & Chesney-Lind, 2008; Lloyd, 1995), which argued that essentialist assumptions about women's psychological makeup and biological purpose condemned them to differential treatment by criminal justice at all stages. In short, women who commit serious offenses are judged to have transgressed two sets of laws: criminal laws and the laws of nature. In Ann Lloyd's (1995) memorable phrase, such women are "doubly deviant and doubly damned."

There is no single "feminist criminology" but rather a diverse set of approaches that make different—and often diverging—claims about the intersections of gender, race, and class within crime, the criminal justice system, and criminology. In their early manifestations, feminist perspectives centered largely on socialization theories and were applied most frequently to constructions of gender in studies of victimization, especially men's violence toward women. However, contemporary interest has broadened to include women offenders, and many feminist theorists have sought to understand unconscious as well as conscious processes that might explain both why some women fail to conform to cultural stereotypes of "femininity" and why legal and media discourses construct and reflect negative public emotions (ranging from antipathy to downright hostility) toward female offenders. Underpinning the discussion that follows, then, are three issues. First is the question of whether women are treated more harshly or more leniently when they come before the courts accused of a serious offense. Second is the question of whether women who commit violent crimes in partnership with a man, or in self-defense against a man, are passive victims of male oppression or active lawbreakers acting out of choice and desire. And third, in light of answers to the previous two questions, how are women who kill represented in the media?

The question of whether women who offend are treated more harshly or more leniently than men has been hotly debated within feminist criminology, with many critics being keen to debunk the so-called "chivalry hypothesis" that presupposes that women "get off lightly" in criminal cases because judges and juries extend to them the same kind of gallantry they would give their female relatives. With regard to "ordinary" offenses, there is still striking disagreement about whether women are treated more or less severely than their male counterparts. Helena Kennedy surmises that women who fulfill society's expectations of the good wife and mother, with all the attendant notions of demure sexuality that these labels imply, are more likely to secure judicial clemency than women who challenge these stereotypes (in Lloyd, 1995). Lloyd further argues that conforming to the stereotype of helpless victim (e.g., of an abusive partner) "can work for a woman" (p. 19), although others have concluded that, while *most* women receive relatively light sentences, *some* female defendants are treated more severely due not only to their perceived conformity to the kind of gender stereotypes already mentioned (marital status, family circumstances, etc.), but also to other factors, such as their class, ethnicity, and age (Morris, 1987).

But whatever the fate of "ordinary" female offenders within the criminal justice system, most feminist commentators assert that when women commit very serious crimes—or commit nonserious offenses but are seen as somehow implicated in their male partners' very serious crimes—they attract more media and public attention, the image created of them is more powerful, and they leave a longer-lasting impression (Heidensohn, 1985; Lloyd, 1995; Worrall, 1990). From Lizzie Borden, who was tried and acquitted of murdering her father and stepmother in Fall River, Massachusetts, in 1893, to Susan Smith, who was convicted of murdering her two young children after strapping them into their car seats and rolling the vehicle into a lake in South Carolina in 1994, women who are implicated or involved in very serious crimes provide the media with some of their most compelling images of crime and deviance (Heidensohn, 1985). It is no wonder that popular discourse even today echoes the famous Rudyard Kipling poem warning that *the female of the species* is more deadly than the male.

In fact, women who commit serious crimes are portrayed in terms very similar to those used to represent children who seriously offend (see Chapter 4). In the absence of any alternative discourse to explain the existence of violence and cruelty in those whom society views as essentially "good," journalists fall back on stock notions of "pure evil," which they illustrate with standard stories, motifs, and stereotypes. As the cover of a supermarket tabloid magazine in Photo 5.1 powerfully illustrates, *women who kill* are represented by the media as hypersexual temptresses, evil monsters, and everything in between.

As we shall see through the course of this chapter, these tried-and-tested narratives often keep aspects of the woman's involvement in the crime hidden or only partially represented, allowing the public to dip into the cultural reservoir of symbolic representations and fill in the gaps as they see fit. Moreover, they combine to render women passive and unstable, lacking in moral agency, and somehow not able to act as fully formed, adult human beings.

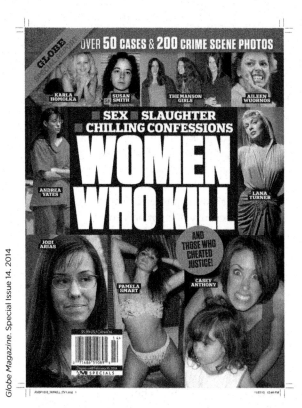

Globe Magazine. Special Issue 14. 2014

PHOTO 5.1
Supermarket
tabloid
salaciously
markets
"women who
kill."

The standard narratives used by the media to construct women who commit very serious crimes are:

- sexuality and sexual deviance

- physical attractiveness (absence of)

- bad wives

- bad mothers

- mythical monsters

- mad cows

- evil manipulators

- non-agents

Sexuality and Sexual Deviance

In Chapter 2's exploration of journalistic news values, it was noted that the media concentrate on crimes of violence that involve the "right sort of victims" (those who lend themselves to constructions of innocence and vulnerability), while those from more marginal groups, who cannot so easily be portrayed as blameless or pure, receive significantly less (and certainly less sympathetic) coverage. This preference for particular sorts of victims also extends to offenders, but conversely it is offenders who can be constructed as, in some sense, "marginal" who are deemed most newsworthy. This makes women who commit serious offenses already of news value by virtue of their relative rarity. However, women offenders become even more newsworthy when they can be further marginalized by reference to their sexuality. In line with the binary classification systems within which children are constructed as either tragic victims or evil monsters, women, their behavior, and their crimes are similarly polarized, often via antithetical constructions of their sexuality and sexual histories. In the simplest form of this system, women are categorized as either sexually promiscuous/deviant or sexually inexperienced/frigid, a dichotomy highlighted in the title of a book on the subject, *Virgin or Vamp* (Benedict, 1992).

It is often suggested that, in its general reporting of women in public life, the press is at its most sanctimonious when it can portray a saintly image of a woman as devoted mother or in faithful support of a man. But real women invariably fail to live up to this impossible ideal and, across the whole range of offenses, women are sexualized by those who work in the criminal justice system. As a result, women are frequently punished—and further punished symbolically by the media—more harshly. Behaviors that would be deemed "normal" patterns of delinquency in young men are reinterpreted as wayward and amoral in young women, the consequence of which is that the "offense" is frequently overdramatized. In fact, noncriminal or status offenses, such as skipping school, drinking alcohol, or perceived sexual misconduct, are more likely to be dealt with formally by social welfare or juvenile justice systems, while the courts are excessively punitive toward adult women who deviate from the maternal, monogamous, heterosexual "norm" (Wilczynski, 1997; cf. Heidensohn, 1985, pp. 47 ff.). According to Meda Chesney-Lind and Michele Eliason (2006), "bad girls," as they are characterized in the popular media, are thus constructed within a masculinist framework, which carries implicit assumptions about crime being the outcome of feminism and equality for women. Meanwhile, cases that could be used by the media to raise questions about the potential dangerousness and culpability of trusted institutions (the family, the education system, social services, the police, and so on) may be reduced to scintillating tidbits reminiscent of a soft porn magazine. During the 1995 trial of British "serial killer" Rose West, just about every derogatory term applicable to women was thrown at her by journalists:

> She was described variously in the news as: depraved, lesbian, aggressive, violent, menacing, bisexual, likes black men, likes oral sex, kinky, seductive, a prostitute, over-sexed, a child abuser, nymphomaniac, sordid, monster, she had a four-poster bed with the word c**t [*sic*] carved on the headboard, posed topless, exhibitionist, never wore any knickers, liked sex toys, incestuous, who shed tears in silence, no sobs, no sound at all. At puberty she developed, allegedly, an obsession for sex and "Fred confided, 'When Rose was pregnant her lesbian tendencies were at their strongest. I had to go out and get her a girl. She gets urges that have to be satisfied'" (*Sun,* November 3, 1995). (Wykes, 2001)

Quite simply, when it comes to the reporting of women who commit serious crimes, constructions of deviant sexuality are almost a given and women whose sexual deviance can be alluded to, if not covered by the tabloid press in salacious detail, represent cardinal folk devils, a contemporary incarnation of criminological positivism's "born female criminal" (Lombroso & Ferrero, 1895). As criminologist Nicole Rafter has described, Lombroso advanced the rather problematic and contradictory position that men were more violent and indeed more "criminal" than women because they were in fact superior to women in every way. However, it is not just female offenders who are denigrated by a media with lofty expectations about appropriate behavior for women; female victims are also subjected to reproach if they fail to comply with conventional and rigidly imposed feminine stereotypes. For example, Maggie Wykes highlights the prurient tone that was also adopted by the popular media regarding the victims of Rose West and her husband Fred. The predictability of their fate was suggested by smug assessments of what happens to wayward girls who leave home young and/or accept rides from strangers. Far from being humanized with details of their lives, family backgrounds, and ambitions, the Wests' victims were portrayed as being "from children's homes; lesbian; illegitimate; runaways; fostered; students; picked up on the 'streets' or hitchhikers" (Wykes, 1998, pp. 238–239). By contrast, there was virtually nothing in the reporting of the West case about the male clients who bought sex from

Fred's 12-year-old daughter, among others, nor about the many policemen who were familiar with the house and its occupants but failed to intervene prior to the murders (Wykes, 1998).

Similarly, Jane Caputi (1989) places the dehumanization and denigration of murdered women on a continuum of systematic violence ranging from domestic violence to rape and murder, which she describes as "gynocide." As she notes, we would assume that the victims and victims' families left behind by serial murderers would be treated empathetically by the news media and society at large. Yet, pointing to two very well known serial murderers who preyed exclusively upon women—Ted Bundy and the then-unnamed "Green River Killer"—Caputi shows how the representation of victims makes it difficult to link all forms of violence against women to the broader gynocidal system. Whereas Ted Bundy's victims were mostly college students and middle-class professionals, the victims of Gary Ridgway, the so-called Green River Killer, were transient sex workers—or by virtue of being his victim "became" such. Drawing out the differences in the perceived worthiness or "grievability" (Butler, 2006) of murdered women, Caputi quotes an investigator assigned to the Green River Task Force, who explained, "There was wide public attention in the Ted [Bundy] case ... because the victims resembled everyone's daughter ... But not everybody relates to prostitution on the Pacific Highway" (1989, p. 449). It seems that Ridgway himself shared the investigator's assumptions about the grievability of his "prestigeless" victims, stating in his confession

> I picked prostitutes as my victims because I hate most prostitutes and I did not want to pay them for sex ... I also picked prostitutes as victims because they were easy to pick up without being noticed. I knew they would not be reported missing right away and might never be reported missing. I picked prostitutes because I thought I could kill as many of them as I wanted without getting caught. (Hickey, 2013, p. 31)

Again, the demonizing of violent women and the dehumanization of murdered women are not solely a function of the American media. In the United Kingdom, derogatory attributions served to dehumanize the victims of "Yorkshire Ripper" Peter Sutcliffe, the overriding impression of whom remains that they were prostitutes (which is not only untrue of many of his victims but also suggestive of low-life squalor that elicits little sympathy), with hardly any attention being paid to their identities as mothers, daughters, partners, students, and so forth. Consider this quote from the assistant chief constable of the West Yorkshire Police:

> [The Yorkshire Ripper] has made it clear that he hates prostitutes. Many people do. We as a police force will continue to arrest prostitutes. But the Ripper is now killing innocent girls ... You have made your point. Give yourself up before another innocent woman dies. (as cited in Chadwick & Little, 1987, p. 267)

The popular press also managed to blame Sutcliffe's wife, Sonia, for his crimes. The *Daily Mirror* (May 23, 1981) ran the following quote from a police detective who investigated the case: "I think that when Sutcliffe attacked his 20 victims he was attacking his wife 20 times in his mind." According to the article, Sutcliffe worshipped his wife, and she dominated and belittled him. As John Upton remarked:

> This was just one of many pieces that put forward Sonia Sutcliffe's failings as a wife—her inadequacies as a sexual partner, her wish not to have children, her mental health difficulties—as the direct cause of his butchery. A woman was expected in the eyes of a prurient, disapproving public not just to stand by her serial killer man but to stand in place of him. (2000, p. 6)

Women's sexual preferences, their enjoyment of sex, or their frigidity have long been used to demonize them and justify their construction in the pages of the popular press as "monsters," even when—as in Sonia Sutcliffe's case—the crimes were not theirs. However, the ascription "monster" comes most readily to the minds of journalists if the sexual preference of the woman in question is for other women. As one newspaper editor reportedly admitted (originally cited in P. Wilson, 1988, p. 55), "If I could get a story of a beautiful lesbian who mows down children at a kindergarten with a machine gun I would be over the moon" (Morrissey, 2003, p. 18). In fact, "real life" provided the next best thing in the form of Australian murderer Tracey Wigginton and her three coaccused—not one lesbian killer on the rampage, but four! (Verhoeven, 1993). In our heteropatriarchal culture, lesbians, prostitutes, and women who are deemed sexually promiscuous are archetypal "outsiders." Within a group already classified as "other," they are *even more* other. As victims, they are invisible; as offenders, they are impossible to ignore.

Jenni Millbank further elaborates on the tendency of the media to view lesbian sexuality as a "cause" of aggressive behavior. In the case of Tracey Wigginton, who, with three friends, picked up a male stranger in her car in Brisbane, Australia, offered him sex, and then murdered him, it is their sexuality that is said to "explain" their crimes. They were lesbian, so they hated men. But "they also hated society and the family—represented by 'the father'—so they killed men who were father figures" (Millbank, 1996, p. 461). Interestingly, in the Wigginton case, of the four women who were accused, only three were convicted. The fourth, who was acquitted, did not conform to cultural stereotypes of lesbians and was portrayed as being not "properly gay," but rather a straight girl led astray (Morrissey, 2003). As far as the media are concerned, lesbians represent an "anomalous" category (Fiske, 1982) positioned precariously on the borderline of maleness and femaleness. Reliant on constructing reality within categories of binary opposition, anomalous beings draw their characteristics from both categories and consequently have too much meaning and are conceptually too powerful. In terms derived from cultural anthropology, lesbians "dirty" the clarity of their boundaries and are subsequently designated taboo (Douglas, 1966; Fiske, 1982). At a psychic level, lesbians represent neither one gender nor the other but can be superimposed onto the social division between masculinity (as active) and femininity (as passive). Quoting a tabloid, Deb Verhoeven demonstrates the precariousness of such classifications in relation to Wigginton, whose gender was presented literally as shifting between femininity and masculinity:

At that time [1987—on meeting her lover Donna] Wigginton rode a motorcycle and took her lover on the pillion. She always exceeded the speed limit. But when Wigginton slipped behind the wheel of the "loving couple's" Commodore car, her character changed completely—to that of the helpless female who always drove cautiously and never exceeded the speed limit. (*Weekend Truth*, February 23, 1991, p. 8, as cited in Verhoeven, 1993, p. 114)

The unsubtle Freudian metaphors used in this piece demonstrate the extent to which psychoanalytical themes are part of the currency of popular discourse. As a consequence, women who are (or who are perceived to be) lesbians are more severely punished when they break the law and are subjected to especially damaging representations by the media (Chesney-Lind & Eliason, 2006). As an anomalous category, lesbianism is often applied to deviant women, whatever the evidence (or lack of evidence) regarding their sexuality. For example, Susan Smith—who in 1994 drew worldwide media attention after she rolled her car into a South Carolina lake, drowning her two young sons locked inside, and then blamed a fictitious "black man" for their abductions—has been subjected to every stereotype discussed in this chapter, including (hetero)sexual promiscuity (the explanation for the crime being reported as her extramarital affair with a man who did not want a "ready-made family") and lesbianism ("toddler-killing mom Susan Smith 'paid off fellow inmate to play guard so she could enjoy lesbian romps with prison girlfriend in cells, closets and even the FREEZER,'" according to a *Daily Mail* headline [Quigley, 2013]).

Another anomalous category for women is that of "rapist"; hence, it is one of the most incomprehensible crimes—to the media and the public at large—for women to be convicted of. While stories involving men who rape are so commonplace that they do not necessarily make the news agenda (unless, as discussed in Chapter 2, they conform to several cardinal news values), women who rape are already newsworthy, although their relative invisibility is not because they do not exist but because the images conjured by a woman rapist do not fit the violent and drug-armed date rapist or the masked stranger who slinks in late at night through an unsecured window. For instance, consider the case of Mary Kay Letourneau, which garnered considerable media attention in the late 1990s. Letourneau, who was then a 34-year-old sixth-grade teacher at Shorewood Elementary School in Burien, Washington, pleaded guilty to "second-degree rape of a child" after admitting to an ongoing sexual relationship and conceiving a child with her 12-year-old student, Vili Fualaau. Sentenced to just a few months in county jail—a very lenient sentence for such a crime—Letourneau quickly violated the terms of her release and a lifetime no-contact order with Faulaau and was subsequently sentenced to seven years in prison (during which she bore a second child by Faulaau who was conceived shortly after her release from jail). Upon her release from prison in 2004 and after the lifetime no-contact order was withdrawn, Letourneau and Faulaau, who was by then 21 years old, married and announced plans to expand their family. Though the underlying offense of "second-degree rape of a child" is not sex-specific, meaning it is carries the same punishments regardless of the sex of the offender or victim, "rape" was not often invoked by the media, and instead much of the coverage of the case suggested that "mental illness" (bipolar disorder) drove Letourneau to leave her successful husband and their four children for the 12-year-old Faulaau. Morrissey (2003) discusses two further cases involving women—Valmae Beck (New Zealand) and Karla Homolka (Canada)—who, with their male lovers, were convicted of abducting, raping, and murdering girls. She notes that the crimes of the women were shown to far outweigh those of their partners, and it was they who received most press attention. In addition, while their male partners—Barrie Watts and Paul Bernardo, respectively—*were* viewed as dangerous psychopaths, they nonetheless remained comprehensible; their lusts were an extreme manifestation of "normal" male fantasies. Their wives, on the other hand, were portrayed as sadists whose deviant sexuality stretched the public's concept of malleable femininity beyond comprehension.

If women offenders cannot be constructed as lesbians or sexual sadists, their deviance will be verified with reference to their previous sexual conduct and sexual history. Basically, if a woman can be demonstrated to have loose moral standards, the portrayal of her as manipulative and evil enough to commit a serious crime is much more straightforward. Conversely, men who commit such crimes are often reported in respectful, even romantic, terms. Wykes notes how the British press referred to the relationship between Fred West and two of his victims (one raped, one murdered) as "sexual intercourse" and an "affair." He was also variously constructed as a good husband, a hard worker, and a reliable provider who was driven by a "mad and terrible love" for his wife (Wykes, 1998, p. 238). Before his suicide in prison left Rose to stand trial alone, Fred had declared that he would take all the blame and that her everlasting love was payment enough (Sounes, 1995, p. 348).

Yet the woman who seems to have suffered most for transgressing the accepted boundaries of feminine sexuality is the supposed "first female serial killer," Aileen Wuornos. A lifelong petty criminal, Wuornos was convicted by the state of Florida in six of the seven murders of men who had solicited her for sex. Through the course of the investigation, it was learned that Wuornos committed the robbery-murders to support herself and girlfriend, Tyria Moore. In the words of filmmaker Nick Broomfield, who produced two documentaries about Wuornos, "the idea of a woman killing men, a man hating lesbian prostitute who tarnished the reputation of all of her victims brought Aileen Wuornos a special kind of hatred" (Human, Broomfield, & Churchill, 2003). Though Wuornos had endured years of serious physical, sexual, and emotional abuse beginning in early childhood and suffered serious mental illness in the years preceding her crimes, much of the media coverage focused on her sexuality, depicting her as a murderous "highway hooker" who simply stalked innocent, vulnerable men for money. Even the critically acclaimed and shamelessly named biopic *Monster* placed considerable emphasis on Wuornos's sexuality, painting her as the dupe of her conniving lesbian lover while downplaying the structural violence of the sex trade. Wuornos received the death sentence in each of six separate trials, and in October 2002, after spending nearly a decade in prison, she was executed by lethal injection by the state of Florida.

Physical Attractiveness

In addition to their sexuality and sexual history, women who kill or who commit other very serious offenses are subjected to intense scrutiny regarding their physical appearance and attractiveness, a fact that is entirely in keeping with general life. Powerfully illustrating these exclusive feminine norms is Charlize Theron's portrayal of Wuornos. Described as "astonishing" and "one of the greatest performances in the history of cinema," the model/actress's transformation and embodiment of Wuornos earned her several honors, including the 2003 Academy Award for Best Actress. Arguably, however, Theron's uncanny mimicry of Wuornos's physical appearance— deep, sunken, searing eyes and crooked, stained teeth—only served to amplify the killer's imagined *monstrosity*. In contemporary societies, the media are engaged in a very particular construction of gender whereby those aspects of femininity that are valued—youth, figure, and sexuality—are constructed to suit the "male gaze" (Wykes & Gunter, 2004). This gendered narrative underpinning media discourses within advertising, women's magazines, tabloid newspapers, and so on extends to news discourses and includes constructions of female criminality. The degree to which media discourses are stuck in a Lombrosian view of female criminality are demonstrated by Australian newspaper reports that portrayed Tracey Wigginton as the epitome of an unfeminine, unnatural woman with "huge buttocks and thighs" and "a personality to match her 17-stone [240-pound] frame—big" (Morrissey, 2003, p. 124). Of her coaccused, the two who were also convicted (and sentenced to life imprisonment and 18 years, respectively) were described in turn as "heavily-built . . . her face fixed in a malevolent glare" and "short and stocky" with a "dumbfounded" expression (p. 124). By contrast, the fourth woman, who was acquitted, was not only regarded as a faux-lesbian but also described as demure and pretty, the most attractive of the accused. Physical appearance was also a factor in the press reporting of Valmae Beck, who assisted her male partner in the abduction, rape, and murder of a 12-year-old girl in Queensland, Australia, in 1987. Her motives, apparently, "lay not in her own sadistic desires, but rather in her insecurity and increasing age" (p. 151).

Yet women, it seems, cannot win. If conventionally attractive, they will be presented as "femme fatales" who ensnare their victims with their good looks but are cold, detached, and morally vacant. A prime example of this characterization is convicted rapist and murderer Karla Homolka, who was presented by the Canadian media as beautiful but shallow. The media also contrived to portray Homolka in positivist terms, as the epitome of beauty and femininity yet revealing "traditionally masculine" traits in her enjoyment of the rapes and of sex generally (M. Campbell, 1995, as cited in Morrissey, 2003).

More recently, in the criminal trial of Jodi Arias, who was eventually convicted by an Arizona court of murdering her boyfriend, coverage focused not only on her attractive appearance but also, more importantly, on how it changed. The local ABC news affiliate covering the trial offered this commentary:

[Newscaster 1] So much of this has been about her appearance, and we want to talk about that today. Arias wore a light blue blouse, hair down, dark-rimmed glasses. ABC15's Monica Lempert spoke with an image consultant, who critiqued Arias' look and how it's really morphed over the years. Monica, we've all noticed this. I understand the image consultant says Arias is using the best tricks in the book to try to portray herself as innocent.

[Newscaster 2] That's right, Katie; everything about her hair, her makeup, even the clothing choice, the colors of the clothing she's been wearing, has been pivotal according to this image consultant that I spoke with. She says her appearance has made her look similar to that of a 12-year-old girl. From her long platinum blonde hair and glossy lips, now to a brunette with bangs, glasses, and hardly any makeup, stylist and image consultant Devy Walker says it's all part of the plan.

[Image Consultant] You know she just looked like a little doll, like a little sex kitten, and now she looks like she's trying to be about 12.

[Newscaster 2] Walker says Arias' clothing, particularly the color, plays a pivotal role in how she's portrayed. In past court appearances, she wore dark colors.

[Image Consultant] With all of the allusion that they're trying to set of her being, you know—young, victim, helpless—I would have thought they'd put her in a soft color like baby pink or baby blue.

[Newscaster 2] That's exactly what she wore taking the stand today—a button-up baby blue blouse—but what about those glasses? While wearing them, Arias was pinned as a librarian lookalike when first taking the stand. Walker says there is a reason for that accessory too.

[Image Consultant] There's a lot that can be said nonverbally with the eyes, so I feel like the glasses are just a way for her to have a little of protection against what she's being accused of.

[Newscaster 2] But nothing caught Walker's attention quite like her choice of accessories when first taking the stand, something she says she hasn't seen since she was a little girl.

[Image Consultant] The barrette yesterday just blew my mind; it's like I haven't seen a woman in a barrette in a long time. Now it's like she's completely transformed that into trying to look like a child. (Lempert, 2013)

In Arias's trial, she was not only predictably portrayed as a crazed "sex kitten" but also accused of manipulating her look to appear as a studious "librarian" or harmless child. Whether this was the case or not, the evening news broadcast transcript above powerfully illustrates how seemingly mundane features of physical appearance inevitably figure into a potent cocktail of feminine sexuality, criminality, culpability, and guilt.

Bad Wives

As discussed earlier, the chivalry hypothesis has been most successfully challenged in relation to women who fit popular, normative images of deviance, either in their dress and appearance or in their behavior. When women do not conform to Victorian-inspired ideals of femininity and domesticity and can therefore be judged as bad wives and mothers, they are much more likely to confound a judge's idea of appropriate womanhood (Kennedy, 1992; Lloyd, 1995). By contrast, marital status, family background, and children have little or no bearing on most cases involving male defendants, whose conformity to conventional notions of "respectability" relies on issues such as employment history rather than factors such as marital status (Lloyd, 1995). Ideally, women should be housewives, content to remain at home, and economically and emotionally dependent on their husbands, who are busy bestriding the public sphere (Worrall, 1990). Women who transgress these codes of conduct and pursue public lives of their own are tolerated only if they continue to put their husbands and families before their careers and occasionally appear beside their husbands as attractive trophies and further evidence of his success.

Little wonder, then, that women who kill their spouse or partner are the epitome of the "bad wife," almost regardless of the provocation that led to the crime. What is perhaps slightly more surprising is that women who are the victims of murder by their spouse or partner are frequently portrayed in a similarly negative light and put on trial for their own victimization. Feminist research has shown that, unlike men for whom there are recognizable patterns of "lifestyle" violence involving public rituals of heavy drinking and fighting, women's violence is mostly confined to the domestic sphere (Heidensohn, 2000; Polk, 1993). Furthermore, in cases where men murder their female spouses or partners, the crimes are often precipitated by jealousy or depression (for example, when the woman threatens to leave or leads the offender to believe she is being unfaithful to him). Women, on the other hand, tend to resort to "spousal homicide" as a response to initial violence from their male partner (Browne, 1987; Lloyd, 1995).

More than any other, the case that thrust spousal homicide into the American cultural imagination is that of Francine Hughes. In 1977, after more than a decade of violent abuse at the hands of her husband, Francine set fire to the couples' bed, killing her husband while he slept and destroying their home. The case, which was later transformed into the popular made-for-TV movie *The Burning Bed,* became a flashpoint for feminist activists and introduced the concept of so-called "battered woman's defense" to the broader public. Interestingly, though Hughes was found not guilty of murder, it was not because of an affirmative self-defense argument but because her representatives effectively argued "temporary insanity."

It is important to note the extent to which there has recently been a backlash against feminist research and theory. For example, despite all evidence to the contrary, Stephen Hornby (1997) concludes that the overrepresentation of men in the criminal justice system must be evidence of a hugely discriminatory system. He also challenges the notion that men are more likely to be violent than women with the glib, unsubstantiated comment that a child is more likely to be hit by its mother than its father. To be clear, to say that men are more violent than women is by no means to accept that all men are violent, violence-prone, or tolerant of violence and that all women are nonviolent or victims of masculine violence. But in some areas of research, it is arguable that anti-feminist sentiments, such as those that underpin Hornby's views, have clouded the real picture of offending and victimization. One such area is that of domestic violence, a subject that has seen vigorous attempts in recent years to cast men as its victims. But despite the salience of male victims of domestic assault in official and popular discourses, research has shown that victimized men are likely also to be perpetrators of domestic violence, especially in male–female partnerships (Gadd, Farrell, Dallimore, & Lombard, 2003). It is interesting to note that even the most "reliable" of official figures misrepresent domestic violence. Farrell and Pease (2007) highlight that there is a fundamental misassumption advanced by official government surveys that people will never be victimized in the same way by the same people more than five times a year. In making this assumption, Farrell and Pease suggest, crime surveys are ignoring 3 million crimes a year, including 2.2 million offenses against the person. Not only are male "victims" less likely than female victims to have been repeatedly victimized or seriously injured, but they are more likely to have the financial resources to allow them to leave the abusive relationship (Gadd et al., 2003). Such misrepresentations illustrate British criminologist Maggie Wykes's assertion that media and legal constructions of male and female violence fit within a framework that emphasizes traditional models of family organization and femininity that is commensurate with a "broader ideological 'claw-back' of feminist 'gains'" (1998, p. 234). The consequence of this emphasis is that traditional conservative family and gender relations are endorsed and celebrated, even when the reality of many of the crimes discussed in this chapter indicates families and marriages as sites of (largely masculine) violence, sexual abuse, and murder.

Bad Mothers

In a Freudian analysis, our psychological makeup means that early dependence on our mothers makes us especially vulnerable to the "fear that an evil mother in human form can elicit" (Morrissey, 2003, p. 23). Not only do they kill, hurt, or neglect when they are "supposed" to care and nurture, but they also represent only a tiny fraction of serious criminals, so they frequently have a perceived "novelty" value that guarantees media interest in them. The "bad mother" motif is so culturally pervasive that it is ascribed to virtually *all* women, whether victims or offenders, actual mothers or nonmothers, and whether they are involved in the murder of children or commit other crimes but also happen to *be* mothers. In the latter category, Tracie Andrews was widely castigated in the British press for committing a crime that carried a life sentence, as this would entail a long separation from her daughter, although in a rare moment of empathy, one news report noted that "this 28-year-old unmarried mother of a little daughter seemed dwarfed by her surroundings . . . it was painful to remember that a verdict of guilty would lead to her daughter Karla being deprived of her mother" (*Birmingham Evening Mail,* July 29, 1997). However, we are reminded in the same article that this is no embodiment of the feminine ideal. Illustrating Lombrosian positivist themes already discussed, Tracie is described as a "bruiser of a woman," a street fighter whose "bottle blonde hair grew more tawny as the trial progressed . . . sometimes obscuring all her features except the heavily-jutting jaw." More controversially, women who lose their children in terrible circumstances may also be portrayed as bad mothers. One of the most notable cases in this respect is that of Lindy Chamberlain, who was convicted of the murder of her infant daughter in Australia in 1982 despite asserting that she had seen a dingo emerging from the tent where her daughter was sleeping. Sentenced to life in prison, Chamberlain had many appeals denied until 1986, when she was acquitted in light of new evidence and mounting public concern. Widely considered the most publicized criminal case in Australian history, it was immortalized by the successful film *A Cry in the Dark,* which earned actress Meryl Streep an Academy Award nomination for her portrayal of Chamberlain.

Bad mother cases are perennial events in the United States, with some confined to regional media markets and others becoming national media spectacles lasting months and sometimes years. The most prominent of the latter variety involved a young single mother in Orlando, Florida, Casey Anthony, and her three-year-old daughter, Caylee. In July 2008, Casey's parents called 911 to report Caylee missing, stating that they had not seen their granddaughter in more than a month and that the trunk of Casey's car smelled as if it had a dead body inside. After making a variety of contradictory if not incriminating statements to police as to what she thought might have happened to her daughter and why she had not immediately reported the child missing, Casey was charged with Caylee's murder. Nearly six months after Caylee disappeared, a local utilities worker discovered her decomposing remains, duct tape still attached. During the trial, which took place in May and June 2011—nearly three years after Caylee's death—prosecutors alleged that Casey, hoping to relieve herself of her motherly duties, killed Caylee by suffocation. To make their case, prosecutors described Casey as a self-centered "party girl" who had been out drinking and dancing and even gotten a tattoo reading "Bella Vita" (Beautiful Life) while her fate hung in the balance. A jury found Casey not guilty of all the serious charges in the matter and only guilty of the lesser charges of lying to investigators. Her punishment was the time she had served awaiting trial. Of course, there was considerable public outrage over the verdict, with numerous celebrities, such as Kim Kardashian (whose father was part of the criminal defense team that had successfully defended O. J. Simpson in his own murder trial), chiming in on social media, "I am speechless." With an updated version of an old moniker, *Time* magazine went so far as to dub the case the "social-media trial of the century" (Cloud, 2011).

Of course, the fascination with bad mothers extends well beyond mediated show trials like those of Andrews, Chamberlain, and Anthony to the domain of formal criminal justice policy. For instance, in 2014, the state of Tennessee amended its criminal code to recognize the "viable fetus of a human being" as capable of criminal victimization. Unsurprisingly, a woman—named Mallory Loyola—was the first person to be charged by the state under the new law just a few weeks after it went into effect. Loyola came to the attention of authorities when, after she gave birth to a baby boy, the child tested positive for methamphetamine. Senate Bill 1391, which as initially written would have carried as much as a 15-year prison sentence, was passed in July 2014 and assigned the crime of misdemeanor assault to mothers who used drugs during their pregnancy. Importantly, SB 1391 does not recognize alcohol as an illegal drug, nor does it apply to the laws governing abortion. Supporters called it a "velvet hammer," arguing that the law would convince needy mothers to accept the state's help with the promise of treatment rather than incarceration. In no short time, however, this proved to not be the case. Fearing arrest or further legal entanglement, some expectant mothers avoided neonatal care, while others, like Brittany Hudson, who with a friend delivered her baby in a car alongside a dirt road, avoided medical care altogether. This was the case with Tonya Martin, the third woman arrested under the law. Martin, who was struggling with opiate abuse, refused drug treatment out of fear of arrest and prosecution. After her son was born and tested positive for opiates, she admitted to using prescription painkillers and eventually pled guilty to charges under the new law. In November 2014, weeks after giving up her son for adoption, Martin committed suicide, hanging herself from a clothesline in her grandmother's yard. Citing Martin's case and others, critics of Senate Bill 1391 see it as a paternalistic attempt to coerce needy mothers into treatment and another example of what some call **carceral feminism,** or the imposition of sometimes harsh punishments, including imprisonment, as a way to protect vulnerable women and their children.

While drug use, welfare dependency, and sexual promiscuity are often reasons for the disproportionate attention heaped upon some women, the bad mother motif is most systematically and vengefully applied to women who are involved in the sexual abuse or killing of children—though it is only relatively recently that society has been ready to come to terms with crimes that challenge the firmly held belief that women are incapable of sexual aggression. Today, however, it is safe to say that the drive to attract audiences and advertisers in a global multimedia environment has resulted in the picture of crime becoming ever more distorted, with atypical offenses frequently being used in a sensationalized manner to indicate wider problems in society and endorse populist political mantras heralding the fall of civil society. When a British nursery worker named Vanessa George was convicted in 2009 for sexually assaulting and distributing indecent images of children in her care, her role as "Public Enemy Number One" (*Sun,* June 12, 2009) was underlined by the news that her two teenage children had disowned her. Meanwhile, the man for whom she had produced the images, Colin Blanchard (a man she had encountered on the Internet but never physically met before the court trial), received far less media coverage and public opprobrium.

However, the archetypal example in the UK of a woman who failed to measure up to the ideals of maternal care perpetuated by a patriarchal media is Myra Hindley. Fifty years after her conviction, Hindley remains a fixture in the popular imagination because, as a woman who was convicted of serious (sexual) crimes against children, she was deemed guilty not only of breaking the law but also of breaking every culturally sanctioned code of femininity and womanhood. Like the murder of two-year-old James Bulger in Liverpool, which has been the subject of detailed discussion in this book, the events surrounding Myra Hindley's offenses, sentencing, and prolonged incarceration occupy a particularly salient place in the UK's collective psyche even half a century after her conviction.

Mythical Monsters

Characterized for decades as "the most evil woman in Britain," Myra Hindley was convicted, along with her lover and coaccused, Ian Brady, in 1966, for her part in the murders of five children between 1963 and 1965. As this chapter will go on to show, there were a

PHOTO 5.2
The now
infamous
booking photo
of Myra Hindley.

number of features about the case that made it especially news-worthy and assured its longevity in the public consciousness—not least that one of the accused was a seemingly very ordinary woman who had, up until she met her boyfriend, led a very ordinary life. In a decade when the tabloid press was gaining a greater foothold in the news market and serious offenders were suddenly very high profile (partly because of the recent abolition of the death penalty, which led to some sections of the media implying that some convicted offenders were literally getting away with murder), Myra's appearance and identity very quickly became public property. Interestingly, the narratives and images that prevailed in media reports of Hindley—and continue to define women who commit serious crimes in the UK, the U.S., and other Anglophone nations—tend toward the "other-worldly." They derive predominantly from pagan mythology, Judeo-Christian theology, and classical art and literature—witches, satanists, vampires, harpies, evil temptresses, "fallen women," and women who conform to Christian notions of Original Sin. These motifs are often interlaced with references to lesbianism, and many mythical monsters defy classification, straddling categories of gods and humans, or the living and the dead. Fitting into neither one category nor the other but deriving from both, they are invested with too much meaning, which has to be controlled by designating it as taboo (Fiske, 1982).

Two favored figures from Greek mythology who can be viewed as anomalous are Medea, an enchantress who, when spurned by her lover, murdered her children, and Medusa, the snake-haired monster who turned her victims to stone with a stare. Tabloid newspapers have made ample use of both symbolic figures over the last 50 years in their coverage of Hindley, which invariably includes her infamous 1966 police arrest photo.

According to Helen Birch, this image, a "brooding presence" that has held a "bizarre grip" over the British public's imagination for four decades, even among those too young to remember the original case, has become detached from its subject (1993, p. 33). It has become a symbolic representation of the "horror of femininity perverted from its 'natural' course" (pp. 34–35), an icon of female deviance. Invoking a Lombrosian physiognomy, many writers seized on Hindley's peroxide-blonde hair and "hooded eyes" and drew inferences from these markers ranging from haughty indifference to irredeemable evil. One such editorial hints at the way the image interpellates the individual viewer and society more broadly through a subtle evocation of mythological monstrosity:

> Myra, Medusa. Medusa, Myra. No matter what she looked like after she was sentenced to life imprisonment in 1966, Myra Hindley was fixed forever in the public eye as the peroxide-haired gorgon of that infamous police snapshot. Look at her defiant, evil eyes, we are meant to say. Spawn of the devil, God knows, she probably had a head of snakes, covered by a blonde wig to fool us, this evil, evil woman. (Glancey, 2002)

The vampiress is another figure of monstrosity invoked in narratives about female killers. Combining sexual desire with violent monstrosity, the figure of the blood-hungry murderous woman has a long, sordid history. Most notably, the 16th-century Hungarian countess Elizabeth Bathory is said to have murdered hundreds if not thousands of peasant girls and woman and bathed in their blood in order to retain her youth. While some suggest that Bathory was a political victim and that the tale was concocted to justify her treatment at the hands of political rivals, tales of the "blood countess" continue into contemporary times, appearing in films and music yet today. In the contemporary moment, perhaps the most notorious use of this imagery comes from the case of Tracey Wigginton, who was described by the Australian press as the "lesbian vampire killer." As several writers have noted, cultural connections have been made between vampirism and lesbianism in film and literature for more than a century, a stereotypical link that is not altogether surprising given that the lust for blood is usually equated with the vampire's role as sexual aggressor (Morrissey, 2003; Verhoeven, 1993). In Tracey Wigginton's case, the vampire appellation came about after her accomplices claimed that she killed her victim to feast on his blood. Despite psychiatric evidence that they were deluded in this respect, the press began to report the story as fact, reveling in stories of gothic horror, cannibalism, and sexual perversion. Although there was *some* speculation in later coverage that Wigginton's accomplices concocted the "lesbian vampire" story to diminish their own roles in the murder and leave her to face trial on her own (Verhoeven, 1993), in general the vampire motif gave the media a fascinating "hook" on which to hang a story that might otherwise have elicited little interest. The willingness of the public to believe the (literally) fantastic stories that were concocted about vampirism was not so surprising. As Verhoeven comments, "if the public could believe a woman would actually kill a man at random, then it was capable of believing anything" (pp. 123–124). This willingness to believe also extended to investigating police officers, who admitted to watching vampire film *The Hunger* in an attempt to find clues as to a motive for the crime (Morrissey, 2003). The vampire motif was stretched almost to the point of incredulity when it was alleged in court that Wigginton combed the streets in search of a victim while listening to the Prince song "Batdance" (Verhoeven, 1993). Even when psychiatrists declared that she was unfit to stand trial and should be subjected to further psychiatric treatment, their diagnosis was skewed to fit the Gothic narrative. The multiple personality disorder with which Wigginton was diagnosed was taken as further evidence of her vampirism and subsequently allowed for a reenactment of other mythical archetypes, such as the witch, the siren, and Jekyll and Hyde (Morrissey, 2003).

The depiction of female killers as vampires clearly serves to make them less woman than monster. Even the reporting of the Tracie Andrews case was humorously constructed with a nod to vampiric motifs and, echoing Tracey Wigginton's musical tastes, the *Sun* quoted a former boyfriend in the headline "Tracie was so crazy in bed she made us do it to [the Meatloaf song] 'Bat out of Hell'" (July 30, 1997). In fact, most women who commit, or who are complicit in, serious crimes get reported in terms that emphasize their conformity to one or more of these ideological constructions of deviant or monstrous femininity. Rather than having tragically lost her child to a wild dingo, Lindy Chamberlain was stereotyped as a witch who sacrificed her daughter in a satanic ritual.

Aileen Wuornos, nicknamed the "damsel of death," was seen as a vengeful lesbian prostitute stalking innocent men to fulfill her inhuman lusts. Beverley Allitt was deemed the "angel of death" who coldheartedly killed babies and children in her care. Anne Darwin was a "hideous, lying bitch"; Monique Olivier was the "Ogress of the Ardennes"; Tracey Wigginton was a "vampire killer"; Karla Homolka was a beautiful but morally vacuous temptress; like Medusa, Tracie Andrews possessed "looks that could kill"; Valmae Beck's confession and court testimony were evidence of her scopophilic desire to watch rape and murder and her sadistic enjoyment in aiding their commission; Joanna Dennehy, who was convicted of killing three men in February 2014, was described by the trial judge as a "cruel, calculating, selfish and manipulative serial killer" with a "sexual and sadistic motivation" and "lust for blood" (*The Guardian,* February 28, 2014).

As Barbara Creed (1996) argues, motifs like these reinforce the notion of female killers as scapegoats for a phallocentric culture. A culture's deepest beliefs and darkest fears about women become entangled with childhood anxieties about supernatural monsters and creatures from the underworld passed down via legend, folklore, and myth. Monstrous images of women become so firmly entrenched in the popular consciousness that it becomes almost impossible to view Myra, Tracy, Aileen, et al. as real women rather than the grotesque caricatures portrayed in the media. For many feminist commentators, this problem is not confined to those women who are constructed via legal and media discourses but also raises important wider issues concerning attitudes toward women: "The dichotomy between 'good' and 'bad' women . . . serves as a means of patrolling, controlling and reinforcing the boundaries of behavior considered 'appropriate' for *all* women" (Morris & Wilczynski, 1993, p. 217). This brings us to another set of stereotypes that dominate "official" discourses on women who offend; namely, that *all* women are potentially mad at certain times of their lives (p. 217).

Mad Cows

While folklore and myth have created one collection of motifs of deviant women, another set of images has been supplied by science and medicine (Heidensohn, 1985). Once more, the "findings" of 19th-century male pioneers, from Lombroso to Freud, have been profoundly influential in constructing notions of female pathology as explanation for women's offending. Most women who commit serious offenses such as murder or manslaughter are advised by their lawyers to use defenses based on psychiatric difficulties; in other words, to plead guilty on grounds of diminished responsibility or infanticide (a crime that applies to women only, referring to the killing of a child under the age of 12 months by its mother when the balance of her mind was disturbed as a result of childbirth). Ania Wilczynski (1997) notes that in cases of filicide (the killing of a child by its parent or stepparent), while 30% of men use psychiatric pleas, over 64% of women do so, resulting in women being twice as likely to receive psychiatric or noncustodial sentences (interestingly, filicide is the only type of homicide that women and men commit in approximately equal numbers). Men tend to utilize "normal" pleas that do not require an "abnormal" state of mind; for example, involuntary manslaughter, which requires an absence of intent to kill or seriously injure the victim (Wilczynski, 1997). Consequently, men are much more likely to receive a custodial sentence when they kill their children (even in cases where a psychiatric plea has been used). Wilczynski further argues that although men who kill their children are sometimes viewed as "sad," they are usually regarded as "bad"; their killings are "less surprising, and they are more in need of punishment and deterrence" (1997, p. 424).

These findings might, at first glance, suggest that the tendency to "psychiatrize" women *can* lead to leniency, especially in cases where women commit infanticide or filicide (Morris & Wilczynski, 1993; Wilczynski, 1997). But several commentators are at pains to point out that psychiatric dispositions are not necessarily "lenient" sentences. They can result in women being labeled "psychotic" or "psychopathic" for life, and there are many documented cases of women who have been incarcerated in mental hospitals, prisons, and other institutions far longer than they might have been had their behavior not been medicalized and had they not been prescribed drugs on which they became dependent (Lloyd, 1995; Wilczynski, 1997). The casualness with which women's crimes are medicalized is well documented (Dobash, Dobash, & Gutteridge, 1986; Lloyd, 1995; Wilczynski, 1997) and is typified by the defense's use of Munchausen's syndrome by proxy (MSBP), an illness that few had heard of prior to the trial of English nurse Beverley Allitt, who was subsequently convicted of murdering four children under her care. In simple terms, MSBP—the "caring disease"—is a condition that affects parents or caregivers, mostly women, who are driven by a psychological need to gain attention by being involved in the medical care of an infant. In such circumstances, it might be assumed that those in the criminal justice system, and in society generally, find it much easier to accept that a woman has committed violent or heinous offenses if she can be categorized as a deluded lunatic or unstable hysteric, even if sentences do not necessarily reflect that sentiment. The word "hysteria" comes from the Greek *husterikos,* meaning "of the womb," and has long been employed to reinforce the notion of women as "other." Additional psychopathological states peculiar to women—for example, pregnancy, child-birth, and lactation—are legally sanctioned explanations of infanticide, while menstruation and menopause are also treated as inherently pathological states that "explain" female offending (Heidensohn, 2000).

Pathologizing the female reproductive cycle also allows the "bad mother" motif to be utilized. Treating women who commit infanticide or filicide as hormonally disturbed perpetuates the "myth of motherhood" (Oakley, 1986) and suggests that "normal" women are naturally maternal and find motherhood constantly fulfilling and joyful. While this is a dominant construction in mediated discourses, especially advertising, it is an image that is at odds with the stark reality that for many women, motherhood can be anything but, for a variety of structural reasons (poverty, lack of support, etc.) as well as physiological and psychological ones (Wilczynski, 1997). Most (in)famously, Otto Pollak, in his 1950/1961 publication *The Criminality of Women,* argues that women's "other" biology not only propels them into crime but also allows them to conceal their criminality, just as they have, for centuries, concealed menstruation, pregnancy, the fatherhood of their children, menopause, and sexual arousal. If women can fake orgasm, Pollack argues, they must be naturally deceitful and are thus better equipped to conceal their deviance. While Pollack has been largely discredited, especially in the feminist literature, the idea that women are ruled by their biology persists in medical, legal, and media discourses about crime. The use of premenstrual syndrome (PMS) to explain and excuse women's violent offending is the most recent manifestation of a biological determinism that has its origins in Victorian ideas about hysterics (cf. Benn, 1993). Meanwhile, men are regarded as rational agents, ruled by their intellect, not their inherent biological drives. Hormonal imbalance is arguably no more likely to result in women's crime as it is men's, although few criminal cases are defended on the grounds that high testosterone levels might explain male outbursts of violence (notwithstanding that in the 1960s and 1970s, some researchers did claim that violent crime was associated with a male chromosome abnormality, dubbed "supermale syndrome"). The tendency to pathologize women's physiological and "natural" traits in order to construct them as artful deceivers brings us to the broader stereotype of women as evil manipulators.

Evil Manipulators

Many of the women mentioned in this chapter did not commit their crimes alone, but in partnership with their male lovers and husbands. Women who form murderous alliances with men are the most problematic for the institutions that seek to understand them and communicate their actions to the rest of society, particularly as their prey are often the archetypal "innocent" victims—children and young women. These female offenders inspire neither sympathy as victims nor celebration as powerful avengers, and, as such, they represent an enigma to mainstream academic and feminist discourses and offer the least possibility for rehabilitation or redemption as far as the legal and media professions are concerned (Morrissey, 2003).

Women who join with their partners in killing cannot be simplistically constructed as lesbians, even if their victims are girls and young women. The media therefore struggle to employ their standard narrative of lesbianism, because their relationships with their male accomplices *insists* on their heterosexuality. Equally, it is usually not possible to easily construct these women as victims or avengers, because rarely is there evidence that suggests either of these defenses. Even if there are grounds for constructing them as victims (as in the case of Homolka, who finally went to the police after months of savage abuse at the hands of her coaccused), their involvement in such terrible crimes (in this example, the abduction, drugging, rape, and murder of young women, including her 14-year-old sister, Tammy Homolka) makes it impossible for the media to elicit any sympathy for them. The media's solution to the problem of heterosexual women who appear to be equal partners, or at least to go along unquestioningly with their men's wishes in very serious crime, is to place the burden of guilt on their shoulders. As a consequence, in all the cases mentioned above, the argument runs thus: The male perpetrators were all evil men, capable of extreme cruelty. But without a submissive woman, a sadistic man would never act. It is only together that they become a "lethal pair" (Morrissey, 2003, p. 152). It is therefore the woman who is instrumental in unleashing the violence and depravity that the man has thus far contained.

The motives of women who form partnerships with men who kill, and assist them in their murderous quests, are complex and contested. Some critics argue that, for the most part, these are "ordinary" women who happen to fall under the influence of a controlling, usually older, man, and that without that fateful first meeting, they would have gone on to live "normal," suburban lives (J. Smith, 1997; Wykes, 1998). Others argue that this conceptualization negates the **agency** and free will of such women, and that they may actually seek out such men because they have similar desires, going along with their partners' murderous plans as a vehicle to their own empowerment (Birch, 1993; Morris & Wilczynski, 1993; P. Pearson, 1998). For these writers, the unpalatable suggestion that these women may have enjoyed their crimes is the main impediment, not only to the invisibility of their roles in the crimes in media and legal discourses but also to an adequate feminist consideration of the cases. It is much harder to defend a person who has apparently willingly committed heinous acts of cruelty than one whose actions resulted from duress or oppression, and, as such, the actual involvement of these women is "repressed out of conscious existence" (Morrissey, 2003, p. 156).

The blurred lines of agency are powerfully revealed in the case of Amy Fisher, whom the media dubbed the "Long Island Lolita." In late 1991, when she was 16, Fisher entered into a sexual relationship with the owner of a local auto body shop named Joey Buttafuoco after she damaged her parents' car and Buttafuoco offered to repair it without notifying her parents. After several months of a torrid sexual affair, Fisher traveled to Buttafuoco's family home, confronted his wife Mary Jo, and shot her in the face with a pistol. Mary Jo survived, and Fisher was quickly arrested and charged with attempted murder. The yearlong media spectacle ended with Fisher pleading guilty to "first-degree assault" and receiving a sentence of 5 to 15 years in prison. After serving seven years, Fisher was released from prison to the status of a minor celebrity, engaged in a well-publicized reunion with her victim Mary Jo, and has since taken up work as a "pornographic actress." As the moniker "Long Island Lolita" might suggest, Buttafuoco's attorney and the news media more generally were successful in placing the blame for the affair and attempt on Mary Jo's life wholly upon Fisher. And though he pleaded guilty to the serious offense of "statutory rape," Buttafuoco escaped with a jail sentence of less than four months and managed to keep his marriage intact. Mary Jo stood by her husband for more than a decade after the shooting, divorcing him in 2003. She has since penned a best-selling memoir, describing her recovery from the shooting and detailing her life with the "sociopath" Buttafuoco.

Non-agents

The conclusion of increasing numbers of scholars, therefore, is that neither academic feminism nor society at large is ready to confront the reality that women can be cruel, sadistic, and violent. The simple truth that men are more aggressive than women not only encourages a widespread cultural ignorance of the fact that women have the potential for violence but also serves to deny psychically the notion that women can kill *as women*. In general, women are viewed either as big children (which is how they were considered by Lombroso and Ferrero a century ago, an idea that still permeates clinical discourse; Morris, 1987) or as men (a view endorsed by the many examples of women who are portrayed as "mannish" lesbians). Monstrous narratives of bloodthirsty vampires and snake-haired medusas also serve to deny women's agency. If a murderess becomes a mythical monster, she loses her humanity and is considered to have acted—but not as a contemporary human woman (Morrissey, 2003).

There are only two crimes for which women may retain their humanity and avoid the ascription of "evil," but both imply that offending women are nonagentic. They are "spousal homicide," where the woman can be seen as acting in self-defense against an abusive partner, and infanticide, where a woman can be viewed as a mixture of "mad" and "sad." In either case, the woman concerned can be regarded as a victim who is not responsible for her actions. Morrissey reflects on constructions of victimization and their wider implications for women generally in relation to spousal murder:

> Many portrayals of women who kill depict them as so profoundly victimized that it is difficult to regard them as ever having engaged in an intentional act in their lives . . . Representations of the murderess as victim, then, function to deny her responsibility, culpability, agency, and often her rationality as well, in their bid to explain her behavior and secure her sympathetic legal treatment. While undeniably often successful in securing reduced sentences, the disadvantages of such a strategy outweigh the benefits in terms of improving general societal attitudes to, and challenging negative myths and stereotypes of, women. (Morrissey, 2003, p. 25)

As discussed earlier, explanations of female criminality that rely on deterministic assumptions about women's physiology and biology arguably have the most far-reaching implications for deviant and nondeviant women alike, and dominant discourses of madness incontestably speak to the nonagency of female offenders. While the Beverley Allitt case provoked the majority of the popular media to fall back on stock notions of psychiatric disorder augmented by their discovery of Munchausen's disease, one lone, contradictory voice was reported in the news media coverage. Dr. David Enoch, an expert on Munchausen's, argued that popular assumptions about Allitt were incorrect:

> She is not mad, she is not psychotic. When you are psychotic you lose insight and delude yourself, you do not know what you are doing. Those who suffer from Munchausen's know that they are not really ill and have insight into their actions . . . she would have known what she was doing with the children. (*Telegraph*, May 19, 1993)

Even women who kill their own children may not fall neatly into the category of "irrational" or "emotional outburst" that is so often constructed for them. Women who are highly emotional at the time of the offense may perpetrate acts of infanticide and filicide, but these acts do not necessarily represent a sudden, irrational loss of control.

The failure of the media to acknowledge the agency of women involved in serious offenses is also apparent in terms of the delicacy with which the media sidestep the actual details of their offenses. Selective reporting is especially evident in cases where women rape and sexually abuse. For example, the crimes of Myra Hindley continue to be held up as perhaps the most heinous ever committed in Britain, yet even many of the journalists who continue using her image to sell newspapers are too young to remember her trial in 1966 and may not actually be fully cognizant of her precise role in the sexual torture and murder of the victims. Despite the collective sense of horror and revulsion at her crimes, few of us know what Myra Hindley *actually did*. Similarly, legal and media constructions of Valmae Beck and Karla Homolka glossed over their participation in the sexual assaults they committed. In fact, Homolka was not convicted of sexual abuse because of the temporary absence of incriminating videotapes at the time of her trial, and in the case of Beck, who *was* convicted of rape, many newspapers did not mention this important aspect of her crimes (Morrissey, 2003). And, while the media enjoyed slavering over the details of Rose West's sexual predilections, the extent to which she was involved in the sexual abuse and murder of the victims remains unclear and legally unproved (J. Smith, 1997; Wykes, 1998). The reticence with which the media confront women's serious sexual crimes is somewhat surprising, especially given the appetite for sex that is often attributed to the popular press and its readership. Morrissey speculates that despite incontrovertible evidence proving women's participation in sex crimes, the media are simply not able to present female protagonists who so clearly deviate from conventional hegemonic, heteropatriarchal conceptions of femininity: "Apparently, so these news stories say, men rape and murder, women watch and help with the clean up" (2003, p. 153). Yet, at the same time, the prudish and partial representation of women's involvement in rape and murder encourages the public at large to dip into the cultural reservoir of symbolic representations and "fill in the gaps."

HONORABLE FATHERS VERSUS MONSTROUS MOTHERS: SOME CONCLUDING THOUGHTS

Psychosocial approaches to "otherness" have provided a useful framework within which to study possible explanations for the bigotry and hysteria that characterizes media and legal discourses of offending women and shed light on the general and deep-seated cultural discomfort generated by women's wickedness. Our inability to view women who commit serious offenses as anything other than—well—"others" may relate to our psychological makeup insofar as early dependence on our mothers makes us especially vulnerable to the fear that evil women can elicit (Morrissey, 2003). Our unconscious fears of feminine evil are then picked up and reinforced by a heteropatriarchal culture that presents any female deviation as intrinsically shocking:

> Those doing the defining, by that very act, are never defined as "other," but are the norm. Those different from the norm—in this case, women—are thus off-centre, deviant. Man is the norm, the objective standard by which others are measured. Men are perceived to be independent, rational, autonomous and responsible. The ... other, the female is therefore dependent, emotional, not entirely adult and irresponsible. She is defined in reference to men. (Lloyd, 1995, p. xvii)

"Otherness" is central to the differential media reporting of men who kill and women who kill. Quite simply, when we consider the narratives used to construct mediated stories about serious crimes, women are characterized as bad mothers even when they are nonmothers and/or have killed adults, not children.

Men, on the other hand, are rarely described as "bad fathers" (although, as with women, stereotypes based on assumptions about class, race, age, and family stability have a bearing on the legal and media discourses constructed around men's offending). Compare the examples of deviant women discussed above with the case of British businessman Robert Mochrie, who, in July 2000, battered to death his wife and four children before ingesting poison and hanging himself. In the press and at least one documentary film, Mochrie was presented as a tragic hero. "Familicide"—or "family annihilation," as it has been dubbed by the media—is usually carried out by middle-aged white men driven to a violent last resort either by marriage breakdown or by their inability to continue providing for their family in the "traditional" manner. To some extent, Mochrie was experiencing both: His wife was involved in a relationship with his former business partner, he was regularly visiting prostitutes, and, following early retirement, he had made some bad investments and was on the verge of bankruptcy. Despite these factors, which might be thought to mitigate against the depiction of a "typical" middle-class family, the discourse constructed by the Mochries' friends and neighbors and presented uncritically by the television documentary filmmakers centered entirely around just that: their sheer averageness. The words that were repeatedly used to describe Robert Mochrie were "ordinary," "normal," "regular," "decent." Cath and Robert Mochrie were "the perfect couple" and Robert "adored" his children. Yet, in the early hours of July 12, 2000, he "meticulously," "calmly," and—according to Cath's best friend—"gently" bludgeoned each member of his sleeping family to death with a hammer, sent a few text messages, canceled the milk, and then hanged himself.

As a newspaper editorial following the documentary observed, the sympathy shown toward Robert by friends, while generous and perhaps rather surprising, is not extraordinary. It was probably a brave attempt to reconcile the man they thought they knew with the unknowable man who took six lives, including his own (McLean, 2003). But the collusion of the filmmakers is more surprising. Not only did they entirely avoid resorting to stock motifs of violent monstrosity, but they also endorsed the idea of Mochrie as a fundamentally decent man driven to the edge by some sort of heartfelt but misguided heroism. The narrator of the documentary concluded that Mochrie's motivation "in a strange and terrifying way, was love." Newspaper columnist Gareth McLean's (2003) comment that Mochrie's motivation was more likely to be fear than love, brought about by a combination of near-psychotic depression and a "desperate, sad, proud and defiantly macho inability to ask for help," once more demonstrates the extent to which psychoanalytic ideas have penetrated popular and media discourses. But of greater interest in the current context is the quietly forgiving response of the community at large to these tragic events. As McLean continues, "try imagining the tsunami of loathing that would descend upon her were a woman to commit those crimes."

It is not being suggested here that all men who murder or commit other serious offenses are tolerated, ignored, understood, or applauded. Most men who commit terrible crimes are not treated with the empathy that was extended to Mochrie, and it is men who are most frequently portrayed by the media as "monsters" or "evil beasts." But the contention is that media and public responses to women who kill and seriously harm are even more exaggerated than they are for men. Male violence is seen to exist on a continuum ranging from the nonviolent to the murderous and sexually bizarre, which results in it being viewed only in terms of degrees (Naylor, 2001). Even the criminological literature on masculinity and homicide couch familicide in terms of "misguided altruism" and as a matter of masculine honor and pride in the face of overwhelming social expectations concerning men's responsibilities for their families' well-being (Alder & Polk, 1996). Put simply, violence is viewed as one of the many possible behavior patterns for men; it is not strikingly unusual, even when extreme. Consequently, when a man kills, he can expect that his crime will be both imaginable and possibly—as in the case of Robert Mochrie—even seen as human. Indeed, male crime is intrinsic to the hegemonic masculine ideal. In all spheres of life—political, social, economic, and above all, cultural—masculine violence is articulated, glorified, even fetishized. Men who commit serious crimes are thus normalized to a much greater degree than women who do so, and their crimes tend not to be accompanied by a sense of collective denial. Yet in cases of women who kill, "vilification operates to displace the offender from her society, to insist on her otherness, thereby avoiding the knowledge that she is produced *by* that society" (Morrissey, 2003, p. 24). No such expulsion is required when men murder; indeed, men's crimes might be said to be but one aspect of a prevailing cultural ideology of aggressive macho values that sustains men's crimes and makes them possible (Ward Jouve, 1988).

Two factors were mentioned at the beginning of this chapter that are paramount in securing a female offender's notoriety. One is her conformity to the key journalistic news values outlined in Chapter 2. Women who murder or sexually abuse form a tiny percentage of an already small, though demonized, group of criminals. This immediately guarantees their coverage; their crimes are novel, and they are negative in essence. But, in addition, they frequently illustrate most or all of the 12 cardinal news values. The horror of their crimes meets the required *threshold*; a grim *predictability* is woven through the account of their crimes via the use of stock stories and familiar motifs (lesbian monster, evil manipulator, etc.); their histories and motives are reduced to the *simplest* of forms (that is, that they must be "mad" or "bad"); their pathology is constructed as *individual* and random, the most meaningless of acts carried out by individuals in whom we are meant to trust—hence any of us (or our children) are at *risk;* their crimes are explained by reference to their *sexuality* or sexual deviance; they frequently achieve a kind of macabre *celebrity;* indeed, some gain iconic status through *graphic imagery,* such as the police mugshot of Myra Hindley, which not only identified her as the "face of the nation's deepest fears" (Upton, 2000, p. 6) in the popular media long after the peroxide had grown out and the lines on her face had appeared but also achieved further immortality in art (e.g., in Marcus Harvey's infamous portrait of her and on covers of The Smiths albums); the victimization of *children* in murders by women further cements their newsworthiness, and even when children are not directly involved, the anomaly of women who kill being *potential* mothers is taken as proof enough of their deviation from notions of traditional womanhood, notions that are at the heart of *conservative ideology.* Finally, murderesses become notorious by virtue of their geographical and cultural *proximity.* The generally ethnocentric nature of our media means that those cases that are culturally and geographically meaningful to an audience in the UK or Australia—except maybe Myra Hindley, and that only because of the ubiquity of her famous mugshot, and Lindy Chamberlain because of the popular film inspired by her case—barely rate a mention in U.S. media.

The fears of some feminist writers that constructions of women who kill have wider implications for all women are understandable, given the evidence put forward in this chapter. Mediated understandings of deviant women do not exist in a cultural vacuum, and negative, potentially damaging stereotypes based on women's appearance, sexuality, and behavior are, of course, not limited to discourses about women who commit very serious crimes. All women who are in the public eye are likely to become the subjects of narratives that construct them in terms of their willingness, or otherwise, to conform to traditional notions of passive, heterosexual, maternal, compliant femininity. However, many commentators have noted that, when it comes to women who kill—and here, once more, we find echoes of the public response to children who kill—a deep cultural unease is provoked by the uncomfortable reality of the human capacity for depravity. Media reports may blithely attribute women's serious crimes to their *in*humanity and "otherness," but Joan Smith (1997) argues that society *needs* the figure of the dominant female killer luring her hapless male partner into crimes he might otherwise not have committed, however far from reality that depiction might be.

SUMMARY

- This chapter has located psychological and sociological concerns with identity and difference within criminological discourses of responses to crime in an attempt to understand the origins of, and reasons for, the fear and loathing that is directed (arguably disproportionately) at a particular group of deviant "others"—women who kill and rape.

- The cultural inclination to view women's deviance as a manifestation of their "otherness" is compounded by its newsworthiness, which is unquestionable, and the proposition that there may never be a prevailing ideological climate that tolerates women who deviate from cultural expectations of "appropriate" feminine behavior.

- It has been argued that, in common with wider media and cultural constructions, women who kill are subject to intense scrutiny—both in legal and media institutions—regarding their sexual proclivities and history, and are frequently judged on their body size, shape, and sexual attractiveness. Paradoxically, conventional constructions of both beauty and ugliness can be used as evidence of a woman's inherent badness, and the media borrow from a range of classical literature and mythology to evoke images of monstrous women. Women who kill (especially those who kill children and young women) are the diabolical antithesis to the myth of the good mother, and much media discourse is constructed around "essentialist" notions of women; in other words, they presuppose that the "essence" of women is different from that of men and that women are biologically predisposed to be caring and nurturing. Women's crimes against children are especially inexplicable and "unreal." Unless an offense can be accounted for in terms of a "sickness" that is compatible with the essential "nature" of womanhood, it will be regarded as "unnatural" and evil (Worrall, 1990). A degree of biological essentialism is also evident in the common theme that women who commit serious crimes—especially when they do so in partnership with a man—are the prime movers in these relationships and are, in essence, evil manipulators.

- If a woman's serious offending cannot be explained as "madness" but appears to be a lucid and rational act, it becomes symbolically disturbing. Women who claim that they acted in an autonomous and calculated manner are so transgressive of societal notions of "proper" (that is, nonagentic) womanhood that the details of their offenses are glossed over in legal and media discourses and explanations for their crimes are curiously absent from feminist readings.

- The discussion has demonstrated that psychosocial and feminist perspectives are far from incompatible, drawing on psychoanalytically informed ways of understanding gendered identities. In the cases discussed in this chapter, psychoanalytic concepts have been used in conjunction with sociologically informed ideas from media studies and cultural studies in order to explore exactly why it is that some individuals generate a level of hysteria and vilification that is arguably disproportionate to their actual offenses. In addition, it has been argued that the media have consistently represented the abuse perpetuated on women and children as extraordinary rather than as the worst outcomes of the institutions of marriage and the family, which historically have enshrined unequal relations between men, women, and children.

STUDY QUESTIONS

Study a range of newspapers and pay close attention to stories involving women offenders.

1. What evidence can you find for the proposition that women are constructed according to their perceived "otherness"? What kinds of motifs and stereotypes are apparent in your chosen news report?

2. To what extent do Lombrosian ideas about "born female criminals," whose deviance is indicated by their very physiology, permeate contemporary discourses concerning women and crime?

3. What sorts of women conform to mediated ideas about "ideal" victims, and which women are invisible in media discourses about victimization?

4. The unwillingness of media, legal, and academic discourses to recognize the possibility of women's agency has arguably resulted in other "omissions" in our understanding of female offending. Explanations centering on women's lust, greed, revenge, or sheer entrepreneurism are curiously absent from criminological inquiries (P. Davies, 2003). What examples of "invisible crimes" can you think of that illustrate this observation?

FURTHER READING

- There is now quite a substantial literature within criminology concerning gender and violence, and much of it draws on media representations to illustrate the circulation of ideas concerning both women's violence and victimization. Meda Chesney-Lind has written extensively about the construction of offending women and

girls; see, for example, her book with Katherine Irwin, *Beyond Bad Girls: Gender, Violence and Hype* (Routledge, 2013); her 2006 article with Mickey Eliason, "From Invisible to Incorrigible: The Demonization of Marginalized Women and Girls," in *Crime, Media, Culture*, 2(1); and her 2006 article "Patriarchy, Crime and Justice:

Feminist Criminology in an Era of Backlash" in *Feminist Criminology, 1*(1).

- In the UK, Maggie Wykes has written about specific cases in her chapters in Gender and Crime, edited by R. Dobash, R. Dobash, and L. Noaks (University of Wales Press, 1995), and in Cynthia Carter et al.'s *News, Gender and Power* (Routledge, 1998). So has Joan Smith in *Different for Girls* (Chatto & Windus, 1997).

- Helen Birch's (1993) *Moving Targets: Women, Murder and Representation* (Virago) is an edited collection that includes chapters on Myra Hindley, Hollywood representations of female killers, mothers who kill their children, and female serial killers.

- Carter et al.'s *News, Gender and Power* (see above) is another edited collection that covers some of the same ground, but from the perspective of gendered institutional working practices in newsrooms.

- Belinda Morrissey's *When Women Kill* (Routledge, 2003) is a more theoretically advanced book, and she discusses many of the cases featured in this chapter (e.g., Homolka, Beck, Wigginton, and Wuornos), which she interprets through a psychoanalytic lens.

- Philip Jenkins discusses serial killers, including female serial killers, in *Using Murder: The Social Construction of Serial Homicide* (Aldine de Gruyter, 1994).

- Lisa Downing's *The Subject of Murder: Gender, Exceptionality, and the Modern Killer* (University of Chicago Press, 2013) provides a thorough analysis of how murder and femininity have combined to produce a distinct sort of criminal subject.

Student Study Site

WANT A BETTER GRADE?

Get the tools you need to sharpen your study skills. Access practice quizzes, eFlashcards, SAGE journal articles, and more at study.sagepub.com/jewkesus.

The Police Image and *Policing* the Image

6

OVERVIEW

Chapter 6 provides:

- A discussion of the changing mediated (or "mediatized") relationship between police and the public.

- Consideration of the relationship between the media and public fears about crime, and the rationality or irrationality of such fears.

- A comparison between "critical criminological" and "left realist" perspectives on fear of crime.

- A consideration of the changing roles of the police and of the symbolic power of the community police officer and the tough-on-crime cop in the contemporary social imagination.

- An analysis of the origins and genre conventions of the long-running "reality" series *Cops*.

- A discussion of how police use social media for crime control purposes and to produce and control the police image.

KEY TERMS

- fear of crime 152
- left realism 152
- legitimacy 159
- new visibility 151

- police image 150
- police power 150
- police/policing 150
- rationality/irrationality 152

- representation/misrepresentation 150
- responsibilization 163
- victimization 151

In December 2014, the New York City Police Department's Midtown South Precinct caused a stir when it tweeted a meme drawn from a popular film and the caption "Motivational Monday—courtesy of Jack Nicholson in 'A Few Good Men.'" The meme (Photo 6.1) refers to the film's climax, where Nicholson's character Colonel

PHOTO 6.1

NYPD "Motivational Monday" tweet invoking the famous "you can't handle the truth!" speech from the film, *A Few Good Men*.

Nathan Jessup, while testifying in the murder trial of a Marine under his command, famously proclaims, "You can't handle the truth!" thereby admitting to ordering the "code red" murder of another of his Marines. In the context of policing, the "motivational" speech, which includes the admonishment from Jessup, "I have neither the time nor the inclination to explain myself to a man who rises and sleeps under the blanket of the very freedom that I provide, and then questions the manner in which I provide it," invokes the clichéd "thin blue line"—which holds that police are all that stands between the law-abiding public and wholesale violence and anarchy—thereby claiming impunity for the NYPD and policing in general against charges of brutality and lethal violence. In addition to questioning the "motivational" qualities of a speech delivered by a character who admitted to ordering and covering up a murder, Twitter users were enraged at the timing of the tweet, noting that it followed just days after thousands of New Yorkers marched in protest of the police killings of Eric Garner and Michael Brown.

And though the tweet was deleted in a matter of hours, it nevertheless demonstrates a number of key issues taken up in this chapter. First, it illustrates how, in the minds of many, the threat of crime necessitates the seemingly ever-expanding reach of U.S. police power and perhaps justifies, for some, instances of wanton brutality. Perhaps more importantly, the tweet demonstrates how social media figure into the production of the police image—how police are viewed in particular cultural and historical contexts (Mawby, 2013). Prior to the advent of the Internet; inexpensive, user-friendly smartphones; and social media platforms such as YouTube, police agencies communicated with the public in what has been characterized as a "few-to-many" or top-down fashion (Lee & McGovern, 2014). As such, research on police and media relations has, until relatively recently, conceived of the relationship as a one-way communication channel. Under this model, whether as unwitting partners or active conspirators, members of the news media are thought to release messages to the public that have been approved by police agencies as part of a broader ideological project intent on advancing a pro-police message, diffusing controversy, and, ultimately, reinforcing police and state authority. Even critical writing of this variety, such as the influential *Policing the Crisis*, focused on the disjuncture or gap between "the facts" of a case and the distorted representation provided by police and their partners in the media (Hall, Critcher, Jefferson, Clarke, & Roberts, 1978/2013). Seen as distinctly separate from police and the media, the public, in this model, tends to be viewed as passive consumers, or simple receptors of signs, messages, and propaganda. As we've discussed, Chibnall's (1977) influential *Law and*

Order News: An Analysis of Crime Reporting in the British Press concerned the ideological production of police authority through the work of elite reporters and the conduit of police–media relations departments (see also Mawby, 2010). Citing laissez-faire market forces, others have pointed out that pro-police propaganda would likely not exist if there wasn't a market it for it (S. Cohen & Young, 1981).

Now, with the proliferation of user-generated content, not only are law enforcement departments likely to release information to the public in ways other than those outlined by Chibnall, but the public is also able to talk back, critique, or praise the police in real time—responding to social media posts, posting images of police misconduct, and so on. As such, we might say that in the contemporary moment, police operate in what sociologist John B. Thompson (2005) and others (e.g., Goldsmith, 2010) have called a **new visibility**, which is to say that mobile and social media have subjected policing to an unprecedented degree of exposure to, and scrutiny by, mainstream and alternative media, activist groups, and everyday people. Therefore, rather than siding with either propaganda or preference, manipulation or market, a more dynamic view and one that perhaps better recognizes the public's agency is to conceive of the public as coproducers equipped with the ability to shape the police image through active interpretation and interaction. Avoiding the troubling dichotomy between the real and represented, we move away from a top-down, one-way conception of the police/media/public interface and toward a dynamic relationship between police and public where communication is a contested and reciprocal process. This chapter begins by considering the ways in which the media's focus on crime might make certain individuals and groups feel more vulnerable than their likelihood of actual **victimization** suggests they should be and, likewise, how this media-induced fear of crime might necessitate or justify the presence and actions of police. Paying special attention to television programs, films, and social media, we then consider how the police image helps to reaffirm policing's power and authority. Finally, we will consider how mobile and social media have altered the ways in which law enforcement agencies communicate with the public and the ability of policing to control its own image.

THE MASS MEDIA AND FEAR OF CRIME

Numerous writers have examined the proposition that the media present crime stories (both factual and fictional) in ways that selectively distort and manipulate public perceptions, creating a false picture of crime that promotes stereotyping, bias, prejudice, and gross oversimplification of particular facts. The general conclusion is that it is not just official statistics that misrepresent the picture of crime, but that the media are also guilty of manipulation and fueling public fears. Studies carried out in both the U.S. and UK indicate that crime reporting in the press is more prevalent than ever before, and that interpersonal crimes, particularly violent and sexual crimes, are consistently over-reported in relation to official statistics. Some studies have also found that newspaper readers overestimate the proportion of crimes solved, and that the police sometimes reinforce journalistically produced concerns about a "crime wave" by feeding reporters stories based on previously reported incidents (Fishman, 1978; Sacco, 2005). This can sometimes provoke fear of a crime surge at a time when, statistically, incidents of that crime are on the decrease (Schlesinger & Tumber, 1994).

The reasons for the media's preoccupation with certain types of crime may be largely pragmatic and economic; they are, after all, in the business of selling newspapers and gaining audience ratings. The strange case of the Brazilian crime program *Canal Livre* provides a particularly outrageous example of how violent crime and hence the fear of crime are packaged as a newsworthy commodity. Produced and hosted by Wallace Souza, a former police officer and politician, *Canal Livre* routinely featured "gore-filled" stories and "specialized in footage of murder victims." The show was a hit for nearly two decades until 2009, when Souza was arrested following testimony of his former bodyguard, who alleged that he had committed at least one murder—on orders from Souza—in order to produce material for *Canal Livre!* Unfortunately, Souza died of natural causes while under armed guard awaiting trial, taking the truth of his former bodyguard's accusations to the grave (Phillips, 2010). Nevertheless, *Canal Livre* demonstrates the reciprocity between the human fascination with violent crime on the one hand and the repulsion and fear it engenders on the other—both of which undoubtedly undergird the public mandate for aggressive policing and increasingly harsher punishments.

Within criminology, discussions of public fears about crime tend to be polarized along theoretical lines. Marxist-inspired critical criminologists argue that politicians, the media, and criminal justice officials set the agenda for public debate about crime and the implementation of crime control projects and collude in perpetuating notions of "enemies within." These agendas then shape public perceptions, not only about their likelihood of being a victim of crime but also about whom they should fear. Steven Box (1983) suggests that the picture of crime that the public receives is manipulated by those in power, and that there is an overconcentration on the crimes of the young, racial minorities, the working class, and the unemployed and an underawareness of the crimes of the well-educated upper and middle classes, the socially privileged, and those in power. He argues that the processes by which the public receives information about crime via the mass media result in perceptions about criminal justice being determined by very narrow legal definitions that tolerate, accept, or even applaud the crimes of the privileged while criminalizing the disadvantaged (see also Tombs & Whyte, 2007; Walters, 2010). Nancy Signorielli goes further, claiming that the way the media construct crime and violence encourages the public to accept increasingly repressive forms of social control: "Fearful people are more dependent, more easily manipulated . . . more susceptible to deceptively simple, strong, tough measures and hard-line postures . . . they may accept and even welcome repression if it promises to relieve their insecurities and other anxieties" (1990, p. 102).

From this vantage point, crime is viewed as an ideological construct that protects the powerful and further marginalizes the powerless. However, there is an implicit assumption in this proposal that **fear of crime** is irrational and unreasonable—that it is a kind of false consciousness produced by those in authority. **Left realist** criminologists hotly dispute this suggestion, arguing that there is a **rational** core to images of crime and to the public concerns they generate. Jock Young (a pioneer of critical, left realist, and cultural criminology), for example, claimed that popular perceptions of crime and justice are largely "constructed out of the material experiences of people rather than fantasies impressed upon them by the mass media or agencies of the State" (1987, p. 337).

In other words, even the most salacious, fear-induced pandering "tends to reinforce what people already know" (Crawford, Jones, Woodhouse, & Young, 1990, p. 76). Of course, these are valid observations, and left realist criminologists have been right to point out that it is not just the media who are to blame for instilling fear of crime. Actual risk of victimization, previous experience of victimization, environmental conditions, race, and confidence in the police and the criminal justice system are among many of the factors interacting through complex processes to influence public anxiety about crime. And, as we have already seen in Chapter 1, the notion of passive audiences soaking up media influences in isolation of their lived experience is regarded as reductive and untenable.

Our interpretation of statistics on fear of crime may thus have to go beyond their face value. For example, crime survey findings suggesting that fear of crime greatly outweighs the likelihood of actually being a victim are sometimes associated with broader structural insecurities, such as those provoked during a prolonged period of economic recession. Furthermore, the fact that the readers of popular newspapers (that is, those that report crime in a sensationalized manner) have the highest levels of fear of crime may simply reflect their actual risk of victimization. Put simply, readers of tabloid newspapers may be of lower socioeconomic or class standing and more likely to live in areas, and behave in ways, that expose them to greater risk of crime and greater surveillance by the police.

But while a specific media effect may be difficult to isolate in a world that is increasingly characterized as multimedia-saturated, we should not dismiss the idea that the media play some part in the distribution of fear. While not reducible to crude causes and "effects," media consumption is centrally implicated in the routines and practices of everyday life and is inextricably interwoven into people's biographies and the stories they tell about themselves. It is impossible to separate situated experience from mediated experience, and so, while women and older people may have genuine grounds for being fearful of violence, their anxiety is constantly and pervasively reinforced by a media that recognizes and perpetuates the newsworthiness of violent crimes against women and the elderly. Quite simply, media coverage of crime and deviance is rarely grounded in fact. Crime has been exploited as commercial entertainment since the earliest days of cinema and remains the most salient theme in television dramas and "reality" shows, which enthusiastically mix fact, fiction, and titillation. Meanwhile, as we have seen in Chapter 2, news about crime and deviance has a strong social control element—"watch and beware." Consequently, media images of crime perpetually reinforce people's anxieties: We are, at one and the same time, fascinated by representations of crime and alarmed by them. It is little wonder, then, that those groups who become most oversensitized to their risk of victimization are the same people whose victimization is overreported and oversensationalized.

The now-decades-old tensions between critical and left realist positions on victimization and fear of crime continue, remaining as fluid as ever. Four days in July 2016 demonstrate this fluidity with powerful and gut-wrenching detail. Just after midnight on July 5 in Baton Rouge, Louisiana, two BRPD officers, who had responded to reports of a man brandishing a handgun, confronted a 37-year-old man named Alton Sterling, who was misidentified as the suspect. A bystander with the activist group "Stop the Killing" was present to record the confrontation and captured Sterling's final moments. The footage shows police tackling Sterling and wrestling him to the ground. As he is flat on his back with the two officers kneeling on his chest and lower body struggling to control his arms, one of the officers announces that Sterling has a gun. In just a few seconds, multiple shots ring out as the officers fire on Sterling, who is still prone, killing him instantly. A day later, on July 6, a 32-year-old Minnesota man named Philando Castile was shot and killed by police during a traffic stop while his partner "live-streamed" it all from the front passenger's seat. According to Philando's partner, during the stop he had told the officer that he was licensed to "conceal and carry" and that there was a handgun in the car, but before he could comply with police commands and produce his driver's license, the officer shot him multiple times, leaving him dead in the seat of his car. The video, beginning seconds after the killing, captures the image of Philando's bloody, lifeless body and the anguished screams of his partner and young daughter. It was posted to Facebook and viewed more than 2.5 million times in less than 24 hours.

The next day in Dallas, Texas, at a protest organized for Sterling and Castile, a 25-year-old U.S. Army reservist named Micah Johnson opened fire, killing five Dallas police officers and wounding another nine. Before ultimately being killed by a police robot armed with explosives, Johnson is said to have pointed to the killings of black people by police as motivation for the attack. A day later, the Bahamian Ministry of Foreign Affairs and Immigration issued a warning to its citizens, urging "appropriate caution" when traveling to the United States. The reason for the warning, according to a Bahamian official, was the "recent tensions in some American cities over shootings of young black males by police officers" (T. Perry, Andrews, & Berman, 2016). The advice to be careful when interacting with the police in a democratic nation might seem reactionary and perhaps unprecedented, but it is not without foundation. The killings of Sterling and Castile, captured in graphic raw footage, were just the latest in an ever-growing list of U.S. citizens killed by police. However, because there has been no enforcement of the federal requirement for police to submit data on shootings, there is not a reliable accounting of lethal police violence (recently taken up by projects like *The Guardian*'s *The Counted*). Nevertheless, left realists would point to "unofficial" data to underline the fact that in a year (2015) when a staggering 1,134 deaths occurred at the hands of police officers, African-American males had cause to be *especially* fearful of interactions with police. Despite making up only 2% of the U.S. population, black males between the ages of 15 and 34 accounted for more than 15% of all those killed by police (https://www.theguardian.com/us-news/series/counted-us-police-killings). Their rate of death was five times higher than that for white men of the same age, despite their being more likely to be unarmed themselves (25% of the African-Americans were unarmed compared with 17% of white people).

To put it in another, equally shocking way, one in every 65 deaths of a young African-American male in the U.S. is a killing by police. In this context, left realists might confirm the advice of the Bahamian government and say quite plainly that, particularly for young black men, the threat is real and the fear warranted. When presented with such an argument, a critical criminologist is likely to agree, while also shifting focus to the scapegoating of young black men as the impetus for ballooning, militarized, and lethal policing. In his highly regarded *City of Quartz*, Mike Davis summarizes this view powerfully:

> The media, whose function in this arena is to bury and obscure the daily economic violence of the city, ceaselessly throw up spectres of criminal underclasses and psychotic stalkers. Sensationalized accounts of killer youth gangs high on

crack and shrilly racist evocations of marauding Willie Hortons foment the moral panics that reinforce and justify urban apartheid. (2006, pp. 224–226)

Interestingly, young people's fears about crime are rarely discussed, while parents' fears for the safety of their children are part of the currency of everyday media discourse. Much like gaming today, television was regarded for decades as a sort of multicolored narcotic, depriving children of healthier forms of interaction and making them vulnerable to ideological manipulation. Likewise, popular music has been seen as a bad influence at least since the earliest days of Elvis Presley. Since then, artists as varied and unrelated as the Rolling Stones, the Doors, Judas Priest, 2 Live Crew, Eminem, Marilyn Manson, Lady Gaga, and Miley Cyrus, to name just a few, have been held up as a corrupting influence of American youth. Concerns about youth culture seem to be exacerbated by new mobile technologies and social media, with worrisome tales of Internet child predators, catfishing, and sexting appearing one after the other. In both the U.S. and the UK, concerns have been expressed about forms of music that glorify gun and drug cultures and promote homophobic and misogynist attitudes.

Any direct causal link between gang-related offenses and wider cultural statements legitimating or glamorizing gang life and gun crime has proved illusory. Yet the lack of relationship between cultural production and violence has not stopped authorities from acting as though music does in fact create violence. In July 2015, for instance, a holographic performance by Chicago rapper Chief Keef at an Indiana hip-hop music festival, "Craze Fest," was interrupted by local police. Because authorities had warned that they would shut down the festival if Chief Keef performed in person, Craze Fest promoters arranged for the rapper to appear via 3D holographic rendering of a live performance given in California. Apparently even a computer-generated analog of Chief Keef was potentially too threatening for local police, who insisted the rapper was "anti-cop, pro-gang and pro-drug use." Explaining the move, the mayor of the town that hosted Craze Fest stated, "It's just this specific case. Gang violence in Chicago is the reality right now, and I'm not going to invite someone that might be a threat to public safety" (Coscarelli, 2015). For the authorities presiding over Craze Fest, the fear of rap music–incited violence was apparently enough to warrant what critics decried as outright censorship. The point here is that fear of crime is a particularly powerful human emotion with far-ranging, sometimes seemingly irrational, consequences.

As powerful as it is, fear is notoriously difficult to define. Often conceptualized as a tangible quantity that we possess in smaller or greater amounts, fear may be more accurately thought of as a mode of perception consisting of a range of diffuse anxieties about one's position and identity in the world (Sparks, 1992). Furthermore, it is very difficult to generalize about "fear of crime 'effects.'" A high-profile crime might cause people to modify their behavior for as long as the offense is newsworthy, but this amplification of anxiety may be periodic, short-lived, and confined to specific social, cultural, and spatial contexts. On the other hand, the relationship between fear and the media might be best conceptualized in subtler and more pervasive terms as contributing to a cultural climate that normalizes male violence and reinforces notions of female submissiveness.

Ultimately, the long-term effects of exposure to mediated images of crime are virtually impossible to gauge. But as already noted, while we should be cautious when making statements about the media "causing" fear (Sparks, 1992), it is also worth bearing in mind that fear of crime is a much more widely experienced phenomenon than victimization. Although victims of crime will probably become more fearful about the likelihood of future victimization as a result of their experiences, many more individuals will experience fear as a result of indirect contact with crime. These vicarious experiences of crime will encompass personal observations, private conversations with victims, and second-, third- and fourthhand accounts passed down through multifarious flows of mediated discourse. Attempts to measure the impact of media reporting on public fears about crime are notoriously problematic. Historically, the majority of people have attributed their knowledge of the risk of crime to information received from television and newspapers (Surette, 1998; P. Williams & Dickinson, 1993), with one study finding that about 66% of people interviewed got their news from television and that half of those reported were more fearful of crime because of it (Keating, 2002). Today, according to recent polling data, the ways in which everyday consumers receive news has shifted decidedly toward the Internet, with as much as 60% of the American public accessing news through social media.

Public polling aiming to measure fear of crime draws out the complicated relationship with what most would consider the material realities of violent crime. Beginning in 1965, the Gallup Poll has asked respondents, "Is there any area near where you live— that is, within a mile—where you would be afraid to walk alone at night?" as a standard fear of crime measure. Responses to this question are relatively consistent, with 39% of those polled (on average) answering in the affirmative. Whereas these data, represented visually, would approximate a horizontal line, rates of violent crime would take on an altogether different shape. In fact, during the same period, the U.S. homicide rate represented similarly would show significant growth in the late 1960s, reaching a peak in the early 1990s, and dropping precipitously in the following decades. All the while, Gallup's "fear of crime" measure would remain relatively stable and appear to act independently.

Relying on statistical measurements to gauge the extent of crime is in itself a problematic endeavor, let alone gauging how large diverse populations *feel* about crime. What is important to recognize is that individual and collective feelings about crime rarely match up with their objective reality, whatever that might be. While the media frequently focus on relatively uncommon issues, such as serial murder, reporting on them in a sensationalized, overblown manner with demands for harsher and more uncompromising punishments can help encourage local responses to crime that are more immediate and explosive. For instance, in June 2015, police in the town of McKinley, Texas, were dispatched to a disturbance at an upscale housing community's swimming pool. According to police, they were called to the pool by residents after many uninvited teens, most of whom were black, climbed the fence to gain access, allegedly assaulting a security officer in the process (it was later shown that the teens had been invited). The arrival of at least a dozen police officers was captured by partygoers on cell phone cameras, as was the behavior of a particularly aggressive officer, Eric Casebolt. Charging into the scene at full sprint while other officers trail behind, Casebolt—cursing—forces several teens to the ground and handcuffs them before engaging another young girl who is wearing only a swimsuit. Slamming 15-year-old Dajerria Becton to the ground, screaming "On your face!" while pushing his knee into the small of her back, Casebolt then draws and aims his handgun at other youth who question Becton's treatment. Uploaded to social media and viewed millions of times in a matter of days, the footage quickly fed into public debates stemming from the police killing of Michael Brown in Ferguson, Missouri, and of Eric Garner in New York. While many called for Casebolt's resignation, an equally large contingent defended the officer's actions, citing the supposed condition of lawlessness that the teens characterized. As one witnessed argued, "they [the police] were just doing the right thing when these kids were fleeing and using profanity and threatening security guards" (Legum, 2015). And though many, including the person who initially called the police, justified Casebolt's actions, citing the necessity of such force to further safety and security, Casebolt was nevertheless suspended and eventually resigned from the McKinley Police Department.

Not only does this case illustrate the relevance of user-generated content and social media to contemporary policing, but it also shows how the fear of crime and a demand for security rationalizes the violent and abhorrent behavior of police. Macro-sociological studies have likewise shown that fear of crime and more specifically the social and economic threat posed by the relative population of racial minorities shares a causal relationship with police force size and strength (see Chamlin, 1989; Stults & Baumer, 2007). Interestingly, demands for more "police on the street" continue, despite a general decline in crime and in the public's respect and faith in the police. In 2004, for instance, 64% of a nationally representative sample of adult Americans voiced a "great deal" of confidence in police, but by 2012 that number had dropped to 56%. The decline in confidence stands in even sharper relief across select demographics, with a "great deal" of confidence among those making less than 20,000 dollars per year dropping from 60% in 2004 to 36% in 2012, and from 41% to 32% among black respondents during the same time period (http://www.albany.edu/sourcebook/pdf/t212.pdf).

Although several studies have shown that deploying more police officers and street patrols is unlikely to significantly reduce crime, quite the opposite persists as a common-sense belief. Not only does this continue to be a key battleground for politicians to prove their "tough-on-crime" credentials, unconditional support of the policing institution, if not individual officers, is an American political imperative. The lazy and misinformed link that is popularly made between policing strength and crime control reflects the journalistic priorities that shape news reporting and the more general limitations of "fear of crime" debates. As David Downes remarks:

> That the "fear of crime" . . . remains most developed in relation to certain forms of street crime is probably more to do with collective representations of unpredictable violence than that which more frequently occurs in the home, or that which is normalized as accidental, or where victimization is indirect and dispersed, as with corporate crime. (1988, p. 182)

It is important to be clear that even though fear of crime and hence the lived realities of crime are undoubtedly cultural, we should caution against assuming an uncomplicated direct relationship whereby a particular media form, such as the nightly news, causes fear. Indeed, as Derek Chadee and Jason Ditton (2005) have shown, in some contexts even the amount of news consumed sometimes has very little to do with fear of crime. It follows, then, that public demands for more police and their often-violent responses may be linked to broader, more deep-seated existential anxieties that have so successfully been exploited by politicians, including Donald Trump—fears of "others," including immigrants, political refugees, people from ethnic minority backgrounds, immigrants, and the homeless. As Leonidas Cheliotis (2013) has argued, the threat of violent crime is a convenient and durable symbol that may obscure or displace similar anxieties brought on by rising inequality, economic precarity, and the certainties of human mortality. In other words, fear, anxiety, and insecurity are pervasive human emotions but are not simply caused by crime. Nevertheless, such emotions are often cited as the impetus of a "fortress mentality" whereby some neighborhoods and housing developments have been turned into fenced, guarded, middle-class ghettos and where residents travel between home, work, and leisure in the assumed safety of oversized tanklike sport utility vehicles (Lauer, 2005). Again we hear from Mike Davis, who concurs:

> The neo-military syntax of contemporary architecture insinuates violence and conjures imaginary dangers. In many instances the semiotics of so-called "defensible space" are just about as subtle as a swaggering white cop. Today's upscale, pseudo-public spaces—sumptuary malls, office centers, culture acropolises, and so on—are full of invisible signs warning off the underclass "Other." Although architectural critics are usually oblivious to how the built environment contributes to segregation, pariah groups—whether poor Latino families, young Black men, or elderly homeless white females—read the meaning immediately. (Davis, 2006, pp. 224–226)

THE POLICE IMAGE: TELEVISION AND FILM

Just how many police officers a given society should employ is a complicated issue, no doubt bound up in competing ideas about the causes and possible remedies of crime and other related social problems. In 2010, a Gallup Poll asked a nationally representative sample of adults, "Which of the following approaches to lowering the crime rate in the United States comes closer to your own view?" When forced to choose between employing more police and making broader structural reforms, 64% of the respondents believed attacking social and economic inequalities associated with crime and increasing funding for education and job training programs to be the best approach to the many problems of crime. Support for broad social and economic approaches to crime control increases among select demographics, with 77% of those aged 18 to 29, 72% of those with some postgraduate education, and 85% of self-identified liberals and blacks favoring job training and education over increased funding for police (www.albany.edu/sourcebook/pdf/t200132010.pdf). Despite these competing views, the insatiable human desire for security helps shield policing as an institution from criticism and significant budget cuts or downsizing, even in times of increasing austerity (consider the million-plus law enforcement personnel in 2011, up from less than half a million in 1980).

To apprehend the ways in which policing reproduces and maintains its position as the mythical thin blue line between order and chaos, we will briefly consider how popular television programs and film produce and affirm a pro-police image. One of the first, if not most, beloved television programs focusing on police in the U.S. is, of course *The Andy Griffith Show*. As sheriff of Mayberry, a small and fictitious North Carolina town, Andy and his bumbling sidekick, deputy Barney Fife, occupied the imaginations of postwar America for eight seasons and nearly 250 episodes. Andy, who famously never wore a gun, dealt with Mayberry's quirks and petty crimes with humor, kindness, and wit, but never force. As such, Andy and Barney offered a small-screen foreshadowing of the later turn toward community policing, one dramatically devoid of the real-world violence and repression that has always been a staple of policing's repertoire (Linnemann & Kurtz, 2014). This is even more the case when considering how the bucolic and all-white Mayberry, fictional as it was, stood in dramatic opposition to much of the U.S. at a time of quickening social change and racial conflict (precisely one nonwhite character had a speaking role in eight seasons). As Don Vaughan put it:

> The serenity of Mayberry was seemingly uninfluenced by hard news. In this respect, Mayberry is like the eye of the hurricane, a place of tranquility in a world of anything but that. Mayberry's problems and stressors were anything but the problems and stressors that most faced in the 1960s: unemployment, overcoming obstacles to voter registration, the quest for civil rights as Americans, sons fighting in a no-cause war, the uneasiness over the risk of nuclear war—the list could go on. (2004, p. 397)

For many, the slow-moving, safe, and profoundly *white* Mayberry stood as a comforting, albeit distorted referent of "real America" in a time of particularly divisive politics and growing calls for a return to "law and order" championed by prominent Republican politicians Barry Goldwater and Richard Nixon.

While *The Andy Griffith* Show was immensely popular and remains a popular trope of the academic literature, the police drama that more accurately foreshadowed the authoritarian politics of the burgeoning tough-on-crime movement was the long-running radio and television program *Dragnet*. As Christopher Sharrett (2012) has argued, *Dragnet* served as a key public relations tool, if not propaganda arm, for the Los Angeles Police Department during some of its most controversial years. Christopher Wilson (2000) has observed a similar marriage between police and crime reporters and news bureaus housed in police precincts, what he calls "cop shops." Wilson notes that numerous best-selling true crime writers launched their careers from cop shops, the least of these being David Simon, writer and executive producer of the acclaimed TV crime drama *The Wire*, who began as the police beat reporter for the *Baltimore Sun*. Cocreated by Jack Webb, a Hollywood insider with right-wing leanings, the iconic cop show grew in prominence at a time when the Los Angeles Police Department and policing in general were mired in conflict and hemorrhaging legitimacy with the urban poor and some sectors of the middle class. But, as Sharrett boldly argues, *Dragnet* was not simply propaganda; it sought to "define 'American values' and to separate the righteous not just from criminals but from all the misfits, oddities, and malcontents who pollute[d] the American landscape" (2012, p. 165). Not only did Webb help create *Dragnet*, but he cast himself in the starring role, as Sgt. Joe Friday, a technocratic authoritarian and supposedly impartial detective seeking "just the facts" from all whom he encountered. The Friday character, and *Dragnet* more broadly, offered Webb a conduit to elaborate his own politics, as well as those of his close personal friend, and avowed white supremacist LAPD chief William H. Parker (Davis, 2006). For 16 seasons and nearly 800 episodes, Webb's particularly Manichean worldview helped to

LIFE
The cities lock up

Fear of crime creates a life-style behind steel

NOVEMBER 19 • 1971 • 40¢

PHOTO 6.2
Life Magazine comments on the growing fear of crime in the early 1970s US.

reify "hippies," "communists," drug users, delinquents, and subversives of all kinds as the target of real-life police and thus the true threats to the American way of life. Beyond the LAPD's direct involvement, the broad cultural influence of *Dragnet* should not be understated, as even its iconic introduction proclaiming to the audience, "What you are about to see is true; the names have been changed to protect the innocent" resonates with the supposed "ripped from the headlines" realism of programs like *Law and Order*.

Perhaps beginning with *Dragnet or The Andy Griffith Show*, police have been a source of endless fascination for film television producers and American viewers alike and thus have a tremendous hold over what the average person knows about the everyday realities of crime and crime control. Yet any discussion of representations of American police, however brief, would not be complete without some mention of Detective "Dirty" Harry Callahan. Making his debut in 1971's *Dirty Harry*, Clint Eastwood would star as the steely-eyed San Francisco detective four more times—*Magnum Force* (1973), *The Enforcer* (1976), *Sudden Impact* (1983), and *The Dead Pool* (1988)—a role that would define his career. Appearing at a time when the fear of crime was a key public issue and a few short months after Richard Nixon declared his "war on drugs," Dirty Harry represented a new kind of cop, tailored perfectly for the rising tide of tough-on-crime authoritarianism.

Armed with his trademark and obscenely oversized and overpowered .44 Magnum handgun, which in one famous scene he describes as "the most powerful handgun in the world" that "would blow your [suspect's] head clean off," Dirty Harry dispensed street justice in such a violent, brutal fashion that he made Sgt. Joe Friday look like Barney Fife. Here Callahan provides for the viewer, a police officer, the exact opposite of the permissiveness and multiculturalism of the 1960s, cutting through the red tape and the "peace and love" of the previous decade with a "Magnum's force." As the influential sociologist of the police, Carl Klockars (1980), put it, Dirty Harry presented the classic problem of liberalism: How might the police uphold law and order without resorting to violent "dirty" means? Of course, others challenge this view (perhaps beginning with the German sociologist Max Weber in 1918), noting that violence always underlies state power, rendering policing the dirty profession par excellence (Neocleous, 2000). It is no coincidence that *Dirty Harry* appeared at a time when policing began to noticeably shift, symbolically at least, from police on the beat to aggressive, heavily armed officers who patrol the city from cars and helicopters (Herbert, 1997). Foreshadowing the coming decades (and the rise of mass imprisonment), Harry Callahan stood on the front lines as a heavily armed soldier in the burgeoning war on crime and drugs.

From crime dramas (*Law and Order, NYPD Blue, True Detective*) to comedies (*The Naked Gun, Brooklyn Nine-Nine*) and even musicals (*Cop Rock*), it is clear that the figure of the policeman (and, to a lesser degree, policewoman) remains a staple of television programming and thus a central figure in the American social imaginary. While there has been little empirical research on the extent to which media representations inform public opinions about the police, and even less about the impact that media have on the police themselves, reality programming featuring police has not entirely escaped academic scrutiny.

COPS AND REALITY TV

First appearing on the Fox network in 1989 and now having aired for 29 seasons, 969 episodes and counting, *Cops* is one of the longest-running programs in U.S. television history. Just as mobile and social media have irrevocably altered interactions between police and public, Aaron Doyle (2003) notes how advances in video camera technology, the television industry's increasing interest in inexpensive "reality"-style programming, and policing's desire to produce pro-police messaging all combined to make *Cops* the first program of its kind (since followed by a raft of similar programs, such as *Alaska State Troopers, S.W.A.T.,* and Joe Arpaio's *Smile . . . You're Under Arrest*). Almost immediately, *Cops* proved tremendously popular among young, lower-class viewers (also the same group typically on the business end of the police in *Cops*), a demographic all but ignored by the major networks to that point. The production and marketing strategies employed by *Cops* fell in line with broader shifts toward tabloid television programming and took a cue from Fox's owner, Rupert Murdoch, who had made a fortune from scurrilous tabloid newspapers. First tagging along with the Broward County (Florida) Sheriff's Department, which patrolled an area that at the time was thought to be one of the highest crime areas in the United States, *Cops* offered viewers a supposedly unvarnished look into the actual day-to-day realities of police work. With the absence of an offscreen narrator and its shaky, raw, cinema verité–style footage, the program normalized a distorted understanding of police work and a broader law-and-order ideology, leaning heavily in the favor of the police and against the "bad boys" it targets (Doyle, 2003). Always filmed from the perspective of its police partners, the program helped its audience identify with police while simultaneously distancing themselves from the program's suspects/subjects. Not unlike *Dragnet*, the program also helped to normalize police violence, through a view of structural disadvantage whereby courageous police officers enter veritable war zones on behalf of the law-abiding public and do battle with an enemy who is at once cunning, dangerous, humorous, and pathetic. This highly stylized and manufactured narrative, of course, inspires viewers to assume that police effectively "get their man" inside the span of three 20-minute segments. All of this combines in a highly visible, popular, and profoundly distorted view of the poor and of racial minorities that further licenses the indiscriminate violence of police.

In his film *Bowling for Columbine*, Michael Moore asked former executive producer of *Cops*, Dick Herlin, why he wasn't interested in a show on "what's causing the crime, rather than just chasing the criminals down." Herlin replied:

It's harder to do that show. I don't know what that show would be. Anger does well, hate does well, violence does well; tolerance and understanding and trying to learn to be a little different than you were last year does less well . . . in the ratings. (Moore, 2002).

In keeping with our understanding of the police image as that which is coproduced by police and public, we might say that the popularity of programs like *Cops* simply reflects a preexisting populist law-and-order ideology. Alternately, and as several studies have shown, such programming also seems to reinforce a profoundly racialized divide in public attitudes toward police (see, e.g., Eschholz, Blackwell, Gertz, & Chiricos, 2002; Hallett & Powell, 1995). In other words, viewers' attitudes toward police, whatever they might be, seem to be amplified by the divisive images advanced by *Cops*.

It is increasingly recognized that the medium of television is situated within, is fully interwoven with, and flows into many other social practices, to the extent that crime, criminals, and criminal justice cannot be separated from their representations on television. While we do not care to make sweeping claims about media "effects" or the media being necessarily responsible for "causing" fear of crime, we can look at the ways in which media in general, and television in particular, are integral to the processes by which we make sense of our everyday lives. For example, although this chapter has deliberately avoided discussion of the many "crime scene investigation" police dramas such as *NCIS* and *CSI,* the phrase "CSI effect" has become commonly used to describe a contested phenomenon in which jury members in criminal trials are thought to base their assessment of the strength of the prosecution's case on the presence or absence of scientific and technical evidence. Not unlike the erroneous belief in the ubiquity of "criminal profilers" who hunt down serial killers, another and perhaps more plausible effect is the rising popularity of degrees in criminology, criminal justice, and the creation of university forensic science programs!

However, as Deborah Landry astutely notes, by uncritically accepting the CSI effect as a real phenomenon, some criminologists contribute to the mistaken assumption of the infallibility of scientific investigation/detection and thus participate in a particularly insidious form of *miseducation* (Landry, 2009, p. 154). Cavender and Deutsch (2007) add that the proliferation of "crime science" programming may have further bolstered the police power with the force of "scientific verisimilitude." Which is to say, not only are the police one of the only domestic institutions with the right to legally administer lethal violence, but now with the distorted view of police work propagated by such programming, they are also thought to wield the supposedly unbiased and infallible power of scientific verisimilitude (truth). Neither Landry nor Cavender and Deutsch suggest that television is necessarily to blame for this new caveat of policing, but, rather, all suggest that such programming taps into, engages, and reinforces preexisting beliefs about scientific knowledge, human nature, crime, and crime control. Nevertheless, these writers and others draw attention to the symbolic power of the televised policeman and its place within American culture. Christopher Wilson powerfully summarizes this view:

Police work is commonly said, meanwhile, to be the most overrepresented profession in prime-time television; likewise, the police disproportionately populate the columns of everyday crime news, the chapters of mystery novels, the action-adventures genres of Hollywood film. Not surprisingly, then, an American child's first idealization of political order, theorists of democratic socialization tell us, is liable to be the mythical beat cop, even ahead of the heroic fireman. (2000, p. 2)

POLICING AND SOCIAL MEDIA

As a central figure in crime news, literature, television, and film, we can hardly over-state the importance of police to American culture. However, the rise of mobile and social media have already further revolutionized the production of the police image and the ways in which it is employed. Pragmatically, Facebook and Twitter are invaluable in publicizing public safety alerts in real time as well as responsibilizing the public, or encouraging them to take up quasi-police work themselves (taking steps to protect themselves and secure their property, engaging in surveillance, etc.). For instance, some community and neighborhood watch groups now use social media platforms like Twitter to communicate with members in real time. As one such community watch participant in Ohio explained, Twitter helps members communicate with themselves and the police:

> Suppose you hear a gunshot somewhere in the neighborhood but you don't know where it came from . . . I might call Dick: "Did you hear that?" And we all—at the same time—we call the police. Because the more police calls, the faster the response. (Associated Press, 2009)

Today, oftentimes in collaboration with providers like Twitter and Facebook, police use social media platforms to alert people of past crimes or the dangers of those ongo-ing; to encourage engagement with crime control programs such as Amber Alert; to monitor and investigate suspects; to obtain information about riots; and to uncover or illustrate criminal networks. And, as of 2016, U.S. Customs and Border Protection asks visitors to the U.S. to voluntarily provide each of their social media user names along with other identifying information (Brandom, 2016). When, in April 2016, the NYPD announced the arrests of 87 "Bronx gang members" (via a press release shared on its numerous social media accounts) in what it described as the "largest takedown in NYC history," news coverage also reported how the police had served an additional 100 search warrants on the social media accounts of others suspected to be involved (Bekiempis, Tracy, & McShane, 2016). As this case illustrates, it is clear that social media is a powerful resource for police, not only to disseminate information but also as a viable landscape in which to search for evidence of criminal activity. Hence, we can say quite literally that police patrol the virtual landscapes of cyberspace as they do city streets (see Jewkes & Yar, 2010; Yar, 2013). Commenting on this new terrain of social interaction, Hayward (2012a) notes that virtual and networked spaces facilitate processes that are productive of their own unique geographies and converge to produce their own material culture, such as "weightless money" and "weightless products" (commodities confined to the virtual/networked spaces of, say, video games). All of this already is presenting interesting questions for police and crime control. For instance, in 2012, a Dutch court convicted a teenager for the theft of property that did not exist outside the virtual world of the game *RuneScape*.

How police access and make use of virtual and networked spaces is further highlighted by a report commissioned by Lexis Nexis Risk Solutions (2012). In the report, an officer describes how he "friended" a suspected drug dealer from a fictitious profile and was then able to verify the suspect's known associates and track his movements. As the officer put it, "he kept 'checking in' everywhere he went so I was able to track him down very easily" (p. 14). In cooperation with the Police Executive Research Forum (PERF), the COPS (Community Oriented Policing Services) unit of the U.S. Department of Justice has also released its own guidelines for policing and social media, which interestingly place significant attention on policing protest. The report notes:

> Social media has now given protesters the ability to informally and very quickly organize and communicate with each other in real time. Police must know how to monitor these types of communications in order to gauge the mood of a crowd, assess whether threats of criminal activity are developing, and stay apprised of any plans by large groups of people to move to other locations.

> Similarly, in the aftermath of an incident of mob violence, police can "mine" social networking sites to identify victims, witnesses, and perpetrators. Witnesses to crime—and even perpetrators—often post photographs, videos, and other information about an incident that can be used as investigative leads or evidence. (U.S. Department of Justice, COPS, & Police Executive Research Forum, 2013, p. 1)

The report also notes the challenges of monitoring social networks, obstacles no doubt faced by the Boston Police Department and the Federal Bureau of Investigation (FBI) when investigating the 2013 marathon bombings (discussed in the Introduction to this volume). As one agent put it, making sense of the vast amounts of information produced by social media is like "trying to take a sip from a fire hydrant" (U.S. Department of Justice, COPS, & Police Executive Research Forum, 2013, p. 60). Of course, we should not assume that the difficulties in making sense of huge amounts of information are any sort of deterrent to police and security agencies. Indeed, since 9/11, policing and homeland security agencies have developed a network of more than 70 "fusion centers" designed to promote the gathering, synthesis, and dissemination of intelligence among agencies such as the Bureau of Alcohol, Tobacco, Firearms, and Explosives (ATF); the FBI; and the Central Intelligence Agency (CIA) down to small, local municipal police departments.

IMAGE MANAGEMENT

Of course, major U.S. police departments are supported by a raft of employees, including press officers, marketing professionals, public relations officers, and corporate identity specialists, all engaged in the business of image work on behalf of the police (Mawby, 2002). As Lee and McGovern (2014) describe, the police press release is a powerful tool for communicating the service's preferred message while making it easier for journalists to write audience-satisfying, sometimes salacious stories about crime and violence. However, the social media platforms now at their disposal help police in managing, or rather *producing,* their image in such a way that frequently bypasses journalists altogether. One of the most widespread yet rarely discussed representational strategies of police image work occurs when police agents report on a major arrest and/or seizure of property and stage promotional "trophy shot" photos with their haul (Linnemann, 2017). Because the most common artifacts of police trophy shots—weapons, drugs, money— are powerful symbols of crime and violence, such images, whether expertly crafted or impromptu, help to produce an affirmative police image by reminding the public of the work done by police on their behalf. In other words, each drug seizure, every firearm taken off the street, and the mountains of untaxed currency represent the violent illegality of the criminal underworld interrupted. As the caption to an NYPD trophy shot shared view Twitter reads, "our officers quick thinking and response, teamwork, and investigatory skills in this incident are helping keep #NYC safe." In images stripped of context, where trophies are celebrated in a manner reminiscent of a hunter posing with the carcass of a dead animal, such image work reinforces the myth of the thin blue line and the view of policing as a stridently "us-versus-them" endeavor, a war for civilization (T. Wall, 2016).

So while police agencies are increasingly called on to be accountable to diverse communities, there is an insidious dimension to their image work. Rob Mawby (2002, 2010) has argued that police may craft a false image or misrepresent themselves in order to mask malpractice, deflect responsibility, or simply insulate themselves from scrutiny. As the police trophy shot might suggest and as Nigel Green (2009) argues, some police forces elevate positive stories while simultaneously burying and diverting attention from cases that represent negative public relations. While the trophy shot is meant to communicate policing's good deeds, what is often obscured or ignored entirely is the practice of civil asset forfeiture—or, as critics describe it, "policing for profit"—in which police are permitted to seize essentially any item they believe is related to criminal activity (M. R. Williams, Holcomb, Kovandzic, & Bullock, 2010).

David Oliver, the so-called "celebrity chief" of the tiny Brimfield, Ohio, police department, provides another particularly interesting example of how police departments employ social media to engage the public and produce an affirmative police image. The BPD did not have a social media presence until Oliver began, in his words, to "call it as it is," offering an unvarnished and reactionary take on police work and lawbreakers. As Oliver explained, "the BPD's reputation within the community had not been great . . . I believed that civilians needed to see what we see and experience some of the highs and

PHOTO 6.3
A police agent poses for a trophy shot of seized drugs and money.

AP Photo/Norwich Bulletin, Khoi Ton

lows. I am also sort of a clown and like humor, so I figured I would write things from that perspective." (Oliver, 2013, as cited in Harper, 2015)

The folksy Oliver, who addressed his followers as "cousins" and took a cue from the TV detective Kojak naming arrestees "mopes," did not shy away from tough moralistic condemnation of his "clientele." Once Oliver began calling the arrested "mopes," posting sensational details about their behavior, offering his opinion on the causes of crime, and responding directly to the posts of the public, the popularity of the BPD's page exploded. At the time of writing, BPD's more than 160,000 Facebook followers eclipse those of larger and more celebrated departments in Boston, Philadelphia, and New York City.

Capitalizing on his popularity, Oliver published a book, *No Mopes Allowed*, and sold a variety of BPD "mope"-related trinkets such as T-shirts and coffee mugs. Interpreting, making claims about the world, or in his words, "telling it like it is," Oliver, like all police, is what Ian Loader calls a "legitimate namer" who possesses the power to "diagnose, classify, authorize and represent both individuals and the world" (Loader, 1997, p. 3). Yet what is perhaps more important to consider in the case of Oliver and the BPD is not only how social media encourage two-way, reciprocal communication but also the type of communication they inspire. Captured in real time through likes, comments, and shares, we are able to observe the coproduction of a distinct dimension of police legitimacy and power. Here Oliver's moralizing condemnation of criminal "mopes" licenses the public to assume and voice similar sentiment while also reaffirming a militaristic us-versus-them understanding of police work and social life. Not unlike those who take to message boards and the comments sections of online news articles and YouTube videos, particularly those dealing with controversial issues, Oliver's foray into social media illustrates how policing offers fertile ground for members of the public to voice staunchly pro-police views. And though a sexual harassment lawsuit forced Oliver to resign from the BDP in 2015 and momentarily muzzled "Chief Babble," other police administrators and public relations experts have no doubt taken notice and are looking to replicate the "overnight Internet sensation's" success in communicating with the public.

While police agencies of all kinds are turning to social media as an image management tool, as the NYPD's "motivational Monday" tweet at the beginning of the chapter details, even large, well-funded departments have yet to master the medium. Once again, the NYPD provides a tremendous example of a social media failure and more broadly how policing fails to control its own image. In early 2014, the New York Police Department launched a public relations social media campaign that encouraged members of the

Popular Resistance
@PopResistance

👤 Follow

#myNYPD trying to stop bystanders filming them is to prevent documentation of #policeBrutality popularresistance.org/street-protest …

We Wouldn't Know this man was Murdered by Cops

If someone hadn't videotaped it.

How many others do we not know about?

RETWEETS 36   LIKES 18

11:22 AM - 9 Aug 2014

↩ 4   ↻ 36   ♥ 18

Popular Resistance, popularresistance.org

PHOTO 6.4
The #mynypd campaign appropriated to publicize the killing of Eric Garner.

public to tweet photos of themselves with NYPD officers. The #myNYPD project quickly backfired, however, as users almost immediately began posting images of police misconduct and violence. Ironically, it was this campaign that helped bring national attention to and condemn the NYPD chokehold killing of Eric Garner.

The #myNYPD case and countless others demonstrate how the public is not simply a passive consumer of the police image but an active player in the contest over the production of the police image and hence police power. The increasingly visible role that mobile and social media play is particularly apparent in violent encounters between police and public where footage, images, and recordings are *absent*. One such instance occurred in the UK in the summer of 2011 when police shot and killed a 29-year-old man named Mark Duggan. After stopping the car that he was riding in, police shot Duggan twice as he attempted to flee, killing him at the scene. The killing touched off a powder keg of tensions directed toward the police, and two days later, riots began on the streets of London, which soon spread to many other cities, constituting the worst civil unrest in a generation. How and why Duggan's killing—which one police insider called a "death by a thousand fuckups"—actually occurred remains disputed and will likely never be known. However, despite witness testimony that Duggan was unarmed and holding only a mobile phone, that he appeared "trapped" and "baffled," held his arms up as if to surrender, and, when he tried to run away, was shot by an officer within five to seven steps of him, British courts found the killing "lawful" (*The Guardian*, January 8, 2014). The Independent Police Complaints Commission (IPCC) declared that Duggan was "probably" throwing a handgun away when he was shot by officers (http://www.bbc.co.uk/news/uk-england-32041119).

While the public may have grown to expect footage of such events and may now raise a skeptical eye when such evidence is absent, this does not mean a visual record will resolve instances of police violence to all parties' understandings. Indeed, one need only consider the recent deaths of Eric Garner, John Crawford III, Walter Scott, Tamir Rice, Alton Sterlin, and Philando Castile, all of which were recorded on handheld cell phone or surveillance cameras, to reckon the contested and sometimes ineffectual nature of video evidence. Yet even before the advent of cell phone cameras and social media, several high-profile cases had already cast significant doubt on the utility of images and video evidence as a method to arrest police violence. The most well-known and widely discussed of these cases, is of course, the 1991 beating of a black motorist named Rodney King by several members of the LAPD and California Highway Patrol. Filmed by a bystander named George Holliday from his apartment's balcony, the footage and King's battered face were seen by many as smoking-gun evidence of the LAPD's brutal history of racist violence and systematic terror. As Ice Cube, rapper, and founding member of Los Angeles's N.W.A. remarked, the sort of beating King suffered had "been happening to us for years. It's just we didn't have a camcorder every time it happened" (Kelley, 2000, p. 47). Despite the shocking footage and considerable public attention, just over a year later a mostly white jury (11 whites, 1 nonwhite) acquitted all four of the LAPD officers charged with brutalizing King. Soon after, riots engulfed Los Angeles. However, as Southern California's *Sublime* commented in their song "April 29, 1992 (Miami)," (you can find the lyrics at http://bit.ly/sublimelyrics), the Los Angeles riots were less about King's beating (and hence the video) and more about a long-standing history of police brutality, not confined to the LAPD.

Attempting to understand how seemingly irrefutable video evidence like Holliday's could fail to convince jurors of the officers' crimes, both Judith Butler (2013) and Allan Feldman (1994) have argued that the American public's embeddedness and complicity in histories of violence and domination prevents them from *seeing* even the most egregious acts of police violence as anything but justified. Here we might say that those who could *see* the savagery of the 56 baton blows suffered by King perhaps did not need to (they'd seen it before), and likewise, those who could not immediately recognize the violent criminality of the police perhaps never would. As Butler (2013) and Feldman (1994) assert, not only had America's legacy of racism prevented jurors from seeing King as anything but a black/criminal and thus deserving of his punishment, but we might also add that the police image (perpetually fabricated through cultural texts like Jack Webb's *Dragnet*) reinforced a worldview that always places the police on the right side of the thin blue line (Katherine Biber, 2007, notes a similar relationship between law and photography but is careful to document how the photograph is legitimized and often unquestioned when offered as evidence by state authorities).

Despite the failure to secure criminal convictions of the officers who battered Rodney King, community activists continue to place their faith in the power of visual evidence and social media as a method to rein in police misconduct (Doyle, 2003). Numerous groups—Cop Watch, Cop Block, Photography Is Not a Crime (to name a few)—organized with the expressed purpose of filming the police and providing training, organizational and tactical instruction, legal assistance, and even mobile phone applications to members of the public interested in the same. Many "cop watchers," in fact, credit Holliday's footage with providing a model of how everyday people might intervene in police violence (Doyle, 2003). Unsurprisingly, most police and police agencies do not welcome the intrusion of the camera-wielding public. Even though U.S. law authorizes photographing and filming of police, agencies and individual police officers continue to challenge the right of the public to record their activities. It is clear that unauthorized photography presents an image management challenge to police. As such, we can say that policing's attempt to control its own image is a recognition of an inversion of the traditional view of the police as the authorized watchers of a given society, to a synoptic relationship where "many in society are increasingly encouraged to watch and admire the ways of the powerful few" (R. Coleman, 2013, p. 142). Perhaps in recognition of the increasing faith the public places in the power of the image, the Obama administration recently committed some 75 million dollars to equip police with body-worn cameras and to study their effectiveness (Jackson, 2015). What this political move fails to recognize or address is that protests of the present are but the latest in a long, unbroken and grotesque train of abuses running through Baton Rouge, Ferguson, and Baltimore of the present; Los Angeles and Washington, DC, of the 1990s; Watts, Detroit, and Newark of the 1960s; and Harlem and Chicago during the earliest days of American policing (the majority of which predate the cell phone). In other words, untouched by the promise of synoptic video activism that tends to focus the camera on the misdeeds of individual officers is the broader question of policing's place in a free democratic society. Nevertheless, the language of "openness" remains embedded in police image work, and "body-cams" will no doubt be held up as an example by police forces as they espouse "open" communications and transparency in the effort to secure public "trust" and "confidence."

SUMMARY

- The media are not solely to blame for inciting fear of crime. Actual risk of victimization, previous experience of victimization, environmental conditions, ethnicity, and previous contact with the police and criminal justice system are among many factors interacting through complex mediated processes to influence public anxiety about crime. As Richard Sparks comments, "the reception by people of media stories about crime and punishment is best grasped ... in situ, in which case many public responses that are commonly deprecated by criminologists and others as 'irrational' or 'hysterical' tend to become substantially more intelligible" (2001, p. 197).

- However, the media might be said to play an important role in creating a cultural climate in which certain types of criminal behavior are portrayed more frequently, and with greater intensity, than others. This distortion may cultivate fears among certain sections of the audience and exaggerate their risk of victimization.

- Some critics argue that, as a consequence of the media's tendency to concentrate on the most atypical crimes and present them in a sensationalistic and voyeuristic manner, women and the elderly are socialized into fear and become oversensitized to their own roles in avoiding becoming victims of crime. However, victimization surveys consistently show that the young (ages 12 to 24) are more likely to be victims of violent crime. Men are slightly more at risk than women and blacks are more at risk than whites (see the most recent National Crime and Victimization Survey data at http://www.bjs.gov/content/pub/pdf/cv14.pdf).

- The mediated fear of crime is coupled with police image, which is produced and reaffirmed by a variety of cultural texts, thereby justifying the place of police in society (and their actions).

- Research shows that programs like *Cops* present a distorted view of police work at the nature of crime and victimization.

- The issue of policing has increasingly come to be understood not simply in its political or social context, but as a set of semiotic practices enmeshed with mediated culture (Ferrell, 2001). "Image work" is central to a police service that is increasingly coming to recognize that policing is as much about symbolism as it is about substance (Mawby, 2002).

- Both traditional media and "new" social media have changed the way that the police do their work and communicate with the public. Platforms such as Facebook and Twitter have a myriad of benefits for the police, from allowing recruitment personnel to covertly check on a candidate's suitability to join the police force to gathering intelligence and responsibilizing the public.

- But, as we've seen, new media have a democratizing role to play on occasions where the police (or individual officers) act inappropriately. During protest events such as demonstrations or riots, the battle to control the "virtual" version of events on Twitter can be every bit as important as what occurs on the ground.

- In recent years, the police have sought to embrace and exploit the media in pursuit of a positive, pro-police image and an impression of legitimacy and accountability.

STUDY QUESTIONS

1. Programs that focus on the police (*Cops, Law and Order, CSI*, etc.) are some of the longest-running and must viewed programs on network television. What accounts for the enduring popularity of such programming, particularly at a time when police seem to be under increased and considerable scrutiny?

2. Lee and McGovern (2014, p. 213) claim that Facebook and Crimestoppers are simply the new Neighborhood Watch: "traditional policing reframed ... through new technologies." Do you agree with this assessment? What can social media enable the police to do which they could not by traditional means?

3. Likewise, some commentators have questioned the ability of visual evidence to bring about substantial reform in the conduct and character of police. Do you agree with this assessment? How has visual evidence made an impact on policing? How has it not?

4. Conduct your own analysis of an episode of *Cops*. Compare and contrast the types of crimes contained therein with crime and victimization statistics provided by the Bureau of Justice Statistics (BJS.gov). How might such a program create a distorted view of police work and of crime and victimization more generally?

FURTHER READING

- The classic text on policing, crime, public disorder, and moral panics remains S. Hall et al.'s *Policing the Crisis: Mugging, the State and Law and Order* (1978), a UK-based book that has found a global audience. In 2013, a 35th-anniversary edition was published, containing two new chapters that explore the book's continued significance as well as a new preface and afterword in which each of the authors takes up a specific theme from the original book and interrogates it in light of current events and contexts.

- For a thorough and engaging take on the figure of the police in American culture from outside criminology, see Christopher Wilson's *Cop Knowledge: Police Power and Cultural Narrative in Twentieth-Century America*. (University of Chicago Press, 2000).

- Rob Mawby's *Policing Images: Policing, Communication and Legitimacy* (Willan/Routledge, 2002) was an early contribution on the "image work" that the police now have to engage in, and M. Lee and A. McGovern's *Policing and Media: Public Relations, Simulations and Communications* (Routledge, 2014) provides an up-to-date analysis.

- Christopher Schneider's *Policing and Social Media: Social Control in an Era of New Media* (Lexington Books, 2016) is another useful recent contribution.

- These other aspects of criminal justice, and their representations in the media, are explored in Yvonne Jewkes's "Media Representations of Criminal Justice" in *Student Handbook of Criminology and Criminal Justice*, edited by J. Muncie and D. Wilson (Cavendish, 2004).

Student Study Site

WANT A BETTER GRADE?

Get the tools you need to sharpen your study skills. Access practice quizzes, eFlashcards, SAGE journal articles, and more at study.sagepub.com/jewkesus.

Crime Movies and Prison Films

OVERVIEW

Chapter 7 provides:

- A consideration of the enduring appeal of crime movies.

- A discussion of some of the most popular crime film genres, including cop films, private eye movies, the Western, pirate films, gangster movies, and the gritty British crime film.

- An analysis of some of the main themes that commonly emerge within these genres, with a particular focus on the various forms of masculinity represented in crime movies.

- A discussion of the prison in cinema, its role as allegory, and its relationship to penal reform.

- A consideration of the documentary film.

- An exploration of what "remakes" of classic crime films can tell us about changing cultural attitudes toward crime and justice, using *The Taking of Pelham 123* as a case study.

KEY TERMS

- audience 172
- catharsis 173
- crime film 172
- documentary 183
- film noir 176
- genre 172
- media criminology 195
- narrative arc 173
- penal spectators 181
- realism 195
- remake 187

The crime movie is arguably the most enduring of all cinematic genres, which makes writing this chapter somewhat daunting. Where does one start and finish with a subject as vast as "**crime film**"? How does one condense into a single chapter movies as diverse as *Bullitt* (1968) and *Batman* (1989), *Murder on the Orient Express* (1974) and *Midnight Express* (1978), *Some Like It Hot* (1959) and *Heat* (1995), *Tightrope* (1984) and *Man on Wire* (2008), *Pirates of the Caribbean: The Curse of the Black Pearl* (2003) and *Captain Phillips* (2013)? The answer is that it is impossible. In its broadest sense, the "crime film" incorporates a wide array of **genres**, including cop dramas, gangster films, pirate movies, Westerns, private-eye films, classic "whodunnits," heist films, anime, and film noir. Because of this breadth, ultimately, all this chapter can do is introduce the reader to a few ideas and encourage further reading, contemplation, and viewing. The chapter discusses crime films, prison films, documentaries, and "remakes," and will largely focus on those films that have enjoyed significant commercial success. This highly selective and deliberately populist stance is in contrast to the method taken up by Nicole Rafter, who in her influential *Shots in the Mirror* chose to address "the best and most important crime films and avoid the worst and most trivial" in order to make observations about the operations of criminological theory in popular culture (2006, p. 8). While we do aim to integrate theory, the more modest aim of this chapter is to raise some interesting but exploratory issues about a handful of somewhat randomly selected films, which tie in to some of the themes raised elsewhere in this volume.

THE APPEAL OF CRIME MOVIES

As we have discussed, crime movies remain an incredibly popular genre among critics, scholars, and the public. While we have yet to put our finger on precisely what accounts for the genre's popularity, we suspect crime films capture the imagination of viewers in the same ways that everyday crime news does. Generally, crime movies focus on a particular criminal or event, a victim or an avenger (Leitch, 2002), and the similarities, differences, and interactions between these adversaries usually constitute an exciting and tension-building narrative. Another possible reason for their attraction is that they incorporate elements that appeal to the **audience**'s own antisocial or deviant tendencies, or their desire to live free outside the law and social order, or to their ambivalence toward the police and other authorities; hence the depiction of a corrupt, dysfunctional criminal justice system, staffed by equally incompetent or corrupt cops and judges. Sometimes viewers find themselves identifying with the villain rather than the hero, with even the most depraved antagonists somehow taking on the charisma of a leading man (Anthony Hopkins's portrayal of serial killer Hannibal Lecter in the 1991 film *The Silence of the Lambs*, for example). In the world of crime film, activities that in real life are in fact mundane or quite administrative—such as policing—can take on an aura of intrigue, glamour, and recklessness.

Some filmmakers and critics maintain that crime movies are, at their core, cathartic, allowing audiences to live out their normally suppressed deviant fantasies in a vicarious but harmless manner and giving them a glimpse of other worlds (from the gritty streets of New York's five boroughs, or a mob-run casino, to an Old West saloon) that may be unknown to them in the real world. In some cases, film may illuminate worlds that are not just unknown but unknowable to many viewers. Movies about prisons and the Mafia are just two examples of hidden social worlds and societies that are surrounded in myth, that fascinate and intrigue. Curiously, then, most people likely better know the silver screen approximation of these worlds than their realities. Likewise, since few people have firsthand experience or knowledge about prison life or organized crime, their expectations about them tend to come straight from the movies, and even more oddly, some may model their identities, personas, or modes of behavior after characters in films who may have never existed (Jewkes, 2002; Larke, 2003; Fiddler, 2007; M. Parker, 2009b).

Audiences may also achieve **catharsis** through the conversion of potentially unbearable social anxieties into entertainment, as latent moral panics are scaled down from the global to the subcultural and threats as diverse as terrorism, invading aliens, and natural disasters are vanquished by charismatic heroes within the comfortably generic lines of the crime film (Leitch, 2002). Alternatively, as noted in Chapter 1, the media's inclination to make all audience members equal in their potential "victimness" may result in an obsessive preoccupation with such narratives. Consequently, like all other media, films may represent a hysterical replaying of the possibility of being a victim and staving it off (Osborne, 1995). It could be that crime movies appeal simply because they permit closure: they reassure us that criminal behaviors *can* be explained and that serious offences *can* be solved. They offer immutable definitions of the "crime problem" and guide our emotional responses to it (Rafter, 2007).

While much of the appeal lies in the thrill inherent in most crime film genres— the pursuit of the killer, the car chase, the shootout, the clever buildup of tension, or whatever—these scenes are often little more than set pieces that would leave the audience disappointed and unfulfilled if left out. Many crime films have a limited **narrative arc** and are relatively predictable in terms of their structure, storyline, and dialogue. For example, each of the five films of the *Dirty Harry* franchise follows the familiar narrative of the ruthless cop running down a collection of rather one-dimensional villains. Likewise, gangster or "mob" movies also tend to have a structure formed, in part, by adherence to a particular formula. Based on unquestioning loyalty to the "family," honoring one's debts, and regarding the "godfather" or gang leader with a mixture of fear and respect, the group is constituted as the supreme social authority and, while the rules are frequently broken, with double-crossing and dealing providing much of the pace and anticipation of the genre (as well as underlining the message that crime doesn't pay), the social structure and unshakable authority of the patriarchal family remains intact. There is a strong, recognizable lineage that takes us from the first gangster films, *Underworld* (1927), *Little Caesar* (1931), *The Public Enemy* (1931), and *Scarface* (1932), through *The Godfather* trilogy (1972, 1974, 1990) and *Goodfellas* (1990) to Guy Ritchie's parodic *Lock Stock and Two Smoking Barrels* (1998) and *Snatch* (2000) and Quentin Tarantino's even more stylized celebrations of gangsterdom in *Reservoir Dogs* (1991) and *Pulp Fiction* (1994). We understand each by reference to the others, and it is partly the audience's assured familiarity with the codes and conventions of the genre that accounts for their continuing success (Langford, 2005). Finally, the message that crime doesn't pay also frequently underpins movies based on real-life stories—for example, *Goodfellas* (1990), *Blow* (2001), *Black Mass* (2015)—even if they have spent the best part of two hours demonstrating quite graphically that it does.

THE CRIME MOVIE: MASCULINITY, AUTONOMY, THE CITY

The comforting familiarity of formula also extends to cinematic themes. Indeed, there are a strikingly small number of key premises and characterizations that shape many crime movies. One theme that appears to run through all crime genres is a particular type of "manliness," a rugged masculinity that combines with heroic agency (Sparks, 1996) to form a self-confident and self-reliant protagonist. The "tough guy" has been a staple of cinema since the first gangster movies of the 1920s and early 1930s. Exemplified by characters such as Tony Camonte in *Scarface* (1932) and Tom Powers in *The Public Enemy* (1931), strong heroes—even if violent criminals—held huge appeal for American audiences in the Depression era who were disenchanted by authority and wanted to take control of their lives (Leitch, 2002).

Since that time, crime films have presented an archetype of individualistic masculinity set against larger forces, whether the wide expanse of the high seas or high plains (and the primitives who inhabit these territories) or the formal, occupational organizations and structures that contain and curtail their individual autonomy and maverick tendencies. Again, cop films are dominated by the myth of the solitary cop who fights crime as well as the bureaucracy and incompetence of his own police department, or at least refuses to play by the rules (Carrabine, 2008). In addition to being monotonous and isolated at work, the cop's personal life is often dogged by alcoholism, interpersonal strife and despair, and a lonely isolation that has been described as "the most immutable of all the genre's conventions" (Leitch, 2002, p. 222). With the "godfather," Don or Boss, standing in as the patriarchal head or alpha male of the genre, the gangster film can thus be read as a "fantasy of a secret society with masculine rituals" (Larke, 2003, p. 128). Likewise, the pirate film—from the swashbuckling epics of the first half of the 20th century that showcased matinee idols such as Errol Flynn and Tyrone Power to the recent *Pirates of the Caribbean* series—has been characterized as "a man fighting for the right in a world that does not understand the right as he sees it" (Parish, 1995, p. 3, as cited in M. Parker, 2009a, p. 174). Regarding the place of the pirate in the contemporary political imagination, Mark Neocleous has recently charged that:

> Johnny Depp has a lot to answer for. If there is one figure that might be said to compete with the Zombie as representing the early twenty-first century zeitgeist, it is the Pirate. Pirates are now one of the most popular children's characters, more than a few sports teams openly identify themselves as pirates . . . there is an "International Talk Like a Pirate Day," radical groups are setting themselves up as Pirate Parties, and cinemas are full with films of swashbuckling and adoringly roguish pirates with whom the audience are clearly meant to identify

or fall in love. I doubt all of these are down to Johnny Depp, but they do all capture some aspect or other of the romantic myth of the pirate as a nomadic and brave figure exercising liberty and alternative form of existence beyond the normal strictures of bourgeois civilization. (Neocleous, 2016, p. 105)

The freedom, solitude, and resourcefulness evoked by the romanticism of the pirate are nearly identical to that of the gunfighters and lawmen of *Westerns*. This sort of fanciful individualism appears to have a near-universal appeal to men and boys, and it is "fair to say that in the minds of many men, even if only for fleeting moments, there's a hankering to be as free and rugged, as engaging and boisterous, as hardworking, daring and independent, as truly American, as the cowboy" (Hassrick, 1974, p. 139, as cited in Parker, 2012, p. 77). Again, the many films of Clint Eastwood, who became a star in Westerns before Dirty Harry Callahan, powerfully illustrate this point. From *A Fistful of Dollars* (1964) and *High Plains Drifter* (1974) to *Unforgiven* (1992), Eastwood's films powerfully display the ideology of redemptive and purgative violence. Here the violence of the Old West represents a temporary regression to a more primitive or natural state, in which violence redeems the "American spirit or fortune," oftentimes by cleansing, eliminating, or purging the outlaw/savage/other from the film's imagined landscape (Plantinga, 1998, p. 65).

Whereas Westerns tend to offer an appreciative and liberatory view of violence, *heist films* tend to feature a decidedly masculine and professional criminality, put to work in pursuit of "one last big score" or the "perfect crime." While the "big job" often provides the means to retire from the criminal career of the professional thief and thus an avenue to freedom, this sort of film also tends to illustrate how the criminal lifestyle takes precedent over family and personal relationships (Rayner, 2003). Take, for instance, Michael Mann's highly regarded film *Heat* (1995), starring Robert DeNiro as Neil McCauley, the masterful leader of a crew of skilled armed robbers, and Al Pacino as Vincent Hanna, the LAPD detective bent on taking him down (both characters are based on real people). In a crucial scene, McCauley and Hanna face off at a diner over coffee and lament the costs of their professions:

> [Vincent Hanna] My life's a disaster zone. I got a stepdaughter so fucked up because her real father's this large-type asshole. I got a wife, we're passing each other on the down-slope of a marriage—my third—because I spend all my time chasing guys like you around the block. That's my life.

> [Neil McCauley] A guy told me one time, "Don't let yourself get attached to anything you are not willing to walk out on in 30 seconds flat if you feel the heat around the corner." Now, if you're on me and you gotta move when I move, how do you expect to keep a . . . a marriage? (Mann, 1995)

As this bit of dialogue details nicely, in the heist film, cop and criminal are inseparable—self-justifying sides of the same coin—locked into a narrative that rarely ends well for the thief and sometimes not for the cop. A more complex narrative is employed by film noir, which may be read as a definition and defense of masculinity as the hard-boiled hero grapples with "the dangers represented by the feminine—not just women in themselves but also any non-'tough' potentiality of his own identity as a man" (Leitch, 2002, p. 72; see also Krutnik, 1991). In short, the hero embodies a charismatic, self-contained hypermasculinity. He may be unusual, unpleasant even, but he is always a "complete man" (Chandler, 1944, as cited in Sparks, 1996). The detective or private eye—who often appears in film noir—is sometimes described as the urban cowboy of the screen, with masculinity once again a defining feature:

> The popular image of the private eye has less to do with his idealized, often obsessive professionalism, however, than with his masculinity. Far more than films about police detectives or amateur detectives, [private eye] films regard detective work as a test of what Frank Krutnik calls the private eye's "self-sufficient phallic potency." This convention is so deeply ingrained in private eye films that it is hard to appreciate how arbitrary and strange it is . . . there is no reason to assume that testosterone ought to be a prerequisite for the job. (Leitch, 2002, p. 197)

Leitch goes on to explain that the genre's celebration of masculinity is exemplified by the classic film *The Maltese Falcon* (1941), in which the private eye hero, Sam Spade (Humphrey Bogart), is pitched against a voracious femme fatale and three men clearly characterized as homosexuals. Spade is thus "admirably, heroically masculine" precisely because he is not female and not gay; thus the private eye's manliness must constantly be confirmed through conflicts with asexual or bisexual characters—or more often with female or gay male characters—whom the film leaves "demystified, disempowered, defeated and dehumanized" (Leitch, 2002, p. 198). That is not to say that all cinematic heroes are the same or even that their (hetero)sexuality is as clearly defined as Leitch's description suggests. As broad as the genre is, crime films invariably provide a multitude of masculinities within a diverse array of settings and narratives (Sparks, 1996). In fact, Jude Davies and Carol Smith (1997, p. 19) go so far as to suggest that since the late 1980s, representations of white males as domesticated, feminized, or paternal have dominated film genres to such a degree that it is only in the films of Quentin Tarantino that "macho masculinity" (which we might characterize as violent and uncompromising, although always underpinned by wit and humor) remains intact. This seems an overstatement and one that overlooks that even "macho masculinity" can have many facets. It is also worth remembering that some of Tarantino's regular cast members have taken a Tarantino-esque version of masculinity into other roles, as the discussion below of John Travolta's character in *The Taking of Pelham 123* will illustrate.

Furthermore, hyperbolized representations of masculinity may be tied to particular political and cultural contexts and thus cyclical. Similar to the observations of Klockars regarding Dirty Harry Callahan (see Chapter 6), Richard Sparks suggests that the exaggerated muscularity of Schwarzenegger, Stallone, and other 1980s action stars may have been in reaction to the instability of masculine gender identity at the time (i.e., the domesticated, feminized, and paternal roles to which Davies and Smith refer).

Relative to the decline of Terminator and Rambo, we have seen a new type of hero emerge, personified by *The Bourne Identity* (2002) and its sequels. While Bourne is undeniably an action hero, actor Matt Damon has said of his character: "Bourne is about authenticity, not fashion, frippery and style. He's about essence and, unlike Bond, you'd never see him watching a girl coming out of the sea with a bikini on. There's none of those old-fashioned macho attitudes" (Lawrence, 2007). Ironically, Bourne might not be directing his gaze at the near-naked female form, but it seems that it is not just representations of women that are erotically charged in mainstream cinema. The appeal—to men rather than women—of the proficient violence of Bourne and muscular physiques of Stallone and Schwarzenegger are summed up by Sparks, following Laura Mulvey, as a "narcissistic identification of the male spectator with images of mastery and omnipotence" (Sparks, 1996, p. 352). To these former action heroes we might add Daniel Craig as James Bond in *Casino Royale* (2006), emerging from the sea in his swimming trunks in a pastiche of the iconic moment in another Bond film, *Dr. No* (1962), where Ursula Andress steps from the sea in a white bikini.

Of course, Johnny Depp as the Keith Richards–inspired camp pirate Jack Sparrow in the *Pirates of the Caribbean* series also embodies the male beauty and joyous love of adventure that marked the classic prewar films about outlaws and pirates and were intended to appeal to men and women equally (M. Parker, 2009a). It is also not the case that there is no female counterpart to the masculine hero; there are, of course, examples of women leads in Westerns (*Calamity Jane*, 1953; *The Missing*, 2003; *Jane Got a Gun*, 2016), cop films (*Blue Steel*, 1989; *Fargo*, 1996), assassin movies (*Kill Bill*, volumes I and II, 2003 and 2004; *Salt*, 2010), films about serial killers (*Natural Born Killers*, 1994; *Monster*, 2003), pirate films (*Cutthroat Island*, 1995), films about outlaws and crime sprees (*Bonnie and Clyde*, 1967; *Spring Breakers*, 2013), buddy/road movies (*Thelma and Louise*, 1991), and "girls-with-guns" (e.g., in countless Japanese anime films—and films starring Angelina Jolie), but they are anomalies. For Martin Parker, these heroines are interesting, and might be celebrated as examples of a feminist politics, but this is largely because there are so few examples of women in these genres, and he notes that, in the main, women are still portrayed in fairly predictable ways:

> The suffering housewife, the raped hostage, the accomplice in love, the golden hearted prostitute and so on. Women usually only make sense in relation to men, and are found in homes, towns and gardens, looking after men, yearning for men, being wounded by men. The Western director Budd Boetticher put it neatly (though without any obvious irony) when he suggested that a woman's job . . . is to react. "In herself she has no significance whatsoever." (M. Parker, 2009a)

Raewyn Connell (formerly Robert Connell)—who popularized the term "hegemonic masculinity"—concurs, arguing that while there is "a bewildering variety of traits considered characteristic of women" (1987, p. 183), there is no superordinate version of femininity that is deemed more structurally powerful than others. *All* versions of femininity are subordinate to the patriarchal power of men.

While numerous crime films have left their mark upon American popular culture, few have had such a widespread and lasting influence as *Scarface* (1983). Taking inspiration from the 1932 film of the same name, *Scarface* was directed by Brian de Palma (*The Untouchables,* 1987; *Carlito's Way,* 1993) and written by Oliver Stone (*Platoon,* 1986; *Born on the Fourth of July,* 1989). Chronicling the meteoric rise of Cuban refugee Antonio "Tony" Montana (Al Pacino) from an exiled, petty street tough to the ruthless kingpin of a Miami cocaine empire, *Scarface* gave viewers a dark and particularly violent view of the American Dream and its terrifying entanglements with the burgeoning war on drugs. Brimming with memorable, repeatable one-liners ("Say hello to my little friend!"), mantras ("The world is yours!"), and scenes like the one where Montana slams his face into a huge pile of cocaine before taking up an assault rifle and shooting it out with members of an invading cartel, the film remains a vibrant cultural referent more than 30 years after its debut.

The staying power of *Scarface* is particularly interesting when one considers that the film was panned by critics for its gratuitous violence and crude racial caricatures and likewise ignored by viewers, managing to take in the relatively paltry sum of 44 million at the box office, a figure that placed it well down the list of the year's top-grossing films. However, since its home video release, *Scarface* has become a cult classic, driven largely by younger viewers. From collector's edition box sets, prints, posters, and T-shirts to replica switchblades, sunglasses, and paraphernalia of all kinds, *Scarface* is its own cottage industry some 30 years on. Yet, as Curtis Marez (2004) suggests, in addition to its violent take on American meritocracy, the film's innovative use of military-grade weapons and gun battles, both as aesthetic props and a narrative device, is perhaps the film's most notable contribution to the crime film genre and popular culture more generally. In fact, *Scarface* is the first major film to make use of a synchronizer that times the frames of the cinematographer's camera with the muzzle flash of automatic weapons fire, thereby making "the automatic weapon an extension of the camera" (Marez, 2004, p. 14). Marez suggests that films like *Scarface* made the assumed overnight success of the drug trade and its violent "get rich or die trying" ethos a key feature of the burgeoning youth hip-hop culture. From rappers like Future, who in his 2012 tune "Tony Montana" sings, "I take over the streets, fresh off the banana boat . . . The money got me geeked like I took a hit of coca, my life is a movie I gotta stay focused," to the subtler nod from Nas's (1994) "The World Is Yours," the material success, ruthlessness, and violent death prominently featured in *Scarface* are themes that continue to pervade hip-hop.

The 1980s also saw the emergence of postmodern fables offering a nightmare vision of middle America. Epitomized by David Lynch's *Blue Velvet* (1986), these portrayals "mingled cloyingly saccharine glimpses" of small-town America with "horrific revelations about its psychosexual underside" (Leitch, 2002, p. 48). Set in a sleepy North Carolina logging town, *Blue Velvet* also powerfully demonstrates how a film's landscape or setting, and the ways in which it is imaged by its producers, oftentimes operates as a character in itself. For a contemporary example, consider the acclaimed 2010 crime thriller *Winter's Bone,* which follows a tough-as-nails teen girl named Ree Dolly, played by Jennifer Lawrence, as she unravels the fate of her missing meth-cook father. Dolly cares for her two younger siblings and invalid mother, rattles the tight-lipped locals for clues about her father's death, and challenges the law, bondsmen, and bankers looking to foreclose the family's home with the tenacity of a dog digging for a "winter's bone." As one critic described, the film "is set in the bleak chill of southwest Missouri in its starkest season, when the trees are black spikes and the hills are bleached silver and rust" (Ulaby, 2011). Shot on location in a "painfully poor" part of the country, "where the illegal methamphetamine trade flourishes," the foreboding backwoods landscape "shapes the bodies and lines the faces of the people who live there," playing a role as central to the film's narrative as is the unbreakable Dolly's (Ulaby, 2011).

While *Blue Velvet* (1986), *Winter's Bone* (2010), and others demonstrate how crime films stretch across landscapes of all kinds, the genre is nevertheless decidedly urban in texture. From the very first gangster "talkie," *The Lights of New York* (1928), to contemporary films such as *The Taking of Pelham 123* (2009), discussed below, New York City in particular has lent vividness, thrill, and menace to the cinematic imagination. This assertion is perhaps best demonstrated by the films of Martin Scorsese, many of which, such as *Mean Streets* (1973), *Taxi Driver* (1976), *Goodfellas* (1990), *Gangs of New York* (2002), and *The Wolf of Wall Street* (2013), are synonymous with his native Queens. Here we might also borrow from David Schmid's observations on the city's role in detective fiction. Schmid argues that in detective fiction—much of which has transitioned from the page to the screen—the scene of the crime is never simply a one-dimensional backdrop but rather is always an active player in the mystery. As such, the city has as much to tell us about crime, violence, and human nature as do the detective, femme fatal, and murderer:

> . . . space is never reduced to a neutral setting or backdrop for the action of the stories; rather, the spaces of detective fiction are always integral to the texts of detective fiction . . . we might say that the "real content" of detective fiction is a "scenic one" (124), in that the spaces of the genre are always "productive" of the crime they contain and structure, forcing the detective to engage with the setting she/he inhabits in order to understand and therefore solve the crime. (Schmid, 1995, p. 244)

Following Schmid, we can say that the crime film has shaped not only how the city is imagined, but how its safety, or lack thereof, is as well. Because of its prominence as a widely recognized world city, the early popularity of film noir, and the subsequent Italian mafia/gangster genre, New York is perhaps the most notable crime-film city, making it feel well known even to those who have never visited except through its depiction in film (television programs, fiction, and song lyrics). Once known for relatively high levels of violent crime and now touted by some as America's safest big city, the foreboding image of 1980s New York City has been and still is the backdrop for countless crime films, and its streets and subways, courtrooms, and police department (NYPD) are familiar to audiences around the world. While Los Angeles and Chicago are also iconic settings (particularly for private eye/film noir and mob films, respectively), no other city comes close to NYC for its number of instantly recognizable locations and landmarks; since 2001, films that feature the World Trade Center have added to its iconic standing.

For instance, *Man on Wire* (2008), the Oscar-winning documentary about Frenchman Philippe Petit's daring tightrope walk between the twin towers in August 1974, and its subsequent dramatic interpretation, *The Walk* (2015), starring Joseph Gordon-Levitt, both depict what has been described variously as a "real-life heist" and "the artistic crime of the century."

THE "PRISON FILM"

The inclusion of the "prison film" in a book about "media and crime" might seem controversial. Crime and punishment are, after all, quite different entities. And though "crime" may only be implied in punishment, prison films almost always take up the subject of crimes, whether they be those committed by corrupt and sadistic prison guards, judges and attorneys, or an actual person responsible for the plight of the wrongly accused and imprisoned. Regardless of issues of definition, we simply must address prison films because of their sheer popularity, both among the cinemagoing public and with academic scholars (see, e.g., Brown, 2009; Jarvis, 2004; P. Mason, 2006; Nellis & Hale, 1982; Rafter, 2000; D. Wilson and O'Sullivan, 2004). As Mike Nellis (1982, p. 6) observes, "no other type of crime film—the gangster movie, the police procedural movie and the characteristically English murder-mystery—has claimed such impressive credentials in its bid for genre status." The author of several publications on the prison film genre, Paul Mason (2008), concurs, commenting that most people could probably name several films about prison, and he speculates that most lists would feature *The Birdman of Alcatraz* (1962), *Cool Hand Luke* (1967), *Papillon* (1973), *Midnight Express* (1978), *Brubaker* (1980), *McVicar* (1980), *Scum* (1983), *The Green Mile* (1999), and, indisputably *The Shawshank Redemption* (1994), which, nearly two decades after its original release, still tops many viewers' polls of their favorite films of all time. Among academic treatments of the genre, *I Am a Fugitive From a Chain Gang* (1932) and *The Big House* (1931) are commonly discussed, and, although unlikely to have been seen by the majority of this book's readers, many of the themes they deal with—the banality and repetitiveness of the prison regime, the limited movement afforded prisoners, the brutality of the chain gang, and so on—are familiar to modern audiences.

However, many "prison films" are not really about prison at all but could actually be set in any number of other environments. Like the mob or gangster movie, the prison lends itself to being used allegorically; and like those genres, a staggering number of American prison films were made in the 1930s—the decade of the economic depression—in part because the prison offered filmmakers a metaphor for the disempowerment, injustice, and isolation felt by the masses (Mason, 2008; see Chapter 1 of this volume for a discussion of "mass society"). Incarceration has also commonly been used as a backdrop for tales about individual perseverance and the indomitable human spirit, whereby the viewer is encouraged to empathize with the prisoner and share in the highs and lows of his or her journey of self-discovery. The central protagonist may have been wrongfully convicted, as Andy Dufresne (played by Tim Robbins) was in *The Shawshank Redemption,* but even when this is not the case, prisoners are often portrayed as old-style romantic heroes struggling to beat (or at least survive) the system.

One of the reasons for the popularity of the prison film is that the prison is a highly ordered, repetitive, and restrictive institution and can therefore give a film an immediate structure and rhythm. Mason (2003b) characterizes the cinematic prison as a dehumanizing "machine" with an impenetrable set of rules and regulations that grind on relentlessly, and he notes that the convention of prison films to continually repeat shots of inmates doing the same tasks—whether it is walking the tiers, moving around the "yard," standing in line for "chow," stamping license plates, or breaking rocks—is a powerful visual reminder to the audience of the brutal monotony of the prison. Just as former prisoner and celebrated author Jack Henry Abbott likened imprisonment to being *In the Belly of the Beast* (1981), Mason notes how the representation of the prison as a machine is fundamental to the prison film, for it is from this metaphor that other themes flow: "escape from the machine, riot against the machine, the role of the machine in processing and rehabilitating inmates, and entering the machine from the free world as a new inmate" (2003b, p. 291).

As with crime films, there are a limited number of plots employed by the prison film genre—Nellis (1982) suggests no more than a dozen—and for the audience there is a certain gratification to be had from the predictability of character traits and plot devices. Images of rock-breaking chain gangs, the admissions process and strip search, the broad black-and-white stripes or bright orange uniform, and terrifying scenes of solitary confinement are part and parcel of most people's understanding of imprisonment and have become iconic symbols associated with loss of liberty. Drawing on Dante Alighieri's *Inferno,* Jewkes (2014) goes further, arguing that the prison must be understood through the lens of darkness and lightness and Heaven and Hell, and that these metaphors—which underpin numerous cinematic portrayals—serve to justify and authorize the prison as an infernal *hell-hole* (on this, recall that solitary confinement, prison within the prison, is commonly known as "the hole"). Of course, prison films also lend themselves to gratuitous and commercially profitable themes such as sex and violence, with violent assaults, riots, and rapes being far more common in cinematic jails than they are in most real-life prisons. Despite the rather large subgenre of sexploitation films that feature women in prison, which no doubt influenced the popular Netflix series *Orange Is the New Black* (2013–), it goes without saying that, with a few dubious exceptions (e.g., *Girls in Prison,* 1956, and *Chicks in Chains,* 1982), prison films are by and large about men.

The Prison Film and the Power to Reform?

That the prison is frequently depicted as a brutal institution that punishes, degrades, and humiliates might be said to present opportunities for those concerned about prison reform to initiate public debates about the futility and inhumanity of incarceration. However, Mason (2008) argues that a closer reading of most prison films reveals not only a reluctance to challenge the existing penal system but also a voyeuristic obsession with interpersonal violence. Mason's observations are similar to those of Michelle Brown (2009), who points to a wide variety of cultural texts, least of all the prison film, as a site where **penal spectators** participate in the moral condemnation inherent in punishment as disconnected observers. Even when the audience is encouraged to empathize with the prisoner protagonist, it is largely at the expense of other prisoners, who are depicted as dehumanized monsters and animals:

> While the prison hero/ine is afforded character, emotional development and agency, the rest of the jail is mere cardboard cut-out and cliché. Consequently, prison is constructed as necessary to keep such psychotic deviants caged and incapacitated and the public safe. (Mason, 2008)

An example that illustrates this point well is the 1997 film *Con Air*, which, if not set in a prison, *is* about prisoners, and stars Nicholas Cage as the "prisoner-good-guy," formerly a highly decorated United States Army Ranger who accidentally killed a man who was attacking his pregnant wife. After seven years in a federal penitentiary, our hero implausibly finds himself on a plane transporting some of America's most violent criminals to a newly built maximum-security prison. Predictably enough, the cons take over the aircraft, killing the prison guards and diverting the plane to Las Vegas. Led by Cyrus "The Virus" Grissom (played by John Malkovich), who charmingly claims to have "killed more people than cancer," this motley bunch of serial killers, drug smugglers, kidnappers, and rapists do nothing to challenge stereotypes of the prison population as almost supernatural inhuman "others." Indeed, in persisting in portraying "the vilest aspects of prison life" (Cheatwood, 1998, p. 210), the movie industry might be said to be endorsing the view that penal reform is undesirable and unachievable.

Thomas Mathiesen (2001) argues that cardboard-cutout and clichéd portrayals of prisoners as brutal, violent, and ultimately irredeemable thugs has a role in making prison population growth acceptable to—or at least unquestioned by—the public. For Mathiesen, the problem is not simply that the American public turns a blind eye to its swelling prison population, but that the picture they *do* receive of imprisonment is grossly misrepresented. Some commentators have suggested that, given that most of us will never even see a prison firsthand (it is probably the least visible part of the penal system), the prison film stands in for the real thing (Fiddler, 2007), and, in celebrating prison violence and encouraging voyeuristic participation among the audience, the prison film even has echoes of the spectacle of public executions described by Foucault (1977) in the *ancien regime,* with the film-viewing audience replacing the crowd at the gallows (Jarvis, 2004; Mason, 2003a; Sparks, 1992). Furthermore, films that are set in the future—*Fortress* (1992), *Face/Off* (1997), *Minority Report* (2002), and *Escape Plan* (2013), among others—may offer a terrifying if not implausible glimpse at the future of criminal punishment (while not a prison film, 1971's *A Clockwork Orange* is a powerful example of such dystopian visions). The prison of the (near) future is automated, dehumanized, and secret, and it is run by sadistic and corrupt wardens working for faceless global corporations. Welcome to the dystopian world of "Technocorrections" (Nellis, 2006, p. 226).

Of course, some might say, "Why *should* cinema have a reforming agenda?" There are many reasons why audiences are drawn to particular films, not least because of the quality or celebrity status of the actors appearing in them, and the notion of being educated at the cinema may not have mass appeal. In the end, films are primarily about entertainment, and even when film producers do try to make a case for prison reform, their efforts may be open to misinterpretation (Nellis, 1982). Further, any inherent messages that movies may carry about the inappropriateness of certain aspects of punishment in a civilized society must compete with other media portrayals that Paul Mason characterizes as "bottom-up pressure from an angry public, driven onwards by screaming red-top headlines, demands [for] more displays of repressive punishment: longer prison sentences, boot camps . . ." (2006, p. 1). This is why, despite the considerable quantity of prison films made over the last 100 years, few (if any) have done anything to challenge the institution of the prison. Indeed, as filmmaking has become more sophisticated, able to show ever more graphic scenes designed to shock and titillate, so society has accepted—demanded, even—more brutal, retributive, and humiliating forms of punishment (Jewkes, 2014). For many observers, it is of little surprise, then, that for most of the last century, the production and popularity of prison cinema has grown in line with actual incarceration rates. It is also why—despite the heart-wrenching depictions of capital punishment in films such as *Dead Man Walking* (1995) and *The Life of David Gale* (2003)—ever-sensationalized real-life offenses are frequently greeted by politicians, commentators, and newspaper readers with demands for its greater use.

THE DOCUMENTARY

Before closing this section on crime films and prison films and going on to discuss the "remake," it is worth considering a genre that has a more explicit agenda in bringing to public attention the social contexts of crime and the realities of the experience of imprisonment—the documentary. Usually made for television rather than theatrical release, there has been a long tradition of postwar television documentaries, which aim to narrate social history from below. Among the most influential is HBO's *Paradise Lost* trilogy, which deals with a small rural community's panic-stricken hunt for the murderer/s of three young boys and the eventual arrest, prosecution, and condemnation of three older boys, labeled "freaks" and "Satanists," ostensibly for their love of heavy-metal music and dark clothing. The first of the series, *Paradise Lost: The Child Murders at Robin Hood Hills* (1996), detailed the shoddy investigation and "modern day witch hunt" in such a stark and convincing manner that it not only spawned two sequels, *Revelations* (2000) and *Purgatory* (2011), but also drew significant public and celebrity attention to the case, thereby fueling an independent investigation that carried on long after the West Memphis 3 (as they had come to be known) had been sentenced to prison. With celebrities such as Henry Rollins, Eddie Vedder, and Johnny Depp as faces of public support, the investigation uncovered evidence that helped free the three, in August 2011, after more than 18 years. Not only was the trilogy instrumental in helping correct an egregious miscarriage of justice, but it has since inspired various commentaries, books, a fourth documentary produced by Peter Jackson (*West of Memphis,* 2012), and a dramatic interpretation of the case staring Reese Witherspoon and Colin Firth (*Devils Knot,* 2013).

Another form of prison documentary is characterized by the popular A&E series *Beyond Scared Straight.* Taking its name from the popular 1970s documentary series *Scared Straight,* the television adaptation, *Beyond Scared Straight,* focuses on delinquent youth ordered to adult prisons for "shock incarceration" and the crude counseling of adult inmates and prison staff. Innovated in the mid-1970s, such programs were widespread in the United States and often assigned as a condition of juvenile probation. The mix of seedy prison life with punitive "in-your-face" scare tactics made both the original *Scared Straight* films (four in total) and the more recent television series quite popular. What is often overlooked, however, is the considerable amount of academic research that has shown such programs not only to be ineffective in their stated mission of reducing youthful offending but also possibly actually encouraging of such behaviors. In fact, research findings were so conclusive that, in the late 1990s, the U.S Department of Justice's Office of Juvenile Justice and Delinquency Programs (OJJDP) defunded "shock incarceration" programs and discouraged their use nationwide. Nevertheless, in 2011, A&E launched its popular series prompting OJJDP officials to disavow "scared straight" tactics, stating, "The fact that [scared straight] programs are still being touted as effective, despite stark evidence to the contrary is troubling" (OJJDP, 2011). In contrast to the positive outcomes of the *Paradise Lost* films and others such as *The Thin Blue Line*, the continued popularity of *Beyond Scared Straight*, despite evidence of its harmful effects and exploitative nature, demonstrates how the documentary continues to be seen by *penal spectators* as simply a form of entertainment, however realistic.

Documentary as Ethnography

Nevertheless, documentaries resonate with the work of ethnographic researchers who revisit the field, seek to create coherent narratives from an excess of material, and confront ethical dilemmas as they investigate the private lives of subjects (Thorne, 2009). Making the case for the documentary film to be viewed as academic text, documentary filmmaker and criminologist David Redmon suggests:

> Documentary criminology embraces an interpretive analysis of lived experience, and adds to written scholarship by actively producing and disseminating audiovisual experiences as sensorial knowledge to help shape a criminological imagination. The substance of sensory knowledge is the fleeting patterns of lived, aesthetic experiences recorded as movements, sounds, colors, and atmospheres. Criminological filmmaking explores, records, and crafts these aesthetic experiences into a documentary with interpretive sensibilities and cinematic conventions that can be disseminated as public criminology. The documentary is an innovative object and also a vibrant representation of knowledge in the public sphere. Documentary criminology therefore creates a vibrant object (e.g., the documentary itself) that can be digitally disseminated as public criminology in various audiovisual formats and popular venues. (Redmon, 2015, p. 426)

While the documentary genre appears to offer transparency and honesty, it is, of course, within the power of the director to control, manipulate, or exploit the medium. Like any sociological analysis, the most interesting variable can be applied retrospectively to make sense of the whole or to give the data a particular slant. Commenting on the popular and long-running British series *Up*, which follows the lives of 14 children beginning in 1964 in a fashion reminiscent of Sheldon and Eleanor Glueck's longitudinal study of delinquent youth, American sociologist and ethnographer, Mitchell Duneier (2009), cites the case of Nicholas, who grew up on a farm and had little structured activity to occupy him. "The world of the seven-year-old can be primitive, even violent," the narrator says as Nicholas discusses his enjoyment of fighting. For Duneier, Nicholas's lack of discipline makes him the same as the East End working-class children in an orphanage who were portrayed as having too much freedom and not enough structure and discipline, but because Nicholas went on to study physics at Oxford and became a university professor, the focus moves to him at age seven saying that when he grew up he wanted to understand the moon, and as an adult saying he had always been interested in technical and scientific things (Duneier, 2009). One of *Up*'s directors, Michael Apted, acknowledges the manipulative possibilities of a genre that purports to tell the truth and confesses that during the making of one of the *Up* installments, he believed Tony (who lived in a lower-income neighborhood and dreamed of being a jockey) would soon be in prison, so he filmed him around dangerous-looking areas for use in later films:

> He lived in a pretty violent environment, and was making quite a lot of cash running bets at an East London greyhound-racing track for some pretty unsavoury looking characters. It didn't look like the future held much promise, so I had him take me round all of the crime hot-spots in anticipation of shooting *28 Up!* in one of Her Majesty's prisons. I was wrong and embarrassed. Tony married Debbie, they had children, and his life took a different course. Tony was decent about it and let me off the hook: "Don't judge a book by its cover, Michael," he told me. (Apted, 2009, p. 362)

Some critics, such as ethnographer Paul Willis, insist that *Up* and thus documentary film more generally promise to capture the texture of real life, no matter the editorial decisions made by producers and directors. From a decidedly Marxist vantage point, Willis laments, "Class still matters to me and that achingness I pick up in Michael's subjects continues to relate to the structured exercise of power, the costs of domination and the pains of subordination" (2009, pp. 349–350).

In this way, the prison documentary promises to bring the exercise of power and pains of subordination into particularly sharp relief. Given our earlier discussion of the failure of prison films to have any positive impact on prison reform, it seems a bold assertion to say that the prison documentary may be one of the few types of prison film that can claim to have made any difference at all to perceptions of prisons and prisoners, but, given Michael Apted's belief that "empathy is at the heart of most documentaries" (2009, p. 360), there may be a case for the suggestion. As we've discussed, some prison documentaries are simply voyeuristic and pander to stereotypes; by contrast, there have been several thoughtful and challenging prison documentaries and series that aim to bring a more empathetic and visceral reading of the prison to their viewers. From an ethnographic standpoint, Michelle Brown has written that with its focus upon injury, harm, and pain, the sociology of punishment in particular is poised to give attention to the role of empathy at precisely those instances of social experience where human connection, understanding, and social knowing are destroyed, avoided, prohibited, or simply impossible. (2012, p. 385)

Following the arguments of Apted, Willis, and Brown, we might find that the greatest utility of the documentary prison film is its ability to convey emotion and elicit compassion. *Fourteen Days in May* (1987), a film concerning the last two weeks in the life of Edward Earl Johnson—the second man to be executed in Mississippi after the national hiatus in capital punishment was ended in 1977—is one such film with undeniable emotional appeal. *Fourteen Days in May* charts the buildup to the execution: the preparations of the gas chamber, the media coverage, and the legal challenges, led by human rights lawyer Clive Stafford Smith. Commenting on the film, Jamie Bennett (2009) says it conveys "an unusual moral depth" by virtue of the fact that it raises specific concerns about the validity of Johnson's conviction, including an alibi witness who came forward who was refused access to the court. As the execution approached, its director, Paul Hamann, became increasingly disturbed by events and started not only to openly sympathize with Johnson but also to raise his concerns with those in authority. The difficulties—and indeed, undesirability—of impartiality on the part of the documentary filmmaker are articulated by Hamann in an interview with Bennett:

> I felt I was in a strange nightmare because it became clear off camera that the prison psychiatrist, the warden, the death row staff, all felt he did not commit the crime he was convicted of. At that moment I stopped being the objective BBC journalist and started doing everything I could to stop the execution . . . In the end it didn't work. The last week of making that film was really horrible, I didn't want to be making it, but morally we had to. Afterwards, myself and Clive Stafford Smith . . . made a follow up film called *The Journey* where we tracked down the man who everyone thought had really carried out the murder . . . the film did prove that Edward Earl Johnson should not have been executed. It was a film made a year too late. (J. Bennett, 2009, p. 47)

In the same interview, Hamann says that he was greatly influenced by the work of Fred Wiseman, an American pioneer of documentary filmmaking in the tradition of cinéma vérité, and by the British documentary filmmaker Rex Bloomstein, particularly his eight-part series *Strangeways* about life inside a British prison. As someone who has shown his work in prisons, has lectured at criminological departments, and is a recipient of two British Academy Film and Television Arts (BAFTA) awards, Bloomstein has to a large degree built his reputation on exposing the realities of prison life and addressing aspects of the criminal justice system that are usually closed to public scrutiny. Employing apparently simple (though in fact highly sophisticated) filmmaking techniques that eschew background music and narrated voice-overs in favor of a more direct focus capturing genuine, spontaneous emotions (sometimes known as "fly-on-the-wall" filming), Bloomstein is widely appreciated for humanizing his subjects while still conveying the complexities of their personalities, motives, and circumstances, a process he has called "undermining the simplicities" (Bloomstein, 2008; cf. J. Bennett, 2006a).

Perhaps the most haunting of Bloomstein's subjects was Steve, an inmate who appeared in two films: *Lifer* (1982) and, 21 years later, the follow-up, *Lifer—Living With Murder* (2003). In the first film, Steve is serving a life sentence for kicking a man to death at the age of 17. Twelve years into his sentence, he is cocky, athletic-looking, restless, and resistant. Prone to responding violently to provocation, he describes how his anger has led him to trash his cell and cause damage to the prison wing on several occasions. He speaks contemptuously of the prison officers, who restrain him physically and with drugs. But 21 years later we see the effects that medication, imprisonment, and *time* have had on Steve. Bloated, dulled, and his speech so slurred that the interview has to be accompanied by subtitles, the effects of 32 years in custody are dramatically conveyed. Now held in the secure wing of a psychiatric hospital and reduced to a shell of his former self, there can be no more graphic or moving illustration of a life inside.

With a prolific back catalog that includes *The Sentence* (1976), *Release* (1976), *Prisoners' Wives* (1977), *Parole* (1979), *Strangeways* (1980), *Lifer* (1983), *Lifers* (1984), *Strangeways Revisited* (2000), *Lifer: Living With Murder* (2003), and *Kids Behind Bars* (2005), Bloomstein has arguably done more than any other single individual to reveal the experience of imprisonment and its effects on inmates and their families. The most published author on Bloomstein's work, Jamie Bennett (see, for example, Bennett, 2004, 2006a, 2006b) is also a prison administrator, while former UK director general of the prison service Martin Narey has cited *Strangeways* as the primary inspiration for his decision to join the service (Narey, 2002). The question remains, however, whether the powerful, reflective, and raw films created by Graef, Hamann, Bloomstein, and others have the ability to challenge public attitudes toward prisoners. Rex Bloomstein firmly believes that documentaries do have the ability to alter entrenched attitudes, and he counsels against underestimating the potential for a change in public attitudes if the complexity of criminal conduct is allowed to be developed in documentary form (R. Bloomstein, 2010, personal correspondence). Just as the beating of Rodney King was seen as abhorrent by some and normal by others (see Chapter 6), the empathy inherent in the documentary process may only be felt by those viewers who already share the narrative's perspective and have preexisting sympathies with its subjects. While prison documentaries such as those described here unquestionably create a profoundly important media space for more considered and thoughtful reflection, the audience may inevitably view them—like any other media text—through the lens of their preexisting political and cultural sensibilities.

THE REMAKE

There is nothing that divides filmgoers more than a remake of a much-loved "classic." While there have been some notable critical and commercial successes (*The Departed*, *The Thomas Crown Affair*, *Ocean's 11*), other remakes have been met with indifference, mirth, or even outrage (*The Italian Job*, *The Wicker Man*, *Psycho*). The most successful remakes are probably those that stay broadly true to their predecessor (perhaps with some oblique references to the original for those in the know) yet also add something new. If a story is compelling yet would benefit from a modern treatment or change of context, so much the better. Some film buffs will always argue that remakes are inferior, but that doesn't mean that the majority of current viewers won't prefer them. In part, the attraction of a remake to modern audiences lies in the quickened pace of action, cutting-edge special effects and computer-generated wizardry, and the inclusion of familiar A-list stars. But what can remakes of classic crime films tell us about changing social attitudes toward crime over the decades?

At a fairly superficial level, they may tell us that filmgoers have a greater appetite for sex and violence (and sexual violence) and graphic language than their forebears, and they certainly indicate more relaxed censorship laws than in previous eras. The remake also tends to highlight that ours truly is a celebrity culture and that sometimes movies become vehicles for high-profile stars even if some critics question the appropriateness of a particular actor in a role. Equally, stars are now more able to move between quite diverse roles as heroes, anti-heroes, or downright villains and are more willing to play psychopaths, killers, and characters who have few, if any, redeeming features. Hollywood movies fully exploit all the technological tools at the filmmaker's disposal, creating spec-tacular, eye-popping, explosive action and underlining the fact that the film industry is a multibillion-dollar enterprise. But can movies help us chart deeper historical transitions and changing social fears and anxieties? Let us consider one film, *The Taking of Pelham One Two Three* (1974), and its remake, *The Taking of Pelham 123* (2009), to see if it can shed light on this interesting proposition.

The Taking of Pelham One Two Three and The Taking of Pelham 123

The Taking of Pelham 123 (directed by Tony Scott, 2009) stars John Travolta as Ryder, the sociopathic leader of a kidnap gang who take over the Pelham 123, a New York subway. Ryder, who was a Wall Street financier sentenced to prison for fraud and was released with all the convict clichés—shaved head, poor complexion, a handlebar mustache, and tattoos—demands 10 million dollars in 60 minutes or he'll start killing the 18 passengers and conductor whom he and his crew have taken hostage. His adversary is Walter Garber—played by the two-time Academy Award winner Denzel Washington—the dispatcher who just happens to be on duty during the siege and becomes an unwilling negotiator. As the film unfolds, we learn that the quiet, modest, and well-meaning Garber has recently been demoted pending an investigation into allegations that he took a bribe (which later is confirmed when Ryder threatens to kill a young man on board the train—his defense is that it was to pay for his kids' college education). The focus of the film is the relationship formed by Ryder and Garber as they engage in a psychological chess game.

In the 1974 original (based on John Godey's 1973 novel of the same name), the vil-lain's adversary was not a train dispatcher but NYPD lieutenant Zachary Garber, played by Walter Matthau (Zach Garber became Walter Garber in the remake, in homage to Matthau). A natural curmudgeon, Matthau's character is terse, cynical, and "hard-boiled" in the classic tradition of cinematic cops and private eyes who have seen it all before. While none of the film's producers have gone on record as to why Garber's occupation changed, we might speculate that the growing ambivalence and anger toward police could be a partial explanation for the decision to make Garber a train dispatcher in the remake. In contrast to Matthau's character, Denzel Washington's Garber is a much softer, more sensitive character, a change universally panned by film critics for being far less interesting than his predecessor. As the *Independent*'s movie reviewer, Geoffrey Macnab (2009), put it:

> We are lumbered with details about his private life: we hear him promising his wife he'll pick up some milk before he gets home in the evening and we learn how he may have had his hand in the till to pay for his daughter's college fees. The remake creaks under the weight of its sentimentality.

The "villain" also diverged quite considerably between the 1974 film and its 2009 successor. Most critics who compared the two films suggested that, despite Travolta's cartoonish Hells Angel appearance and expletive-ridden dialogue (both of which owe a debt to the character he played in Tarantino's *Pulp Fiction*), the urbane Robert Shaw was much more successful in conveying quiet menace and a cold-blooded and calculating attitude toward the hostages. Travolta's frenetic characterization suits the faster pace of the action. Where Shaw was quietly chilling, Travolta is a loose cannon "willing to kill innocents not out of necessity but out of spite" (Ordoña, 2009), perhaps reflecting contemporary fears that violent crime is random and indiscriminatory. Although writing several years before *The Taking of Pelham 123* was made, Thomas Leitch might have been talking about the film when he said that violence was becoming

> more and more successful, and more and more in demand, in selling movies to a generation of teenagers who had grown up with remote controls that had sharpened their impatience, discouraged the deferred gratifications of slow-moving films, and reintroduced . . . [the] principle of slapstick comedy. (Leitch, 2002, pp. 45–46)

In the original movie, the gang members are disguised in identical conservative suits, large-framed glasses, and false mustaches and answer to color-coded names, with Shaw going by Mr. Blue (to which Quentin Tarantino paid homage in *Reservoir Dogs* 20 years later). The original movie thus follows the common convention of the time of setting up relatively clear-cut distinctions between "evil" and "good" (personified by Mr. Blue and Lt. Garber). By the time of the remake, it was more usual to find distinctions blurred between "good" people and "bad" people, and adversaries were frequently portrayed as mirror images or similarly morally ambiguous ("You're just like me!" says Ryder to Garber).

An immediate and obvious difference between the 1974 film and the 2009 version are the cultural attitudes toward "minorities" and the use of language to express intolerance. While today's cinema audiences are more tolerant of frequent use of the "f-word" (which does appear in the original but with far less frequency and to much more shocking effect), they are less broadminded about language that reveals sociopolitically motivated hatred of others. The original film was a very 1970s production, containing casual misogyny ("I gotta watch my language just because they let a few broads in?"), racism ("Shut your mouth, n****r"), and xenophobia (a supposedly comic scene has Matthau referring to Japanese visitors as "Chinamen" and "monkeys" to their faces, unaware that they speak perfect English; Scherick & Sargent, 1974). Technology, both in terms of cinematography and narrative plot, makes notable distinctions between the two films. In the recent version, the gang makes use of a Wi-Fi booster so that Ryder may access his laptop underground and monitor the Dow Jones index (he has short-sold the market and invested in gold, earning him a profit far larger than the ransom money). Unknown to the kidnappers, however, a young male passenger has an active laptop with a webcam, which has been knocked to the floor but is facing the interior of the carriage with a decent view of the action. It reconnects using the same Wi-Fi network, reestablishing a previously used videochat to his girlfriend's PC. When she realizes what she's witnessing on her webcam, she provides the feed to the local television station, thus providing a perfect example of synopticism to titillate, terrify and, panic the TV audience watching at home (Mathiesen, 1997).

Some critics felt that the producer of the remake employed technical trickery simply because it was available and to cover up for a much thinner plot than the original had (hectic camera action, high color contrast, and frenetic editing are the hallmarks of Tony Scott's films). The more mundane plot devices of the earlier film are also preferred by many:

> It's all in the sneeze. If you want to know why 1970s thrillers are so much better than their counterparts today, you just need to pay attention to the part that flu and coughing play in the original ... The film-makers don't rely on the visual pyrotechnics that characterise Scott's movie, in which the camera never seems able to stay still for more than a moment. Instead, key plot points are conveyed in far more subtle fashion. Who needs a line of dialogue or a final-reel shootout when you can have a character giving himself away by blowing into a handkerchief? What better way to depict a corrupt and ineffectual mayor than to show him in bed with flu, being scolded by a nurse? (Macnab, 2009)

In 2009, the conflict takes place in the control room between Garber, his boss, and a professional hostage negotiator, but in the original movie, all the conflict occurs within the gang and on board the train as Mr. Blue fights to control dissent and disharmony among his men. In 1974, the gang is portrayed as a disparate band of thieves, but by 2009 they reflect the zeitgeist by initially appearing as terrorists and then being revealed as the new enemies of the people: bankers and hedge fund operators (French, 2009). Terror striking on an underground train retains some currency as a modern urban nightmare. One need only recall the attack on a Tokyo subway in 1995, when the deadly virus sarin was released on several lines, killing 12 people, or the suicide bombings on the London underground in July 2005, which killed the four bombers and

52 others, to reckon the potential terror of the subway. Nevertheless, in a post-9/11 world, the train no longer has quite the same symbolic potency as the passenger plane as a source of fear. Added to that, the remake of *The Taking of Pelham 123* remains faithful to the 1974 original's simple plot device of having the hijackers fool the authorities into believing they are still aboard the train when they have in fact escaped. Employing the same, relatively low-tech method, they lock the driving lever in the full-speed position, bypassing the "dead man's switch" meant to shut the train down in the event of an incapacitated (dead) conductor. Even the energetic pace that is maintained throughout Scott's version and the obligatory high-speed chase at the end of the film (a new addition since the 1974 version) do not prevent the remake from having a rather quaint, old-fashioned feel. Most surprising of all is that Scott's film makes no reference to 9/11 itself:

> Tony Scott's version of The Taking of Pelham 123 makes one very curious omission. It doesn't foreground at all the event that changed everything—the September 11, 2001 attacks on the World Trade Center. This gives the film's portrayal of New York a time-warp feel. The hijackers and the cops alike both seem to be playing by old-fashioned rules. We're not in the realm of suicide bombing or apocalyptic destruction. The robbers want a ransom, not necessarily to bring western democracy tumbling down. (Macnab, 2009)

Negation of the effects of 9/11 is especially puzzling because, although much of the action takes place beneath New York, *The Taking of Pelham 123*, like so many other films, is in part a fable about the city itself. As film critic Geoffrey Macnab implies, the character of the city mayor is an allegory for the health of New York City more generally. In the original film, the mayor is a neurotic, bloated, and sickly figure who can be read semiotically as a symbol of the bureaucratic mess that New York was in and of the U.S.'s political vulnerabilities following the Vietnam War and Watergate scandal. The original screenplay is rife with references to the instabilities troubling New Yorkers ("We don't want another Attica, do we?" in reference to the most serious prison riot in U.S. history that occurred in 1971; "There's another strike taking place"; "The city is broke" [Macnab, 2009]). As Macnab (2009) notes, 1970s New York was represented as a city "coming apart at the seams"; it had "something apocalyptic about it." John Carpenter famously captured this vision in his 1981 dystopian classic, *Escape From New York*, which begins with the premise that the entire city has become a maximum-security prison. In the remake of *The Taking of Pelham 123*, the mayor, played by James Gandolfini (of *Sopranos* fame), is a slick, sardonic, financially savvy manager in command of a technologically sophisticated multimedia environment, while New York is similarly clean-cut and efficient, sporting subway cars remarkably free of graffiti. The comparison of the gritty New York of old with the slick, technocratic city of the remake also usefully evokes the contested "city that became safe" thesis advanced by criminologists like Frank Zimring (2011) and conservative politicians such as former Mayor Rudolph Giuliani, who credit broken windows, order maintenance, and hotspots policing for New York's crime decline. The remake's sentimental final shots are perhaps the most telling—if still somewhat oblique—reference to the legacy of 9/11. Flying in a helicopter over the beautifully lit Manhattan skyline at sunset, the official hostage negotiator remarks to Garber that the city's beauty reminds him of what he's fighting to preserve.

DISCUSSION

The analysis above has highlighted some of the differences between two versions of a film separated by 35 years and what they have to tell us about changing perceptions of, fears about, and attitudes toward crime. To broaden this discussion and generalize somewhat, the films of the 1960s were about art burglars, jewel thieves, bank robbers, or Cold War spies, and the individuals who perpetrated them were essentially gentlemen who played by the rules. Crime was cool, and the movies of this period were filled with dashing heroes, dastardly villains, and glamorous but merely decorative women. However, by 1970, fears about violent, interpersonal crime were increasing, and the shock of rising urban crime rates in the U.S. was hitting home—literally. In 1969, the murder of Sharon Tate (an American actress and wife of film director Roman Polanski who was heavily pregnant at the time of her death) and four others at Tate's home and then, two days later, the equally brutal murder of Rosemary and Leno LaBianca in their home stunned and repulsed the American public. It was reported that the gang that committed the crimes—Charles Manson and his "family" of followers—had precipitated the murders by breaking into several homes, sometimes stealing items but sometimes simply moving them around in what they called "creepy crawlies." The violation of the domestic space—particularly these homes in attractive, suburban, affluent neighborhoods—have since become the theme of countless crime and horror movies (*The Last House on the Left,* 1972, remade in 2009; *Funny Games,* 1997, remade in 2007; and *Panic Room,* 2002; Simon, 2009; cf. Lowenstein, 2005).

As discussed elsewhere in this chapter, the 1970s also gave rise to several cop and private eye movies featuring a lone hero taking on conspiracies and corruption by state, municipal, and police organizations (*Dirty Harry,* 1971; *Chinatown,* 1974). By the 1980s, the maverick police officer was still around but by then had morphed into an all-action hero with a heavily muscled body to make up for his limited dialogue. It is somewhat ironic that California, which Vanessa Barker (2009) notes has been the leader and thus ground zero of mass imprisonment, is also the home of the movie industry and for a time was governed by Arnold Schwarzenegger. Another iconic cop film of this period, cited in many policy documents, academic studies, and media reports, is *Robocop.* The first of the series released in 1987, *Robocop* foresaw—in a fantasy-driven, science fiction fashion— changes in policing that many felt were overdue. In the UK, a series of riots that set police against the public spurred demands for police to get "tooled-up" like American police. As riot shields, full-face helmets, rubber bullets, and tear gas were introduced and "zero tolerance" and "order maintenance" policing were imported from the United States, many commentators also began to draw parallels between the traditional English "Bobby" and man/machine Robocop. The motif still retains sufficient currency in both countries, as one critic of the handling of the London riots quipped that "Police dressed up as Robocop act like him too" (Graef, 2009) while, in the U.S., it is a common practice for police to earn the nickname "Robocop" for displaying particularly violent and heartless behavior. One officer, William Melendez, who earned the "Robocop" tag through a particularly virulent reputation for violence, has reportedly cost the already beleaguered City of Detroit (also where the films are set) millions in legal settlements. And of course, since the "militarization of police" became a public issue following the 2014 death of Michael Brown, commentators have used the Robocop motif in a broader critique of police violence. As journalist Glen Greenwald wrote in the midst of the Ferguson protests:

> Americans are now so accustomed to seeing police officers decked in camouflage and Robocop-style costumes, riding in armored vehicles and carrying automatic weapons first introduced during the U.S. occupation of Baghdad, that it has become normalized. But those who bear the brunt of this transformation are those who lack loud megaphones; their complaints of the inevitable and severe abuse that results have largely been met with indifference. (Greenwald, 2014)

The early 1990s saw the rise of the serial killer movie (*Silence of the Lambs,* 1991; *American Psycho,* 1991; *Se7en,* 1995), which Brian Jarvis (2007) links to the rise of a voracious consumer culture: society's greed and vanity in this period were transmuted into themes of cannibalistic consumption, orgiastic gluttony, and fetishism in the movies. The decade also brought another kind of "excess"—computer-generated imagery (CGI)—to most films, although the decade closed with an exceedingly low-budget "found footage" riposte to CGI, *The Blair Witch Project* (1999). Since then, movies (at least movies aimed exclusively at adults—we'll leave aside the pirates and magicians who have conquered the box office in recent years) have been dominated by technology, terrorist attacks, environmental disasters, and other apocalyptic global threats to the human race.

To an extent, this is simply art imitating life and life imitating art. Stories in cinema run parallel to stories in the news, and filmmakers are merely picking up on the issues that audiences will recognize and that provoke the strongest reactions. Thus, many of the themes that have been highlighted in this chapter—drama; predictable storylines and themes; a simple narrative arc; masculine individualism, autonomy, and lack of normative social ties; the risk of random, violent (and sexual) crime; the importance of A-list celebrity actors, etc.—all spectacularly and graphically portrayed thanks to the technological toolbox at directors' disposal—are precisely the values that news journalists use to structure their reporting of crime (see Chapter 2). It is not surprising that the spate of films about children being left unsupervised by their parents (most famously, *Home Alone,* 1990) coincided with several real-life "home alone" cases, or that recent cinema releases have reflected contemporary moral panics, including a sensitively handled movie about the rape and murder of a little girl by a pedophile neighbor (*The Lovely Bones,* 2009) and a film about a four-year-old child abducted from her apartment, the release of which was postponed when British child Madeleine McCann disappeared from a holiday apartment in Portugal (*Gone Baby Gone,* 2007).

CONCLUDING THOUGHTS

The question of what makes a film a crime film is a tricky one, and this chapter—by including pirate movies, Westerns, prison films, and documentaries—has pushed the definition about as far as possible. But the truth is that there are few films that contain zero visual references to crime, deviance, antisocial behavior, policing, punishment, justice, or any number of other criminological themes. Is *Superman* a crime film? Or *Some Like It Hot*? What about *The Truman Show*?

While academics attempt to address the thorny question of why people become criminals via recourse to competing theories such as "rational choice," disadvantageous life chances, genetic predispositions, environmental factors, and so on, crime films offer a similarly diverse range of motivations for criminal behavior. Gangster, pirate, and outlaw movies link crime to a sociopathic alienation from a remote or uncaring society combined with excessive vanity or megalomania. Private eye and classic cop films blame institutional corruption or a malfunctioning system. Modern police films link criminal behavior to psychopathy. Heist movies and kidnap films peg it on simple greed. Film noir blames sexual victimization by a predatory femme fatale. British films use class, and sometimes race, to explore how the disenchantment of those who are economically and culturally at the margins of society can turn into aggression and violence. For the criminologist, the themes of crime films may overlap with academic interests, but, equally, their appeal might be that they deal with matters beyond the range of academic criminology:

> Philosophically, [crime films] raise questions concerning the nature of good and evil. Psychologically, they encourage viewers to identify with victims and offenders—even serial killers—whose sexualities, vulnerabilities and moralities may be totally unfamiliar. Ethically, they take passionate moral positions that would be out of place in academic analyses. Crime films constitute a type of discourse different from academic criminology, one with its own types of truth and its own constraints. (Rafter, 2007)

In fact, part of the appeal of writing scholarly treatments of crime movies may also be that they permit more passion and moral positioning than most "criminological" subjects; certainly, academic analyses of film usually betray the personal predilections of the author. All of this presents an opportunity for us to introduce one of our personal favorites, *Battle Royale* (2000). Directed by Kinji Fukasaku, the movie is a kitsch Japanese take on teenage delinquency that contains cartoonish, bloody brutality similar to that seen in Tarantino's *Kill Bill* films (Tarantino has discussed in many interviews his debt to Fukasaku and his son, Kenta Fukasaku, who wrote the screenplay). The film has a simple plot. While on a school field trip, 42 students are taken hostage and find themselves on a remote island where they must play a fascist government–sponsored game called Battle Royale. They are each made to wear a collar that will explode, killing them instantly, if they break any rules, and each randomly assigned a different weapon and told that they must fight each other to the death. They have three days to kill each other until one survives—or they all die. The film has a quality that is part video game and part reality TV. What does *Battle Royale* tell us about its sociopolitical context and about public attitudes toward crime in the 21st century? Must it be viewed differently in the light of the ghastly attack waged by Anders Breivik on Utøya Island in July 2011 (Chapter 2)? These are discussions that will have to wait for another time . . .

SUMMARY

- This chapter has attempted to account for the enduring appeal of crime and prison films, both to scholars of media criminology and to the wider public. It has offered several possible explanations for their attraction to audiences, ranging from an appeal to everyone's innate desire to be deviant to a cathartic satisfaction in seeing offenders get their just desserts.

- It has been argued that a relatively small number of generic themes dominate crime film. This chapter has chosen to focus on three: masculinity, autonomy, and the city, all of which are examined via some of the most popular subgenres, including the Western, the gangster movie, the pirate film, the spy franchises, the classic American cop movie, the private eye or film noir, and gritty British cinematic realism.

- The "prison film" has been included because of its sheer popularity and longevity. It has been noted that, while most academic scholars are content to analyze crime films without going much beyond their entertainment value, there have historically been greater demands of prison films to educate and influence the public on matters of penal reform. It is generally recognized, however, that

prison films have on the whole not succeeded in this endeavor and have instead continued to create and perpetuate stereotypes of prisoners as a dangerous and violent underclass.

- The documentary has arguably had more success in informing the viewing public about the pains of imprisonment, although its claims to realism may be compromised, as the discussion of Apted's *Up* films has demonstrated. Like other forms of ethnography, the documentary cannot be separated from the beliefs, motives, and agenda of its originator, and, like all other media content, the documentary also has a mission to entertain.

- The cinematic remake has much to tell us about changing sociopolitical climates and attitudes toward crime and punishment over the decades. Our discussion of two versions of *The Taking of Pelham 123*, made three decades apart, illustrates the ways in which audiences' perceptions of offenders, crime, the police, and other authorities have evolved; the different entertainment imperatives that viewers bring with them; and the sentimental affection with which New York is held, especially since 9/11.

STUDY QUESTIONS

1. Reflect on some of your own favorite crime and prison films and why it is that you enjoy them. In what ways do you think your responses might be different from those of your parents' and grandparents' generation?

2. Write a review comparing an original crime film and its remake. From this comparative analysis, what can you observe about emerging social anxieties and changing attitudes toward crime and justice over the years covered by the two films you have reviewed?

3. Given this volume's earlier discussions about media influence and effects (and the problems with making causal links between screen violence and real-life offending behaviors), how would you characterize the relationship between crime movies and criminals?

4. Why have prison movies, despite their popularity, failed to inform penal reform agendas? Do you agree with Rex Bloomstein that documentaries such as those he produces have greater potential to change public perceptions of prisoners and lead to less punitive attitudes more widely?

FURTHER READING

Just as there are a vast amount of crime films to choose from, there seem to be an almost equally daunting array of academic commentaries on them, making any particular recommendations appear highly subjective.

- However, one book we thoroughly recommend is *Criminology Goes to the Movies: Crime Theory and Popular Culture,* by N. Rafter and M. Brown (New York University Press, 2011). The authors base each chapter on a criminological theory and apply it to a famous Hollywood movie—for example, strain theories and *Traffic;* feminist criminology and *Thelma and Louise.* Although inevitably highly selective in the films they discuss (like this chapter), Rafter and Brown provide an inventive and very readable treatment of many of the theories discussed in Chapter 1 of this volume.

- Other than that, we will limit our suggestions to two books: *Crime Films,* by T. Leitch (Cambridge University Press, 2002); and *Captured by the Media: Prison Discourse in Popular Culture,* edited by P. Mason (Willan/Routledge, 2006).

- In addition, we would urge readers to follow up on the references to some of the criminologists mentioned here who have written about film, among them Mike Nellis, Jamie Bennett, Michael Fiddler, Richard Sparks, Eamonn Carrabine, Michelle Brown, and Nicole Rafter; as well as some of the media/cultural theorists who are interested in crime movies, including Martin Parker, Steve Chibnall, and Brian Jarvis.

Crime and the Surveillance Culture

8

OVERVIEW

Chapter 8 provides:

- An overview of recent revelations concerning the covert surveillance and spying activities of U.S. security agencies over their own citizens and the citizens of numerous other countries.

- A consideration of the dominance of the panopticon as a metaphor for contemporary surveillance techniques.

- A discussion of the extent to which surveillance technologies and systems are linked to form carceral networks of disciplinary power.

- An exploration of the institutional rationales and motivations that have led to a dramatic expansion of surveillance over the last two decades.

- An analysis of the ways in which media and popular culture have helped us to conceptualize various forms of surveillance through their representation in newspapers, television, films, music, art, and so on, and how the "viewer society" that traditional and "new" media have given rise to synthesizes panoptic and synoptic models of surveillance.

KEY TERMS

- carceral society 203
- control of the body 203
- cybersurveillance 203
- fifth estate 218
- fourth estate 218
- governmentality 205
- panopticon/panopticism 200
- profit 203
- security 203
- surveillant assemblage 202
- synopticism 213
- voyeurism 203

THE NSA AND A NEW AGE OF SURVEILLANCE

Everyone Is Under Surveillance Now, Says Whistleblower Edward Snowden

People's privacy is violated without any suspicion of wrongdoing, former National Security Agency contractor claims.

The US intelligence whistleblower Edward Snowden has warned that entire populations, rather than just individuals, now live under constant surveillance.

"It's no longer based on the traditional practice of targeted taps based on some individual suspicion of wrongdoing," he said. "It covers phone calls, emails, texts, search history, what you buy, who your friends are, where you go, who you love." (Associated Press, 2014)

In 1965, Gordon Moore, cofounder of Fairchild-Semiconductor and later the tech giant Intel, observed that the relative processing power of the then-nascent integrated circuit doubled every year. Known now as Moore's law, this observation has mapped the dizzying pace of technological advance, from those earliest days of computer engineering to a present where, as theoretical physicist and futurist Michio Kaku notes, a smartphone has more computing power than the machines used by NASA in 1969 to place two astronauts on the moon (http://mkaku.org). As others have noted, the advance of communication technology charted by Moore's law, has provided governments a frightening ability to peer into the lives of their subjects. Yet we should caution against a view of the age of the smartphone as altogether unique or exceptional. As *Time Magazine* reported in 1966:

> The government has been electronically spying on its citizens for years. The Internal Revenue Service, for example, has admitted bugging public and private phones and even rooms where IRS auditors called businessmen for questioning, on the theory they might reveal something when IRS men left the room (*LIFE Magazine,* The Big Snoop, May 20, 1966).

In fact, as soon as electronic communications were developed, so too were engineered methods for eavesdropping and documenting the activities of foreign agents and ordinary people. During the Civil War, for instance, both the Union and Confederate armies pioneered techniques and technologies in order to monitor their opponent's telegraph lines. But while electronic surveillance is hardly new, it may be that the centrality of technology to everyday life has created some degree of compliancy and perhaps a condition where much of the public sees intrusive surveillance as a necessary evil, such has been the volume of news concerning state surveillance and the attendant whistleblowing of activists, military personnel, computer experts, and former security employees. In fact, it might appear scarcely believable that WikiLeaks, the online organization that publishes "secret," sensitive, and classified information, only came to many people's attention in 2010 when the extent of war crimes committed by coalition troops in Afghanistan was published. What may be new is that these electronic surveillance practices no longer appear to be targeted and governed by the rule of law but instead are broad and indiscriminate.

The UK newspaper *The Guardian* has been at the forefront of bringing revelations about the U.S.'s National Security Agency (NSA) surveillance activities to a global audience. In June 2013, Edward Snowden, a former systems administrator for the Central Intelligence Agency (CIA) and Defense Intelligence Agency (DIA) and then a contractor working for an intelligence and security company in Hawaii, allegedly downloaded 1.5 million secret files about the NSA's covert and highly controversial practices before flying to Hong Kong to meet journalists. He then flew on to Moscow where he was granted asylum while, in his absence, the U.S. Department of Justice charged him with violating the Espionage Act, an offence punishable by 30 years' imprisonment. Among Snowden's revelations were that the NSA, together with the British Intelligence Agency, collected the phone records of millions of citizens, accessed and collected data from Google and Facebook accounts via a program called Prism, mined personal data from smartphone apps such as "Angry Birds," hacked computers, intercepted phone and Internet communications (including those of foreign politicians attending G20 meetings), carried out offensive cyberattacks and infected more than 50,000 computer networks worldwide with malware designed to steal sensitive information, shared raw intelligence data with Israel in an information-sharing agreement, bugged offices of the European Union, spied on at least 38 foreign embassies using a variety of electronic surveillance methods, tapped the private phone of German chancellor Angela Merkel, sifted through vast amounts of email and text communications of its own citizens and those of many other countries, and harvested millions of faces from web images for use in a previously undisclosed facial recognition database (Szoldra, 2014). While these examples are fairly wide-ranging, they merely represent the tip of the iceberg (see Szoldra, 2014, for a full list of "everything we've learned in one year of unprecedented top-secret leaks"). Snowden's fate remains uncertain, but, while the U.S. government has branded him a traitor and criminal, his alter-ego as patriot and hero have been underlined by his appointment, in February 2014, as Rector of Glasgow University and also by his nomination and serious contention for the 2016 Nobel Peace Prize.

At the time of writing, the scale of the U.S. and UK governments' surveillance programs is still unfolding, with new revelations steadily coming to the fore. A decade ago, much of the academic writing in the field of surveillance—surveillance studies—was concerned with closed-circuit television (CCTV), and experts could scarcely have envisaged how pervasive and invasive surveillance was actually becoming. With the oft-cited estimation that the average person living and working in a major city could be filmed up to 300 times a day, surveillance became a cornerstone of the literature on "target hardening," "defensible space," and victimization. Some studies examined whether visual surveillance technologies such as CCTV were effective in cutting crime or whether they simply displace it to surrounding areas (with contradictory findings). Others focused on the capacity for visual surveillance systems to reduce public fears about personal safety. On the basis that these issues are dealt with at length in other books (e.g., R. Coleman &

McCahill, 2010), this chapter will take a different approach and discuss some of the key motivations behind the rapid expansion of surveillance and its potential for social classification and social control. The chapter will also attempt to blend voices from criminology with those of the most prominent writers in the fields of sociology and cultural studies. But first let us consider the primary motif that unites debates about surveillance across all academic disciplines: the panopticon.

PANOPTICISM

In the popular consciousness, many forms of surveillance are dominated by the figure of "Big Brother," George Orwell's creation of an all-seeing, all-knowing, invisible superpower. In academic discussions of surveillance, however, the dominant metaphor has been that of the **panopticon**, an image that lends itself especially well to discussions of surveillance technologies that allow some individuals to monitor the behavior of others. The panopticon, developed by 18th-century reformer Jeremy Bentham, was an architectural design that could be used for prisons, schools, factories, workhouses, and any other social institutions that required the management of large groups of people by a small number of individuals with authority over them. While Bentham's vision was essentially a benign one, the panopticon became a motif for punitive prison regimes, and although it is often written that Bentham's model was never realized, several prisons have been and continue to be constructed according to the broad principles of **panopticism**. In brief, Bentham's design consisted of a circular building with individual cells built around its entire circumference, and a central watchtower in which the activities of the prisoners could be constantly watched. A system of lighting that illuminated the cells but kept the inspection tower in darkness made it possible for just one person to monitor many inmates, each of whom knew they were under surveillance but did not know exactly when. They were therefore obliged to behave as if they were being monitored at all times, and conformity and passivity were assured. The mental state of being seen without being able to see the watcher induced a fear that eliminated the need for visible deterrents or overt force.

Writing about the plague at the end of the 17th century, Michel Foucault (1977) describes how certain areas of a town were cordoned off and kept under continuous vigil, with guards inspecting every part of the town to ensure that no one escaped to spread the disease further. Consequently, like the inmates in Bentham's prison, the town's populations were not simply observed; the surveillance of them was designed to act as a deterrent, a caution to encourage them to behave in a certain way. Thus, for Foucault, Bentham's architectural design was not only a blueprint for future surveillance technologies that would allow a small, unseen few to observe the lives of the masses, but it was also a means of dispersing control over a conforming, docile population.

The panopticon was subsequently appropriated by others following Foucault's example, who took the ideological concept behind the design and used it to demonstrate the potential of new communication and information technologies. Most notably, Stan Cohen (1985) considered numerous manifestations of surveillance, including community penalties, neighborhood watch, private security, and the use of public surveillance cameras, and argued that they have enabled the "dispersal" of social control. Among the consequences of dispersal is the move to informal, private, and communal controls that "widen the net" of the formal system by bringing about "an increase in the total number of deviants getting into the system in the first place" (Cohen, 1985, p. 44). At the same time, there is a "thinning of the mesh" that increases "the overall level of intervention, with old and new deviants being subject to levels of intervention (including traditional institutionalization) which they might not have previously received" (p. 44). In short, surveillance has a tendency to disperse and become operative in a wide range of social settings not merely found *within* the criminal justice state but also *alongside* it, and to subject a large number of individuals and groups to being criminalized or labeled as deviants who formerly would not have been (cf. Coleman & McCahill, 2010).

THE SURVEILLANT ASSEMBLAGE

The pertinence of the panoptic model is obvious in relation to the widespread surveillance of private data and communications by governments, as revealed by Ed Snowden. Panopticism has also been evoked to explain the insidious presence of CCTV, although, as Norris and Armstrong (1999) demonstrate, the panoptic effects of CCTV systems, first introduced as a "closed circuit" of dedicated cameras, are limited. Three shortcomings are highlighted. First, CCTV systems that operate in public spaces, such as streets, are impossible to monitor continuously, and it is relatively easy for those intent on behaving deviantly to disguise their appearance or move outside the camera's gaze. Second, even when deviance is observed, the ability to mobilize a rapid response is constrained. In most cases, CCTV operators themselves are not authorized to deal with incidents, and neither are they in a position to demand swift intervention by the police. Third, the disciplinary power of CCTV is only complete when one-way total surveillance is combined with additional information about the individual being monitored. Clive Norris (2003) suggests that despite the massive expansion of CCTV surveillance, its operators' inability to routinely link a person's image to any more detailed knowledge or information about them places a severe limitation on CCTV as a panopticon; such surveillance is, as Haggerty and Ericson note, "often a mile wide but only an inch deep" (2000, p. 618). To put it in its simplest terms, there is not much the police can do with a recorded image of an offense that has already taken place unless further data can be gathered about the offender—name, whereabouts, address, previous convictions, and so on—hence the use that the police make of television programs like *America's Most Wanted* in appealing to the public to "fill in the blanks."

Having now been in widespread commercial use for a half century, CCTV may be best thought of as the first and now surpassed wave of electronic visual surveillance. Likewise, we might be forced to reconsider the panoptic model and metaphor with the proliferation and ubiquity of surveillance cameras, particularly those capable of perpetually recording what they see and maintaining the footage in cloud-based storage. When paired with facial recognition software that can match characteristics of the human face to images drawn from other databases such as those managed by departments of motor vehicles or Facebook, these sorts of perpetually archiving surveillance systems transcend the limitations of both the "closed circuit" and the "television"—fashioning a kind of artificially intelligent, never-sleeping CCTV 2.0. Likewise, innovations in automatic license plate recognition (ALPR) technology operate in much the same way. Not only do ALPR units affixed to police patrol cars perpetually and indiscriminately "run" the license plates of everyday citizens for outstanding warrants and traffic infractions, but they also automatically geocode each vehicle to a specific location, thereby creating a massive searchable database of vehicle locations. It does not take much imagination to reckon how a database mapping vehicle locations across time and space might be used for nefarious, perhaps unconstitutional purposes. As geographer and artist Trevor Paglen (2016) has recently reported, private industry has already paired with police to make ALPR technologies part of an incredibly lucrative entrepreneurial venture. In early 2016, a company named Vigilant Solutions partnered with several cities in Texas to provide ALPR technology, training, and support as well as access to their massive database of ALPR records free of charge in exchange for a percentage of any traffic fines or court costs their equipment helped to collect. The deal works like this: When police stop a "flagged" vehicle associated with outstanding fines, the driver is given two options: she or he can pay the fine on the spot using equipment provided by Vigilant Solutions, plus a 25% "service fee" that goes directly to the company, or she or he can be arrested. This arrangement also gives Vigilant Solutions proprietary ownership over any data gathered by their systems, thereby enlisting public servants (police) in the production of digital capital. As Paglen put it, "the political operations here are clear. Municipalities are incentivized to balance their budgets on the backs of their most vulnerable populations, to transform their police into tax-collectors, and to effectively sell police surveillance data to private companies" (Paglen, 2016, p. 20).

The stitching together of once-discrete surveillance systems, such as surveillance cameras, ALPRs, DMV records, and credit card usage, has been dubbed the "surveillant assemblage," marking a point at which we have witnessed the "disappearance of disappearance" (Haggerty & Ericson, 2000, p. 619). This raises the interesting question of whether our electronic identities have taken precedence over our "real" identities. Once information (be it visual or textual) about a person is entered onto a networked surveillance system, their identity is "fixed" even if it is "false." In much the same way as a person's legal identity is constructed from a mass of facts taken from the beginning to the end of life—birth certificate, passport, employment histories, medical and dental records, criminal record, post mortem, and so on—a cumulative mass of documents that captures and fixes them, so an individual can be captured in a web of nondocumentary, visual surveillance as a virtual entity or "data double" (Haggerty & Ericson, 2000).

Writing well before the advent of social media, Mark Poster prophetically noted that, increasingly, in any major serious crime investigation, both the victim(s) and the suspect will have their movements, consumption patterns, reading tastes, personal contacts, sexual histories, and various other aspects of their private lives compiled into a detailed "dossier that reflects the history of his [sic] deviation from the norm" (Poster, 1990, p. 91). But even before the ubiquitous Facebook was invented, information was coalesced and then made public knowledge via the mainstream media. As our discussion of the Boston Marathon bombing in the introduction of this volume described, seemingly disparate pieces of security and surveillance technology—ATM cameras, GPS-coded smartphone images, social media "check-ins," etc.—are increasingly stitched together into a singular assemblage to do the work of crime control. One early example that illustrates the depth of information that can be achieved when fragments of data are coalesced is the police hunt for British 12-year-old Shevaun Pennington, who disappeared with a 31-year-old U.S. Marine named Toby Studebaker in July 2003 after "meeting" him in an Internet chat room. Following Shevaun's safe return home, it was reported that, despite her family's pleas for information about their missing child and her abductor, the police had known their whereabouts all along, thanks to a GPS (global positioning satellite) system picking up the suspect's mobile phone transmissions. Not only did this allow the police to triangulate the phone's location to within a few feet, but also they were reportedly able to activate the phone even when it was switched off. In addition, the police alerted credit card companies so that an alarm was automatically triggered when the suspect used his credit card to buy airline tickets. Meanwhile, police in Studebaker's Michigan hometown were examining his personal computer, where they found downloaded child pornography, and his criminal records that revealed that he had previously been charged with molesting another 12-year-old child. On the other side of the Atlantic, police examined Shevaun's computer, and it was discovered that, unbeknownst to her parents, she had been in communication with Studebaker for over a year. Perhaps most bizarrely, it was reported that the former Marine had planned the abduction with military precision. Forensic analysis of his computer apparently revealed that his rendezvous and escape with Shevaun "smacked of special forces 'in-hit-out' tactics" (Morris & al Yafai, 2003).

This case demonstrates that surveillance is far from a unitary technology and hasn't always relied on social media. But even when we confine our discussion to the mundane monitoring of "ordinary" citizens by government agencies, as discussed previously in relation to Snowden's NSA revelations, we are in fact referring to a nexus of computers, telecommunications, and people. Taken together, these networks are said to constitute a carceral society (Foucault, 1977), whereby more and more aspects of life are becoming subject to the kind of disciplinary power that we usually associate with the panopticon and the prison. Moreover, these systems of discipline and domination are driven by a common set of motives and desires on the part of those who instigate and operate them. In a slight modification of Haggerty and Ericson's (2000) typology, these rationales for surveillance will be further explored in this chapter under the following headings: control of the body, governance and governmentality, security and cybersurveillance, profit, and voyeurism and entertainment.

Control of the Body

A great deal of surveillance is directed toward monitoring, codifying, and controlling the human body. Surveillance of specifically targeted groups can be achieved via an interface of technology and corporeality that can range from direct physical contact between flesh and technological device to more oblique or covert methods of producing information (Haggerty & Ericson, 2000). The former would include the various forms of "electronic tagging" that are now commonplace, such as securing an electronic tag around newborn babies' wrists or ankles in hospitals that not only contains personal information about the child and its medical condition but also triggers an alarm if the infant is moved beyond a secure area. The electronic monitoring of probationers via an ankle bracelet or ignition interlock system, and the use of microchips inserted under the skin of pets to monitor their whereabouts, are also examples of the diversity of applications that exploit the flesh-technology-information amalgam. Less direct forms of surveillance that rely on distantiated monitoring of corporeality include the computer monitoring of keystrokes to assess output and efficiency in offices and the visual surveillance of shop workers' body language to ensure that they are conveying the customer service ethos of their employer (see below).

When it comes to techniques of identification, bodily or "somatic surveillance" (Monahan & Wall, 2002) extends beyond individuals and discrete groups to entire populations. In this respect, identity verification is achieved by means of "biometrics," which are identification techniques based on physical attributes—fingerprints, palm scans, retina identification, body fluids, and so on. In the global surveillance society, one is no longer identified by what one has (for example, a driver's license or passport) or by what one knows (social security, student identification number, date of birth), but increasingly by what one *is*—a collection of unique body parts (Aas, 2005). Ironically, we have returned to the anthropometric preoccupations of the positivist school of criminology with their measurements of the body, skull, and so on—albeit in a more sophisticated guise. There is, then, nothing intrinsically new about the "informization of the body" (van der Ploeg, 2003, p. 58). Primitive forms of biometric identification have existed for centuries, and advancements in photography and fingerprinting at the end of the 19th century coincided with the centralization and bureaucratization of administration and record keeping. In fact, fingerprinting is a good example of a form of surveillance that has lost a great deal of its stigma through familiarity and diversity of use. Once used uniquely by law enforcement agents to identify suspected criminals, with all the negative connotations that such an application would evoke, the use of fingerprinting has expanded to include privileged cardholders, frequent flyers, club members, library users, and children. What *is* new is that information has "lost" its body (Aas, 2005). Again, to take the example of forensic crime investigations, traditional fingerprinting is being superseded by "genetic fingerprinting," otherwise known as DNA testing. Many criminal cases that had been consigned to police files years or even decades ago have been belatedly solved by recourse to DNA tests on items of clothing, weapons, or other items that have been touched by a suspect and stored by investigators. But despite the fact that DNA provides a unique identifier that cannot be transferred between individuals, no system dependent on human hands is foolproof. DNA can be cloned, "planted," or, in the case of suicide bombers and terrorist "martyrs," rendered irrelevant. Even if an effective form of everyday personal identification incorporating DNA could be found, as with other technological advancements, it is likely that human ingenuity would remain one step ahead of the police.

Governance and Governmentality

A salient theme in the surveillance literature has been its contextualization within "actuarial" discourse. In other words, surveillance occupies a central role in a broad strategy of social control that has moved from being "reactive" (i.e., only activated when rules are violated) toward one that is "proactive," "predictive," or "pre-crime" (Zedner, 2007)—that is, that tries to predict rule violations before they happen. Visual surveillance systems are thus seen as just one element within a raft of risk-calculating crime control strategies that also embrace risk assessments of "dangerousness" in relation to prisoners and those on parole, a national register for sex offenders and the notification of communities about pedophiles in their midst, community safety partnerships and neighborhood watch programs, and attempts to "design out" crime in architecture and town planning. Not only do surveillance systems underpin crime control policies, then; they have, in fact, figured into a distinct mode of governance. The "rehabilitative ideal" with its promise of "treating" the sickness that causes individuals to offend, and its evocation of a benevolent state concerned to eradicate poverty, deprivation, and hardship, dominated criminological discourse throughout much of the 20th century. But in recent years, as concerns about crime and the perceived failures of the criminal justice system have intensified, the focus has turned to one of predicting and preventing criminal acts through "zero tolerance" and "tough-on-crime" strategies.

The new discourse of governance is also reflected in the reemergence of "classical" criminological theories that view crime as opportunistic and "normal," that is, requiring no particular maladjustment on the part of the offender. The salience of these theoretical perspectives in recent years has been accompanied by a shift from policies directed at the individual lawbreaker to those aimed at "criminogenic situations," including unattended parking lots, bar and nightclub districts, disadvantaged neighborhoods, poorly lit streets, subways, schools and colleges, shopping centers, and sports stadia. While one objective of the new **governmentality** is to develop methods of situational crime control, a related aim is to single out those who do not "belong" in certain environments and take preemptive action to monitor and exclude them. Thus, rather than attempting to tolerate, understand, and rehabilitate the different and the dangerous, there has been an ideological shift toward the less expensive and simpler task of displacing them from particular locations and from opportunities to obtain goods and services; of restricting mobility and behavior; and of managing them rather than changing them. These shifting attitudes are increasingly being seen not simply as attempts to govern crime but also to involve "government through crime"; a new "governmentality" (Simon, 1997). Unfortunately, it is targeted disproportionately at people of color and poor whites, who are being increasingly segregated into ghettoized spaces that function as "human garbage dumps, where survival, excitement and success and opportunities for entrepreneurship depend increasingly on involvement in illegal economies" (Stenson, 2001, p. 18; cf. Ferrell, 2002). Mike Davis, writing about Los Angeles, detects a similar segregation of new core business zones from the ghetto areas, a process of sequestration which, he observes, carries "ominous racial overtones" (1994, p. 4).

The move to render large populations legible and quantifiable through technological identification, classification, and differentiation is achieved through a complex network of strategies to predict and manage threat and risk. As more and more of contemporary society's ills are represented as problems of "criminality," individuals and organizations are being encouraged to view themselves as potential victims and to action in order to protect themselves. Governance through crime is thus a project of not only the state and its police but also the insurance industry, communities, employers, retail managers, and individuals themselves. Often justified in terms of their ability to monitor "risk" groups who pose a significant threat to economic stability or social order, the surveillance measures adopted by these diverse bodies can quickly lead to much broader definitions of threat, danger, and risk. For example, despite the objections of civil liberties groups, police in the United States have the varying ability to collect DNA and to maintain it in large databases for use as evidence in subsequent investigations.

There are few questions that divide people to the extent that a national DNA database does. Many people feel quite uncomfortable with the fact that a society governed by calculations of risk makes everyone a potential suspect. This, of course, reaches a terrifying extent when one considers that DNA does more than establish identity—it provides a *complete genetic profile*. The Combined DNA Index System (CODIS) is an umbrella service maintained by the FBI to coordinate the various DNA databases that exist throughout the United States. Today, more than half of all states and the federal government collect DNA samples from arrested suspects, while the others collect DNA samples upon conviction. This has led to significant criticism and formal legal challenges of preconviction collection practices on the grounds that they constitute illegal searches. In the landmark 5–4 Supreme Court ruling in *Maryland v. King,* the legality of DNA collection prior to conviction was upheld. Yet, in his strongly worded dissent, then–associate justice Antonin Scalia, who typically sided with police power, held that such practices violated Fourth Amendment rights and warned, "Make no mistake about it: As an entirely predictable consequence of today's decision, your DNA can be taken and entered into a national DNA database if you are ever arrested, rightly or wrongly, and for whatever reason" (Ross, 2014).

Critics continue to voice concerns over the potential for human error in processing or the outright misuse of such evidence and note that regardless of genetic variation, the DNA of any two human beings is 99.9% identical. Nevertheless, the ascendancy of such technology continues to present significant concerns and challenges. As Marcus Feldman, a professor of biological sciences at Stanford University, warned, "There are clear differences between people of different continental ancestries . . . It's not there yet for things like IQ, but I can see it coming. And it has the potential to spark a new era of racism if we do not start explaining it better" (Harmon, 2007). Professor Sir Alec Jeffreys, the UK scientist who discovered DNA, has joined in the public criticism of current practices, likening the database to creating a "presumption of likely future guilt" (Casciani, 2009).

The growing body of research into how specific genes can predict future substance addiction, sexual orientation, and criminal and violent tendencies is also of concern to many, who argue that DNA profiling could lead to the stratification of society, creating a *Brave New World* based upon genetic elitism. Proponents of the use of DNA technology in criminal justice repeat the dominant security mantra, "If you have nothing to hide, you have nothing to fear," and insist that DNA has proven invaluable to police and has led to a growing number of exonerations. Still, critics counter that while such evidence is useful, it is not prioritized in all criminal cases. For instance, nearly 400,000 untested "rape kits" collected after sexual assaults has led many to suggest that violence against (mostly) women is a secondary priority for police and criminal justice in general.

Security and "Cybersurveillance"

There are two aspects of security commonly discussed in the criminological literature on surveillance: personal safety and the security of property (from theft to an act of terror). In relation to the former, one of the outcomes of the processes of governance and capitalism outlined above is that, as urban space has become progressively fragmented and fortified, the population that inhabits that space become subject to feelings of insecurity and paranoia. Nearly two decades ago, Keith Bradsher writing for the *New York Times* noted that the fear of crime was so pervasive that it was readily apparent in a wide range of seemingly disparate consumer products—clothing to sport utility vehicles—styled to display a "high level of aggression" (Bradsher, 2000). He writes:

> The United States is in some ways becoming a medieval society, in which people live and work in the modern equivalent of castles—gated communities, apartment buildings with doormen and office buildings with guards—and try to shield themselves while traveling between them. They do this by riding in sport utility vehicles, which look armored, and by trying to appear as intimidating as possible to potential attackers. (Bradsher, 2000)

Extending Bradsher's observations and assertions, Josh Lauer (2005) suggests that the popularity of the SUV lies in widespread beliefs about crime, the unpredictability of violence, and the necessity of security. The SUV, which is meant to sit above other vehicles and appear intimidating and fortified, essentially signifies armored transport, which is particularly attractive for those moving between fortified environments such as secure office parks and gated communities. Despite the unwanted and undesirable being marooned in spaces *between* controlled urban spaces, there is a tendency for those who occupy the newly privatized public realm to nonetheless demonize them. As discussed elsewhere (and as exemplified by the new president and his ban on immigrant travel to the U.S.), when difference and diversity are not tolerated, far less celebrated, the inclination to regard some people as alien and fear them as a result becomes more pronounced.

In such a climate, visible surveillance technologies may further increase public anxieties and contribute to the image of public spaces as dangerous places. Paradoxically, the solution most frequently put forward to counter the public insecurity that is, in part, generated by the prevalence of surveillance systems is to introduce yet more surveillance systems and security measures. Hence, a greater level of exclusion is created and a "fortress mentality" of segregation and ghettoization is reinforced. For example, personal and home security devices, including do-it-yourself CCTV systems, are increasingly commonplace in urban and rural areas alike. Architects and planners around the world are following the American example of fortified "gated communities," offering security to residents with high walls, ID-protected gates, and 24-hour (un)armed guards. As depicted in the 2002 film *Panic Room*, there is a growing demand among affluent homeowners for indoor bunkers capable of withstanding various types of biological, chemical, and armed attacks. These rooms contain a panic button to alert police and video surveillance monitors to allow the homeowner to view the rest of the property in relative safety. A similar security obsessed sentiment underpins the vibrant "prepping" community, which imagines all manner of potential threats—crime waves and urban riots, war, pandemics, and even the "zombie apocalypse"—and offers an equally expansive range of security measures and products in response (Linnemann, Wall, & Green, 2014).

There is little doubt that surveillance technologies have radically destabilized the public/private boundary, and no other issue has generated public disquiet about surveillance to the extent that fears about loss of privacy have. Yet anxieties about acts of terror have altered people's tolerance to surveillance and, in the wake of the terrorist attacks on America in September 2001, the political and public stance toward government intrusion appears to have relaxed, or shifted altogether. For instance, on the HBO political talk show *Real Time* (June 7, 2013), host Bill Maher admitted, "You know, the fact that a city can be just demolished in one second kind of tips the scale for me. So, I'm not saying to look into your emails is the right thing, I'm just saying, I'm not going to pretend it's because I'm brave; it's because I'm scared" (Johnson & Arria, 2016). If he reflects the broader sentiment, the American public may indeed be willing to tolerate increasingly intrusive security measures for fear of the next calamity. For instance, policymakers in the U.S. and elsewhere see networked "national" identity cards as a panacea to the problems of illegal immigration, crime, and terrorism. These so-called "smart" ID cards hold a wide range of coded data and can incorporate national identity, driver's license, health details, and passport information as well as eye scans or thumbprints.

It is often assumed that technological progress has made it much more difficult for those with "spoiled" (that is, criminal or illegal) identities to hide the unfavorable elements of their past and that identity cards would ensure that goods and services would be allocated on the basis of entitlement. However, two somewhat contradictory issues must be considered. First, it has never been easier to "fabricate a more acceptable self" (Finch, 2003, p. 93). Identity theft is an undeniable problem, exacerbated by the ease with which it can be achieved via the Internet. As Emily Finch notes, the "carceral network" of documentation "fixing" the identity of the individual is, in some senses, subverted by the Internet, which offers the identity thief a "plethora of "new" identities to "try on" (2003, p. 96). Furthermore, a relatively high-integrity identity can be constructed by accumulating a collection of relatively low-integrity documentation (Finch, 2003; Stalder & Lyon, 2003). Many forms of identification can be bought via the Internet, including fake passports, driving licenses, birth certificates, electronic PINs, and credit card numbers, and, as Stalder and Lyon observe, no matter how sophisticated an ID card is, it is only as reliable as the document on which it is based. Administrative identity may be established by reference to a series of documents, but the reliability of the final document, the ID card, will be defined by the weakest link in this chain of references. If a person possesses a convincing counterfeit birth certificate, she or he can acquire an ID card, which will duplicate whatever information happens to be on this certificate. In addition, the scope for bribing officials to issue a genuine document in the knowledge that it contains incorrect information makes these systems much more vulnerable than their "high-tech dazzle might suggest" (Stalder & Lyon, 2003, p. 84).

The second point to be considered is that not all criminals and terrorists have spoiled identities. Even a relatively sophisticated ID system could not have prevented the terrorist attacks on the Pentagon and World Trade Center from taking place in September 2001, as most of the "terrorists" had valid visas, no criminal record of any sort, and were not on suspect lists. As Stalder and Lyon (2003, p. 85) note, terrorists, particularly the ones willing to kill themselves in the attack, belong to a special class of criminal. They rarely have prior convictions; thus, background checks are rarely revealing. There are no repeat suicide bombers. Moreover, the overwhelming tendency, fueled by the popular media, to assume that all terrorists are Muslim and affiliated with networks such as ISIS and al-Qaeda means that so-called, "home-grown," "lone-wolf" perpetrators sometimes operate beneath or beyond the carceral net. Thomas Mathiesen cites a report that notes that of 174 prevented and successful terrorist attacks in Europe in 2011 (of which 63% were caused by separatists from France and Spain), "no al-Qaeda affiliated or inspired attacks were carried out in EU Member States" (TE-SAT, 2012, as cited in Mathiesen, 2013, p. 72). It was in that year, however, that Anders Breivik, a right-wing, anti-Islamist extremist, killed 77 people in Norway. As Mathiesen argues, Breivik's case raises numerous important questions, not least how this man was unknown to police in the years during which he was plotting the massacre and why it took police so long to act on intelligence received during his murderous spree when they could possibly have saved lives. In part, he suggests, Breivik was allowed to slip under the radar precisely because he was a white, blond-haired Norwegian, dressed on the day in question in a police officer's uniform. He didn't "look" like a terrorist, and in the months leading up to the attacks, the only thing the police had registered was that he had legally bought large amounts of fertilizer online (to make bombs), which did not alert undue suspicion as he lived on a farm.

These shortcomings have done nothing to thwart the seemingly relentless drive by governments to oversee and regulate the activities of their citizens, as the revelations by Ed Snowden have demonstrated, and it is state surveillance that remains of greatest concern to many commentators. While current fears about terrorism may have mollified the general public into accepting a greater degree of surveillance (and there is no convincing evidence that this is the case), many political commentators, human rights campaigners, and civil liberties organizations have expressed extreme disquiet about the license that governments take in unstable times.

For the U.S., the principal legislative response to 9/11 was the legislation titled "Uniting and Strengthening of America to Provide Appropriate Tools Required to Intercept and Obstruct Terrorism Act of 2001" (the USA PATRIOT Act), hastened into law the month after the attacks on New York and Washington. This act expanded powers to require businesses to turn over records to the FBI and Internet service providers (ISPs) to preserve all data specific to a client for a specified period of time. The act also included proposals that require college and university administrators to provide authorities with any information on foreign students suspected of being involved in terrorism and proposals to make medical records of suspects available to investigators (Coleman & McCahill, 2010). Not everyone feels secure in the knowledge that state authorities have this level of power to monitor the communications and movements of individuals, not least because they frequently fail to identify and act on a known threat, for example, the Boston Marathon bomber, Tamerlan Tsarnaev, who had previously been investigated by the FBI at the request of officials in the Russian Federation. More worrying for many in the aftermath of the "War on Terror" is that American governments have a long and troubled history of defining deviants, miscreants, and people displaying the "wrong kind" of patriotism, and post-9/11 fears that persons with "Arab" or "Muslim" backgrounds are among the primary targets of intensive surveillance at airports or border checkpoints (Lyon, 2003) have not receded. Dissenters claim that the sweeping legislation brought in by governments around the world in response to the fear of terrorist attack is applied indiscriminately—or indeed applied very discriminately and knowingly to individuals and contexts that pose no terrorist threat but are being surveilled for other reasons. For example, in Spain, anti-globalization protestors have complained of monitoring by security forces who equate them with "terrorists" (Coleman & McCahill, 2010). The U.S. intelligent search agent "Echelon," which intercepts and monitors traffic on commercial communications satellites and is essentially a sophisticated "eavesdropping" device, was justified on grounds of terrorism and crime but has been found to routinely intercept valuable private commercial data (Hamelink, 2000).

Of course, surveillance does not necessarily rely on technology. The disciplinary and repressive character of the panopticon was exemplified by its ability to influence behavior and transform selves. Using only a fairly primitive lighting system, the panoptic prison engendered a climate of fear and paranoia. History shows that the most oppressive political regimes do not necessarily require high-tech methods to achieve the same aim. For example, the Romanian dictator Nicolae Ceausescu (who ruled between 1965 and 1989, when he and his wife were overthrown and executed) and the former leader of Iraq, Saddam Hussein, both created a low-tech climate of fear based on a culture of enforced eavesdropping that effectively amounted to a total surveillance society, with secret police mandated to employ brutal torture to ensure that self-imposed censorship was upheld. But the Internet has taken whispering campaigns to a new and potentially dangerous level—described by Claire Valier as "transnational vengeful networks" (2004, p. 103)—as the man mistaken for notorious British child killer Jon Venables found when a Facebook page was created urging vigilantes to kill him. Moreover, the monitoring of communications by governments in the West might be seen as no more lawful, for all its high-tech gloss and covert methods, than the practices of Ceausescu and Hussein. As communications intelligence has moved its operations from narcotics trafficking, money laundering, and terrorism to intercepting "ordinary" citizens' mobile phone communications, emails, and Internet traffic, notions of what is "acceptable" in the interests of security are ambiguous and nevertheless controversial.

Profit

As we've seen in Paglen's discussion of Vigilant Solutions, one of the most significant drives behind the expansion of surveillance comes from the companies who manufacture the hardware and software, many of which were once suppliers of military equipment, but have adapted to a changing global market. As the technology becomes more sophisticated, the commercial market for surveillance equipment sets to grow even further, promising to reveal new avenues toward marketization. Video surveillance systems are themselves big business: In the period of rapid expansion of CCTV in the 1990s, the

United Kingdom invested 75% of its crime prevention budget in CCTV technologies, which over a decade amounted to a quarter of a billion pounds (over 315 million U.S. dollars; Norris, 2003). The NSA Utah Data Center, a massive 1.5-million-square-foot facility outside Salt Lake City, was designed to archive Internet traffic to the tune of 12 exabytes or greater. Reflecting on the sheer capacity of the Utah NSA facility, researchers of the University of California at Berkeley's School of Information Management and Systems, estimated in 2003 that "all words ever spoken by humans since the dawn of time" would be the equivalent to 5 exabytes of information (Klinkenborg, 2003). Of course, the massive facility, which cost $1.5 billion to construct and will cost nearly $50 million a year to operate, has been a boon for all those in the business of national security, from construction conglomerates on down to individual tech contractors.

The desire for profit has interesting social implications. When Foucault (1977) developed his vision of surveillance as a form of hierarchical social control, he emphasized the power that panoptic surveillance techniques had over the masses, stating that surveillance did more than observe and monitor people. For Foucault, panoptic surveillance targets the soul, disciplining the working populace into a form of self-regulation designed to meet the requirements of the developing factory system. However, Zygmunt Bauman (1992) argues that surveillance is becoming less about discipline and repression and more to do with classifying individuals according to their conspicuous wealth and consumption patterns, seducing those deemed "desirable" into the market economy. With the advent of networks of computers, "data mining" has become operational through the extraction of information about individual citizens and can be used to classify high and low value customers for corporations in just the same way that it can be used to assess and rank "high" or "low" risk groups in relation to criminal behavior (Coleman & Norris, 2000). We probably all immediately recognize that there are a number of outcomes of this process. First, surveillance can be used to construct and monitor consumption patterns so that detailed consumer profiles can be put together. Second, these profiles can then be used to predict future behavior or consumption habits, lure customers to a rival organization, or even encourage people to buy items they may not otherwise have purchased on the basis that they fit a preexisting aspect of their lives. This increases potential profits for corporations based on knowledge of consumer behavior in the name of "efficiency" (Coleman & McCahill, 2010). Third, surveillance can be used to differentiate between populations, limiting the movements of some on the basis of their identity profiles, consumption habits, or spending power. The meeting of certain criteria by desirable (i.e., relatively affluent) consumers might then determine anything from preferential credit ratings to rapid movement through customs and airports (Haggerty & Ericson, 2000).

These processes combine to create what Oscar H. Gandy (1993) terms the "panoptic sort": a situation in which *all* individuals are continuously identified, assessed, and sorted into hierarchies, which are then used to manage and control their access to goods and services. Furthermore, they have taken place against a backdrop of changes that have resulted in the supremacy of conspicuous consumption and the commodification of the city. No longer are Western cities characterized by industrialization and an emphasis on welfare. Now big budgets are made available for advertising the virtues of cities, and the role of video surveillance has been recast as not simply a means of deterring criminals but also as a friendly eye in the sky promoting the "feel-good factor" for those who work, visit, or are at leisure there. Shopping malls have become the cathedrals of the age but were, from the start, designed with a darker touch of the panoptic prison where visibility and surveillance prevailed (Langman, 1992). The mall's primary defining characteristic is that it is enclosed and more or less isolated from the larger environment. Moreover, within its boundaries, everything, from temperature to the movement of people and the shop displays, is rigorously controlled.

But within these cathedrals of capitalism, the weak create their own "spaces," inflicting damage on the strategic interests of the powerful. Michel De Certeau (1984) uses the language of warfare, arguing that subordinates are like guerrillas, appropriating space as a means of resistance; an apt metaphor for the "mall rats" who gather in shopping centers. Presdee also elaborates on this subject in his study of unemployed youth in a South Australian town, 80% of whom visit the local shopping mall at least once a week, aggressively "invading the space" of those with a legitimate right to be there (Presdee, 1986, p. 13). These "outsiders" are tricking the system, consuming images, warmth, and places of consumerism without any intention of buying its commodities. At the same time, they offend "real" consumers and security personnel by asserting their difference within, and different use of, the glittering palaces (Presdee, 1986; Fiske, 1989). They appropriate the space for subversive performance and resistance, including illegal drinking, provoking security guards, and crowding around shop windows, preventing "real" customers from seeing the displays or entering the stores. Little wonder, then, that the "policing" of malls has become progressively more rigid and uncompromising in recent years, as witnessed by the ban on young people wearing "hoodies" in many retail outlets. The desire to remove "undesirables" is an economic one: "The malls are there to make profits, to sell goods and services, not to provide environments for 'deviants' who refuse to spend or who cannot afford to spend" (Bocock, 1993, p. 107).

The drive to exclude some individuals from certain public spaces raises questions about the kind of society that is left as a result. There is a danger that the moral engineer has replaced the social engineer (Stenson, 2001), as "difference" is eliminated and those who do not conform are displaced to the dark, and often dangerous, corners of the city where their capacity to "convey a negative image" is less material (Norris & Armstrong, 1999, p. 45). Numerous writers have drawn on themes of cleanliness and dirt in attempting to characterize the ordering of contemporary public spaces. For example, Geoff Mulgan (1989) describes how surveillance is used to purify space of the homeless and alcoholics in order to create a convivial atmosphere for those who conform to the demands of the consumerist environment. Lyon (2003, p. 22) further notes that the poor are "cleaned away" from cities for tourism, and Jeff Ferrell's recent and current work employs Matza's notion of "drift" to conceptualize how the poor and disenfranchised are constantly moved from space to space to avoid "contamination" of commercial districts. Meanwhile, Bauman (1997, p. 14) refers to the "new impure," who are prevented from responding to the enticements of the consumer market and are thus dismissed as "the dirt of post-modern purity." These analogies all recall the work of anthropologist

Mary Douglas (1966), who argues that the elimination of "dirt" is a positive effort to organize the environment; dirt invites social control because it is perceived as a threat to order. There has also been, in recent years, a more literal manifestation of this idea, with restrictions in many city centers on litter dropping, alcohol consumption, smoking, and traffic. McCahill (2002) further notes that in the city center shopping mall he observed, banned activities included walking a dog, pushing a bicycle, eating, sitting on the floor, and lying down. When these kinds of behaviors were observed via video surveillance, a security worker would be dispatched to request that the miscreant "position their body in a way conducive to the commercial image of the mall" (p. 128). In this respect, the flawed consumers who come under surveillance in shopping malls are, quite simply, as Douglas (1966) reminds us, "matter out of place"—dirt (p. 2).

Voyeurism and Entertainment

While many commentators argue that recent developments in systems of surveillance and social control have augmented an intensification of panopticism (where the few observe the many), an emerging theme in the sociological and criminological literature on surveillance has been that of "synopticism," where the many observe the few (Mathiesen, 1997). Synopticism has been accelerated by the proliferation of mobile phone cameras, which have led to a number of instances where members of the public have filmed events that were not "meant" to be seen, or have simply arrived on the scene before journalists, and either posted the footage online or sold it to national television networks for broadcast around the world. As Tyler Wall and Travis Linnemann have noted, the American security state, which is dependent on coercive-looking practices—from electronic surveillance to routine police patrol and observation—is averse to synopticism and is in fact quite "camera shy" (Wall & Linnemann, 2014, p. 135). They observe a so-called "war on cameras" and "war on photography" that emerges when members of the public attempt to film the everyday actions of police. As CopBlock, an activist group dedicated to synoptic "film the police" activities, has written:

> Across the country, police officers and other government officials are waging a war on cameras. People everywhere are being harassed, detained, threatened, assaulted, and even arrested just for legally taking photographs or filming. Government officials are even unlawfully confiscating cameras and destroying photographs and videos. (www.copblock.org/cameramap)

While in most instances, U.S. law permits citizens to film the police, unsurprisingly, police agents and agencies routinely ignore the law and harass, coerce, and arrest photographers and confiscate and destroy equipment and images. All of this, CopBlock suggests, reveals the political potential of synoptic power, or what they call the "counter-stare."

In fact, the drive is not only to look, but also to be looked at. In the 21st century, to be watched elicits a positive as well as a negative response, a synoptic development that suggests that video surveillance and mobile/webcam footage is as much about entertainment as it is control. The popularity of social networking sites such as Facebook,

Instagram, Snapchat Flickr, Vine, and Twitter are a testament to the desire to see and be seen. These new turns in visual communication were preceded by the "reality TV" genre, which was also aided by surveillance technologies and cheap user-friendly home movie equipment. Where television documentaries and news-based programs were once "normal, safe, middle class and secure," surveillance bystander footage of serious and spectacular crimes, accidents, and disasters have taken these formats into the realm of incendiary, the "raw" and the dangerous (Dovey, 1996, p. 129). The ubiquity of "real" footage is of course aided by platforms like YouTube, which make grassroots production of news content possible for a larger segment of the global population than at any time preceding.

Other media genres similarly exploit the information and entertainment potential of surveillance technologies. As we saw in Chapter 6, surveillance clips are an integral component of news broadcasts and interactive programs, as are light entertainment programs that show the police and emergency services at work. In the postmodern quest for the hyperreal, the desire to be part of the "action" may be satisfied by the ability to see it played out as it was caught on camera. Although clearly a more secondhand experience than actually being there, it may constitute the "next best thing"—or arguably the "best thing" insofar as one can "witness" a criminal, dangerous, or spectacular event from the safety of one's home. Not only do news programs, documentaries, and tabloid entertainment shows routinely make use of video footage of everything from high-speed police car chases to air disasters, but there is a burgeoning trade for such material on the Internet. Newspapers also use stories involving video footage to fill their pages. McCahill (2003) suggests that video surveillance footage constitutes a "good news story" because it illustrates many of the key journalistic news criteria and "adds value" to already newsworthy stories. As we saw in Chapter 2, the mainstream media frequently deal in binary oppositions, and McCahill reports that this is no less true in the reporting of surveillance-related stories than in that of any other news event.

So, surveillance is a common theme in mediated culture. Indeed, we find that art, science fiction, comic books, jokes and cartoons, film, advertising, and popular music have all anticipated and even inspired surveillance systems and their applications (for a tremendous critique of our contemporary technological culture, see the BBC and now Netflix anthology series *Black Mirror*). As the sociologist Gary Marx (1995) suggests, these cultural texts help us understand the depth, complexity, and indeed the implications of electronic surveillance by providing an alternative language of visual metaphors (for example, Sting's "classic" pop song "Every Breath You Take" offers a plethora of metaphors for omnipresent and omnipotent surveillance; p. 114). These texts remind that the field of surveillance is always a contest of power. (Charlie Chaplin's 1927 film *Modern Times* contains surveillance themes to illustrate the relationship between controller and controlled, manager and worker.) Many cultural artifacts convey the profound ambivalence of our culture toward surveillance technologies that can both protect and violate (take two Bob Dylan songs—"Subterranean Home Sick Blues" and "Talkin' John Birch Paranoid Blues"—by way of example). Yet we can often see that the meaning is not in the object but in the context and in how it is interpreted (most people would agree that the song "Santa Claus Is Coming to Town"—Santa "knows where you are sleeping, he knows when you're awake, he knows if you've been bad or good, so be good for goodness' sake"—is an illustration of benign panopticism). There is, as several commentators have observed, nothing inherently threatening or sinister in the technology itself. Finally, cultural material raises new questions for social research, such as, what is the effect of popular media creating an environment that welcomes, tolerates, or opposes new surveillance? Does constant media exposure normalize, routinize, domesticate, or trivialize surveillance? (Marx, 1995, p. 106ff.).

Marx reminds us that cultural material must be viewed against the backdrop of the times, and a detailed analysis such as his can tell us much about technological evolution and public attitudes to surveillance. For example, Hitchcock's dark depiction of voyeuristic surveillance, *Rear Window* (1954), was released at the height of the Cold War when a climate of suspicion prevailed and people distrusted even their neighbors. The television series *The Prisoner* (1967) was broadcast at a time when fears about technological progression collided with the ubiquity of the gadget-laden secret agent in popular fiction, television, and cinema. Following the period of McCarthyism, when political attention was directed toward the enemy within, as opposed to the enemy without, *The Prisoner* both reflected this theme and anticipated the impending Watergate scandal, perfectly encapsulating the escalating conspiracy theories of the period. More recently, films such as Spielberg's *Minority Report* (2002; based on the short story of the same name, written by Philip K. Dick) reflect current developments in face and eye recognition techniques as well as underlying concerns about the potential applications of new surveillance technologies. Set in a police state, circa 2054, *Minority Report* seamlessly combines current allegiances to proactive "pre-crime" strategies with an equally contemporary faith in "new age" prescience to raise questions about the ethics of taking predictions as "facts" (a point that brings to mind the newly proposed charge of "grooming," which is causing concern among civil liberties groups because it is designed to target adults who meet a child after contact has been made on the Internet but *before* any offense has taken place; this "real-life" example raises the same question as Spielberg's movie, that is, whether *thinking* about criminal acts is the same as committing them).

In short, perhaps, what Marx's analysis demonstrates most forcefully is that over the last century, surveillance has been consistently viewed, at best, with ambivalence, and at worst with paranoia and hostility. Indeed, all the examples above are centrally concerned with the question, who has the right to look? It may be that the power of surveillance technologies has evolved to an extent that would outshine the prescience of Orwell, but the sentiments with which they are viewed by society at large—complacency and horror—show a significant degree of cultural continuity (Marx, 2002).

FROM THE PANOPTICON TO SURVEILLANT ASSEMBLAGE AND BACK AGAIN

Of course, the categories discussed—control of the body, governance, security, profit, and entertainment—are far from mutually exclusive. A brief consideration of recent developments in school surveillance serves to illustrate the constitutive nature of surveillance rationales. Originally justified by the fear of external threats, surveillance technologies have inevitably been turned inwards, and students now come under the scrutiny of their educators. In 2010, a particularly shocking example came to light in the Lower Marion suburb of Philadelphia. As part of a technology integration plan, the Lower Marion School District had distributed nearly 2,500 MacBooks—equipped with theft tracking and remote-viewing "spyware"—to district students. Alarms were soon sounded when one student was confronted and punished for behavior alleged to have occurred in his home. A subsequent investigation found that district administrators used the laptops to remotely monitor this particular student, accessing his webcam, taking screenshots, and monitoring his chat logs in hopes of documenting criminal behavior.

An ongoing investigation found that the district had undertaken widespread spying practices, accessing webcams to capture nearly 70,000 images of students in their homes and elsewhere. A class action lawsuit was settled later that year, with the school district agreeing to pay more than 600,000 dollars to two plaintiffs and their lawyers. This case illustrates that the notion of trust has been supplanted by suspicion, aided by the relative ease of electronic surveillance. In the workplace, powerful surveillance systems are in regular use to deter theft, monitor areas that were previously the responsibility of supervisors, assess training needs, ensure that the correct organizational procedures are followed, monitor compliance with health and safety regulations, check that goods are not being damaged during loading and unloading procedures, observe workers taking unauthorized breaks, and encourage punctual time-keeping (cf. McCahill, 2002, p. 153ff.). In all these practices, the governance-security-profit alliance can be discerned in various guises and formations. Moreover, it is not just employees but also *potential* employees who are vulnerable to forms of surveillance. As Jewkes (2003a) discusses, there exists software capable of sifting through any written communication and spotting when the writer is lying or confused about the facts. One of the potential applications of this high-tech lie detector is for companies to recognize embellished or falsified resumes, which they can then reject on principles very closely aligned to the governance-security-profit motives discussed above. On the other hand, many employers may prefer the cheaper and simpler method of checking out applicants' profiles on their Facebook site to make judgments about their suitability for employment.

But it is arguably surveillance that targets the body as an object to be monitored and controlled that is most alarming to the majority of employees. Examples of surveillance technologies that are being introduced in work environments around the world are toilet bowls that automatically check for drugs and surveillance cameras in cubicles that then film the people who test positive, sensors monitoring whether workers wash their hands after visiting the washroom, smart badges that track employees' movements, high-tech clocking-on procedures, and various "Big Brother" systems that check the performance quality of staff in call centers and other telephone-based work environments—including the number of calls taken and the number of calls with a "successful" outcome in a given time period (Hamelink, 2000; Jewkes, 2003a). Even more insidious are the workplace surveillance systems that monitor employees' presentation of self; for example, ensuring that service industry workers are always smiling and using appropriate body language. In these circumstances, the employee becomes the "bearer of their own surveillance" and the panoptic model is once again recalled:

> In the enclosed and controlled setting of the workplace CCTV can easily become an instrument of disciplinary power exercised through the architecture of the panopticon, allowing management to see everything without ever being seen themselves ... In the name of "customer service" employees' gestures, facial expressions and body language all become subject to the disciplinary gaze ... The anticipatory conformity that this induces in employees who recognize that they are always potentially under surveillance presents management with an extremely powerful managerial tool. (McCahill, 2002, pp. 162–163)

And if there seems little voyeuristic entertainment value in these workplace examples, consider the case of Australian police officers caught on camera having sex, drinking alcohol, and taking drugs while at work, a series of misdemeanors made more embarrassing by the fact that they were subsequently broadcast on television networks around the world. Relatedly, there is an ever-growing list of cases where comments made by a disgruntled employee on social media quickly result in the termination of that person's employment.

"BIG BROTHER" OR "BRAVE NEW WORLD"? SOME CONCLUDING THOUGHTS

Much of this chapter has been concerned with the ways in which surveillance systems are bound up with wider relations of power and discipline, reinforcing existing inequalities along traditional lines of class, gender, ethnicity, and age. This stance is in line with most critical criminologists who have been generally skeptical (if not downright hostile) toward the idea that surveillance technologies liberate, empower, and comfort the general citizenry. The panoptic model of top-down scrutiny is exemplified by Roy Coleman and Joe Sim's (2000) analysis of Liverpool's CCTV program in which they argue that the surveillant gaze is turned almost continuously downward on those who are already disenfranchised. By contrast, they say, there is a virtual absence of "upward" surveillance of the powerful, "whose often socially detrimental and harmful activities remain effectively beyond scrutiny and regulation" (p. 637). However, several commentators have taken exception to the idea that the powerful are exempt from the watchful gaze and argue that power does not entirely reside in the hands of those at or near the top of social and occupational hierarchies. There are numerous examples that could be offered that support this, not least the whistleblowers who expose wrongdoing by those in power. While WikiLeaks source Chelsea (formerly Bradley) Manning and Ed Snowden are the highest-profile whistleblowers of recent years—together with the journalists they cooperated with to bring their disclosures to a global audience—good old-fashioned investigative journalism remains a cornerstone of the fourth, and indeed, fifth estate. Further, as Haggerty and Ericson (2000) comment, and as Snowden's disclosures about the extent of government snooping appear to bear out, contemporary surveillance transforms traditional social hierarchies because people from all social backgrounds are now under surveillance in many aspects of their everyday lives. Indeed, those most subject to surveillance are likely to be the relatively privileged and most affluent who use regularly use credit cards, mobile phones, and computers.

Haggerty and Ericson (2000, p. 617) concede that the targeting of surveillance *is* differential but assert that it has nonetheless "transformed hierarchies of observation," allowing for the scrutiny of the powerful by both institutions and the general population. Examples of "bottom-up" surveillance include the introduction of CCTV systems into police custody suites and cells, allowing the activities of custody officers to come under just as much scrutiny as those of the inmates, and the proliferation of phone cameras that has resulted in numerous recordings of police brutality and government abuses of human rights.

It is not just bottom-up or lateral surveillance that may enhance due process, fairness, and legitimacy (Marx, 2002). Those who operate conventional top-down CCTV systems have also been known to resist the "higher" authority of the police in a show of solidarity with their subjects. McCahill (2013) notes that many of the security personnel in the shopping center he observed were from the same part of town as the people they spent their days observing and monitoring; they went to school together, played on the same football team, and knew each other's families. This degree of familiarity between the observers and the observed is interesting for three reasons. First, it endorses Gillespie and McLaughlin's (2002) findings that a less-punitive attitude toward "offenders" is adopted when a "deeper knowledge" of their background is known. Second, it challenges the notion implicit in the moral panic thesis that exaggerated public responses to deviants are magnified when the perceived threat is "close to home." Third, the fact that watchers and watched are known to each other inevitably places limits on the disciplinary potential of the surveillance systems:

> [Some] security officers are not always willing to co-operate with the police. For instance, the local beat officer has given the security personnel a list of "wanted" persons and asked them to give him a ring . . . if they see any of these suspects on camera. However, whether or not this information reaches the beat officer depends upon the degree of familiarity between the security officers and the local "surveilled" population . . . Recall, for example, the security officer who said, "I wouldn't grass . . . on Tommo 'cause he's all right, he's never given me any bother. (McCahill, 2002, p. 199)

Even in the workplace, the notion of surveillance as panopticism is not universally endorsed. Zureik (2003, p. 44ff.) summarizes several studies that challenge the view that all surveillance by managers of workers is exploitative and disempowering. One report (D. Mason, Button, Lankshear, & Coats, 2000) provides evidence from several work environments to support their argument that both workers and unions generally accept surveillance as an extension of traditional monitoring in the workplace and have no problems with it as long as it is transparent, based on collective agreement, and does not contravene the law (cited in Zureik, 2003). In fact, many workers welcome the "electronic supervisor" because it provides protection against unfair work distribution, violence and bullying, and accusations of negligence or poor productivity.

On the whole, though, a distinction is drawn between surveillance of work and surveillance of the worker, with only the former being deemed acceptable. For example, one report from a government agency recommends that monitoring should not violate trust nor be excessive and "should not intrude unnecessarily on employees' privacy and autonomy" (cited in Zureik, 2003). Marx believes that this recommendation is not being heeded by many employers, and that the "information-gathering net" is constantly expanding to encompass aspects of workers' private lives, personal characteristics, appearance, and so on. Genetic testing and screening are being introduced into the workplace to allow employers to assess the behavioral dispositions of potential employees and their propensity to certain illnesses. Because they claim to rely on precise scientific evidence, they have been characterized as "total surveillance" (Regan, 1996, p. 23), a feature that makes these forms of surveillance qualitatively different from the CCTV cameras and their operators in McCahill's English shopping center.

It might be argued, then, that discussions of surveillance have a tendency to flatten the terrain of power, control, and the role of individuals in social systems, and that a more finely nuanced approach is required. The panopticon has been a useful metaphor for the notion of surveillance as social control and has given rise to several theoretical developments of the original concept: synopticism (Mathiesen, 1997), "super-panopticism" (Poster, 1990), and "postpanopticism" (Boyne, 2000), to name a few. But the main limitation of the panoptic thesis is that it overstates the power of systems, institutions, and processes and underplays the importance of the individual actor. The human element is often forgotten or ignored (a response known as "technological determinism"), but as Lyon reminds us, sociotechnical surveillance systems are affected by people complying with, negotiating, or resisting surveillance (Lyon, 2003, 2007). One of the foremost commentators on surveillance and social sorting, Lyon has always argued that surveillance is ambiguous and that technologies that permit surveillance can be positive and beneficial, enabling new levels of mobility, efficiency, productivity, convenience, and comfort. In the contemporary everyday world of telephone transactions, Internet surfing, affordable domestic as well as international air travel, street-level security, and work, the metaphors of Big Brother and the panopticon may indeed seem increasingly less relevant. What is more, a general ethos of self-surveillance is encouraged by the availability of home testing kits and do-it-yourself health checks, allowing people to test for alcohol level, pregnancy, AIDS, and hereditary or potentially fatal medical conditions (Marx, 2002). Such innovations empower people and offer them personal choice (for example, whether to have a child if there is risk of it being born with a congenital illness) on an unprecedented scale.

The subject of surveillance thus remains contradictory and contested. In the pursuit of the goals discussed in this chapter—control, governance, security, profit, and voyeuristic entertainment—surveillance would seem to go hand in hand with suspicion and segregation. But several commentators have highlighted the extent to which surveillance can be played with and used for fun, seduction, and narcissism, even exhibitionism. Perhaps more significant than any other development is the centrality of mobile phones and social networking sites to the ways in which we communicate with and "keep tabs" on each other. Online social networking has taken Mathiesen's "viewer society" to a completely new level and created scopophiles of us all. The increasing numbers of (especially) young women willing to expose intimate details of their private thoughts, lives, and bodies through online diaries and blogs, reality TV shows, and bedroom-based webcams challenges the idea of "panopticism" with its rather threatening implications of authoritarian control (Koskela, 2006; see also Chapter 9). But the fact that we've become a culture that enjoys watching and being watched "socially" may make us more inured to other forms of surveillance, that is, those introduced in the name of "security." Younger generations in particular may be so accustomed to the Internet and increased social visibility that they do not think about, let alone protest, the erosion of civil liberties; quite simply, "the general tide of surveillance washes over us all" (Haggerty & Ericson, 2000, p. 609).

However, while most of us barely notice the extent to which we are at the center of a surveillance society, so easily have we internalized the changes in our conduct (using swipe cards instead of keys to access our workplaces; banking online rather than in person; keeping in touch with our friends using mobile phones, email, and social networking sites, and so on), there can be no doubt that the Internet has also changed the ways in which "private" information is shared, controlled, and compromised. Now when *any* serious crime occurs (or, for that matter, other stories, such as suicides and fatal accidents), the first port of call for journalists is the social network site of each of the individuals involved, and the millions of users who regularly upload personal information into cyberspace with relatively little control over how it may eventually be used and abused may end up regretting their self-disclosures, as Amanda Knox and Raffaele Sollecito surely must. Convicted of the sexual assault and murder of Leeds University student Meredith Kercher in Perugia, Italy, in November 2007, they found aspects of their characters exposed to a global media audience when—before they were even formally charged—the press reproduced text and images from their social media pages (including pictures of them individually posing with weapons) and linked this content to the police allegations against them (see Chapter 2 and also Gies & Bortoluzzi, 2016, for a comprehensive set of discussions about this case).

Like any technological innovation, then, surveillance must be viewed as part of a network of systems that operate within a wider context of political, cultural, technological, and economic currents. For Lyon (2006), the conundrum at the heart of surveillance is that the more stringent and rigorous the panoptic regime—for example, compulsory biometric ID cards—the more it generates active resistance, whereas the softer and subtler the panoptic strategies (e.g., social networking sites), the more it produces docile subjects. Dystopia or utopia? You decide!

SUMMARY

- Advances in technology have resulted in the disciplinary gaze being extended beyond the confines of closed and controlled environments, such as the school, prison, or factory, to encompass society as a whole. The exponential growth of surveillance techniques in most areas of contemporary life has led some commentators to suggest that the primary advantage of technological advancement is the potential that arises for risk management at a distance. Discussions of surveillance have been dominated by pessimistic images of "Big Brother" and the panopticon, metaphors that have helped to perpetuate the notion that surveillance technologies are linked to insidious and repressive forms of regulation and social control. However, in recent years, the idea of the "synopticon" has emerged to challenge this cynical and despairing view. Views of surveillance systems are now split between those who hold that technologies such as CCTV constrain people's activities, restrict their behavior, and are used to regulate demonized "others" and those who characterize surveillance as essentially liberating and democratizing.

- It has been suggested that we are increasingly witnessing the convergence of once-disconnected systems to the point that we can now speak of a "surveillant assemblage" (Haggerty & Ericson, 2000). The systems of discipline and domination that make up this convergence of once discrete systems are driven by five principal motives: control of the body, governance, security, profit, and entertainment, all of which have significant social and cultural implications. An analysis of surveillance in the workplace has served to illustrate these motives in situ and has demonstrated the arguments for and against the regulation and monitoring of individuals.

- The subject of surveillance remains an ideological battleground, but whatever view one takes of its purposes and outcomes, it must be remembered that technologies such as CCTV do not exist in a cultural vacuum and are inextricably entwined with the human motives, values, and behavior of both observers and observed.

STUDY QUESTIONS

1. Due to limitations of space, this chapter has discussed in detail only a few of the systems and practices that can broadly be defined as "surveillance." How many other applications of surveillance (in both its guises as coded data collection and visual monitoring) can you identify on your campus or workplace?

2. Gary Marx (1995) demonstrates that surveillance motifs are pervasive in popular culture. They range from themes of erotic fantasy (of secret watching) to political paranoia about the "enemy within." What are the impacts of the widespread cultural treatment of surveillance as entertainment on the public at large? Do they help to "normalize" surveillance and make it acceptable, or do they increase public fears and anxieties about crime?

3. For all their benign appearance, are sites like Facebook and Twitter simply the most instant and global means of surveillance on the planet? Are they just the most effective way of keeping in touch, or do they legitimize people spying on each other and make the notion of privacy (and indeed friendship) a thing of the past?

4. As of October 2016, the CODIS DNA database stores 2,521,974 arrestee profiles and 738,992 forensic profiles, but there are frequent

discussions about whether it should be extended, even to the entire United States population. What are the pros and cons of keeping samples taken from the entire population on a national DNA database? Would such a move reduce discrimination, or might it create "at risk" categories that reinforce racial and ethnic stereotypes (Nelkin & Andrews, 2003)?

5. From your reading of this subject, would you say that on the whole, surveillance systems empower or constrain?

FURTHER READING

So vast has the subject of surveillance now become, and so expansive is the criminological literature on the subject, that this chapter has been able to do no more than scratch the surface. By including discussions of surveillance as entertainment and the surveillant properties of Internet sites like Facebook, we have selectively chosen themes that strike a chord with discussions throughout this volume. Inevitably, however, this has been at the expense of more detailed analyses of the surveillance-governance-security nexus, which is more commonly addressed in criminological circles.

- The most comprehensive and up-to-date overviews of surveillance are *Surveillance and Crime,* by R. Coleman and M. McCahill (SAGE, 2010); *Towards a Surveillant Society,* by T. Mahiesen (Waterside Press, 2013); and—with a particular focus on the surveillance of children—*Surveillance Futures: Social and Ethical Implications of New Technologies for Children and Young People,* edited by E. Taylor and T. Rooney (Routledge, 2016).

- Also excellent are *New Directions in Surveillance and Privacy,* edited by B. Goold and D. Neyland

(Willan/Routledge, 2009); *Technologies of InSecurity: The Surveillance of Everyday Life,* edited by K. F. Aas, H. O. Gundhus, and H. M. Lomell (Routledge, 2008); and *The New Politics of Surveillance and Visibility,* edited by K. Haggerty and R. Ericson (Toronto University Press, 2006).

- David Lyon has been prolific on the subject of surveillance, and all his books are worth a look, including his published "conversation" with Zygmunt Bauman, *Liquid Surveillance* (Polity, 2012).

- There is an excellent e-journal devoted to surveillance—*Surveillance and Society*—which can be accessed at http://www.surveillance-and-society.org/ojs/index.php/journal, and *Crime, Media, Culture: An International Journal* also embraces new research on surveillance technologies as well as other "new" and alternative media (http://cmc.sagepub.com).

- Finally, it is worth reading the *Guardian*'s reports on the Snowden revelations and their repercussions at http://www.theguardian.com/world/series/the-snowden-files.

Student Study Site

WANT A BETTER GRADE?

Get the tools you need to sharpen your study skills. Access practice quizzes, eFlashcards, SAGE journal articles, and more at study.sagepub.com/jewkesus.

The Role of the Internet in Crime and Deviance

9

OVERVIEW

Chapter 9 provides:

- A brief overview of the ways in which linked, mobile, digital technologies have revolutionized the ways in which (especially young) people communicate and interact with each other.

- Discussion of the "digital divide" and an analysis of the ways in which the Internet and World Wide Web are shaping the development of China as it moves from totalitarianism to "market authoritarianism" and partial democracy.

- A description of some of the "ordinary" cybercrimes that most frequently appear in the news.

- Reflection on the ways in which the Internet is transforming not only young people's leisure and pleasure habits but specifically and explicitly their sexual development.

KEY TERMS

- cyberbullying 230
- cybercrime 227
- cyberspace 228
- cyberterrorism 228
- sexting 236
- social networking 224
- trolling 230

Over the last two decades, the perpetual growth of the Internet has resulted in radical and far-reaching changes in both industrialized nations and, increasingly, the "developing world." Even since the first edition of this book was published in the UK (in 2004, just as Mark Zuckerberg was setting up Facebook as a localized college directory and messaging service at Harvard University), most people's working, shopping, financial, and leisure patterns have altered dramatically as a result of linked, mobile, digital technologies, and the World Wide Web. At the vanguard of profound social, cultural, political, and economic changes, Facebook had, as of the end of 2016, 1.79 billion active users, was worth 50 billion dollars, and was being accessed by 1.18 billion people every day (http://newsroom.fb.com/company-info/).

While **social networking** sites are used by people of all ages, they have particularly revolutionized the ways in which young people communicate, compete, and interact. We may have seen the emergence of the "kidult," as the media have termed adults who enjoy a prolonged (or permanent!) state of adolescence, but young people use new communications technologies differently to their parents' generation. By way of example, in July 2009, 15-year-old Matthew Robson, working with the Media and Internet Research Team at global financial services company Morgan Stanley, wrote a report on *How Teenagers Consume Media*. In it, Matthew describes a mediascape that has become a great deal more confusing and complicated in some respects and considerably easier, more mobile, and more accessible in others. The report reveals that teenagers do not listen to the radio, preferring to use their PCs and phones to access online streaming sites, which are free of ads and allow users to choose the songs they want instead of listening to what the radio presenter chooses. They rarely purchase music but do download tracks and albums illegally. No one in their mid to late teenage years regularly reads a newspaper, as most do not have the time and cannot be bothered to read pages and pages of text when they could view a short summary of the news on the Internet or on TV. By the time they are 15, youth go to movies less frequently because they have to pay the adult price, opting instead to locate a pirated copy somewhere online. The report further informs us that girls are a lot more prone to spend their time on social networking sites than boys but that, unlike their male counterparts who spend the majority of their free time gaming, "only about one in fifty" girls plays console games, though the dominance of the Nintendo Wii is put down to girl gamers and its status as a console that the whole family can enjoy. Most widely and sensationally reported by the media was Matthew's observation that young people don't use Twitter. As he drily observes, Twitter is "pointless," "strictly for the elderly."

What is abundantly clear from these brief details of Robson's report is that the continuing development of networked computer technologies has transformed how we communicate and consume, work and play, and engage with others across the spheres of economic, political, cultural, and social life. So embedded have these technologies become that it is easy to forget just how profound the changes have been and how rapidly new forms of social action and interaction have become normalized, taken for granted, even mundane. eBay (established in 1995), Google (1998), Wikipedia (2001), YouTube (2005), Facebook (2006), Twitter (2007), WhatsApp (2009), and Instagram (2010) are among the most ubiquitous brands in contemporary life. Yet it is worth remembering that 30 years ago, the Internet was known only to a small and specialized community largely confined to academic and scientific institutions. From this position of marginality, the subsequent expansion of the Internet has been exponential (Jewkes & Yar, 2010).

REDEFINING DEVIANCE AND DEMOCRATIZATION: DEVELOPING NATIONS AND THE CASE OF CHINA

While there have been far-reaching developments in the rise of "new" media technologies in the West, the transformations that are taking place in some parts of the developing world are arguably even more profound. Having said that, we should not lose sight of the continuing global "digital divide," which, as Vincent Miller (2010) explains, means that the move to the digital age is greatly enhancing the position of the advanced, industrialized economies over those of the developing world, allowing them to play by a fundamentally different set of economic rules. Startup costs of Internet access are still prohibitively high for the poorest people in the world, where many do not even have access to a telephone service. Moreover, regional growth in Internet use is not always smooth and continuous, but may be disrupted by war, disaster, or displacement. For Miller, it is quite simply the case that, without some form of intervention, developed countries will benefit from increased access to knowledge, increased economic flexibility, and increased communication efficiency, while developing nations are at risk of being ever more victimized and marginalized by these trends. The optimism that once accompanied the Internet revolution has begun to fade in light of the realization that our culture has transformed the Internet more than the Internet has transformed our culture (V. Miller, 2010).

To illustrate further the digital divide, usage statistics from www.internetworldstats.com now put the global Internet population at 3,675,824,813, or 50.1% penetration (representing 918.3% growth since 2000). Leading the world table is North America, where 89% of the population is online. At the other end of the scale, just 28.7% of Africa's population has Internet access. Of the total world Internet users by region, 50.2% are in Asia; 16.7% are in Europe; 8.7% are in North America; 10.5% are in Latin America and the Caribbean; 9.3% are in Africa; 3.8% are in the Middle East; and 0.8% are in Australasia/Oceania. In terms of languages, 948.6 million Internet users communicate in English, followed next by Chinese language speakers at 751.9 million. China provides a fascinating case study because it illustrates in dramatic ways how digital technologies are implicated in social, political, and economic change. Use of the Internet in China grew from 22 million in 2000 to 721,434,547 million by mid-2016. The biggest distributor of online video in China is Yukou Tudou, which has overtaken YouTube with over 1 billion megabytes of data transfers every day. The Mandarin search engine Baidu has more hits than Google, and Chinese entrepreneur Jack Ma has set up Taobao to compete with eBay.

These examples are all the more remarkable given the Chinese authorities' fears about the potential uses of the Internet by "subversives." Over the last two decades, China has undergone immensely important economic reforms, which have given rise to tensions involving the Chinese media industries. With a population of nearly 1.4 billion and an increasingly important role to play in the global political economy, the Chinese media have been described as being in transition between totalitarianism and market authoritarianism (Winfield & Peng, 2005). Nowhere is the dual role that Chinese media play—simultaneously commodities in the market and ideological apparatuses—more apparent than in relation to new information and communication technologies; in particular, Internet restriction and censorship. A study conducted in 2002 found that of approximately 200,000 websites to which access was attempted, 19,032 sites accessible from the U.S. were inaccessible from China on multiple occasions, suggesting that even allowing for temporary technological glitches, the vast majority of these sites were deliberately blocked via government-maintained web filtering systems (Zittrain & Edelman, 2003). In 2004, an Amnesty International report revealed that the Chinese government was becoming increasingly heavy-handed with people using the Internet to circulate anti-government beliefs (Jewkes, 2013). All Chinese Internet service providers (ISPs) have to register with the police, and all Internet users must sign a declaration that they will not visit forbidden sites. Among those routinely blocked are news, health, and education sites, although pornography sites are virtually unregulated. In January 2010, Google declared that it was no longer going to censor search results on Google China, and two months later the company announced that it was moving its Chinese operation from the mainland to Hong Kong to avoid the rules and restrictions imposed by the authorities in Beijing, such as the blocking of results for searches using sensitive words and phrases, for example, "Tiananmen Square 1989." In 2014, as the 25th anniversary of Tiananmen approached, many Western news agencies reported that the Chinese government had further cracked down on access to information about the unrest of June 4, 1989, when troops shot dead hundreds of pro-democracy protesters gathered in central Beijing. The Chinese authorities have never publicly admitted how many people were killed, and many people born in China after these events may be unaware that it ever happened.

As *The Guardian* (March 22, 2010) noted, "the furore highlighted the challenges of doing business in China for western companies and drew a line under the era of unfettered optimism about the Internet's ability to change the country" (Branigan, 2010). For all its reputation as a wild frontier, then, the truth is that the Net can be used as just another means of constraint by those governments around the world who wish to discourage free thought, speech, and action. Nevertheless, there has been some softening in attitudes on the part of Beijing in recent years, even if benevolence is somewhat inconsistently applied. In May 2008, it was reported that the Chinese government had responded to the devastation caused by an earthquake in the Sichuan province, in which tens of thousands of people perished, by moderating its control of the Internet. This meant that those affected by the tragedy could use video sharing sites, blogs, chat rooms, instant messaging services, and the like to circulate graphic pictures and accounts of their experiences. For these new citizen journalists, the government's relaxation of its generally tough stance on Internet content brought an unprecedented level of freedom, and, as noted in Chapter 2, citizen journalism has changed the relationship between traditional news producers and audiences and taken the "immediacy" of news and its synoptic power to a new level. User-generated content is particularly powerful when produced by ordinary people in regions where professional journalists and camera operators have been unable to get to the scene quickly enough or where reporters are banned for political or military reasons.

China has also become the home of much activity that criminologists usually refer to by the shorthand term "cybercrime"—a word that encompasses both "computer-assisted" and "computer-oriented" crimes. The former refers to those offenses that, while predating Internet technology and having an existence independent of it, find a new lease of life online. For example, falling under this category are certain types of fraud, such as selling nonexistent, defective, substandard, or counterfeit goods; theft of monies through credit card and bank fraud; investment frauds such as pyramid schemes and fake stocks and shares; intellectual property offenses, including the unauthorized sharing of copyrighted content such as movies, music, digitized books, images, and computer software; posting, sharing, and selling obscene and prohibited sexual representations; and harassment, "stalking," bullying, sexual predation, and forms of hateful or defamatory speech. These offending behaviors are not unique to the online world (having long-established terrestrial counterparts) and have thus been described as "old wine in new bottles" (Grabosky, 2001). However, if we stick with this analogy, we can certainly appreciate that we are dealing with *an awful lot of wine* in very many differently shaped and capacious bottles (Jewkes & Yar, 2010). This point is illustrated by the fact that the first cybercrime in China took place in the mid-1980s, which was two decades later than the first active digital crime in the West, when the Chinese banking system was defrauded. Throughout the 1980s and 1990s, the growth of cybercrime in China was slow and steady, but today cybercrime in China is a vast self-perpetuating criminal industry and is proliferating partly because current law is wholly inadequate to deal with it (Qi, Wang, & Xu, 2009).

In addition to "computer-assisted" crimes, we have those that are "computer-oriented." This category of offense takes as its target the electronic infrastructure (both hardware and software) that constitutes the "fabric" of the Internet itself. Examples include various forms of "malicious software" (viruses, worms, Trojans) that corrupt files and hard drives; "denial of service attacks" that overload server capacity and effectively "crash" websites; and various forms of "defacement" through which web content is manipulated, changed, and/or deleted without permission or authorization. Again, to take the example of China, it was the emergence of a hitherto unknown phenomenon, a computer virus in the form of a malware program known as "Ping Pong," that first drew cybercrime to the attention of the Chinese public. According to one report, Beijing is now home to the world's largest collection of malware-infected computers (nearly 5% of the world's total), and research by the security company Sophos showed that China has overtaken the U.S. in hosting webpages that secretly install malicious programs on computers to steal private information or send spam emails (www.msnbc.com/id/19789995/).

Cyberwarfare and Cyberterrorism

The decision by Google to pull out of China is said to have followed a cyberattack it believes was aimed at gathering information on Chinese human rights activists. Most recently, attention has been directed toward the possibility of attacks on computer infrastructure by terrorist groups ("cyberterrorism"). For example, Dorothy Denning (2010) has outlined six areas of terrorist practice that have been substantially altered or enhanced by the Internet and the Web: media operations, attacks, recruitment, learning, finance, and security. However, while most commentators have focused on the specific threats from named terrorist cells and networks, state-authorized and government-sponsored attacks also appear to be on the rise and, again, China has suddenly appeared alongside nations that are more usually identified as posing a threat. The Military Balance 2016 is an annual study published by the International Institute for Strategic Studies (IISS) and is an assessment of global military capabilities that now includes analysis of cyberterrorism and cyberwarfare (http://www.iiss.org/publications/military-balance/). According to IISS, terrorism and warfare in cyberspace may be used to disable a country's infrastructure, meddle with the integrity of another country's internal military data, confuse its financial transactions, or accomplish any number of other possibly crippling aims (ibid.). In June 2009, the Pentagon created U.S. Cyber Command, and in Britain it was announced that a cybersecurity operations center would be established at GCHQ in Cheltenham. Yet governments and national defense establishments at present have only limited ability to tell when they were under attack, by whom, and how they might respond.

While these measures may give cause for alarm and seem to be in response to threats that might come from a Hollywood movie, we should not overstate the threat of cybercrime, cyberterrorism, or cyberwarfare. Further, it has not been our intention here to paint China as a particular problem; rather, it has been presented as a fascinating case study illustrating the speed and scope of Internet penetration and the consequent shifts in local and global power that occur. However, we must retain a healthy skepticism about claims made in the West regarding the threats posed by rapidly developing nations such as China. Put bluntly, media commentators, politicians, criminal justice actors, and security professionals may have strong vested interests in overplaying the risks presented. As Majid Yar (2010) has intimated, much of the debate about Internet regulation and censorship appears to be based on speculative notions of the antisocial and harmful impacts it may have at some point in the future rather than actual, current levels of victimization. Some of the concern expressed by authorities in the West about China as a source of cybercrime, cyberterror, and cyberwarfare therefore might reasonably be said to emanate from economic and political fears about Chinese growth and dominance in arenas and markets that other countries (particularly the U.S.) have owned for many decades. Maggie Wykes (2010) concurs and suggests that the media have been instrumental in heightening public fears about the possibility of terrorist attack. It is her view that since 9/11, the media have consistently reported that terrorist groups use Internet technologies to organize and plan both terrestrial and cyber attacks, and that these accounts have supported the concept of an ever-present global threat and underwritten policy from the U.S. and its allies regarding the "War on Terror." Wykes suggests that the meaning of terrorism in the 21st century has been reconstructed and allied to the Internet through hyperrealistic criminalizing practices and fear-inducing discourses that have legitimated policies, alliances, laws, actions, and—as we saw in Chapter 8—invasive surveillance methods, with profound implications for netizens, citizens, and the exercise of power (Wykes, 2010). Although global acts of cyber-facilitated warfare and terrorism are certainly possible and their consequences terrifying to contemplate, it is the more mundane, "ordinary" cybercrimes that affect millions of people worldwide that are of most concern to most of us, so let us take a brief overview of some of the offenses that come under the heading of "cybercrime."

"ORDINARY" CYBERCRIMES

Electronic Theft and Abuse of Intellectual Property Rights

One of the most obvious consequences of the new information and communications revolution is its creation and distribution of unimaginably more information-based products that force us to reevaluate traditionally held ideas about crime and criminality. For example, theft has commonly involved one person taking something belonging to another person without his or her permission—the result being that the first party no longer has possession of the property taken. Investigation of this type of offense is usually relatively straightforward insofar as it involves property that is tangible, visible, and atom-based (Goodman, 1997). But in a virtual context, it is quite possible for one person to take something that belongs to another person without permission and, in some cases, make a perfect copy of the item, the result being that the original owner still has the property even though the thief now has a version as well. Intellectual property can take a number of recognized forms— patents, trademarks, trade secrets, industrial designs, and copyright. Such acts challenge conventional and legal definitions of offenses and render traditional copyright laws irrelevant (D. S. Wall & Yar, 2010). Electronic reproduction of data can take many forms. One of the most common is "peer-to-peer" (or P2P) file sharing, which has arguably returned to the Internet a sense of the liberal, collective ethos, and benign anarchy that characterized its early days in the 1960s and 1970s. But for the film and music industries who are losing millions of dollars in lost sales, this form of "digital piracy" taking place in teenagers' bedrooms the world over is every bit as unlawful as the knowing and criminal use of the Internet to market or distribute copyrighted software (Yar, 2006).

Moreover, it is not just young people who believe that it is morally acceptable to illegally download movies, music, and software: a U.S. survey found that only 26% of professionals oppose piracy (Yar, 2010). The industry has been slow to respond to the problem of file sharing, and broadband technology has made it even quicker and easier to download music and movies illegally. The Record Industry Association of America (RIAA) is taking legal action against individuals it alleges offer file-swapping services on university campuses, and the Movie Picture Association of America is attempting to close down sites that distribute films online. But many believe that big corporations are being forced into playing cat-and-mouse games they can't possibly hope to win because—as the RIAA's infamous closure of Napster demonstrated—when the illegal business of one outfit is terminated, numerous others will appear in its wake.

HATE CRIME

Hate crime may be racist, religiously motivated, homophobic, gendered, disablist (Chakraborti & Garland, 2009), or, as we shall see, simply a violent reaction to a particular lawbreaker who has been in the news. The promotion of hatred is widespread, and the Internet is a relatively cheap and accessible means of connecting similarly minded people across the world and coalescing their belief systems. The Net is also a sophisticated tool for recruitment and unification, providing links between hate movements that were previously diverse and fractured and facilitating the creation of a collective identity and empowering sense of community (B. Perry, 2001). In fact, while the potential of the Internet as a weapon of warfare has already been discussed, it must also be remembered that the Internet has increased the global reach of terrorist groups, such as ISIS and al-Qaeda, who can use computer and telecommunication links, email, and cellular and radio networks to conduct operations over long distances while dispensing with the need for fixed physical presence. Coleman and McCahill (2010) note that a former radical Muslim claimed that more than half of young Saudis who had embraced a radical ideology were recruited through the Internet. In Europe, various groups on the political far right—neo-Nazis, skinheads, and groups with ties to the Ku Klux Klan—use the Net to target a youthful and impressionable audience with racist, anti-Semitic, and homophobic propaganda with little fear of the kind of legal sanction that might accompany the circulation of such material in more "traditional" forms. Although Germany and many other European countries have criminalized the publication and distribution of hate propaganda, the Internet remains largely unregulated, and there is little the police can do unless a specific crime is reported. Moreover, the constitutional protection afforded to "free speech" in the U.S. makes it difficult to challenge the global dissemination of messages of hate. Although often targeted at broad demographic groups, religions, and so on, hate crime is increasingly taking the form of vigilantism against individuals. Accordingly, anti-fascist (Antifa) groups regularly use social media to "out" members of far-right racist organizations who wish to remain anonymous. More legally ambiguous are "hate" behaviors that might be termed "cyberbullying" or "trolling." As we shall see later in this chapter, some bullying among children and young people is linked to sexual behavior, but, much like traditional bullying, it may range from name calling to serious threats of assault and blackmail. Like its "real-life" equivalent, cyberbullying behaviors may be covered by legislation, but much of it consists of low-level abuse, gossip, and rumor, which, while potentially very upsetting to the recipient, are not usually a criminal offense. "Trolling," on the other hand, is usually associated with more serious behavior. Formerly known as "flaming," trolling has become associated with the worst displays of hatred, misogyny, racism, and homophobia, usually in public online forums, and has, in several cases, resulted in the victim taking his or her own life. While there is no federal legislation aiming to address cyberbullying, every U.S. state has some form of anti-bullying law.

INVASION OF PRIVACY, DEFAMATION, AND IDENTITY THEFT

The entitlement to security of person is regarded as a fundamental human right, yet the scope and pervasiveness of digital technologies open up new areas of social vulnerability. Invasion of privacy takes many forms from "spamming" to online defamation, stalking, and violence. Spamming has thus far been considered little more than an extension of conventional junk mail, although it is increasingly being recognized as an insidious and frequently illegal activity. It can encompass everything from electronic chain letters and scams claiming that there are extensive funds—for example, from over-invoiced business contracts or a deceased relative's will—available for immediate transfer into the target's bank account, to phony cancer cures and bogus test kits for anthrax. One increasingly prevalent crime, originating particularly in countries in West Africa and targeting women in Europe and the U.S., is online dating scams, whereby fraudsters post bogus photographs and establish relationships with vulnerable victims (sometimes over several months) before persuading them to send them money. In addition, the past few years have seen a massive rise in incidents of so-called "phishing," in which communications purporting to come from legitimate organizations such as banks and building societies target Internet users, inducing them to voluntarily surrender sensitive financial information, which can then be used to defraud them.

In providing a forum for discussion among discrete groups, the Internet inevitably makes public what might be assumed to be private, as some students have discovered when fined by their universities for "breaking the rules" on post-exam celebrations and posting photographic "evidence" on Facebook. In addition, staff at several universities have reportedly checked personal profiles on networking sites to make decisions about whether or not to admit individual students. Another cybercrime related to privacy is the theft of personal identity, a practice that has dramatically increased in the last few years. Identity theft encompasses a full range of offenses from the appropriation and use of credit card numbers to the wholesale adoption of someone else's persona. It can be mundane and opportunistic; for example, many identity thieves rummage through dustbins for discarded credit card statements or pick up receipts left at bank ATMs. However, more high-tech versions include hacking into an individual's personal computer in order to steal his or her bank and credit card details, using software programs designed to work out or randomly generate PIN numbers, and "skimming" credit cards in shops and restaurants to produce a near perfect copy of the original card. Apart from financial fraud, identity theft has come to be viewed as an important "precursor" enabling a range of further offenses, including illegal immigration and human trafficking using stolen identities.

There may be a generational divide in levels of public anxiety about identity theft. On the whole, fears appear to be more strongly experienced by older people (illustrated, perhaps, by the fact that in 2004, sales of shredders increased by 50% at one international supplies company, with 1.3 million units sold in a single year; Jewkes & Yar, 2010). But, as Russell Smith (2010) points out, although young people may be more cavalier about their potential for victimization, the expansion in social networking sites has left young people at greater risk of identity crime. By way of example, he notes that one in seven users on Facebook log into their profile virtually all the time during office hours, rendering both themselves and their organizations open to criminal activity.

EBAY FRAUD

Identity theft clearly can be a prelude to fraud, but fraud can be perpetrated via the Internet without recourse to stealing someone else's bank account details, credit card number, or other aspects of their documentary identities. A growing number of criminal offenses are facilitated via online auction site eBay, including the sale of knives and other weapons, metabolic steroids, hardcore pornography, and abusive images of children. More mundanely, however, it is goods that are counterfeit, or which breach intellectual copyright laws or are knowingly stolen, faulty, or damaged, that make up the bulk of the criminal transactions that occur on eBay. Most individual consumers do not pursue legal action when the "designer" goods they purchase arrive and are clearly not genuine. But the global corporations that trade on their luxury brand names have the finance and motivations to act when they feel their brand has been damaged. In a landmark legal ruling in 2008, a French court ordered eBay to pay 19.28 million euros to Louis Vuitton Malletier and 17.3 million euros to its sister company Christian Dior Couture for damage to their brand images and for causing "moral harm." Damages were sought over two issues: First, it was argued that eBay had committed "serious errors" by not doing enough to prevent the sales of fake goods, including Louis Vuitton bags; second, it was argued that eBay had allowed unauthorized sales of perfume brands owned by the group. The company's view was that, whether the perfumes were real or fake, an offense had been committed because the sale of real goods and perfumes on eBay violates the company's authorized distribution network, which only allows sales through specialist dealers (*Guardian,* July 1, 2008). While these kinds of offenses can cost luxury brand companies millions, more pervasive in terms of perpetration and victimization are offenses involving handling stolen goods, financial fraud, obtaining property by deception, or instances where sellers simply fail to provide goods to buyers. According to one report, police investigate an alleged eBay scam every hour, some of which have moved beyond the cyber realm and precipitated "real-world" crimes, including burglary, assault, possession of firearms offenses, civil disputes, harassment, and an arson attack (*Daily Mail,* October 8, 2008). Users of the auction website reported an estimated total of more than 8,000 crimes in 2007 prompting eBay to respond by offering training to 2,000 police officers to tackle suspected Internet fraud.

Hacking and Loss of Sensitive Data

eBay has also been the target of hackers. In May 2014, the auction site was forced to ask 145 million users to change their passwords when it was revealed that hackers had stolen email addresses, birth dates, and other identity information in a significant data breach. Other reports suggest that hackers in Russia are infiltrating people's Apple devices, blocking them, and demanding payment from their owners to unblock them; that Chinese hackers have targeted U.S. defense and European security industries and stolen data relating to satellite, aerospace, and communications; and that the Bank of England "is to let hackers loose on Britain's biggest banks to test their defenses against cyber-attacks" (*Independent,* June 10, 2014). Most sensationally, following the somewhat surprising (to many people in America and the rest of the world) election of Donald Trump as U.S. president in 2016, several high-profile commentators have suggested that Russian hackers were instrumental in his victory and in the discrediting of his opponent, Hillary Clinton. One of outgoing President Barack Obama's final acts while in office was to expel nearly three dozen Russian intelligence agents from the U.S. At the same time, the FBI and National Cybersecurity and Communications Integration Center (a branch of the Department of Homeland Security) published a report outlining Russia's "malicious cyber-enabled activities" (NCCIC & FBI, 2016).

Hackers can, then, be driven by a wide range of motives. In addition to the acts of "cyberterrorism" and "cyberwarfare" described earlier, hacking can emanate from a relatively benign belief in freedom of access to information for all. Alternatively, hackers may claim the moral high ground in cases such as the Russian hack team Fancy Bears, who in 2016 stole athletes' medical records from the World Anti-Doping Agency (WADA) and published details of many high-profile sports stars' alleged drug misuse on grounds of believing in "clean competition" (fancybear.net). Hacking may even simply be a desire for mastery for its own sake (P. A. Taylor, 2003). There are, then, inherent complexities in the term "hacking," some of which will be perceived by society at large as more legitimate than others. Indeed, "hacking from the moral high ground" is a fascinating subject, and hacking is one of very few cybercrimes that can elicit social tolerance and even a grudging admiration for its audacity and the technical skill required. The authorities of most countries take a different view, however, especially the United States post 9/11. Gary McKinnon, a 42-year-old Briton accused of breaking into Pentagon computers and raiding U.S. Army, Navy, and NASA networks in 2001 and 2002 (he claimed he was looking for evidence of UFOs), faced the full wrath of the American criminal justice system and was facing extradition and up to 70 years in an American prison under terrorist charges, despite support from dozens of high-profile British politicians, academics, and celebrities who claimed that, as a man with severe Asperger's syndrome, McKinnon should be tried not as a terrorist but as a man with a social disability. In the end, the British government stepped in and blocked his extradition, and Mr. McKinnon was told that he would not be prosecuted in the UK either, bringing a 10-year legal battle to an end. However, Lauri Love, another British man with Asperger's syndrome facing similar charges, may not be so fortunate. In 2016, the British home secretary authorized his extradition, and he is, as this book goes to press, facing 99 years in an American jail for breaching U.S. government security.

The penetration of any security system may be damaging enough, but the Pentagon—headquarters of the U.S. Department of Defense—may be regarded as one of the greatest prizes by hackers around the world. Yet what is striking about the stories of Gary McKinnon and Lauri Love is how easily they accessed potentially sensitive data. As Jon

Ronson (2009) rather colorfully puts it, McKinnon "spent between five and seven years roaming the corridors of power like the Invisible Man, wandering into Pentagon offices, rifling through files." When he was eventually arrested in November 2002, British arresting officers told him to expect a few months' community service. But they underestimated how draconian the U.S. administration had become in the aftermath of the War on Terror, and Ronson notes that

> US prosecutors saw him not as a north London nerd who had allowed his addictive actions to escalate stupidly, but as the man who had committed "the biggest military computer hack of all time" and thus threatened the safety of every single American citizen. (2009)

McKinnon and Love both admitted their hacking but strenuously denied having malicious motives of the kind alleged by the U.S. authorities. Described by Ronson as essentially "idiotic but harmless" conspiracy theorists who spent their time on the Internet because they were "too nerdy to make it on the outside," Gary McKinnon and Lauri Love may simply be "a social type US prosecutors don't recognize" (2009).

Child Pornography and Online Grooming

Pornography is a subject that provokes fear and fascination in equal measure, and, while online porn (depicting adults and children) was the force that propelled the rapid growth of the Internet and demonstrated its commercial potential, equally it was child pornography that precipitated the establishment of some of the most high-profile organizations that police the Net. "Adult" cyberporn has democratized sexual gratification and provided greater freedom of access to women as well as its traditional customers, men (Jewkes & Sharp, 2003), yet at the same time it has reignited debates about the exploitation of women and the relationship between pornography and sexual assault and provoked a significant degree of technological determinism whereby blame is attributed to the Internet itself. The death of British music teacher Jane Longhurst, who was sexually assaulted and murdered by an acquaintance who reportedly downloaded images and accounts of necrophilia and asphyxiation to fuel his deviant sexual desires, was reported under the sensational headline "Killed by the Internet" (*Daily Mirror*, February 4, 2004; see Jewkes, 2007). Characterized by Yar (2010) as a "signal crime," the mediated public outcry following this case led to legislation criminalizing the possession of "violent pornography."

Despite such alarmism, which invariably reinvigorates debates about greater self-regulation, tougher legislation, and even censorship of the Internet, reported cases involving adult victims are extremely rare, and the most intensive focus continues to fall on pornography featuring children. It has been argued elsewhere in this volume that pedophilia constitutes *the* moral panic of our age (although that ascription has also been problematized), with all the attendant implications that moral panics tend to have on government and policing priorities. In common with broader news values, the issue is largely kept in the public eye through cases involving high-profile "offenders," including celebrities and newsworthy "victims."

Many believe that the police have taken too long to address the problem of online child sexual abuse and have, for many years, been playing catchup with online offenders. Limited resources, lack of technological expertise, a tendency to target "low-hanging fruit," and an occupational culture resistant to new challenges are among the impediments to successfully policing online abuse of children (Jewkes, 2010b; Jewkes & Andrews, 2005), but, thankfully, law enforcement is now beginning to reflect the changing technological and cultural landscape. One of the advancements made by those aiming to safeguard children has been to develop a proactive strategy based on specialist intelligence. An initiative that has proved reasonably successful is the employment of undercover officers posing as children on fake websites and in chat rooms to lure pedophiles (popularized by the NBC program *To Catch a Predator*). However, the charge of "grooming" has caused concern among civil liberties groups because it is designed to target adults who meet a child after contact has been made on the Internet but *before* any offense has taken place, raising the question of whether *thinking* about sexual acts is the same as committing them. Even if a case reaches court, proving intent is notoriously difficult for the police and prosecutors. In most cases, police are permitted to carry out "sting" operations by posing as children in Internet chat rooms; however, questions often remain regarding entrapment.

CHILDHOOD, CYBERSPACE, AND SOCIAL RETREAT

Interestingly, anxieties about crime and safety, especially of children, have been significant factors in many aspects of life becoming isolated and atomized activities. Numerous forms of "social retreat" have become commonplace, including the growing numbers of gated communities, ownership of four-wheel-drive vehicles, the popularity of home leisure systems including social gaming platforms, and many others. For young people, new social trends including the all-pervasiveness of the Internet and the tendency for parents to accompany their children in every public sphere constitute profound changes in the way that identities are shaped and social skills learned. At the same time, and partly as a consequence, of this privatization of social discourse and interaction, the Internet has become something of a scapegoat for a myriad of deviant human behaviors and conditions from sexual aggression and homicidal urges to attention deficit disorder and obesity. Unsurprisingly, it is children and young people who are considered most vulnerable to the potentially harmful effects of "new" media technologies and most likely to be victims of predators wishing to exploit or abuse them.

As noted in Chapters 3 and 4, childhood has been transformed, especially since the pedophile emerged to haunt our collective imagination in the mid-1990s. In the 21st century, adventure is for many children a virtual pleasure; competitiveness is honed at the games console rather than on the sports field; and sexual development occurs in chat rooms, on social networking sites, and via mobile phones (Jewkes, 2010b). Unfortunately, this means that some children and young people put themselves at risk of victimization and engage in more "extreme" behaviors online than they would in the "real" world.

Among the "risky" behaviors to emerge in recent years is sexting, where an individual sends nude or suggestive photos of themselves over their mobile phone. While such pictures are usually sent by young women to their boyfriends, police report that predatory adults are taking advantage of the willingness of young people to experiment with their sexuality over the Net by engaging in sexually explicit chat and by exposing their bodies in front of a webcam. So widely reported has sexting become (including stories of young celebrities who have found their "private" photos posted online) that governments have launched education campaigns aiming to educate young people about the dangers of the practice and warn them of the consequences, which can include bullying, harassment, sexual assault, and even suicide, as in one case in Cincinnati where an 18-year-old woman killed herself following months of taunting and bullying after nude images that she had sent to her boyfriend were circulated, first across her high school and subsequently far beyond.

The "normality" of cybersurveillance and the apparent willingness of children to take risks with their online activities and to flaunt their emerging sexuality within a forum that they mistakenly believe to be private is illustrated by the case of a sexual assault on a 13-year-old girl. Investigating police said they were exploring whether there was a connection between the attack and the fact that she described herself on her webpage as a "Bebo whore" (*Sunday Mercury*, April 14, 2008), although that line of inquiry probably ended as soon as they realized the routine frequency with which girls describe themselves as whores to indicate their attachment to social networking sites. Similarly, research conducted by an educational sociologist found that more than 25,000 users of Bebo (a former Facebook rival) had "slut" in their usernames (Ringrose, cited in the *Times*, August 5, 2009), again, illustrating to each other (if not to any pedophiles viewing their sites) that there has been a cultural shift in the meaning of such terms. Hille Koskela (2006) suggests that some young women who charge people to view their home pages may not have grasped that they are effectively turning images of themselves into pornography. New communications technologies also have reportedly facilitated novel kinds of aggressive and sexually aggressive behaviors among children and young people, including sexual cyberbullying. For example, police report that children as young as 10 are posing as predatory pedophiles on Internet networking sites to frighten other children they have fallen out with (*Guardian*, January 9, 2009), and, in 2007, a 16-year-old schoolboy was charged with sexually assaulting a 14-year-old girl and another was charged for filming the attack and distributing the pictures on his mobile phone (*Sunday Times*, February 4, 2007).

It is ironic, then, that as childhood has been privatized, the private sphere has itself become a source of anxiety, so inextricably is domestic space now intertwined with cyberspace. Hardly a week goes by without some new moral panic being generated about Facebook (which, once again, may say as much about its economic presence as its social and cultural importance). But long before the development of the Internet, children bullied, and their sexual experimentation has always, on occasion, had a dark side. In his partially autobiographical account of the James Bulger murder case, Blake Morrison (1997) recalls the rape of a 14-year-old girl at a party he attended when he was 15. He uses the story to illustrate that most of us experienced events in our youth of which we are now embarrassed or ashamed; after all, children can be promiscuous and unimpeded by perceptions of risk. Perhaps social networking sites and mobile phones simply offer a new means and a new lexicon with which children can explore their identities, including their psychosociosexual makeup, and to exert power over their peers.

The pervasiveness of images of young women asserting their sexual agency on networking sites and on YouTube may be unsettling, but it is arguable that they are simply using a new channel to express what is essentially "normal" adolescent behavior, especially in a culture that increasingly attaches more emphasis on the desire to look and to be watched and less stigma to nudity, intimate confession, and explicit material in published diaries and blogs. The open displays of sexuality by young women that one encounters on social networking sites are arguably the inevitable consequence of a surveillance-rich and surveillance-tolerant society (as discussed in Chapter 8). In today's "celebrity culture," women are urged to live up to prevalent feminine codes epitomized by celebrities such as Kim Kardashian regarding their domestic roles, body shape, dietary habits, dress sense, sexuality, and sexual performance. While, for some, this imposed self-surveillance may result in negative responses, including disgust and shame at their failure to live up to these ideals, for others, the ability to make public their private bodies via webcams, phone cameras, and social networking sites may constitute empowerment, albeit nonetheless a form of "obedience to patriarchy" underpinned by a "pervasive feeling of bodily deficiency" (Bartky, 1988, pp. 81–82; cf. Coleman & McCahill, 2010).

CONCLUDING THOUGHTS

This chapter has discussed a range of "cybercrimes" and included more detailed discussion of two very different case studies. At the beginning of the chapter, we considered the role that the Internet is playing in the development of China as an economic and cultural superpower, briefly dwelling on issues as diverse as cyberwarfare and citizen journalism. Later, we reflected on young people's sexual experimentation online, the freedoms it affords them that they may be denied in other spheres of life, and the deviant and criminal consequences that can result. These examples illustrate the extent to which the evolution of the Internet may be characterized as a "chronicle of contradiction" (Curran, 2010). From its military origins and the massive investment put into its development by a U.S. government seeking military and technological superiority over the Soviet Union during the Cold War, to the "hippie," liberal counterculture in which the World Wide Web was conceived in the 1980s and the era of deregulated media in the 1990s which allowed the newly commercialized Internet to flourish, the history of the Internet has combined paradoxical influences and outcomes. In its post-military phase, it amalgamated the values of academic science, American counterculture, and European public service ideals. But having come to public life as a profoundly democratic concern, it eventually had to offer itself to commercial interests and, then, to private and state bodies who wanted to use it for surveillance of populations (Curran, 2010). Vestiges of the counterculture ethos remain intact and arguably are evident in the sexual and political freedoms afforded to users, as described in this chapter. But it is also true that the liberty and democracy that many of us take for granted have more negative, even sinister, connotations.

SUMMARY

- This chapter has discussed two examples of online activity that raise urgent social, cultural, and political questions and illustrate some of the complexities and paradoxes inherent in our uses of the Internet in the 21st century: namely, its facilitation of democracy and freedom on the one hand, and repression and risk on the other. Our focus could have been any number of online behaviors that would illustrate the contradiction and dilemmas thrown up by the Internet, but the two chosen—its role as a conduit of power within China and between China and the West; and its radical reformulation of the ways in which children and young people communicate, interact, and negotiate sexual relations—are in keeping with broader themes that underpin this entire book.

- Like so many other issues examined throughout this volume, the Internet crystallizes social attitudes toward youthful deviance and highlights both the ambiguous status occupied by adolescents (simultaneously infantilized and adultified) and also the paradoxical relationship between young people as victims and, conversely, as offenders or deviants.

- Chapter 9 has also offered a broad introduction to the types of activities that may be described as "cybercrimes," including electronic theft and abuse of intellectual property rights; hate crime, invasion of privacy, defamation, and identity theft; eBay fraud; hacking and loss of sensitive data; child pornography; and online grooming.

STUDY QUESTIONS

1. Do you behave, or have you ever behaved, online or using any form of digital/mobile technology in ways that you would not risk in "real life"? Why do you think that sometimes different rules and moral codes apply in cyberspace?

2. Both this chapter and the preceding one have highlighted that we live in a scopophilic, synoptic society. What are the social messages underpinning this "mass looking exercise" (Coleman & McCahill, 2010)? Exactly what is being looked at and with what social consequences?

3. What do you understand by the term "digital divide"? Can it be applied in local as well as global contexts?

4. Are there negative consequences of the democratization of access to information that the Internet has brought?

5. How newsworthy is cybercrime? Give reasons for your answer.

FURTHER READING

There are now a number of useful collections that discuss many kinds of "cybercrime," although understandably they become outdated very quickly!

- *Handbook of Internet Crime,* edited by Y. Jewkes and M. Yar (Willan/Routledge, 2009), and the second edition of M. Yar's *Cybercrime and Society* (SAGE, 2013) are useful references.

- Covering many of the issues raised in both this chapter and the previous one is the second edition of *Globalization and Crime,* by K. F. Aas (SAGE, 2013); see especially Chapter 8 on "Controlling Cyberspace?"

- David Wall's extensive writings on cybercrime include *Policing Cybercrime: Networked and Social Media Technologies and the Challenges for Policing* (with M. Williams; Routledge, 2014) and *Cybercrime: The Transformation of Crime in the Information Age* (Polity, 2007).

- A fascinating discussion of growing up in the surveillance age, with chapters on sexting, mobile phone surveillance, and monitoring of young people's favorite websites, can be found in E. Taylor and T. Rooney's *Surveillance Futures: Social and Ethical Implications of New Technologies for Children and Young People* (Routledge, 2016).

- A comprehensive collection looking at the phenomenon of sexting is *Sexting and Young People,* by T. Crofts, M. Lee, A. McGovern, & S. Milivojevic (Palgrave, 2015).

Student Study Site

WANT A BETTER GRADE?

Get the tools you need to sharpen your study skills. Access practice quizzes, eFlashcards, SAGE journal articles, and more at study.sagepub.com/jewkesus.

(Re)Conceptualizing the Relationship Between Media and Crime

10

OVERVIEW

Chapter 10 provides:

- Some thoughts on how an interest in media criminology might extend to conducting research.

- Criticisms of existing scholarship in the field, particularly in relation to the methodologies employed.

- A bringing together of the main themes of the book.

- An examination of the significance of "mega-cases."

KEY TERMS

- audiences 247
- images 244
- media criminology 242

- media text 243
- mega-cases 251
- methodologies 243

- otherness 249
- signal crimes 252

In this final chapter, we would like to reflect on what this book has been about and offer some concluding thoughts about how some of the primary themes that have emerged might help us to better understand the complex relationship between media and crime. First, though, it is likely that many of the readers of this volume will be students planning to write a thesis or dissertation in this area, so it is worth dwelling briefly on how the study of the field may be approached. The chapter will be divided into two parts; it will end with some thoughts on what we have learned from our discussions so far, but first we will consider the business of doing media-crime research.

DOING MEDIA-CRIME RESEARCH

Researching the kinds of issues discussed throughout this book is an exciting prospect, but conducting studies that aim to enhance our understanding of any aspect of the relationship between media and crime should not be undertaken lightly; the very best studies in the field have not compromised on theoretical depth or methodological rigor. For example, Cohen's (1972/2002) model of moral panics has proved impressively enduring, and many followers have sought to emulate it. It is more easily understood than many media theories; it is more tangible than some subjects (e.g., those that appear to belong in the "virtual" world of cyberspace); and it seems relatively easy to research, compared to, say, criminal justice agencies (or, for that matter, news agencies) that can be difficult to access. However, despite its continuing popularity, the moral panic thesis is frequently misrepresented or cannibalized in contemporary scholarship, and even established academics may cherry-pick the bits of it that make their point while ignoring much of its theoretical substance and empirical exactitude.

Few research studies since Cohen's famous analysis have come close to the empirical rigor and diversity of methods with which he approached his subject. Cohen's documentary sources included national and local press cuttings from the entire two-and-a-half year research period; tape recordings of most radio and television news bulletins over the bank holiday weekends during which the incidents took place; local publications with restricted circulation (parish newsletters, council minutes, and the like); Hansard reports; and letters received by the National Council for Civil Liberties alleging police malpractice. In addition to these secondary sources, Cohen administered questionnaires to trainee probation (parole) officers; interviewed news editors; held informal discussions with local hotel owners, shop assistants, taxi drivers, and so forth; interviewed 65 members of the public who had witnessed the clashes between the mods and rockers; wrote letters to politicians and other public officials, some of which were followed up with interviews; talked to local action groups; and participated as a volunteer worker for a youth project in one of the seaside towns in which conflict had occurred (Cohen, 1972/2002, pp. 173–177). It is perhaps precisely this methodological thoroughness that helps to explain both why this kind of empirical research is now so rare and why many contemporary studies of moral panic are hackneyed and unconvincing.

Although today's students may not be able to devote the time and resources to a project of this scope (apart from PhD students, that is, which Cohen was when he conducted the *Folk Devils and Moral Panics* study), that does not mean that they should compromise on theoretical and empirical robustness or that doing any kind of media research should be viewed as an easy option. Chris Greer has voiced his concern about "the types of research that appear increasingly to be defining the field," and he urges new scholars to engage in "more fully interdisciplinary, theoretically and methodologically rigorous, qualitative engagement with the crime-media nexus" (2009, p. 1). Implicit in his critique is an appeal to students of media and crime to take risks and push the boundaries of existing knowledge. Explicit is his criticism that media criminology sometimes seeks to shed light on the role of media in society without any grounding in sociology or sometimes even any reference to the vast literature that has been born out of media studies and cultural studies. Put bluntly, some scholars in criminology adopt an insular stance that leads, at best, to partial understanding of the issues being studied. In addition to theoretical parochialism, Greer is disparaging about what he describes as the growing distancing between the researcher and the object of enquiry, when "methods are designed for detached quantification and counting rather than engaged, in-depth understanding, and the main objective is the routinized production of quick, clean datasets" (Greer, 2009, p. 4). Greer's aversion to quantitative methods is shared by Ferrell, Hayward, and Young (2015), who lament that methodologies designed explicitly to "exclude ambiguity, surprise, and 'human error' from the process of research result in 'lifeless, stale, and inhuman' data" (p. 165).

Jewkes (2010b) has explored the kinds of research that can be undertaken into the media-crime nexus by breaking the field into four distinct parts. In brief, and to take them in reverse order, she discusses the role of *media within the criminal justice system* and the part that research can play in illuminating aspects of a system that is usually not only hidden from public gaze but can also be shrouded in a certain amount of myth and mystique. Unfortunately, negotiating access, getting past "gatekeepers," persuading busy criminal justice professionals and wary "clients" to grant interviews, and treading fine ethical lines are all potential obstacles to carrying out research in the relatively "closed" settings of police stations, legal practices, courtrooms, and prisons, which is why such projects are arguably the least commonly undertaken, with some notable exceptions. Hardly more straightforward are ethnographic studies into media organizations. As we saw in Chapter 2, in the 1970s, 1980s, and 1990s, several groundbreaking studies were conducted in the newsrooms where crime correspondents worked, but the practicalities of immersing oneself in the field of news production and spending a great deal of time with journalists, both on and off duty, in order to explore the full range of institutional and sociocultural factors that shape and determine news output, have caused a sharp decline in the number of projects carried out in these environments.

Rather more easily embarked upon are studies examining *media audiences*. Large-scale mail or email surveys examining public perceptions of mediated crime are usually beyond the financial means and time constraints of most students, although small-scale questionnaires, especially when administered online, are popular and can yield valuable responses. Focus groups and semistructured interviews are also commonly undertaken because they are cheap and relatively easy to organize and are useful for obtaining rich data in participants' own words and developing deeper insights than would be elicited from a questionnaire. Finally, media texts may be the subject of research, and content analysis or discourse analysis might be the chosen method. Newspapers, TV news bulletins, films, social media exchanges, or any other "readable" text can be studied, and this approach is particularly useful for examining the kinds of biases, prejudices, and omissions in media reporting that were discussed in the first six chapters of this volume. There now exist several searchable online databases and newspaper digital archives, which make content and discourse analysis relatively cheap and easy—and therefore attractive to students with limited means and numerous competing pressures on their time and attention.

It is for these reasons that we want to dwell a moment on online news archives and exercise a word of caution. The problem with research tools like LexisNexis is that they only provide the researcher with flat text, as Greer et al. caution:

> Reduced to words on a computer monitor, printed "news" becomes decontextualized, shorn of structure and style, disconnected from defining images and surrounding stories—and so, ultimately, left with little similarity to the increasingly spectacular, brilliantly colourful products that media audiences consume on a daily basis. (Greer, Ferrell, & Jewkes, 2007, p. 6)

Actual newspaper digital archives might be considered superior insofar as a story can be viewed online as a facsimile of the original news page, along with accompanying photographs and other images, and the stories composed around it. These aspects of news reporting—images and composition—are important elements to any news story, and it is frequently instructive to look beyond a single report and examine other elements that are constructed around it in order to fully grasp the meaning encoded in it. For example, when they were both alive, British news reports about Diana, Princess of Wales, and child murderer Myra Hindley were frequently published alongside each other in the popular press, together with mirroring photographs of the two women (e.g., close-up images of their faces). While the accompanying headline would sometimes make reference to binary oppositions such as "Angel" and "Devil," it was not always necessary to spell out so blatantly the intended meaning, given that the juxtaposed images were of the invariably photogenic Diana and the unflattering police mugshot of Myra (see Figure 5.2).

Another common practice, especially in the local and regional press, is to publish lots of small-crime stories, often taken from court reports, on a single page to give the impression of a crime wave. The overall effect of this kind of composition is frequently lost if the researcher is using only a keyword search to isolate particular stories.

The Importance of the Visual

Echoing Greer et al.'s concerns about the relative neglect of visual images in media criminology, a growing collection of scholars have argued that it is in the realm of the visual—or the "graphic image," to use the news-values terminology employed in Chapter 2—that meaning is most immediately and powerfully conveyed (see, for instance, the introduction to the 2014 special issue of the journal *Theoretical Criminology*, Visual Culture and the Iconography of Crime and Punishment by Nicole Rafter). Any story can be manufactured in such a way that it is deemed newsworthy, but it is the incorporation of images that most directly communicates the intended message. Tammy Ayres and Yvonne Jewkes (2012) demonstrated this in a small-scale analysis of UK press coverage of the "moral panic that never was"—the predicted arrival of a crystal methamphetamine epidemic from the United States. Crystal meth was a drug that British people may have known little about beyond the fact that self-confessed user Andre Agassi was seemingly able to continue his professional career, appearing on television numerous times, playing, and being interviewed, while looking the picture of health and not arousing suspicion.

So, in their bid to shock readers out of any complacency about the harms caused by crystal meth, several newspapers published lurid "before and after" pictures of meth addicts, the latter graphically illustrating the facial deformities and chronic aging effects accompanying use of the drug.

These "shock pictures of what new danger drug can do to you" (*Mirror*, March 2, 2006, as cited in Ayres & Jewkes, 2012, p. 317) were crucial in conveying the moral message of the story and communicating a sense of awe and fear about the next anticipated crime wave to hit these shores from the United States. As Brown (2009, p. 23) and Linnemann et al. (Linnemann, Hanson, & Williams, 2013, p. 612) have further commented, looking at and judging the lives of others (e.g., meth users) harnesses a "peculiar energy" bound up in the enduring human fixation on the traumatic and grotesque. In a similar way to passing the scene of an accident and feeling compelled to look, shocking images are a defining feature of spectatorship (Linnemann et al., 2013). More importantly, though, the "faces of addiction," as they were described, were used as a driver for broader drugs legislation and policy, a highly visible manifestation of the need for an American-style "war on drugs" to be waged on *all* drugs, including cannabis. Linnemann (2013) calls this "governance through meth" and argues that it is part of a broader politics of security that underpins all of crime control. He also notes that analyses of the centrality of visual images to a story like meth use—including an advertising campaign that employed graphic images accompanied by headlines such as "15 Bucks for Sex Isn't Normal. But on Meth It Is" and "Before Meth I Had a Daughter; Now I Have a Prostitute"—demonstrates what Greer and colleagues had earlier observed; that "the visual constitutes perhaps the central medium through which the meanings and emotions of crime are captured and conveyed to audiences . . . a sort of inflationary spiral of shock and enticement designed to sustain commercial buoyancy" (Greer et al., 2007, p. 5). In this sense, and as Ayres and Jewkes (2012) further note, the mugshots of meth users performed a similar function to the photographs on cigarette packets showing the damaging effects of nicotine. Ostensibly designed to act as a visual deterrent, yet frequently having the opposite effect, especially among young smokers, it might be suggested that the graphic depictions of crystal meth users reproduced in the newspapers had similar intentions and effects.

Taking Media-Crime Research Seriously

We would argue that by far the best way to research any cultural text, including newspaper content, is to get hold of the actual texts themselves; indeed, many believe that the ways in which we engage with the physicality of newspapers are radically different to the ways in which we use online news sources. This is not just because newspapers *have* a physicality (they have a certain smell; they crackle as you turn the pages; they are frequently large and cumbersome, especially if you are trying to read one in a restricted space, such as on a train; some still leave inky marks on your fingers), but it is because when we browse "real" newspapers, we have a healthy lack of control. By exercising control through our choice of searchable keywords when we conduct research, we limit our opportunities to chance upon stories that are of interest and relevance to our research topic but that did not contain the words we inputted. On the other hand, "actual" newspapers can be difficult to get hold of, especially if your desired sample is very large or goes back several years/decades. In any case, it is estimated that more people now get their news online than from old-fashioned newspapers. For example, a U.S. survey found that 37% of Americans go online for news compared to 27% who only read a print newspaper (http://people-press.org/report/444/news-media). People who consume news in this way may interact with the journalist, editor, and other readers via comment pages, networking sites, and blogs, and they may also access video clips as well as still images, all of which will be absent from an online news search. We are not saying don't use Nexis, but *do* supplement it with other research tools and approaches.

For example, in the study by Ayres and Jewkes (2012) described above, it was impractical to get hold of and analyze actual newspapers. Instead, a twofold methodological approach was adopted. First, a keyword search was undertaken using both the InfoTrac newspaper database and LexisNexis for the key terms "crystal meth" and "crystal methamphetamine." These searches yielded approximately 1,254 articles in UK national newspapers published between 2004 and 2011, which were then reduced to 537 by removing irrelevant articles and non-news stories (including TV guides, book reviews, and quizzes). Then, the second stage involved a more focused online search in which 52 key articles incorporating visual images were isolated. Of these, 20 (38%) were accompanied by the faces of crystal meth users. At this stage, Ayres and Jewkes emailed the newspapers concerned and requested "hard copies" of the ones that contained the images, in which they were interested. This allowed the pair to conduct a detailed semiotic analysis of the photographs used *and* to consider the relationship between written text and image. They also analyzed the pages on which the stories were situated in order to understand intra- and intertextual relationships and how news stores are composed and juxtaposed on the page (or across double pages) to subtly suggest a particular ideological worldview (Ayres & Jewkes, 2012). For example, they were able to see how stories about crystal meth were printed alongside stories about other drugs (ranging from cannabis to heroin) and also alongside reports of serious crimes, including gun offenses. The overall impression was that experimenting with, say, cannabis, may represent the "thin end of the wedge," leading unavoidably to addiction to more serious drugs such as meth; and that crime and drug use are inextricably and inevitably linked.

The crystal meth study demonstrates the importance of going beyond a simple textual analysis using word-search software. The message, then, is to take media-crime research seriously, applying the same kinds of theoretical and methodological standards as you would to any other area of criminological research while nonetheless exercising your imagination and enthusiasm. Be cognizant of the field's interdisciplinary roots, but be prepared to go beyond a faithful adherence to orthodoxies. In these endeavors, we may succeed in (re)conceptualizing the relationship between media and crime in the 21st century.

STIGMATIZATION, SENTIMENTALIZATION, AND SANCTIFICATION: THE "OTHERING" OF VICTIMS AND OFFENDERS

The notion of (re)conceptualizing the media-crime nexus brings us to some concluding thoughts on what we have learned from this book. Although ostensibly about the relationship between media and crime particularly in the U.S., but also in the UK and elsewhere, this volume has touched on many wider issues that continually circulate in media discourse and partially define contemporary society—among them, the sexual exploitation of children, the different cultural responses to men and women who kill, racism and violence of police, and the threat of the "outsider." This latter concern is perceived as sufficiently troubling to legitimate the demonization of certain individuals and groups—on the basis of age, ethnicity, style, and a range of other, usually visible, indicators—and to justify the repressive surveillance of public spaces. The examples discussed throughout the book indicate a clear selectiveness in the mediated constitution of offenders and offenses as well as victims who capture the public imagination.

If we were able to ask the readers of this book, "What have been the three most important, significant, and newsworthy crime stories reported in the last decade?" we imagine that most people's replies would *not* include the worldwide recall of millions of cars by Toyota in 2009 and 2010 after mechanical defects reportedly caused severe injury and the deaths of 52 people in the United States. Nor would most readers point to the case of Bernard Madoff, who defrauded thousands of investors and, in June 2009 was given a maximum prison sentence of 150 years. The severity of punishment in itself guaranteed the story's newsworthiness (Madoff's lawyer had pushed for 12 years), but the scale of the invested money lost ($65 billion) in the midst of a global recession and at a time when bankers and financiers were regarded as folk devils also accounted for the case's widespread coverage. In fact, what this book perhaps best illustrates is that contemporary mediascapes deliver story after story in a seemingly uninterrupted flow, making some crimes such as the salacious sexual murder committed by Jody Arias eminently visible and the crimes of presidential administrations, predatory financiers, and local police essentially invisible. That said, the recent election of Donald Trump to the office of U.S. president may well be the exception that proves the rule. Already inherently newsworthy for a whole range of reasons, Trump is finding his financial affairs and potentially inflammatory opinions under close scrutiny by the world's media.

Such is the nature of news in the "global village" that all the cases described throughout this volume might also come to the minds of readers in other countries, although there will, of course, be local variations. Readers outside the United States might not be familiar with the details of cases such as Madoff's, though and, when it comes to crime news, the U.S. pretty much operates in a void! As we have tried to make clearer, the U.S. arguably is a great deal more newsworthy than any other country from a crime news perspective, but it still takes events of a significantly high threshold or magnitude to register with audiences outside the States. The point is that in our increasingly individualized culture, where offending is regarded as the inflicting of harms by some individuals onto other individuals, mediated articulations of crime and punishment can still be seen as vehicles for connecting people and making a personal tragedy somehow emblematic of a wider social malaise or cause. As noted in Chapter 4, stories about crime and justice perform a similar role as sporting events, bringing communities together and mobilizing common responses, sometimes on either side of a single issue. Yet even the most extreme crime, murder, is subject to differing levels of interest, with only certain murders—of certain victims—containing sufficient human interest to touch everyone with the emotional intensity required to constitute a climate of public vilification and mourning. Appealing to the consensual values of an "imagined community" (Anderson, 1983), the media stigmatize offenders, sentimentalize victims, and sanctify those deemed particularly vulnerable or tragic. And, in relation to the latter, it is not just victims of serious and violent offenses that attain such elevated status but, in some cases, their relatives too (consider John Walsh from *America's Most Wanted,* for instance).

The rewriting of this book, originally published in the UK in 2004, for an American audience has proved instructive in thinking about how certain crimes come to public attention and stay in the mass consciousness, subtly contributing to our sense of selves, our perceptions of others, our cultural values, our levels of tolerance, and our national identity. In the 12 years or so since Yvonne Jewkes wrote the first edition of *Media and Crime,* new tragedies have come to occupy the collective psyche. Many of the offenses inflicted on the victims we all now we feel we "know" have already passed from being "current events" to "historical events," living on in the shared memory and serving to frame future mediated public discourses on crime and punishment. As mediated witnesses to tragic events, we come to occupy a terrain that Moira Peelo (2006) terms "virtual victimhood" or what Mark Seltzer (1998) calls our national "wound culture," a condition where an offense to one empathetically or otherwise becomes an offense to all. Furthermore, as Lynn Chancer argues, when a crime becomes so high profile that it blurs into a "social cause," it not only alters the contours of future public discourse about similar events but also creates an irresolvable tension when it enters the arenas of the legal system. Put simply, the law cannot be impartial and objective in cases that generate feverish media and public debate, especially those that appear to emphatically lay down markers that highlight broader social problems. Whether intentionally or unwittingly, then, individuals involved in judicial proceedings have a profound influence on understandings of subsequent cases, which are tried in the knowledge, and under the influence, of what has occurred previously (Chancer, 2005).

But why, in the case of JonBenét Ramsey, for instance, does the murder of a six-year-old in 1996 still occupy such a powerful place in the collective psyche when there have been so many similarly brutal crimes since that have failed to register in most minds? Why do only certain criminal events become thrust into the public sphere with sufficient vigor and emotional intensity to shape public fears of victimization? Why do some crimes invoke a public reaction so forceful that they become embedded in the cultural fabric of society, while other, almost identical, incidents fail almost to register on the media radar, still less capture the collective imagination? Why do some very serious crimes cast a much longer shadow than others, and some offenders become iconic representations of pure evil while others fade into quiet obscurity? Why, for example, are the names Jeffry Dahmer and John Wayne Gacy infamous and the name Wayne Williams not? And why do pedophiles who target children unknown to them merit such extreme hostility that the deep, enraged seething that bubbles quietly under society's surface occasionally erupts into violent, bloody, and frequently indiscriminate action, when the level of abuse occurring within families is largely ignored?

While it does not claim to provide all the answers, this book has attempted to shed light on some of the most troubling questions that continue to vex scholars of media and crime. While we didn't set out to write a book about "self" and "other," the finished project has had much to say about the ways in which "we"—the audience—in an ever-expansive mediascape, are influenced in our understandings of those who transgress legal and moral boundaries. We have concentrated on some of those crimes that are most sensationalized by the media and, as a consequence, have a peculiarly strong hold on U.S. culture and identity. But there are many "outsiders"—"the threatening outcast, the fearsome stranger, the excluded and the embittered" (Garland, 1996, p. 461)—who provide the "others" against whom we measure ourselves. As Michel Foucault (1988) suggests, we judge the criminal, not the crime, and for all our "postmodern" sophistication, the beginning of the 21st century finds us still falling back on the positivist discourses of 19th-century criminology. Attributing irrationality, oversensitization, and lesser reasoning to women, children, adolescents, the dangerous classes, those who lead "unconventional" lifestyles, people from different ethnic backgrounds from our own, and people with mental illnesses, it is perhaps not surprising that these "lesser mortals" are the very groups who are considered to be most susceptible to media "effects." It is also they who are most consistently demonized by the media, as these ascribed attributes then become the lens through which we view crime and violent behavior. No one who lives in today's media-saturated society is immune to the winner–loser/self–other/insider–outsider culture—little wonder, then, that to many U.S. citizens, the police and criminal justice system are viewed as, at best, ineffective and, at worst, threatening (Reiner, Livingstone, & Allen, 2001).

It has long been established that the media is not a window on the world but a prism subtly bending and distorting our picture of reality. In most versions of this argument, the reader, viewer, or listener is characterized according to varying degrees of passivity, unarmed and ill prepared to cognitively filter out the prejudices, biases, and slants that may be subtly conveyed or overtly apparent. But in this book, we have argued that the relationship between media and audience in defining the parameters of social (in)tolerance and social control is not only complex but also one of collusion. To be blunt, crime is constructed and consumed in such a way as to permit the reader, viewer, or listener to sidestep reality rather than confronting or "owning up" to it. Many of the cases discussed in this volume have been described as the unthinkable and unknowable, but perhaps they simply alert us to our collective unwillingness to think and to know. We have suggested that the crimes that conform to journalistic perceptions of "newsworthiness" elicit a deep cultural unease that we, as a society, can confront only if we detach ourselves from the perpetrator(s) emotionally, morally, and physically. Through a process of alienation and demonization, we establish the "otherness" of those who deviate and (re)assert our own innocence and normality (Blackman & Walkerdine, 2001).

Our premodern responses to postmodern problems are also evident in the media's overwhelming tendency to denounce acts as "evil." Since Cohen popularized the notion of the "folk devil" four decades ago, the symbolic potency of that image has been weakened and has, in recent times, been replaced by a more powerful icon—the "evil monster." When very serious offenses are committed, the evil nature of the act is projected onto the perpetrators and "evil" comes to be seen not as the element that sets this crime apart as an abnormal and isolated event but as the common factor in all crimes that can be reported as components of a single moral panic. Thus, children who kill—in breaching our ideal of childhood innocence—and women who commit very serious crimes—in challenging traditional notions of acceptable femininity—become doubly vilified. Meanwhile, pedophiles are universally condemned as unequivocal folk devils, set apart from "normal" society, inherently evil and incapable of reform (Critcher, 2003). The commonly felt emotions of guilt, denial, and repression that characteristically follow serious crimes perpetrated by women and children and by pedophiles give their crimes a superordinacy that lifts them above other, equally horrible, crimes and secures for them a powerful symbolic place in the collective psyche. Constructed as evil monsters or subhuman beasts, their complexity can be denied and their evil can be exorcized by their exclusion from society (Critcher, 2003; Kitzinger, 1999). It is, then, precisely for this reason that some crimes, extreme and terrible as they are, fail to spark the interest of the media and public. The point, then, is this: Crimes do not become the stuff of media sensation because the constitutive features of the case cannot be consigned to the unknown and unknowable margins. Certain crimes are so terribly ordinary and in fact so close to us that they invite society to recognize that it is not simply "evil" or "mad" people who are capable of killing, but our friends and relatives, and this is an unpalatable truth that society is simply not ready to negotiate.

It would also seem that media-orchestrated infamy is shaped by the representational resources available to report a case. Since the infamous "Watergate" tapes that brought down the Nixon presidency, mediated sounds and images have themselves frequently become part of a crime story and help not only to elevate public awareness at the time but also to ensure that a crime remains in the collective imagination long after the trial is over. There are many examples of chilling-with-hindsight snippets and snapshots from audiotapes, film, cell phones, and surveillance cameras that help to explain the potent symbolic resonance of certain crimes. The audiotape played in court of one of the child victims of Ian Brady and Myra Hindley crying and begging to go home; the amateur video film of Rodney King being brutally beaten by the LA police; the television footage shot from a police helicopter of O. J. Simpson driving slowly down the highway trying to evade the LA police that was seen on television by approximately 100 million viewers; the 14-minute tape played in court of Nicole Brown Simpson pleading for help from a 911 emergency operator as O. J. could be heard in the background threatening and abusing her. All these haunting moments are seared into the memories of those who have witnessed them and into our collective culture.

Of course, many of the criminal cases discussed in this volume have no such audio-visual "extras," and it is not being suggested that crime stories must have these media adjuncts to be deemed newsworthy. Nonetheless, it has become virtually impossible in contemporary society to separate the real from the mediated, and every "true crime" that comes to public attention becomes inseparable from the media discourses and images that communicate it, which, once again, underlines the importance of a holistic approach to media-crime research. Of course, there is no video footage of the 1959 murder of the Clutter family, but that case is virtually impossible to separate from the imagery conjured by Truman Capote's classic *In Cold Blood* and the numerous analyses, commentaries, documentaries, and biopics that followed.

As a final thought, it must be remembered that in order to construct offenders as "others," their "outsider" status must be unequivocal and incontestable. All mediated discourses are narrative devices, but there are always counternarratives, even if they are not represented by the media. Revenge is a common theme in the defenses of many notorious killers, and many claim that they acted out of a sense of grievance that they perceive as legitimating their crimes. Aileen Wuornos's explanation for her murder of seven men was that she had acted in self-defense; Thomas Hamilton, who in March 1996 massacred 16 children and their teacher in a primary school in Dunblane, Scotland, was said to have acted out of revenge against a community from which he felt persecuted and ostracized; Timothy McVeigh, who killed 168 people when he detonated a truck bomb outside a government building in Oklahoma, described it as a "retaliatory strike, a counter attack" against the U.S. government for their botched raid on a cult headquarters in Waco, Texas, and their treatment of Iraqis and their own troops through the use of chemicals (McVeigh, 2001). Numerous perpetrators of crimes that are, at one and the same time, so horrific that they result in life prison sentences yet so mundane (because they are committed by men against women and children) that they barely register a flicker of interest from the media, were either neglected in childhood or grew up in foster care and, in either case, were frequently the victims of sexual and physical abuse by adults in whom they should have been able to trust. Even Leopold and Loeb, as famously argued by Clarence Darrow, might be said to have had mitigating circumstances for the brutal murder of Robert Franks. Of course, all these defenses can be read as cynical ploys by the actors involved, or their supporters, to shift their status from that of offender to that of victim. But the crucial point is that, in downplaying their defenses, the media demonstrate the profound discomfort and denial with which our culture views these counternarratives. Whether this denial arises from a fear of the potential for "evil" that is within all of us or more generally of the unwillingness to accept that, sometimes, horror lies beneath the most ordinary façades, is debatable. But the fact remains that the truly "unthinkable" and "unknowable" are those crimes that take place behind closed doors and never reach public attention.

SUMMARY

This chapter has sought to do two things in conclusion:

- First, it has offered some thoughts on how an interest in media criminology might extend to conducting research (perhaps for a dissertation or thesis) into some or other aspect of the media-crime nexus. It has also highlighted some of the criticisms of existing scholarship in the field and warned against taking certain shortcuts when carrying out your own study.

- Second, the chapter has attempted to draw together some of the main themes that have emerged from the discussions throughout this volume. It has noted that not all offenders, victims, and crimes are treated equally by the media and that there is a tendency to concentrate on the most unusual, serious, and atypical offenses and report them in such a way as to characterize the offenders as "absolute others" with no hope of rehabilitation or redemption. At the same time, the victims of these horrible but thankfully rare offenses are sentimentalized sometimes to the point of sanctification. All these processes ensure that "mega-cases" take on a significance far greater than might be the case for other criminal events. They become socially, culturally, politically, and historically important, bringing audiences together as "mediated witnesses" or "virtual victims" and uniting them in an imagined community.

STUDY QUESTIONS

1. Given the criticisms raised here about media criminology sometimes lacking methodological rigor and theoretical interdisciplinarity, what do you think might provide fruitful areas for future research?

2. What do you imagine might be some of the barriers to conducting the kind of research that cultural criminologists like Jeff Ferrell and his colleagues have undertaken?

3. Compile a list of "mega-cases" or "**signal crimes**." How would you characterize their place in the collective psyche, and what kinds of wider social, cultural, and legal implications have they had?

4. Are mega-cases always brutal homicides, or do other types of offenses have the capacity to move from being "current events" to "historical events," living on in the collective memory and serving to frame future mediated public and legal discourses on crime and punishment? Can you think of any state crimes, corporate crimes, eco-crimes, or cybercrimes that could be described as mega-cases?

FURTHER READING

- Books devoted to the relationship between media and crime are growing in numbers, but the one we would most strongly recommend is *Crime and Media: A Reader*, edited by C. Greer (Routledge, 2009), which is a collection of "classic" and more unusual readings accompanied by insightful original commentaries written by the editor.

- In a similar vein is Y. Jewkes's *Crime and Media: Three Volume Set* (SAGE, 2009).

- As its title suggests, *Crime, Culture and the Media*, by E. Carrabine (Polity, 2008), goes beyond the media to analyze the role of crime in other cultural forms, including art and literature.

- An engaging and thought-provoking collection that demonstrates the importance of the visual in crime reporting is K. Hayward and M. Presdee's *Framing Crime: Cultural Criminology and the Image* (Glasshouse-Routledge, 2010).

- Finally, *Crime, Media, Culture: An International Journal* (http://cmc.sagepub.com) should be required reading for all students studying media and crime and is still one of the few "criminology" journals to incorporate photographs, cartoons, and other graphic illustrations.

Student Study Site

WANT A BETTER GRADE?

Get the tools you need to sharpen your study skills. Access practice quizzes, eFlashcards, SAGE journal articles, and more at study.sagepub.com/jewkesus.

Glossary

adultification: a term that hints at the ill-defined and variable nature of childhood, referring to the tendency to see children and young people as possessing similar capacities of reasoning and knowledge as adults. While this may be to their advantage in human rights terms, it also leads to an inclination—in the UK, at least—to criminalize children at a very young age.

agency: the notion that individuals act independently out of a sense of moral choice and free will, as opposed to being "acted upon" by social forces and structures.

agenda-setting: the ways in which those who work within the media decide what is important enough to be reported and what is ignored, thus setting public agendas of debate. Crime is a particularly striking example of the agenda-setting process because it is considered to be inherently **newsworthy**—although certain types of crimes, offenders, and victims are more prominent on the news agenda than others.

anomie: a concept deriving from the work of Durkheim and developed by Merton, who suggest that anomie characterizes certain groups who experience a conflict between culturally desired goals (for example, material wealth) and legitimate means of attaining such goals. It is sometimes held that the media and culture industries are among the primary culprits in creating a desire for success, wealth, and so on that are unobtainable by means other than criminal or deviant.

audience: the assumed group at whom media texts are aimed. Recent media theory has reconceptualized the notion of audience from an agglomeration of individual receivers who are fragmented and passive to sophisticated and active meaning-makers. In the light of developments in "reality television," it might be argued that the lines between producers and audiences are becoming increasingly blurred.

behaviorism: an empiricist approach to psychology developed by J. B. Watson in the early years of the 20th century. Becoming the dominant perspective in psychology in the 1960s, this school is concerned with the objective study of observable behavior and represents an antithetical challenge to psychoanalysis.

binary oppositions: the notion that the media (picking up on a human inclination to do the same) presents the world through polarized constructions of **difference** that are fixed and immutable—man/woman, black/white, good/evil, **tragic victim/evil monster**, and so on. The media's tendency to deal largely in binary oppositions is said to further entrench biased or prejudiced public attitudes toward marginalized groups.

carceral feminism: the view held by some feminists which holds that the criminal justice system should be relied upon predominately to protect women against violence and abuse and also to punish the abusers.

carceral society: the idea (derived from Foucault, 1977) that systems of surveillance are extending throughout society so that many more areas of social life are becoming subject to observation, categorization, and control, resulting in an increasingly compliant population.

catharsis: sometimes held to be a media "effect" and used to counter the argument that there is too much violence in the media, catharsis literally means "cleansing" or "purging" and implies that consuming violent media content allows viewers to release their feelings of anger, frustration, or aggression in a vicarious but safe manner. The designers of violent computer games are among proponents of catharsis theory, arguing that their products constitute a harmless outlet for players' negative emotions.

celebrity: one of the 12 cardinal **news values** of the late 20th/early 21st century referring to a person who is globally famous. Celebrity is said to carry cultural weight as a key signifier of how media culture operates (Osborne, 2002), and it intersects with crime insofar as celebrities who commit offenses, or who are victims of crime, are eminently **newsworthy**, while some "ordinary" offenders and victims become celebrities by virtue of the crimes associated with them.

children: a relatively neutral term (compared to the more negative ascriptions "adolescents," "youths," and "juveniles") that nonetheless is inclined to take on somewhat sinister undertones in the aftermath of serious crimes committed by the very young.

citizen journalism: a form of democratic participation brought about by mass ownership of mobile phones with built-in cameras, image-sharing networking sites including YouTube and Twitter, and the popularity of blogs. **User-generated content** from citizen journalists has transformed news, particularly of events where either professional journalists and camera operators have been unable to get to the scene quickly enough or where reporters have been banned for political or military reasons.

consensus: the achievement of social unity through shared agreement. **Critical criminologists** suggest that, far from being conceived in terms of consensus, societies are actually characterized by *conflicts* between social groups and classes whose interests are opposed and incompatible. Some of these groups exercise power and hold positions of advantage over others. In this interpretation, consensus is seen as constructed and imposed in order to maintain the privileged position of dominant groups. Consensus might thus be achieved subtly and **hegemonically**.

control of the body: an aspect of surveillance achieved via an interface of technology and corporeality that can range from direct physical contact between flesh and technological device to more oblique or covert methods of monitoring and codifying the body.

crime: conventionally, crime is a violation of the law, but this is not a unitary concept and it has been extended to incorporate social harms. Its meaning is historically and culturally relative and depends to a large extent on the theoretical position adopted by those defining it.

crime film: here used simply to denote a film made for cinema release or television that has a narrative/visual reference to criminal activity and/or criminal justice.

crime news: news stories about **crime** are ubiquitous in modern society and are invariably "novel" and "negative" in essence. In addition, crime news conforms to 12 **news values** that not only help us to understand the relationship between journalists, editors, and the **audience** but also tell us much about prevailing cultural and ideological assumptions.

criminalization: the application of the label "criminal" to particular behaviors or groups, this term reflects the

state's power—transmitted via the media, among other institutions—to regulate, control, and punish selectively.

critical criminology: a Marxist-inspired, "radical" school of criminology that emphasizes the relationship between routine, everyday life and the surrounding social structures. Critical criminology has parallels with the political economy approach within media studies in their common emphasis on the connections among class, state, and crime control.

crowdsource: the strategy of enlisting a large group of often disconnected people to work toward a common goal.

cultural criminology: an approach that embraces postmodernism's concerns with the collapse of meaning, immediacy of gratification, consumption, pleasure, and so on and emphasizes the cultural construction of crime and crime control and the role of image, style, representation, and performance among deviant subcultures.

cyberbullying: a "catchall" term describing any form of abusive behavior online that threatens, harasses, or harms others, particularly over a sustained period.

cybercrime: any criminal activity that takes place within or by utilizing networks of electronic communication such as the Internet.

cyberspace: the interactional space or environment created by linking computers together into a communication network.

cybersurveillance: surveillance of individual internet users and of the Internet more broadly.

cyberterrorism: activity that seeks to realize political ends by unlawful (and usually violent) means, and that (a) utilizes electronic communication networks to further those ends (such as the dissemination of propaganda, fund-raising, or recruitment) and/or (b) targets computer networks and information systems for attack.

dangerousness: a term that sums up widespread fear of individuals and groups who appear to pose a significant threat to order or to individuals' personal safety (references to the "dangerous classes" were common in 19th-century Britain) but is increasingly being supplanted by the actuarial and politically charged concept of **risk**.

demonization: the act of labeling individuals or groups whose norms, attitudes, or behavior is seen to constitute "evilness." Those who are demonized are traditionally characterized as **folk devils** and are the subjects of **moral panic** (Cohen, 1972/2002), although it is arguable that ascriptions of "pure evil" are becoming more salient than the rather less potent image of folk devilry.

deviance: a social, and usually moral (as opposed to legal), concept to describe rule-breaking behavior.

deviancy amplification spiral: the moral discourse established by journalists and various other authorities, opinion leaders, and moral entrepreneurs, who collectively demonize a perceived wrongdoer (or group of wrongdoers) as a source of moral decline and social disintegration, thus setting off a chain of public, political, and police reaction.

difference: a concept often used in a negative sense to encapsulate cultural diversity, whereby the patterns of behavior of certain groups are identified as "differing" from some presumed norm. Cultural difference—most unequivocally expressed in **binary oppositions**—is frequently seen as the key factor in designating some groups as "others," "outsiders," or "strangers," all of which can lead to **criminalization** and **demonization**.

documentary: usually a visual genre that has a claim to realism—that is, is based on the attempt, in some form or other, to document "reality" (although the line between "fact" and "fiction" can be somewhat blurred).

doli incapax: the principle that children under a certain age are incapable of understanding the difference between right and wrong, and therefore cannot be held criminally responsible for their actions.

effects research: a tradition of research that focuses on the impact or effects of media texts on audience attitudes or behavior. Although a popular explanation for serious and juvenile crime (particularly and, somewhat ironically, within the media), much effects research has been discredited for isolating media influence from all other variables.

essentialism: the belief that behavior is determined or propelled by some underlying force or inherent "essence." Essentialism informs many "commonsense" views on crime and criminality and provides the basis of a great deal of stereotyping about offenders.

ethnocentrism: when a country's news organizations value their own nation over others. In a famous study originally published in 1979 by Herbert J. Gans, ethnocentrism was found to be the enduring value in American news. He describes it as coming through most explicitly in foreign news "which judges other countries by the extent to which they live up to or imitate American practices and values" (2004, p. 42). The clearest expression of ethnocentrism in all countries appears in war news that relies on unsubtle and unmitigated notions of "the enemy."

evil monsters: a (post)modern version of **folk devils** whereby media, political, and legal discourses intersect to construct serious offenders in **essentialist** terms as absolute **others** and beyond the normal values that bind the **moral majority** together.

fake news: deliberate hoaxes, propaganda, and disinformation purporting to be real news and using social media to drive web traffic and amplify their effect. There were numerous fake news stories around the time of the 2016 U.S. presidential election, leading to suggestions that the election result was influenced by a widespread belief in fake news among Trump supporters.

familicide/family annihilation: reported to be an increasingly common phenomenon whereby a man is driven by fear of failure to kill himself and his family. It is often characterized as "misguided alturism," or a matter of masculine honor and pride in the face of overwhelming social expectations concerning men's responsibilities for their families' well-being. The relatively sympathetic coverage afforded by the media to men who commit familicide stands in contrast to media reporting of women who kill and demonstrates public tolerance of men's violence.

fear of crime: a state of anxiety or alarm brought about by the feeling that one is at risk of criminal victimization. Much discussion of individuals' fear of crime centers on whether such fear is rational (that is, that there is some tangible basis to the fear, such as previous experience of victimization) or irrational (that is, that fear is engendered by overblown and sensational media reporting of serious but untypical crimes).

feminism: in criminology, feminism emerged in the 1970s to challenge traditional approaches and their inability, or unwillingness, to explore the relationship of sex/gender to crime or criminal justice systems. Feminist criminologies are diverse and evolving and have been instrumental in introducing theories from psychoanalysis and cultural studies into criminology. One recent concern has been the portrayal of offending women as active agents exercising choice and free will rather than simply as passive victims of male oppression.

fifth estate: traditionally used to describe the poor, the fifth estate now usually refers to social media users and bloggers who are not part of the mainstream media, but the term has also been used, in a film of the same name, about WikiLeaks.

filicide: the killing of a child by its parent or stepparent, filicide is the only type of homicide that women and men commit in approximately equal numbers.

film noir: a highly stylized cinematic crime genre usually characterized by hard-boiled cynicism (on the part of the police officer, detective, or private eye) and sexual motivations (on the part of a ubiquitous femme fatale).

folk devils: the term popularized by Cohen (1972/2002) to describe an individual or group defined as a threat to society, its values, and its interests who become the subjects of a media-orchestrated **moral panic**. Folk devils are frequently young people who are stereotyped and scapegoated in such a fashion as to epitomize them as *the* problem in society.

fourth estate: although its meaning has changed over time, the fourth estate is generally regarded as being the press, in the form of powerful press barons like Lord Beaverbrook, William Randolph Hearst, and latterly Rupert Murdoch.

framing: the shared cultural narratives and myths that a news story conveys via recourse to visual imagery, stereotyping, and other journalistic "shortcuts."

genre: a category of usually musical, literary, or media composition characterized by a particular style, form, or content.

governmentality: Foucault coined this term to describe the growing inclination of the state to intervene in the lives of its citizens, not only via overt forms of regulation such as surveillance systems but also through the dynamic relations of power and knowledge circulated intellectually and linguistically across institutions.

hegemony: a concept derived from Gramsci that refers to the ability of the dominant classes to exercise cultural and social leadership and thus to maintain their power by a process of consent rather than coercion. The notion of hegemony is typically found in studies that seek to show how everyday meanings and representations (for example, to be "tough on crime") are organized and made sense of in such a way as to render the class interests of the dominant authorities a natural, inevitable, and unarguable general interest, with a claim on everybody.

heteropatriarchy: a society in which the heterosexual male/masculine is assumed to be the norm and anyone or anything that differs from this is defined as "**other**" and is subject to censure or discrimination.

hypodermic syringe model: an unsophisticated model of media effects whereby the media are seen as injecting ideas, values, and information directly into the passive receiver, thus producing a direct and unmediated effect.

ideology: a complex and highly contested term referring to the ideas that circulate in society and how they represent and misrepresent the social world. Ideology is often reduced to the practice of reproducing social relations of inequality in the interests of the ruling class.

imagined community: a term suggesting collective identity based on, and encompassing attitudes toward, class, gender, lifestyle, and nation. An imagined community is sustained via its representation, expression, and symbolization by various social and cultural institutions, including the media.

infanticide: the homicide of an infant under 12 months old by its mother while she is affected by pregnancy or lactation.

infantilization: while recent times have seen a certain "**adultification**" of children, particularly in legal and criminal discourses, they have simultaneously been subjected to a much greater degree of protective control and regulation than in former times. In addition, social, political, and economic forces have resulted in many young people having to delay the "rites of passage" (marriage, home ownership, and so on) that have traditionally marked the transition from adolescence to adulthood, thus condemning them to a prolonged period of infantilization.

labeling: a sociological approach to crime and deviancy made famous by Becker (1963) that refers to the social processes by which certain groups (politicians, police, the media, and so on) classify and categorize others. Deviance is thus not inherent in any given act but is behavior that is so labeled.

late modernity: a term used to describe the condition or state of highly developed, present-day societies that denotes their state as a continuation or development of what went before ("modernity") rather than as a distinct new state ("post-modernity").

left realism: a "radical" criminological perspective that emerged in Britain in the 1980s that views crime as a natural and inevitable outcome of class inequalities and patriarchy and that proposes to take both **crime** and **fear of crime** seriously.

legitimacy: the process by which a group or institution achieves and maintains public support for its actions. For example, **critical criminologists** have argued that while the media frequently construct violence by protesters as unacceptable and deviant, violence on the part of the police is legitimated on the grounds that it is seen as necessary and retaliatory.

Marxism: a theoretical approach that proposes that the media—like all other capitalist institutions—are owned by the ruling bourgeois elite and operate in the interests of that class, denying access to oppositional or alternative views. Crime is regarded as one of the ways in which class conflicts are played out within a stratified society.

mass media: the term used to describe the means of mass communication via electronic and print media made popular following the rise of the mass circulation newspaper in the 19th century and fully realized with the growth of radio in the 20th century. "Mass media" encapsulates the notion of large numbers of individuals being part of a simultaneous audience; thus—in this book—it has been used sparingly. In the postmodern media environment, the plurality of **media texts** available and the increasing move toward "narrowcasting" rather than "broadcasting" make the notion of a "mass" media increasingly untenable.

mass society: a term from sociology suggesting that in industrial/capitalist societies, individuals are directly controlled by those in power and are atomized and isolated from traditional bonds of locality or kinship, making them particularly susceptible to the harmful effects of the **mass media**.

media criminology: the academic study of the relationship between the media and crime in all their forms.

media text: a media text is any media product (for example, film, advertisement, television program, Internet home page, radio jingle, newspaper article) in which meaning is inscribed and from which meaning can be inferred.

mediated: in general usage, to mediate is to connect, not directly, but through some other person or thing. In this book, the term "mediated" is used throughout to mean "mediated via the media." While semantically incorrect, this avoids using the clumsier but perhaps less ambiguous "mediatized."

mega-cases: are those that take on a significance far greater than might be the case for other criminal events. They become socially, culturally, politically, and historically important, bringing audiences together as "mediated witnesses" or "virtual victims" and uniting them in an **imagined community**.

moral majority: a term that encapsulates the **imagined community** to which the popular press address themselves. Encompassing notions of conservativeness, respect for the law and its enforcers, and a certain version of "Britishness," it assumes **consensus** on the part of the readership and can be summed up as the *Daily Mail* view of the world.

moral panic: hostile and disproportional social reaction to a condition, episode, person, or group defined as a threat. According to some, crime has moved so emphatically to the center of the media agenda, and has become so commercialized, that a virtual permanent state of moral panic exists.

murderabilia: a term identifying collectibles related to murderers, murders, or other violent crimes, especially artifacts used or owned by murderers and items (often artwork) created by them.

narrative arc: the pattern of progression in a storyline; put simply, a beginning, middle, and end.

new visibility: with the proliferation of inexpensive camera and cellphone technology, some suggest that we all live in an age of increased or hyper-visibility. Cellphone recordings of police violence captured by bystanders, for instance, underscore this point.

news values: the professional, yet informal, codes used in the selection, construction, and presentation of news stories.

newsworthiness: a term that encapsulates the perceived "public appeal" or "public interest" of any potential news story. Newsworthiness is determined by **news values**; the more news values a potential story conforms to, the more newsworthy it is perceived to be.

otherness: the term "other" denotes a symbolic entity (for example, one or more individuals) located outside the self. Otherness involves the perception of the self as distinct from the not-self, the latter being a vast category subdivided according to learned **differences**. Otherness is frequently used as an explanation for the **demonization** and **criminalization** of those who differ in background, appearance, and so on from oneself or "us" and relies on notions such as **moral majority**, **imagined community**, and so forth to provide the norm against which others are perceived and judged.

pedophile: in clinical psychology, "pedophilia" denotes an erotic preference for prepubescent children—that is, those under 11 years of age. In common currency, "pedophile" refers to adults who are sexually attracted to children of any age, including pubescents of 12 years or older, although these individuals are more accurately described as "hebephiles." Applying the term indiscriminately to both "lookers" (for example, those who download abusive images of children from the Internet) and "doers" (those who actually abuse children themselves), the media also frequently refer to offenders as "convicted pedophiles," although no such offense exists in law.

panopticon/panopticism: the panopticon was a prison design created by Jeremy Bentham that has been used as a blueprint for analysis of surveillance, social control, and the exercise of power within society as a whole. Panopticism can be summed up as "the few observing the many."

paradigm: a shared set of ideas; the dominant pattern of thinking at any given time. Movements in theoretical understanding (for example, from modernity to postmodernity or from Marxism to pluralism) are often referred to as "paradigm shifts."

penal spectators: spectators who engage in the act of punishment vicariously through cultural texts such as films and documentaries and consumer experiences such as prison tours.

pluralism: an idea, deriving from sociology, suggesting that all opinions and interests should be equally represented and equally available. The promotion of a plurality of ideas has led some to criticize pluralism as a factor in the "dumbing down" of culture.

police/policing: the term "policing" refers to a diverse array of tasks, skills, and procedures involving monitoring, regulation, protection, and enforcement. Even "the police" themselves are becoming part of a more diverse assortment of bodies with such functions, and the array of activities we term "policing" is becoming increasingly diffuse. Policing has come to be understood as a set of semiotic practices enmeshed with mediated culture, an activity that is as much about symbolism as it is about substance.

police image: the totality of social and cultural meanings tied to policing within a particular social and historical context.

police power: the broad range of powers extending beyond the uniformed police, which are exercised by a variety of agencies and institutions concerned with the production and maintenance of social order.

political economy: a sociological tradition that analyses society and social phenomena, including the media, in terms of the interplay between politics, economics, and ideology.

populism/populist punitiveness: "populism" means an appeal to the masses; "populist punitiveness" is a term often used interchangeably with "penal populism," referring to the perception that the public demands more punitive justice and punishment strategies to deter would-be offenders from committing crime.

positivism: the 19th-century theoretical approach that argues that social relations can be studied scientifically and measured using methods derived from the natural sciences. In criminology it draws on biological, psychological, and sociological perspectives in an attempt to identify the causes of crime that are generally held to be beyond the individual's control. In media studies, positivism has also been influential in the development of experimental, especially **behaviorist**, research, and has been particularly central to studies of media effects.

postmodernism: postmodernism embraces a rejection of claims to truth proposed by the "grand theories" of the past and challenges us to accept that we live in a world of contradictions and inconsistencies that are not amenable to objective modes of thought. Postmodernism is arguably most prominent in cultural studies where it is used to emancipate meanings from their traditional usage and emphasize pleasure, feelings, carnival, excess, and dislocation. Within criminology, postmodernism implies an abandonment of the concept of crime and the construction of a new language and mode of thought to define processes of criminalization and censure.

precautionary principle: this is a line of reasoning grounded on "worst-case" thinking, reflecting a shift from probabilistic, "what might happen" scenarios to possibilistic, "what could happen" scenarios.

profit: in the context of this book, "profit" has been highlighted as a key term in relation to surveillance and social control. Surveillance and **security** represent big business and are driven largely by profit-motivated corporations who want to make their products attractive to the "right kind" of consumer.

psychoanalysis: a theoretical approach developed by Freud and more recently popularized through the work of Lacan, psychoanalysis studies people's unconscious motivations for their actions and has been especially influential as a theory of constructions of sexuality and of masculinity/femininity.

psychosocial: explanations that rely on perspectives that draw on both **psychoanalysis** and social/sociological understandings, particularly in the pursuit of knowledge about gendered identities. It is often useful to employ psychoanalytic concepts in conjunction with sociologically informed ideas from, for example, feminism, media studies, and cultural studies, in order to explore why some individuals generate a level of media-orchestrated and publicly articulated hysteria and vilification disproportionate to their actual crimes.

public appeal/public interest: two related but different concepts that are frequently confused. "Public appeal" can be measured quantitatively in sales figures and ratings and is frequently used to justify the growing dependence on stories with a dramatic, sensationalist, or celebrity component. "Public interest" may involve qualitative assessments of what the public should and should not be made aware of. It therefore connotes interference from corporations or, more commonly, politicians.

rationality/irrationality: in debates about public fear of crime, it has frequently been proposed that such fears are irrational because the crimes that people fear most are those they are least likely to fall victim to. However, in recent years, **left realists** and **cultural criminologists** have argued that there is a rational core to most people's anxieties. For example, the former suggest that people will fear crime if they have previously been victimized,

while the latter argue that the modern media are so saturated with images of, and discourses about, crime, that it is increasingly difficult to separate the "real" from the "mediated."

realism: an approach to painting, literature, filmmaking, and so on that attempts to describe something "as it is" without idealization or romantic subjectivity.

reception analysis: an alternative term for "audience research" that has taken an increasingly sophisticated view of the "receivers" of media texts. No longer are audiences conceived of in terms of what the media *do* to them, but, rather, the concern of reception analysts is "What do audiences *do with* the media?"

remake: generally refers to a movie that uses an earlier film as the main source material as opposed to a second, later-movie based on the same source (e.g., a novel or comic book), although remakes do not necessarily share the same title as the original.

representation/misrepresentation: the ways in which meanings are depicted, communicated, and circulated. Although the media are sometimes conceptualized as a mirror held up to "reality," in fact they are arguably more accurately thought of as a means of representing the world within coherent, if frequently limited and inaccurate, terms.

responsibilitization: as public services have been privatized over the last four decades, individuals and communities have been encouraged to take the responsibility for these services as their own. In the realm of education for instance, parents are now asked to volunteer at their children's schools to replace services once provided by paid staff. In the realm of crime control, neighborhood watch is an example of the responsibilization process.

risk: a concept that emerged to dominate discussions of late modernity in the 1990s, the term "risk society" was coined by Beck to denote the social shift from the pre-industrial tendency to view negative events as random acts of God or nature to the post-industrial preoccupation with manmade dangers and harms. The media are frequently conceptualized as the most prominent articulators of risk (and thus the primary source of people's **fear of crime**) because of their seeming obsession with health scares, panics over food and diet, and, of course, **crime**.

scopophilia: Taking pleasure in looking; having a desire to see.

security: one of the five aspects of surveillance that has significant social and cultural implications. Paradoxically, surveillance technologies may make people feel both more secure and more paranoid about their personal safety.

sexting: one of the fastest-growing harms involving young people; a form of peer-to-peer grooming or exploitative behavior in which sexually explicit messages and images are shared on mobile phones, via texting, instant messaging, or social networking sites. The phenomenon is linked to **cyberbullying** because victims are often threatened or blackmailed, and to revenge porn when used as retaliation.

signal crime: bearing some similarity to **moral panics** and the theory of "broken windows," signal crimes are incidents or offenses that, when seen or experienced, may trigger a change in public beliefs or behavior. It has become a familiar concept in policing because signal crimes can have a negative disproportionate impact on public perceptions of security.

social constructionism: a perspective that emphasizes the importance of social expectations in the analysis of taken-for-granted and apparently natural social processes. Constructionism avoids the conventional **binary opposition** of **representation**/reality by suggesting that there is no intrinsic meaning in things but that meaning is conferred according to shared cultural references and experiences.

social networking: The practice of encountering, interacting, and forming social relations with others using Internet-based sites or services designed for this purpose.

social reaction: the social process characterizing responses to crime and deviance. Encompassing public, political, criminal justice, and media reactions, the term is often used to signify the processes of **labeling, stereotyping**, and **stigmatizing** of certain individuals and groups.

spousal homicide: the unlawful killing of an individual by her or his spouse or partner, this offense has led to a great deal of research, especially within **feminist** criminology, regarding the mediating factors that have to be taken into account in studies of offending and **victimization**.

stereotyping: the process of reducing individuals or groups to oversimplified or generalized characterizations, resulting in crude, and usually negative, categorizations.

stigmatizing: the process by which an individual or group is discredited because of some aspect of their appearance or behavior. Stigmatization helps to explain why some perceived **deviants** are subjected to marginalization and social exclusion and are the recipients of hostile reporting and censure by the media.

stranger danger: a term that gained popularity in the U.S. in the late 1970s, reflecting the widespread concern for the threats posed to women and children by kidnappers and sex offenders. Importantly, this concern eclipses crimes that occur within the family.

subculture: generally used to describe groups of young people whose appearance, norms, and behavior differ from those of the mainstream or "parent" culture.

surveillant assemblage: the depth, or intensity, of surveillance that is achieved via the connection of different and once discrete technologies (for example, digitized CCTV systems and computer databases) and institutions (for example, the police and private security companies; Haggerty & Ericson, 2000).

synopticism: an emerging theme in the sociological and criminological literature on surveillance, synopticism describes a situation where the many observe the few (as opposed to **panopticism**, where the reverse is true). The late modern trend toward synopticism is evident in the development of the **mass media** and is exemplified by the "reality television" boom that has taken place in recent years.

tragic victims: the term frequently used in **binary opposition** to that of **evil monsters**, whereby the innocence and vulnerability of a victim of crime become the primary aspect of their representation in the media to the point of sentimentalization and sanctification.

trolling: formerly known as "flaming," the posting of defamatory and/or threatening messages on online forums, including personal Twitter accounts. Internet trolls divide opinion. Some maintain that freedom of speech, however tasteless or offensive, must be preserved. Others argue that the prison sentences handed out to trolls who have targeted **newsworthy** victims are justified.

unconscious: the term used in **psychoanalysis**, and central to the work of Freud, to refer to that which is repressed from consciousness.

user-generated content, or UGC: refers to various kinds of media content that is publicly available and is produced by end users. In news contexts, these end users are known as **citizen journalists**.

victimization: the experience of being a victim of crime. The study of the relationship between the victim and the offender—or "victimology"—has become a key concern and might be said to constitute a subdiscipline within criminology.

vigilante viewers: where penal spectators might engage vicariously in punishment through mediated cultural texts, television programs such as the long standing *America's Most Wanted* and other cultural texts encourage viewers to actively engage in the act of crime control and to "be on the look out" for criminal suspects.

voyeurism: originally used to describe the act of watching the sexual activities of others, voyeurism is now used more widely to describe spectatorship of what is usually held to be a private world.

youth: the imprecise period between infancy and adulthood. In media reporting of crime, youth tends to be more frequently linked to offending than victimization.

References

Aas, K. F. (2005). *Sentencing in the Age of Information: From Faust to Macintosh.* London, UK: Glasshouse-Cavendish.

Agnew, R. (2012). The ordinary acts that contribute to ecocide: A criminological analysis. In N. South and A. Brisman (Eds.), *Routledge international handbook of green criminology* (pp. 58–72). London, UK: Routledge.

Alder, C. M., & Polk, K. (1996). Masculinity and child homicide. *British Journal of Criminology, 36*(3), 396–411.

Aldridge, M. (2003). The ties that divide: Regional press campaigns, community and populism. *Media, Culture & Society, 25,* 491–509.

Allcott, H., & Gentzkow, M. (2017, Spring). Social media and fake news in the 2016 election. *Journal of Economic Perspectives, 31*(2), 211–236. Retrieved from https://web.stanford.edu/~gentzkow/research/fakenews.pd

Almog, S. (2012). Representations of law and the nonfiction novel: Capote's *In Cold Blood* revisited. *International Journal for the Semiotics of Law–Revue Internationale de Sémiotique Juridique, 25,* 355–368.

Anderson, B. (1983). *Imagined communities: Reflections on the origins and spread of nationalism.* London, UK: Verso.

Apted, M. (2009). Michael Apted responds. *Ethnography, 10*(3): 359–367.

Ashenden, S. (2002). Policing perversion: The contemporary governance of paedophilia. *Cultural Values, 6*(1 & 2): 197–222.

Associated Press. (2009, August 11). Fighting crime, one tweet at a time. *CBSnews.com.* Retrieved from http://www.cbsnews.com/news/fighting-crime-one-tweet-at-a-time/

Associated Press. (2014, May 3). Everyone is under surveillance now, says whistleblower Edward Snowden. *The Guardian.* Retrieved from https://www.theguardian.com/world/2014/may/03/everyone-is-under-surveillance-now-says-whistleblower-edward-snowden

Avedon, R. (1966, January 7). Horror spawns a masterpiece. *Life Magazine, 60*(1), 58–76.

Ayres, T. C., & Jewkes, Y. (2012). The haunting spectacle of crystal meth: A media-created mythology? *Crime, Media, Culture: An International Journal, 8*(3), 315–332.

Barak, G. (1994). Media, society, and criminology. In G. Barak (Ed.), *Media, process, and the social construction of crime.* New York, NY: Garland.

Barker, V. (2009). *Politics of imprisonment: How the democratic process shapes the way America punishes offenders.* Oxford, UK: Oxford University Press.

Bartky, S. L. (1988). Foucault, femininity, and the modernization of patriarchal power. In I. Diamond & L. Quinby (Eds.), *Feminism and Foucault: Reflections of resistance.* Boston, MA: Northeastern University Press.

Baudrillard, J. (1981). *For a critique of the political economy of the sign.* St. Louis, MO: Telos.

Baudrillard, J. (1983). *Simulations.* New York, NY: Semiotext(e).

Bauman, Z. (1992). *Intimations of postmodernity.* London, UK: Routledge.

Bauman, Z. (1997). *Postmodernity and its discontents.* Cambridge, UK: Polity Press.

Becker, H. (1963). *Outsiders: Studies in the sociology of deviance.* New York, NY: Free Press.

Bekiempis, V., Tracy, T., & McShane, L. (2016, April 28). 87 Bronx gang members responsible for nine years of murders and drug-dealing charged in largest takedown in NYC history. *New York Daily News.* Retrieved from http://www.nydailynews.com/new-york/nyc-crime/100-bronx-gang-members-busted-largest-takedown-nyc-history-article-1.2615933

Benedict, H. (1992). *Virgin or vamp.* Oxford, UK: Oxford University Press.

Benn, M. (1993). Body talk: The sexual politics of PMT. In H. Birch (Ed.), *Moving targets: Women, murder and representation.* London, UK: Virago.

Bennett, J. (2004). Life lessons: Rex Bloomstein's *Lifer* films. *Journal for Crime, Conflict and the Media, 1*(3), 43–54. Retrieved from http://www.jc2m.co.uk/Issue%203/Bennett.pdf

Bennett, J. (2006a). Undermining the simplicities: The films of Rex Bloomstein. In P. Mason (Ed.), *Captured by the media: Prison discourse in popular culture* (pp. 122–136). Cullompton, UK: Willan.

Bennett, J. (2006b). "We might be locked up, but we're not thick": Rex Bloomstein's *Kids Behind Bars. Crime, Media, Culture: An International Journal, 2*(3), 268–285.

Bennett, J. (2009). The interview: Paul Hamann. *Prison Service Journal, 184,* 45–50.

Bennett, W. J., Dilulio, J. J., & Walters, J. P. (1996). *Body count: Moral poverty . . . and how to win America's war against crime and drugs.* New York, NY: Simon & Schuster.

Berman, M. (1983). *All that is solid melts into air: The experience of modernity.* London, UK: Verso.

Berntzen, L. E., & Sandberg, S. (2014). The collective nature of lone wolf terrorism: Anders Behring Breivik and the anti-Islamic social movement. *Terrorism and Political Violence.* Retrieved from http://www .tandfonline.com/doi/abs/10.1080/ 09546553.2013.767245

Biber, K. (2007). *Captive images: Race, crime, photography.* London, UK: Routledge.

Birch, H. (1993). If looks could kill: Myra Hindley and the iconography of evil. In H. Birch (Ed.), *Moving targets: Women, murder and representation.* London, UK: Virago.

Blackman, L., & Walkerdine, V. (2001). *Mass hysteria: Critical psychology and media studies.* Basingstoke, UK: Palgrave.

Bloomstein, R. (2008, November 5). *Crime and the camera: Making prison documentaries: The work of Rex Bloomstein.* Presentation as part of the Scarman Lecture Series, Department of Criminology, University of Leicester, Leicester, UK.

Blumler, J. (1991). The new television marketplace. In J. Curran & M. Gurevitch (Eds.), *Mass media and society* (pp. 194–215). London, UK: Arnold.

Bocock, R. (1993). *Consumption.* London, UK: Routledge.

Bonilla-Silva, E. (2012, February). The invisible weight of whiteness: The racial grammar of everyday life in contemporary America. *Ethnic and Racial Studies, 35*(2), 173–194.

Boulahanis, J., & Heltsley, M. (2004, June). Perceived fears: The reporting patterns of juvenile homicide in Chicago newspapers. *Criminal Justice Policy Review, 15*(2), 132–160.

Box, S. (1983). *Power, crime and mystification.* London, UK: Tavistock.

Boyne, R. (2000). Post-panopticism. *Economy and Society, 29*(2), 285–307.

Bradsher, K. (2000). Ideas & trends; The latest fashion: Fear-of-crime design. *New York Times.* Retrieved from http://www.nytimes.com/2000/ 07/23/weekinreview/ideas-trends- the-latest-fashion-fear-of-crime- design.html

Brake, M. (1980). *The sociology of youth culture and youth subcultures: Sex and drugs and rock 'n' roll.* London, UK: Routledge & Kegan Paul.

Brandom, R. (2016, June 24). US Customs wants to collect social media account names at the border. *TheVerge.com.* Retrieved from http:// www.theverge.com/2016/6/24/1202 6364/us-customs-border-patrol- online-account-twitter-facebook- instagram

Branigan, T. (2010, March 23). Google angers China by shifting service to Hong Kong. *The Guardian.* Retrieved from https://www .theguardian.com/technology/2010/ mar/23/google-china-censorship- hong-kong

Bright, M. (2002, December 15). The vanishing. *Observer Magazine.* Retrieved from https://www .theguardian.com/theobserver/2002/ dec/15/features.magazine57

Brown, M. (2009). *The culture of punishment: Prison, society, and spectacle.* New York, NY: New York University Press.

Brown, M. (2012). Empathy and punishment. *Punishment and Society, 14*(4), 383–401.

Browne, A. (1987). *When battered women kill.* New York, NY: Macmillan/ Free Press.

Bunz, M. (2010, February 10). Q&A: BBC World Service director Peter Horrocks on social media and news. *The Guardian.* Retrieved from http://www.guardian.co.uk/media/ pda/2010/feb/10/peter-horrocks- social-media

Butler, J. (2006). *Precarious life: The powers of mourning and violence.* New York, NY: Verso.

Butler, J. (2013). Endangered/endangering: Schematic racism and white paranoia. In R. Gooding-Williams (Ed.), (2013). *Reading Rodney King/ reading urban uprising* (pp. 15–22). New York, NY: Routledge.

Cameron, D., & Frazer, E. (1987). *The lust to kill: A feminist investigation of sexual murder.* Cambridge, UK: Polity Press.

Campbell, M. (1995, February 9). Partnerships of perversion under study. *Globe and Mail* [Toronto].

Capote, T. (1993). *In cold blood: A true account of a multiple murder and its consequences.* New York, NY: Penguin Books. (Original work published 1965)

Caputi, J. (1989). The sexual politics of murder. *Gender and Society, 3*(4), 437–456.

Carlen, P. (2008). Imaginary penalties and risk-crazed governance. In P. Carlen (Ed.), *Imaginary penalties*. Cullompton, UK: Willan.

Carrabine, E. (2008). *Crime, culture and the media*. Cambridge, UK: Polity.

Carrington, K., & Hogg, R. (Eds.). (2002). *Critical criminology: Issues, debates, challenges*. Cullompton, UK: Willan.

Carter, C. (1998). When the "extraordinary" becomes "ordinary": Everyday news of sexual violence. In C. Carter, G. Branston, & S. Allen (Eds.), *News, gender and power* (pp. 219–232). London, UK: Routledge.

Casciani, D. (2009, May 7). Q&A: The national DNA database. *BBC News*. Retrieved from http://news.bbc.co.uk/1/hi/uk/7532856.stm

Cavender, G., & Deutsch, S. K. (2007). CSI and moral authority: The police and science. *Crime, Media, Culture, 3*(1), 67–81.

Cere, R., Jewkes, Y., & Ugelvik, T. (2013). Media and crime: A comparative analysis of crime news in the UK, Norway and Italy. In S. Body-Gendrot, M. Hough, K. Kerezsi, R. Lévy, & S. Snacken (Eds.), *The Routledge handbook of European criminology* (pp. 266–279). London, UK: Routledge.

Chadee, D., & Ditton, J. (2005). Fear of crime and the media: Assessing the lack of relationship. *Crime, Media, Culture, 1*(3), 322–332.

Chadwick, K., & Little, C. (1987). The criminalisation of women. In P. Scraton (Ed.), *Law, order and the authoritarian state*. Buckingham, UK: Open University Press.

Chaffin, M., Levenson, J., Letourneau, E., & Stern, P. (2009). How safe are trick-or-treaters? An analysis of child sex crime rates on Halloween. *Sexual Abuse, 21*(3), 363–374.

Chakraborti, N., & Garland, J. (2009). *Hate crime: Impact, causes, and consequences*. London, UK: SAGE.

Chalfant, H., & Silver, T. (1983). *Style wars* [Broadcast documentary film]. United States: PBS.

Chamlin, M. B. (1989). A macro social analysis of change in police force size, 1972–1982. *Sociological Quarterly, 30*(4), 615–624.

Chancer, L. S. (2005). In *re* the legal system. In *High-profile crimes: When legal cases become social causes* (pp. 115–172). Chicago, IL: University of Chicago Press.

Cheatwood, D. (1998). Prison movies: Films about adult, male, civilian prisons: 1929–1995. In F. Bailey & D. Hale (Eds.), *Popular culture, crime and justice* (pp. 95–130). Belmont, CA: Wadsworth.

Cheliotis, L. K. (2013). Neoliberal capitalism and middle-class punitiveness: Bringing Erich Fromm's "materialistic psychoanalysis" to penology. *Punishment and Society, 15*(3), 247–273.

Chermak, S. (1994). Crime in the news media: A refined understanding of how crimes become news. In G. Barak (Ed.), *Media, process, and the social construction of crime*. New York, NY: Garland.

Chesney-Lind, M. (1997). *The female offender*. Thousand Oaks, CA: SAGE.

Chesney-Lind, M., & Eliason, M. (2006). From invisible to incorrigible: The demonization of marginalized women and girls. *Crime, Media, Culture: An International Journal, 2*(1): 29–47.

Chesney-Lind, M., & Pasko, L. (1997). *The female offender: Girls, women and Crime* (2nd ed.). Thousand Oaks, CA: SAGE.

Chibnall, S. (1977). *Law and order news: Crime reporting in the British press*. London, UK: Tavistock.

Cloud, J. (2011, June 16). How the Casey Anthony murder case became the social-media trial of the century. *Time Magazine*. Retrieved from http://content.time.com/time/nation/article/0,8599,2077969,00.html

Cohen, S. (1980). *Folk devils and moral panics: The creation of the mods and rockers* (2nd ed.). Oxford, UK: Martin Robertson.

Cohen, S. (1985). *Visions of social control: Crime, punishment and classification*. Cambridge, UK: Polity Press.

Cohen, S. (2002). *Folk devils and moral panics: The creation of the mods and rockers* (3rd ed.). London: Routledge. (Original work published 1972)

Cohen, S., & Young, J. (1973). *The manufacture of news: Deviance, social problems and the mass media*. London, UK: Constable.

Cohen, S., & Young, J. (1981). *The manufacture of news: Social problems, deviance and the mass media*. Thousand Oaks, CA: SAGE.

Coleman, C., & Norris, C. (2000). *Introducing criminology*. Cullompton, UK: Willan.

Coleman, R. (2013). Confronting the "hegemony of vision": State, space and urban crime prevention. In A. Barton, K. Corteen, D. Scott, & D. Whyte (Eds.), *Expanding the criminological imagination* (pp. 38–64). New York, NY: Routledge.

Coleman, R., & McCahill, M. (2010). *Surveillance and crime*. London, UK: SAGE.

Coleman, R., & Sim, J. (2000). "You'll never walk alone": CCTV surveillance, order and neo-liberal rule in Liverpool city centre. *British Journal of Criminology, 41*(4), 623–639.

Connell, I. (1985). Fabulous powers: Blaming the media. In L. Masterman (Ed.), *Television mythologies* (pp. 88–93). London, UK: Comedia.

Connell, R. W. (1987). *Gender and power: Society, the person and sexual politics*. Cambridge, UK: Polity.

Coscarelli, J. (2015, July 26). Hologram performance by Chief Keef is shut down by police. *New York Times*. Retrieved from https://www.nytimes.com/2015/07/27/arts/music/hologram-performance-by-chief-keef-is-shut-down-by-police.html?_r=0

Cowburn, M., & Dominelli, L. (2001). Masking hegemonic masculinity: Reconstructing the paedophile as the dangerous stranger. *British Journal of Social Work, 31*, 399–415.

Crawford, A., Jones, T., Woodhouse, T., & Young, J. (1990). *Second Islington Crime Survey*. London, UK: Middlesex Polytechnic.

Creed, B. (1996). Bitch queen or backlash? Media portrayals of female murderers. In K. Greenwood (Ed.), *The things she loves: Why women kill* (pp. 120–135). Sydney, Australia: Allen & Unwin.

Critcher, C. (2003). *Moral panics and the media*. Buckingham, UK: Open University Press.

Cross, S. (2014). Mad and bad media: Populism and pathology in the British tabloids. *European Journal of Communication, 29*(2), 204–217.

Curran, J. (2010). Reinterpreting Internet history. In Y. Jewkes & M. Yar (Eds.), *Handbook of Internet crime*. Cullompton, UK: Willan.

Davies, J., & Smith, C. R. (1997). *Gender, ethnicity and sexuality in contemporary American film*. Edinburgh, UK: Keele University Press.

Davies, P. (2003, Autumn). Women, crime and work: Gender and the labour market. *Criminal Justice Matters, 53*, 46–47.

Davis, M. (1994). *Beyond Blade Runner: Urban control—the ecology of fear*. Open Magazine Pamphlet series. New York, NY: New Press.

Davis, M. (2006). *City of quartz: Excavating the future in Los Angeles* (new ed.). New York, NY: Verso.

Debord, G. (1997). *The society of the spectacle*. London: Verso. (Original work published 1967)

De Certeau, M. (1984). *The practice of everyday life*. Oakland, CA: University of California Press.

Denning, D. E. (2010). Terror's web: How the Internet is transforming terrorism. In Y. Jewkes & M. Yar (Eds.), *Handbook of Internet crime*. Cullompton, UK: Willan.

Dilulio, J. J. (1995, November 27). The coming of the super-predators. *Weekly Standard*. Retrieved from http://www.weeklystandard.com/the-coming-of-the-super-predators/article/8160

Ditton, J., & Duffy, J. (1983). Bias in the newspaper reporting of crime news. *British Journal of Criminology, 23*(2), 159–165.

Dobash, R., Dobash, R., & Gutteridge, S. (1986). *The imprisonment of women*. Oxford, UK: Blackwell.

Douglas, M. (1966). *Purity and danger: An analysis of concepts of pollution and taboo*. London, UK: Routledge and Kegan Paul.

Dovey, J. (1996). The revelation of unguessed worlds. In J. Dovey (Ed.), *Fractal dreams: New media in social context*. London, UK: Lawrence & Wishart.

Downes, D. (1988). The sociology of crime and social control in Britain, 1960–87. In P. Rock (Ed.), *A history of British criminology*. Oxford, UK: Oxford University Press.

Downes, D., & Rock, P. (1988). *Understanding deviance: A guide to the sociology of crime and rule breaking*. Oxford, UK: Oxford University Press.

Doyle, A. (2003). *Arresting images: Crime and policing in front of the television camera*. Toronto, Ontario, Canada: University of Toronto Press.

Duneier, M. (2009). Michael Apted's *Up!* series: Public sociology or folk psychology through film? *Ethnography, 10*(3), 341–345.

Durkheim, E. (1964). *The rules of sociological method*. New York, NY: Free Press. (Original work published 1895)

Eagleton, T. (2010). *On evil*. New Haven, CT: Yale University Press.

Education ban on paedophiles targeting schools. (1998, December 2). *BBC News*. Retrieved from http://news.bbc.co.uk/1/hi/education/225532.stm

Ehrlich, J. (2016). How a documentary on slain journalist James Foley reclaims his legacy. *Rolling Stone*. Retrieved from http://www.rollingstone.com/movies/news/how-a-documentary-on-slain-journalist-james-foley-reclaims-his-legacy-20160203

Ericson, R., Baranek, P., & Chan, J. (1987). *Visualising deviance: A study of news organisations*. Buckingham, UK: Open University Press.

Eschholz, S., Blackwell, B. S., Gertz, M., & Chiricos, T. (2002). Race and attitudes toward the police: Assessing the effects of watching "reality" police programs. *Journal of Criminal Justice, 30*(4), 327–341.

Farrall, S., & Gadd, D. (2004). The frequency of the fear of crime. *British Journal of Criminology, 44*(1), 127–132.

Farrell, G., & Pease, K. (2007, June). Crime in England and Wales: More violence and more chronic victims. *Civitas Review, 4*(2). Retrieved from https://pdfs.semanticscholar.org/2b5f/1da0debd0502836e9eb27bf01e0822dd7ddd.pdf

Federal Bureau of Investigation. (2014). *Crime in the United States, 2014*. Retrieved from https://ucr.fbi.gov/crime-in-the-u.s/2014/crime-in-the-u.s.-2014

Feldman, A. (1994). On cultural anesthesia: From desert storm to Rodney King. *American Ethnologist, 21*(2), 404–418.

Ferrell, J. (1996). *Crimes of style: Urban graffiti and the politics of criminality*. Boston, MA: Northeastern University Press.

Ferrell, J. (2001). Cultural criminology. In E. McLaughlin & J. Muncie (Eds.), *The SAGE dictionary of criminology* (pp. 103–106). London, UK: SAGE.

Ferrell, J. (2002). *Tearing down the streets: Adventures in urban anarchy*. New York, NY: Palgrave/St. Martin's.

Ferrell, J., Hayward, K., & Young, J. (2015). *Cultural criminology: An invitation* (2nd ed.). London, UK: SAGE.

Fiddler, M. (2007). Projecting the prison: The depiction of the uncanny in *The Shawshank Redemption. Crime, Media, Culture: An International Journal, 3*(2): 192–206.

Finch, E. (2003). What a tangled web we weave: Identity theft and the Internet. In Y. Jewkes (Ed.), *Dot.cons: Crime, deviance and identity on the Internet* (pp. 86–104). Cullompton, UK: Willan.

Fishman, M. (1978). Crime waves as ideology. *Social Problems, 25*(5), 531–543.

Fiske, J. (1982). *Introduction to communication studies*. London, UK: Routledge.

Fiske, J. (1987). *Television culture*. London, UK: Routledge.

Fiske, J. (1989). *Reading the popular*. London, UK: Routledge.

Foreman, T. (2006). Diagnosing missing white woman syndrome [Blog post]. *Anderson Cooper 360 Blog*. Retrieved from http://www.cnn.com/CNN/Programs/anderson.cooper.360/blog/2006/03/diagnosing-missing-white-woman.html

Foucault, M. (1977). *Discipline and punish*. London, UK: Allen Lane.

Foucault, M. (1988). *Politics, philosophy, culture: Interviews and other writings, 1977–1984*. London, UK: Routledge.

Frayn, M. (1965). *The tin men*. London, UK: Collins.

Freeman, M. (1997). The James Bulger tragedy: Childish innocence and the construction of guilt. In A. McGillivray (Ed.), *Governing childhood*. Aldershot, UK: Dartmouth.

French, P. (2009, August 1). *The Taking of Pelham 1 2 3. The Guardian*. Retrieved from https://www.theguardian.com/film/2009/aug/02/taking-of-pelham-123-review

Furedi, F. (1997). *Culture of fear: Risk-taking and the morality of low expectation*. London, UK: Cassell.

Furedi, F. (2013). *Moral crusades in an age of mistrust: The Jimmy Savile scandal*. London, UK: Palgrave Pivot.

Gadd, D., Farrell, S., Dallimore, D., & Lombard, N. (2003, Autumn). Male victims of domestic violence. *Criminal Justice Matters, 53*.

Galtung, J., & Ruge, M. (1973). Structuring and selecting the news. In S. Cohen & J. Young (Eds.), *The manufacture of news: Deviance, social problems and the mass media*. London, UK: Constable. (Original work published 1965)

Gandy, O. (1993). *The panoptic sort*. Boulder, CO: Westview Press.

Gans, H. J. (2004). *Deciding what's news* (2nd ed.). Chicago, IL: Northwestern University Press.

Garland, D. (1996). The limits of the sovereign state: Strategies of crime control in contemporary society. *British Journal of Criminology, 36*(4), 445–471.

Garland, D. (2008). On the concept of moral panic. *Crime, Media, Culture: An International Journal, 4*(1), 9–30.

Gelsthorpe, L., & Morris, A. (Eds.). (1990). *Feminist perspectives in criminology*. Buckingham, UK: Open University Press.

Gergen, K. J. (1991). *The saturated self*. New York, NY: Basic Books.

Gies, L., & Bortoluzzi, M. (2016). *Transmedia crime stories: The trial of

Amanda Knox and Raffaele Sollecito in the globalised media sphere. London, UK: Palgrave Macmillan.

Gillespie, M., & McLaughlin, E. (2002, Autumn). Media and the making of public attitudes. *Criminal Justice Matters, 49,* 8–9.

Girling, E., Loader, I., & Sparks, R. (2000). *Crime and social change in Middle England: Questions of order in an English town.* London, UK: Routledge.

Glancey, J. (2002, November 16). Image that for 36 years fixed a killer in the public mind. *The Guardian.* Retrieved from https://www.theguardian.com/uk/2002/nov/16/ukcrime.jonathanglancey

Goldsmith, A. J. (2010). Policing's new visibility. *British Journal of Criminology, 50*(5), 914.

Goldson, B. (2003, April 22–24). *Tough on children . . . tough on justice.* Paper presented to "Tough on Crime" . . . Tough on Freedoms? The European Group for the Study of Deviance and Social Control Conference, Centre for Studies in Crime and Social Justice, Edge Hill College, Liverpool, UK.

Goode, E., & Ben-Yehuda, N. (1994). *Moral panics: The social construction of deviance.* Oxford, UK: Blackwell.

Goodman, M. (1997). Why the police don't care about cybercrime. *Harvard Journal of Law and Technology, 10,* 465–494.

Grabosky, P. (2001). Virtual criminality: Old wine in new bottles? *Social & Legal Studies, 10,* 243–249.

Graef, R. (2009). Roger Graef: Police dressed up as Robocop act like him too. *Independent.* Retrieved from http://www.independent.co.uk/voices/commentators/roger-graef-police-dressed-up-as-robocop-act-like-him-too-1804743.html

Green, D. A. (2008a). Suitable vehicles: Framing blame and justice when children kill a child. *Crime, Media, Culture: An International Journal, 4*(2), 197–220.

Green, D. A. (2008b). *When children kill children: Penal populism and political culture.* Oxford, UK: Oxford University Press.

Green, N. (2009, December 7). Are readers being robbed of the facts? *MediaGuardian,* p. 6.

Greenwald, G. (2014, August 14). The militarization of U.S. police: Finally dragged into the light by the horrors of Ferguson. *The Intercept.* Retrieved from https://theintercept.com/2014/08/14/militarization-u-s-police-dragged-light-horrors-ferguson/

Greer, C. (2003). *Sex crime and the media: Sex offending and the press in a divided society.* Cullompton, UK: Willan.

Greer, C. (2009). *Crime and media: A reader.* London, UK: Routledge.

Greer, C., Ferrell, J., & Jewkes, Y. (2007). It's the image that matters: Style, substance and critical scholarship. *Crime, Media, Culture: An International Journal, 3*(1), 5–10.

Greer, C., & Jewkes, Y. (2005). Images and processes of social exclusion. *Social Justice, 32*(1), 20–31.

Grochowski, T. (2002). The "tabloid effect" in the O.J. Simpson case: The *National Enquirer* and the production of crime knowledge. *International Journal of Cultural Studies, 5*(3), 336–356.

Haggerty, K. D., & Ericson, R. V. (2000). The surveillant assemblage. *British Journal of Sociology, 51*(4), 605–622.

Hall, S. (1978). The treatment of football hooliganism in the press. In R. Ingham (Ed.), *Football hooliganism.* London, UK: Inter-Action.

Hall, S., Critcher, C., Jefferson, T., Clarke, J., & Roberts, B. (Eds.). (2013). *Policing the crisis: Mugging, the state and law and order* (2nd ed.). London, UK: Macmillan. (Original work published 1978)

Hallett, M., & Powell, D. (1995). Backstage with *Cops:* The dramaturgical reification of police subculture in American crime info-tainment. *American Journal of Police, 14,* 101.

Halloran, J. (1970). *The effects of television.* London, UK: Panther.

Halloran, J., Elliott, P., & Murdock, G. (1970). *Demonstrations and communication: A case study.* Harmondsworth, UK: Penguin.

Hamelink, C. J. (2000). *The ethics of cyberspace.* London, UK: SAGE.

Harmon, A. (2007). In DNA era, new worries about prejudice. *New York Times.* Retrieved from http://www.nytimes.com/2007/11/11/us/11dna.html

Harper, J. (2015, January 22). No more mopes: Who was Brimfield Police Chief David Oliver? A timeline of his career. Retrieved from http://www.cleveland.com/akron/index.ssf/2015/01/who_was_brimfield_police_chief.html

Hayward, K. J. (2012a). Five spaces of cultural criminology. *British Journal of Criminology, 52*(3).

Hayward, K. (2012b). Pantomime justice: A cultural criminological analysis of "life stage dissolution."

Crime, Media, Culture: An International Journal, 8(2), 213–229.

Hayward, K., & Presdee, M. (Eds.). (2010). *Framing crime: Cultural criminology and the image.* Abingdon, UK: GlassHouse-Routledge.

Hebdige, D. (1979). *Subculture: The meaning of style.* London, UK: Routledge.

Hebdige, D. (1989, January). After the masses. *Marxism Today,* pp. 48–53.

Heidensohn, F. (1985). *Women and crime.* New York, NY: New York University Press.

Heidensohn, F. (2000). *Sexual politics and social control.* Buckingham, UK: Open University Press.

Henry, S., & Milovanovic, D. (1996). *Constitutive criminology.* London, UK: SAGE.

Herbert, S. K. (1997). *Policing space: Territoriality and the Los Angeles police department.* Minneapolis: University of Minnesota Press.

Herman, E., & Chomsky, N. (1992). *Manufacturing consent: The political economy of mass media.* New York, NY: Vintage.

Hickey, E. W. (2013). *Serial murderers and their victims.* Boston, MA: Cengage Learning.

Hickman, T. (2005). "The last to see them alive": Panopticism, the supervisory gaze, and catharsis in Capote's "In Cold Blood." *Studies in the Novel, 37,* 464–476.

Hornby, S. (1997). *Challenging masculinity in the supervision of male offenders.* Social Work Monograph 157, University of East Anglia, Norwich.

Horrocks, P. (2008, January 7). The value of citizen journalism. *BBC News.* Retrieved from http://www.bbc.co.uk/blogs/theeditors/2008/01/value_of_citizen_journalism.html

Horton, D., & Wohl, R. (1956). Mass communication and para-social interaction. *Psychiatry, 19,* 215–219.

Hough, M., & Roberts, J. (1998). *Attitudes to punishment.* Home Office Research Study No. 179. London, UK: HMSO.

Hughes, J., Rohloff, A., David, M., & Petley, J. (2011). Foreword: Moral panics in the contemporary world. *Crime, Media, Culture: An International Journal, 7*(3).

Human, J. (Producer), & Broomfield, N., & Churchill, J. (Directors). (2003). *Aileen: Life and death of a serial killer* [Documentary film]. United States: Lafayette Films.

Innes, M. (2003). Signal crimes: Media, murder investigations and constructing collective memories. In P. Mason (Ed.), *Criminal visions: Media representations of crime and justice* (pp. 51–72). Cullompton, UK: Willan.

Innes, M. (2004). Crime as signal, crime as memory. *Journal for Crime, Conflict and the Media, 1*(2), 15–22.

Irwin, K., & Chesney-Lind, M. (2008). Girls' violence: Beyond dangerous masculinity. *Sociology Compass, 2*(3), 837–855.

Jackson, D. (2015, May 1). Obama team will fund police body camera project. *USA Today.* Retrieved from https://www.usatoday.com/story/news/nation/2015/05/01/obama-police-body-cameras-josh-earnest-baltimore/26696517/

Jarvis, B. (2004). *Cruel and unusual: A cultural history of punishment in America.* London, UK: Pluto.

Jarvis, B. (2007). Monsters Inc.: Serial killers and consumer culture. *Crime, Media, Culture: An International Journal, 3*(3), 326–344.

Jefferson, T. (2002). For a psychosocial criminology. In K. Carrington & R. Hogg (Eds.), *Critical criminology: Issues, debates, challenges.* Cullompton, UK: Willan.

Jenkins, P. (1992). *Intimate enemies: Moral panics in contemporary Great Britain.* New York, NY: Aldine de Gruyter.

Jenkins, P. (1994). *Using murder: The social construction of serial homicide.* New York, NY: Aldine de Gruyter.

Jenkins, P. (2001). *Beyond tolerance: Child pornography on the Internet.* New York, NY: New York University Press.

Jenkins, P. (2009). Failure to launch: Why do some social issues fail to detonate moral panics? *British Journal of Criminology, 49*(1), 35–47.

Jewkes, Y. (2002). *Captive audience: Media, masculinity and power in prisons.* Cullompton, UK: Willan.

Jewkes, Y. (2003a). *Dot.cons: Crime, deviance and identity on the Internet.* Cullompton, UK: Willan.

Jewkes, Y. (2003b). Policing the Net: Crime, regulation and surveillance in cyberspace. In Y. Jewkes (Ed.), *Dot.cons: Crime, deviance and identity on the Internet.* Cullompton, UK: Willan.

Jewkes, Y. (2007). *Crime online.* Cullompton, UK: Willan.

Jewkes, Y. (2008). Offending media: The social construction of offenders, victims and the probation service. In S. Green, E. Lancaster, & S. Feasey (Eds.), *Addressing offending* behaviour (pp. 58–74). Cullompton, UK: Willan.

Jewkes, Y. (2010a). The media and criminological research. In P. Davies, P. Francis, & V. Jupp (Eds.), *Doing criminological research* (2nd ed., pp. 245–261). London, UK: SAGE.

Jewkes, Y. (2010b). Much ado about nothing? Representations and realities of online soliciting of children. *Journal of Sexual Aggression, 16*(1), 5–18.

Jewkes, Y. (Ed.). (2013). *Crime online.* London, UK: Routledge.

Jewkes, Y. (2014). Punishment in black and white: Penal "hell-holes," popular media and mass incarceration. *Atlantic Journal of Communication [Special Issue on Reframing Race and Justice in the Age of Mass Incarceration], 22*(1), 42–60.

Jewkes, Y., & Andrews, C. (2005). Policing the filth: The problems of investigating online child pornography in England and Wales. *Policing & Society, 15*(1), 42–62.

Jewkes, Y., & Sharp, K. (2003). Crime, deviance and the disembodied self: Transcending the dangers of corporeality. In Y. Jewkes (Ed.), *Dot.cons: Criminal and deviant identities on the Internet.* Cullompton, UK: Willan.

Jewkes, Y., & Wykes, M. (2012). Reconstructing the sexual abuse of children: "Cyber-paeds," panic and power. *Sexualities, 15*(8), 934–952.

Jewkes, Y., & Yar, M. (Eds.). (2010). *Handbook of Internet crime.* Cullompton, UK: Willan.

Johnson, A., & Arria, M. (2016). 20 of the dumbest, most bigoted things Bill Maher has ever said. *Alternet.* Retrieved from http://www.alternet.org/media/19-dumbest-most-bigoted-things-bill-maher-has-ever-said

Katz, J. (1990). *Seductions of crime: Moral and sensual attractions in doing evil.* New York, NY: Basic Books.

Keating, M. (2002). Media most foul: Fear of crime and media. In A. Boran (Ed.), *Crime: Fear or fascination.* Chester, UK: Chester Academic Press.

Kelley, R. D. (2000). Slangin' rocks . . . Palestinian style: Dispatches from the occupied zones of North America. In *Police brutality: An anthology.* New York, NY: W. W. Norton.

Kennedy, H. (1992). *Eve was framed.* London, UK: Chatto & Windus.

Kidd-Hewitt, D., & Osborne, R. (Eds.). (1995). *Crime and the media: The post-modern spectacle.* London, UK: Pluto.

Kitzinger, J. (1999). The ultimate neighbour from hell? Stranger danger and the media framing of paedophiles. In B. Franklin (Ed.), *Social policy, the media and misrepresentation* (pp. 207–221). London, UK: Routledge.

Klinkenborg, V. (2003). Editorial observer; Trying to measure the amount of information that humans create. *New York Times.* Retrieved from http://www.nytimes.com/2003/11/12/opinion/editorial-observer-trying-measure-amount-information-that-humans-create.html

Klockars, C. B. (1980). The Dirty Harry problem. *Annals of the American Academy of Political and Social Science, 452*(1), 33–47.

Knopf, T. (1970, Spring). Media myths on violence. *Columbia Journalism Review,* pp. 17–18.

Koskela, H. (2006). "The other side of surveillance": Webcams, power and agency. In D. Lyon (Ed.), *Theorizing surveillance: The panopticon and beyond* (pp. 163–181). Cullompton, UK: Willan.

Kotulak, R. (1980, February 20). The zombie murderers. *Montreal Gazette,* p. 94.

Krutnik, F. (1991). In a lonely street: Genre, film noir, masculinity. London, UK: Routledge.

Lacey, N. (1995). Contingency and criminalization. In I. Loveland (Ed.), *Frontiers of criminality.* London, UK: Sweet & Maxwell.

Landry, D. (2009). Faux science and the social construction of a risk society: A Burkean engagement with the CSI debates. *Journal of the Institute of Justice and International Studies, 9,* 145.

Langford, B. (2005). *Film genre: Hollywood and beyond.* Edinburgh, UK: Edinburgh University Press.

Langman, L. (1992). Neon cages: Shopping for subjectivity. In R. Shields (Ed.), *Lifestyle shopping: The subject of consumption.* London, UK: Routledge.

Larke, G. S. (2003). Organized crime: Mafia myths in film and television. In P. Mason (Ed.), *Criminal visions: Media representations of crime and justice* (pp. 116–132). Cullompton, UK: Willan.

Lauer, J. (2005). Driven to extremes: Fear of crime and the rise of the sport utility vehicle in the United States. *Crime, Media, Culture: An International Journal, 1*(2), 149–168.

Lawrence, W. (2007). Matt Damon: "Jason Bourne has done so much for me." *The Telegraph.* Retrieved from http://www.telegraph.co.uk/culture/film/starsandstories/3667144/Matt-Damon-Jason-Bourne-has-done-so-much-for-me.html

Lea, J., & Young, J. (1984). *What is to be done about law and order?* Harmondsworth, UK: Penguin.

Leacock, V., & Sparks, R. (2002). Riskiness and at-risk-ness: Some ambiguous features of the current penal landscape. In N. Gray, J. Laing, & L. Noaks (Eds.), *Criminal justice, mental health and the politics of risk* (pp. 199–218). London: UK: Cavendish.

Le Bon, G. (1960). *The crowd: A study of the popular mind.* New York, NY: Viking. (Original work published 1895)

Lee, M., & McGovern, A. (2014). *Policing and media: Public relations, simulations and communications.* London, UK: Routledge.

Legum, J. (2015, June 17). Local homeowners defend Texas cops who brutalized black teens at pool party. *ThinkProgress.* Retrieved from https://medium.com/m/global-identity?redirectUrl=https://thinkprogress.org/local-homeowners-defend-texas-cops-who-brutalized-black-teens-at-pool-party-8933617ca43c

Leitch, T. (2002). *Crime films.* Cambridge, UK: Cambridge University Press.

Lemert, E. (1951). *Social pathology: A systematic approach to the theory of sociopathic behaviour.* New York, NY: McGraw-Hill.

Lempert, M. (2013). Jodi Arias trial: Image consultant says Valley woman uses "best tricks" to portray innocence. *ABC15.* Retrieved from http://www.abc15.com/news/region-phoenix-metro/central-phoenix/image-consultant-says-jodi-arias-uses-best-tricks-to-portray-innocence www.abc15.com

Lexis Nexis Risk Solutions. (2012). *Survey of law enforcement personnel and their use of social media in investigations.* Irvine, CA: Author.

LIFE Magazine. The big snoop (1966, May 20). New York: author.

Linnemann, T. (2013). Governing through meth: Local politics, drug control and the drift toward securitization. *Crime, Media, Culture: An International Journal, 9*(1), 38–60.

Linnemann, T. (2015). Capote's ghosts: Violence, media and the spectre of suspicion. *British Journal of Criminology, 55*(3), 514–533.

Linnemann, T. (2017). Proof of death: Police power and the visual economies of seizure, accumulation and trophy. *Theoretical Criminology, 21*(1), 57–77.

Linnemann, T., Hanson, L., & Williams, L. S. (2013). "With scenes of blood and pain": Crime control and the punitive imagination of The Meth Project. *British Journal of Criminology, 53*(4), 605–623.

Linnemann, T., & Kurtz, D. L. (2014). Beyond the ghetto: Police power, methamphetamine and the rural war on drugs. *Critical Criminology, 22*(3), 339–355.

Linnemann, T., Wall, T., & Green, E. (2014). The walking dead and killing state: Zombification and the normalization of police violence. *Theoretical Criminology, 18*(4), 506–527.

Lloyd, A. (1995). *Doubly deviant, doubly damned: Society's treatment of violent women.* Harmondsworth, UK: Penguin.

Loader, I. (1997). Policing and the social: Questions of symbolic power. *British Journal of Sociology, 48*(1), 1–18.

Lombroso, C., & Ferrero, W. (1895). *The female offender.* London, UK: Unwin.

London, S. (n.d.). How the media frames political issues. Retrieved from http://www.scottlondon.com/reports/frames.html

Lowenstein, A. (2005). *Shocking representation: Historical trauma, national cinema, and the modern horror film.* New York, NY: Columbia University Press.

Lyon, D. (2003). Surveillance as social sorting: Computer codes and mobile bodies. In D. Lyon (Ed.), *Surveillance as social sorting: Privacy, risk and digital discrimination* (pp. 13–30). London, UK: Routledge.

Lyon, D. (2006). The search for surveillance theories. In D. Lyon (Ed.), *Theorizing surveillance: The panopticon and beyond* (pp. 3–20). Cullompton, UK: Willan.

Lyon, D. (2007). *Surveillance studies: An overview.* Cambridge, UK: Polity Press.

MacKay, C. (1956). *Extraordinary popular delusions and the madness of crowds.* New York, NY: Harmony Books. (Original work published 1841)

Macnab, G. (2009, June 11). The Taking of Pelham 123—Why remake a seventies classic? Independent. Retrieved from http://www.independent.co.uk/arts-entertainment/films/features/the-taking-of-pelham-123-why-remake-a-seventies-classic-1702936.html

Mander, J. (1980). *Four arguments for the elimination of television.* New York, NY: Harvester.

Mann, M. (Producer & Director). (1995). *Heat*. [Motion picture] United States: Warner Bros.

Manning, P. (2001). *News and news sources: A critical introduction*. London, UK: SAGE.

Marez, C. (2004). *Drug wars: The political economy of narcotics*. Minneapolis: University of Minnesota Press.

Marx, G. T. (1995). Electric eye in the sky: Some reflections on the new surveillance and popular culture. In J. Ferrell & C. R. Sanders (Eds.), *Cultural criminology* (pp. 195–218). Boston, MA: Northeastern University Press.

Marx, G. T. (2002). What's new about the "new surveillance"? Classifying for change and continuity. *Surveillance & Society, 1*(1), 9–29.

Mason, D., Button, G., Lankshear, G., & Coats, S. (2000). *On the poverty of a priorism: Technology, surveillance in the workplace and employee responses*. Unpublished manuscript, University of Plymouth, Plymouth, UK.

Mason, P. (2003a). (Ed.). *Criminal visions: Media representations of crime and justice*. Cullompton, UK: Willan.

Mason, P. (2003b). The screen machine: Cinematic representations of prison. In P. Mason (Ed.), *Criminal visions: Media representations of crime and justice* (pp. 278–297). Cullompton, UK: Willan.

Mason, P. (2006). (Ed.). *Captured by the media: Prison discourse in popular culture*. Cullompton, UK: Willan.

Mason, P. (2008). Entries in Y. Jewkes & J. Bennett (Eds.), *Dictionary of prisons and punishment*. Cullompton, UK: Willan.

Mathiesen, T. (1997). The viewer society: Michel Foucault's "panopticon" revisited. *Theoretical Criminology, 1*(2), 215–234.

Mathiesen, T. (2001). Television, public space and prison population: A commentary on Mauer and Simon. *Punishment & Society, 3*(1), 35–42.

Mathiesen, T. (2013). *Towards a surveillant society: The rise of surveillance systems in Europe*. Hook, Hampshire, UK: Waterside Press.

Matza, D. (1964). *Delinquency and drift*. New York, NY: Wiley.

Mawby, R. C. (2002). *Policing images: Policing, communication and legitimacy*. Cullompton, UK: Willan.

Mawby, R. C. (2010). Police corporate communications, crime reporting and the shaping of policing news. *Policing & Society, 20*(1), 124–139.

Mawby, R. (2013). *Policing images*. Cullompton, UK: Willan.

McCahill, M. (2002). *The surveillance web: The rise of visual surveillance in an English city*. Cullompton, UK: Willan.

McCahill, M. (2003). Media representations of surveillance. In P. Mason (Ed.), *Criminal visions: Media representations of crime and justice*. Cullompton, UK: Willan.

McCahill, M. (2013). *The surveillance web*. New York, NY: Routledge.

McChesney, R. (1999). *Rich media, poor democracy*. New York, NY: New Press.

McLean, G. (2003, July 30). Family fortunes. *The Guardian*. Retrieved from https://www.theguardian.com/world/2004/sep/25/2020.madeleinebunting

McNair, B. (1998). *The sociology of journalism*. London, UK: Arnold.

McRobbie, A., & Thornton, S. (1995). Rethinking "moral panic" for multi-mediated social worlds. *British Journal of Sociology, 46*(4), 559–574.

McVeigh, T. (2001, May 6). The McVeigh letters: Why I bombed Oklahoma. *The Guardian*. Retrieved from https://www.theguardian.com/world/2001/may/06/mcveigh.usa

Merton, R. K. (1938). Social structure and anomie. *American Sociological Review, 3*, 672–682.

Millbank, J. (1996). From butch to butcher's knife: Film, crime and lesbian sexuality. *Sydney Law Review, 18*(4), 451–473.

Miller, B. (2013). Lance Armstrong says reality is uncomfortable for many. *USA Today*. Retrieved from https://www.usatoday.com/story/sports/cycling/2013/07/22/lance-armstrong-reality-uncomfortable/2576417/

Miller, V. (2010). The Internet and everyday life. In Y. Jewkes & M. Yar (Eds.), *Handbook of Internet crime* (pp. 67–87). Cullompton, UK: Willan.

Minsky, R. (1998). *Psychoanalysis and culture: Contemporary states of mind*. Cambridge, UK: Polity Press.

Mokrzycki, P. (2015). Lost in the heartland: Childhood, region, and Iowa's missing paperboys. *Annals of Iowa, 74*(1), 29–70.

Monahan, T., & Wall, T. (2002). Somatic surveillance: Corporeal control through information networks. *Surveillance and Society, 4*(3).

Moore, M. (2002). *Bowling for Columbine* [Film]. United States: United Artists/Alliance Atlantis.

Morley, D. (1992). *Television audiences and cultural studies*. London, UK: Routledge.

Morris, A. (1987). *Women, crime and criminal justice*. Oxford, UK: Blackwell.

Morris, A., & Wilczynski, A. (1993). Rocking the cradle: Mothers who kill their children. In H. Birch (Ed.), *Moving targets: Women, murder and representation* (pp. 198–217). London, UK: Virago.

Morris, S., & al Yafai, F. (2003, July 17). Girl flies home to family as US marine arrested in Germany. *The Guardian*. Retrieved from https://www.theguardian.com/uk/2003/jul/17/childprotection.society

Morrison, B. (1997). *As if*. London, UK: Granta.

Morrissey, B. (2003). *When women kill: Questions of agency and subjectivity*. London, UK: Routledge.

Mulgan, G. (1989, March 18–25). A tale of two cities. *Marxism Today*, pp. 18–25.

Muncie, J. (1999). Exorcising demons. In B. Franklin (Ed.), Social policy, the media and misrepresentation (pp. 174–187). New York, NY: Routledge.

Muncie, J. (2001). *Youth and crime: A critical introduction*, London, UK: SAGE.

Muncie, J. (2009). *Youth and crime: A critical introduction* (3rd ed.). London, UK: SAGE.

Mythen, G., & Walklate, S. (2006). Communicating the terrorist risk: Harnessing a culture of fear? *Crime Media Culture: An International Journal, 2*(2), 123–142.

Narey, M. (2002). Human rights, decency and social exclusion. *Prison Service Journal, 142*, 25–28.

National Conference of State Legislatures. (2017). *Juvenile age of jurisdiction and transfer to adult court laws*. Retrieved from http://www.ncsl.org/research/civil-and-criminal-justice/juvenile-age-of-jurisdiction-and-transfer-to-adult-court-laws.aspx

Naylor, B. (2001). Reporting violence in the British print media: Gendered stories. *Howard Journal, 40*(2), 180–194.

Nelkin, D., & Andrews, L. (2003). Surveillance creep in the genetic age. In D. Lyon (Ed.), *Surveillance as social sorting* (pp. 94–110). London, UK: Routledge.

Nellis, M. (1982). Notes on the American prison film. In M. Nellis & C. Hale (Eds.), *The prison film*. London, UK: RAP.

Nellis, M. (2006). Future punishment in American science fiction films. In P. Mason (Ed.), *Criminal visions: Media representations of crime and justice*. Cullompton, UK: Willan.

Nellis, M., & Hale, C. (Eds.). (1982). *The prison film*. London, UK: RAP.

Neocleous, M. (2000). *The fabrication of social order: A critical theory of police power*. London, UK: Pluto Press.

Neocleous, M. (2016). *The universal adversary: Security, capital and "the enemies of all mankind."* New York, NY: Routledge.

New York State Division of Parole. (2006). New York State Division of Parole announces Operation Halloween: Zero Tolerance [Press release]. Retrieved from http://www.doccs.ny.gov/PressRel/2006/CS_Operation_Halloween.html

Newburn, T., & Jones, T. (2005). Symbolic politics and penal populism: The long shadow of Willie Horton. *Crime, Media, Culture: An International Journal, 1*(1), 72–87.

Norris, C. (2003). From personal to digital: CCTV, the panopticon, and the technological mediation of suspicion and social control. In D. Lyon (Ed.), *Surveillance as social sorting: Privacy, risk and digital discrimination* (pp. 249–281). London, UK: Routledge.

Norris, C., & Armstrong, G. (1999). *The maximum surveillance society: The rise of CCTV*. Oxford, UK: Berg.

Oakley, A. (1986). *From here to maternity: Becoming a mother*. Harmondsworth, UK: Penguin.

Ordoña, M. (2009). "Taking of Pelham 1 2 3" stars Travolta, Denzel. *SFgate.com*. Retrieved from http://www.sfgate.com/entertainment/article/Taking-of-Pelham-1-2-3-stars-Travolta-Denzel-3228679.php

O'Rourke, S. (2011, November 2). NOW silent on Occupy Wall St sex assaults. *Fox News*. Retrieved from http://nation.foxnews.com/wall-street-protests/2011/11/02/now-silent-occupy-wall-st-sex-assaults

Osborne, R. (1995). Crime and the media: From media studies to postmodernism. In D. Kidd-Hewitt & R. Osborne (Eds.), *Crime and the media: The postmodern spectacle*. London, UK: Pluto.

Osborne, R. (2002). *Megawords*. London, UK: SAGE.

O'Sullivan, T., & Jewkes, Y. (Eds.). (1997). *The media studies reader*. London, UK: Arnold.

Oz, M. (2011, May 29). Bath salts: Evil lurking in your corner store. *Time Magazine*. Retrieved from http://content.time.com/time/magazine/article/0,9171,2065249,00.html

Paglen, T. (2016). Invisible images (Your pictures are looking at you). *New Inquiry*. Retrieved from https://thenewinquiry.com/invisible-images-your-pictures-are-looking-at-you/

Parker, K. (2012). The boomerang generation: Feeling OK about living with Mom and Dad. Retrieved from Pew Research Center: Social & Demographic Trends website: http://www.pewsocialtrends.org/files/2012/03/PewSocialTrends-2012-BoomerangGeneration.pdf

Parker, M. (2009a). Tony Soprano on management: The Mafia and organizational excellence. *Journal of Cultural Economy, 2*(3), 379–392.

Parker, M. (2009b). Pirates, merchants and anarchists: Representations of international business. *Management and Organizational History, 4*(2), 167–185.

Parker, M. (2012). *Alternative business: Outlaws, crime and culture.* London, UK: Routledge.

Pearson, G. (1983). *Hooligan: A history of respectable fears.* Basingstoke, UK: Macmillan.

Pearson, P. (1998). *When she was bad: How and why women get away with murder.* Toronto, Ontario, Canada: Random.

Peelo, M. (2006). Framing homicide narratives in newspapers: Mediated witness and the construction of virtual victimhood. *Crime, Media, Culture: An International Journal, 2*(2), 159–175.

Perry, B. (2001). *In the name of hate: Understanding hate crimes.* New York, NY: Routledge.

Perry, T., Andrews, T. M., & Berman, M. (2016, September 28).

Police fatally shoot black man they say took "shooting stance" in San Diego suburb, sparking protests. *Washington Post.* Retrieved from https://www.washingtonpost.com/news/morning-mix/wp/2016/09/28/police-shoot-black-man-in-san-diego-suburb-sparking-protests-circumstances-remain-unclear/?utm_term=.180176d2941b

Petley, J. (1997). In defence of video nasties. In T. O'Sullivan & Y. Jewkes (Eds.), *The media studies reader.* London, UK: Arnold.

Phillips, T. (2010, July 27). Wallace Souza, Brazilian TV host who murders to boost ratings, found dead. *The Guardian.* Retrieved from https://www.theguardian.com/world/2010/jul/27/wallace-souza-brazil-tv-dies

Plantinga, C. (1998). Spectacles of death: Clint Eastwood and violence in "Unforgiven." *Cinema Journal, 37*(2), 65–83.

Platt, A. M. (2009). *The child savers: The invention of delinquency.* Seattle, WA: Rutgers University Press.

Plunkett, J. (2013, February 22). Jimmy Savile case: Jeremy Paxman's view. *The Guardian.* Retrieved from http://www.theguardian.com/media/2013/feb/22/jeremy-paxman-on-jimmy-savile

Polk, K. (1993). Homicide: Women as offenders. In P. Easteal & S. McKillop (Eds.), *Women and the law.* Canberra, Australia: Australian Institute of Criminology.

Pollak, O. (1961). *The criminality of women* (2nd ed.). New York, NY: Perpetua. (First edition published 1950)

Poster, M. (1990). *The mode of information.* Chicago, IL: University of Chicago Press.

Pratt, J. (2002). *Punishment and civilization: Penal tolerance and intolerance in modern society.* Thousand Oaks, CA: SAGE.

Pratt, J. (2007). *Penal populism.* London, UK: Routledge.

Presdee, M. (1986). *Agony or ecstasy: Broken transitions and the new social state of working-class youth in Australia.* South Australian Centre for Youth Studies Occasional Paper.

Presdee, M. (2000). *Cultural criminology and the carnival of crime.* London, UK: Routledge.

Presdee, M. (2011). *Burning issues: Young people and the fascination for fire.* Retrieved from http://www.culturalcriminology.org/papers/presdee-fire.pdf

Punch, M. (1996). *Dirty business: Exploring corporate misconduct.* London, UK: SAGE.

Qi, M., Wang, Y., & Xu, R. (2009). Fighting cybercrime: Legislation in China. *International Journal of Electronic Security and Digital Forensics, 2*(2), 219–227.

Quigley, R. (2013, October 2). Toddler-killing mom Susan Smith "paid off fellow inmate to play guard so she could enjoy lesbian romps with prison girlfriend in cells, closets and even the FREEZER." *Daily Mail.* Retrieved from http://www.dailymail.co.uk/news/article-2441945/Susan-Smith-paid-fellow-inmate-play-guard-enjoy-lesbian-romps-prison-girlfriend.html

Rafter, N. (2000). *Shots in the mirror: Crime films and society.* Oxford, UK: Oxford University Press.

Rafter, N. H. (2006). *Shots in the mirror: Crime films and society* (2nd. ed.). New York, NY: Oxford University Press.

Rafter, N. (2007). Crime film and criminology: Recent sex-crime movies. *Theoretical Criminology, 11*(3), 403–420.

Rafter, N. (2014). Introduction. In special issue on visual culture and the iconography of crime and punishment. *Theoretical Criminology, 18*(3), 127–133.

Rayner, J. (2003). Masculinity, morality and action: Michael Mann and the heist movie. In P. Mason (Ed.), *Criminal visions: Media representations of crime and justice.* Cullompton, UK: Willan.

Reagan, R. (1982, September 11). Radio address to the nation on crime and criminal justice reform. Retrieved from The American Presidency Project website: http://www .presidency.ucsb.edu/ws/?pid=42952

Redmon, D. (2015). Documentary criminology: Expanding the criminological imagination with "Mardi Gras—Made in China" as a case study (23 minutes). *Societies, 5*(2), 425–441.

Regan, P. M. (1996). Genetic testing and workplace surveillance: Implications for privacy. In D. Lyon & E. Zureik (Eds.), *Computers, surveillance and privacy* (pp. 21–46). Minneapolis: University of Minnesota Press.

Reinarman, C., & Levine, H. G. (1997). *Crack in America: Demon drugs and social justice.* Oakland, CA: University of California Press.

Reiner, R. (2001, Spring). The rise of virtual vigilantism: Crime reporting since World War II. *Criminal Justice Matters, 43,* 4–5.

Reiner, R., Livingstone, S., & Allen, J. (2001). Casino culture: Media and crime in a winner–loser society. In K. Stenson & R. R. Sullivan (Eds.), *Crime, risk and justice: The politics of crime control in liberal democracies.* Cullompton, UK: Willan.

Ronson, J. (2009, August 1). Gary McKinnon: Pentagon hacker's worst nightmare comes true. *The Guardian.* Retrieved from http://www.guardian .co.uk/world/2009/aug/01/gary-mckinnon-extradition-nightmare

Roshier, B. (1973). The selection of crime news by the press. In S. Cohen & J. Young (Eds.), *The manufacture of news* (pp. 28–39). London, UK: Constable.

Ross, V. (2014). Forget fingerprints: Law enforcement DNA databases poised to expand. *PBS.org.* Retrieved from http://www.pbs.org/wgbh/nova/next/body/dna-databases/

Sacco, Vincent F. (2005). When crime waves. Thousand Oaks, CA: SAGE.

Sandberg, S., Oksanen, A., Berntzen, L. E., & Kiilakoski, T. (2014). Stories in action: The cultural influences of school shootings on the terrorist attacks in Norway. *Critical Studies on Terrorism, 7*(2), 277–296.

Schechter, D. (2003). How media has changed since "the day that changed everything." *Cold Type.* Retrieved from http://www.coldtype.net/Assets/danny/DS.9–11.pdf

Scherick, E. J. (Producer) & Sargent, J. (Director). (1974). *The taking of Pelham One Two Three* [Motion picture]. United States: Pallomar Pictures.

Schlesinger, P., & Tumber, H. (1994). *Reporting crime: The media politics of criminal justice.* Oxford, UK: Clarendon.

Schmid, D. (1995). Imagining safe urban space: The contribution of detective fiction to radical geography. *Antipode, 27*(3), 247–269.

Schnur, A. C. (1958). The new penology: Fact or fiction? *Journal of Criminal Law, Criminology and Police Science, 49*(4): 331–334.

Scraton, P. (2002). The demonisation, exclusion and regulation of children: From moral panic to moral renewal. In A. Boran (Ed.), *Crime: Fear or fascination* (pp. 9–39). Chester, UK: Chester Academic Press.

Scripps Howard News Service. (2005, December 2). News coverage ignoring missing minority children. *Gainesville Sun.* Retrieved from http://www.gainesville.com/news/20051202/news-coverage-ignoring-missing-minority-children

Seltzer, M. (1998). *Serial killers: Death and life in America's wound culture.* New York, NY: Psychology Press.

Sharrett, C. (2012). Jack Webb and the vagaries of right-wing TV entertainment. *Cinema Journal, 51*(4), 165–171.

Signorielli, N. (1990). Television's mean and dangerous world: A continuation of the cultural indicators project. In N. Signorielli & M. Morgan (Eds.), *Cultivation analysis: New directions in media effects research.* Newbury Park, CA: SAGE.

Silverman, J., & Wilson, D. (2002). *Innocence betrayed: Paedophilia, the media and society.* Cambridge, UK: Polity.

Simon, J. (1997). Governing through crime. In L. Friedman & G. Fisher (Eds.), *The crime conundrum: Essays on criminal justice* (pp. 171–189). Boulder, CO: Westview Press.

Simon, J. (2009, November 27). *Governing through crime.* Paper presented to Architecture and Justice conference, University of Lincoln, Lincoln, NE.

Smart, C. (2013). *Women, crime and criminology: A feminist critique.* New York, NY: Routledge.

Smith, J. (1997). *Different for girls: How culture creates women.* London, UK: Chatto & Windus.

Smith, R. (2010). Identity theft and fraud. In Y. Jewkes & M. Yar (Eds.), *Handbook of Internet crime.* Cullompton, UK: Willan.

Smith, S. J. (1984). Crime in the news. *British Journal of Criminology, 24*(3).

Snyder, G. J. (2011). *Graffiti lives: Beyond the tag in New York's urban underground.* New York, NY: New York University Press.

Soothill, K., & Walby, S. (1991). *Sex crime in the news.* London, UK: Routledge.

Sounes, H. (1995). *Fred and Rose.* London, UK: Warner Books.

South, N., & Brisman, A. (2013). (Eds.). *Routledge international handbook of green criminology.* London, UK: Routledge.

Sparks, R. (1992). *Television and the drama of crime: Moral tales and the place of crime in public life.* Buckingham, UK: Open University Press.

Sparks, R. (1996). Masculinity and heroism in the Hollywood "Blockbuster": The culture industry and contemporary images of crime and law enforcement. *British Journal of Criminology, 36*(3), 348–360.

Spillius, A. (2009, October 5). Barack Obama cancels meeting with Dalai Lama "to keep China happy." *The Telegraph.* Retrieved from http://www.telegraph.co.uk/news/worldnews/barackobama/6262938/Barack-Obama-cancels-meeting-with-Dalai-Lama-to-keep-China-happy.html

Stalder, F., & Lyon, D. (2003). Electronic identity cards and social classification. In D. Lyon (Ed.), *Surveillance as social sorting: Privacy, risk and digital discrimination* (pp. 77–93). London, UK: Routledge.

Stenson, K. (2001). The new politics of crime control. In K. Stenson & R. R. Sullivan (Eds.), *Crime, risk and justice: The politics of crime control, in liberal democracies* (pp. 15–28). Cullompton, UK: Willan.

Stillman, S. (2007). "The missing white girl syndrome": Disappeared women and media activism. *Gender and Development, 15*(3), 491–502.

Stokes, E. (2000). Abolishing the presumption of *doli incapax:* Reflections on the death of a doctrine. In J. Pickford (Ed.), *Youth Justice: Theory and Practice,* London, UK: Cavendish.

Stults, B. J., & Baumer, E. P. (2007). Racial context and police force size: Evaluating the empirical validity of the minority threat perspective. *American Journal of Sociology, 113*(2), 507–546.

Surette, R. (1994). Predator criminals as media icons. In G. Barak (Ed.), *Media, process, and the social construction of crime.* New York, NY: Garland.

Surette, R. (1998). *Media, crime and criminal justice.* Belmont, CA: West/Wadsworth.

Szoldra, P. (2014, June 7). Snowden: Here's everything we've learned in one year of unprecedented top-secret leaks. *Business Insider.* Retrieved from http://www.businessinsider.com/snowden-leaks-timeline-2014-6

Taylor, I., Walton, P., & Young, J. (1973). *The new criminology: For a social theory of deviance.* London, UK: Routledge & Kegan Paul.

Taylor, P. A. (2003). Maestros or misogynists? Gender and the social construction of hacking. In Y. Jewkes (Ed.), *Dot.cons: Crime, deviance and identity on the Internet* (pp. 126–146). Cullompton, UK: Willan.

Thompson, J. B. (2005). The new visibility. *Theory, Culture and Society, 22*(6), 31–51.

Thomson, K. (1998). *Moral panics.* London, UK: Routledge.

Thorne, B. (2009). The *Seven Up!* films: Connecting the personal and the sociological. *Ethnography, 10*(3), 327–340.

Tierney, J. (1996). *Criminology: Theory and context.* Harlow, UK: Pearson.

Tombs, S., & Whyte, D. (2007). *Safety crimes.* Cullompton, UK: Willan.

Turner, J. (2015). Seeing like an Orientalist state: The three deaths of Neda Agha-Soltan. *Critical Criminology, 23*(1), 85–103.

Ulaby, N. (2011, August 18). On location: The frozen Ozarks of "Winter's Bone." *NPR.org.* Retrieved from http://www.npr.org/2011/08/18/139753185/on-location-the-frozen-ozarks-of-winters-bone

Upton, J. (2000, October 17). The evil that women do. *The Guardian,* p. 6.

U.S. Department of Justice, Community Oriented Policing Services, & Police Executive Research Forum. (2013). *Social media and tactical considerations for law enforcement.* Retrieved from http://www.police forum.org/assets/docs/Free_Online_Documents/Technology/social%20media%20and%20tactical%20considerations%20for%201aw%20enforcement%202013.pdf

U.S. Department of Justice, Office of Juvenile Justice and Delinquency Prevention. (2011). Justice Department discourages the use of "scared straight" programs. *OJJDP News @ a Glance*. Retrieved from https://www.ncjrs.gov/html/ojjdp/news_at_glance/234084/topstory.html

Valier, C. (2004). *Crime and punishment in contemporary culture*. London, UK: Routledge.

van der Ploeg, I. (2003). Biometrics and the body as information: Normative issues of the socio-technical coding of the body. In D. Lyon (Ed.), *Surveillance as social sorting: Privacy, risk and digital discrimination* (pp. 57–74). London, UK: Routledge.

Vaughan, D. R. (2004). Why *The Andy Griffith Show* is important to popular cultural studies. *Journal of Popular Culture, 38*(2), 397–423.

Verhoeven, D. (1993). Biting the hand that breeds: The trials of Tracey Wigginton. In H. Birch (Ed.), *Moving targets: Women, murder and representation*. London, UK: Virago.

Waddington, P. A. J. (1986). Mugging as a moral panic: A question of proportion. *British Journal of Sociology, 37*(2), 245–259.

Wall, D. S., & Yar, M. (2010). Intellectual property crime and the Internet: Cyber-piracy and "stealing" informational intangibles. In Y. Jewkes & M. Yar (Eds.), *Handbook of Internet crime* (pp. 603–630). Cullompton, UK: Willan.

Wall, T. (2016 *Antipode, 48*, September). Ordinary emergency: Drones, police, and geographies of legal terror. (4), 1122–1139.

Wall, T., & Linnemann, T. (2014). Staring down the state: Police power, visual economies, and the "war on cameras." *Crime, Media, Culture: An International Journal, 10*(2), 133–149.

Walters, R. (2010). *Eco-crime and genetically modified food*. London, UK: Routledge-Cavendish.

Ward Jouve, N. (1988). *The street-cleaner: The Yorkshire Ripper case on trial*. London, UK: Marion Boyars.

Watney, S. (1987). *Policing desire: Pornography, aids and the media*. London, UK: Methuen.

White, R. (2013). *Environmental harm: An eco-justice perspective*. Bristol, UK: Policy Press.

Wilczynski, A. (1997). Mad or bad? Child killers, gender and the courts. *British Journal of Criminology, 37*(3), 419–436.

Wilkins, L. (1964). *Social deviance: Social policy, action and research*. London, UK: Tavistock.

Willis, P. (2009). The accidental ethnographer and the accidental commodity. *Ethnography, 10*(3), 347–358.

Williams, M. R., Holcomb, J. E., Kovandzic, T. V., & Bullock, S. (2010). The abuse of civil asset forfeiture. Retrieved from Institute for Justice website: http://www.ij.org/images/pdf_folder/other_pubs/assetforfeituretoemail.pdf

Williams, P., & Dickinson, J. (1993). Fear of crime: Read all about it? The relationship between newspaper crime reporting and fear of crime. *British Journal of Criminology, 33*(1), 33–56.

Wilson, C. P. (2000). *Cop knowledge: Police power and cultural narrative in twentieth-century America*. Chicago, IL: University of Chicago Press.

Wilson, D., & O'Sullivan, S. (2004). *Images of incarceration: Representations of prison in film and television*. Winchester, UK: Waterside Press.

Wilson, P. (1988). Crime, violence and the media in the future. *Media Information Australia, 49*, 53–57.

Winfield, B. H., & Peng, Z. (2005). Market or party controls? Chinese media in transition. *International Communication Gazette, 67*(3), 255–270.

Worrall, A. (1990). *Offending women*. London, UK: Routledge.

Wright, A. (2013). *Monstrosity: The human monster in visual culture*. New York, NY: Palgrave Macmillan.

Wykes, M. (1998). A family affair: The British press, sex and the Wests. In C. Carter, G. Branston, & S. Allen (Eds.), *News, gender and power* (pp. 233–247). London, UK: Routledge.

Wykes, M. (2001). *News, crime and culture*. London, UK: Pluto.

Wykes, M., with Harcus, D. (2010). Cyber-terror: Construction, criminalization and control. In Y. Jewkes & M. Yar (Eds.), *Handbook of Internet crime* (pp. 214–229). Cullompton, UK: Willan.

Wykes, M., & Gunter, B. (2004). *Looks could kill: Media representation and body image*. London, UK: SAGE.

Yar, M. (2006). *Cybercrime and society*. London, UK: SAGE.

Yar, M. (2010). Public perceptions and public opinion about Internet crime. In Y. Jewkes & M. Yar (Eds.), *Handbook of Internet crime* (pp. 104–119). Cullompton, UK: Willan.

Yar, M. (2013). Cybercrime and society. Thousand Oaks, CA: SAGE.

Young, J. (1971). *The drug takers: The social meaning of drug use.* London, UK: MacGibbon and Kee/Paladin.

Young, J. (1974). Mass media, drugs and deviance. In P. Rock & M. McKintosh (Eds.), *Deviance and social control.* London, UK: Tavistock.

Young, J. (1987). The tasks facing a realist criminology. *Contemporary Crises, 11,* 337–356.

Zedner, L. (2007). Pre-crime and post-criminology? *Theoretical Criminology, 11*(2), 261–281.

Zimring, F. E. (2011). *The city that became safe: New York's lessons for urban crime and its control.* New York, NY: Oxford University Press.

Zittrain, J., & Edelman, B. (2003, March/April). Empirical analysis of Internet filtering in China. *IEEE Internet Computing.* (Also available at http://cyber.law.harvard.edu/filtering/china/)

Zureik, E. (2003). Theorizing surveillance: The case of the workplace. In D. Lyon (Ed.), *Surveillance as social sorting: Privacy, risk and digital discrimination* (pp. 31–56). London, UK: Routledge.

Index

documentary, 183–187
film noir, 175–176
genres, 172
heist films, 175–176
masculinity theme, 174–178
media criminology appeal, 195
narrative arc of, 173–174
penal spectators, 181–182
police image in, 158–161
prison film, 180–183
realism approach, 195
remake, 187–192
Robocop, 192–193
study guide, 171, 195–196
urban theme, 178–180
Western genre, 175
women's image, 177, 181
Crime news, 42, 254
Crime news production:
  agenda-setting, 43
  binary opposition, 51
  celebrity criminals, 57–58
  celebrity news stories, 69–73
  celebrity news value, 55–57
  children's image, 52–53, 56–57,
    58, 60–62, 65–66
  citizen journalism, 73–76
  conflict news value, 62–63
  conservative ideology news
    value, 66–69, 145
  crime news, 42
  ethnocentrism, 59
  fake news, 42
  framing of story, 43–44
  graphic imagery news value,
    63–65, 145
  high-status persons, 58
  individualism news value,
    51–53, 145
  moral panic model, 82–83
  murderabilia, 57–58
  news values, 43, 44, 46–69, 76,
    145–146
  newsworthiness, 43, 45–46
  newsworthiness examples,
    69–73
  political diversion news value,
    66–69

populism, 75
populist punitiveness, 67
predictability news value, 48–49,
  83, 145
proximity news value, 59–62,
  145–146
public appeal, 43
public interest, 43
racism, 68
retaliatory hate crime, 68
risk news value, 51, 53–54
sexuality news value,
  54–55, 145
simplification news value,
  49–51, 83, 145
social constructionism, 66
stranger-danger, 55
study guide, 41–42, 77–78
superpredator theory, 67
television coverage, 45
threshold news value, 47–48,
  83, 145
underlying factors of, 42–43
user-generated content
  (UGC), 73–76
victimless crimes, 67–68
violence news value, 62–63, 83
women's image, 54–55
of women's image, 54–55,
  123–143
xenophobia, 68
Crime rate:
  public opinion (1989-2011), 14*f*
  reduction in crime, 14
Crimes Against Children
  Research Center, 61
Crimes of Style (Ferrell), 35
*Criminality of Women,
  The* (Pollak), 139
Criminalization:
  defined, 254
  as theoretical perspective, 22
Criminal Minds, 45
Criminology research:
  moral panic model, 80–81, 98
  theoretical perspectives, 12–13,
    16, 19, 21–26, 29, 30,
    33–36

Critcher, Chas, 22, 24, 29, 68, 150
Critical criminology:
  defined, 254
  as theoretical perspective, 22,
    25–26
Critical criminology research:
  police image, 152–154
Crowdsource:
  Boston Marathon bombing
    (2013), 2
  defined, 254
CSI, 162
Cultural criminology:
  defined, 254
  as theoretical perspective, 33–36
Cultural research, 20, 29–30
Cyberbullying:
  defined, 254
  Internet role, 230–231
Cybercrime:
  defined, 254
  Internet role, 227, 229–230
Cyberspace:
  defined, 254
  of Internet, 228, 235–237
Cybersurveillance:
  defined, 254
  in surveillance culture, 207–210
Cyberterrorism:
  defined, 254
  Internet role, 227–229, 230
Cyberwarfare, 227–229

Dahmer, Jeffery, 57, 109
Daily Express, 80
Daily Mail, 107, 128, 232
Daily Mirror, 126–127, 234
Daily Star, 108
Daily Telegraph, 83
Damon, Matt, 177
Dangerousness:
  children's image and, 109
  defined, 254
Darrow, Clarence, 106, 251
Darwin, Anne, 138
Davis, Mike, 154–155
Dead Pool, The (1988), 160
Dean, James, 89

Matthau, Walter, 188–189
Matza, David, 80
McCann, Madeleine, 193
McKinnon, Gary, 233–234
McMartin Preschool child abuse
    case (1987), 109
McVeigh, Timothy, 5, 57, 251
Media-crime relationship, 242–246
    within criminal justice
        system, 243
    in graphic imagery, 244–245
    media audience, 243
    media text, 243
    online newspapers, 244,
        245–246
    otherness of criminals,
        246–251
    study guide, 241, 251–252
Media criminology:
    crime film appeal, 195
    defined, 257
Media effects, 13–20
Media ownership, 25
Media research:
    theoretical perspectives of,
        12–13, 21–26, 29–30
    moral panic model, 98
Mediated discourse:
    defined, 257
    theoretical perspective, 28
Media text:
    defined, 257
    media-crime relationship, 243
Mega-case:
    defined, 257
    moral panic model, 80
Megan's Law, 110
Melendez, William, 193
Mericle, Robert K., 52–53
Merkel, Angela, 199
Merton, Robert, 20
Military campaigns, 32
Military-industrial complex, 23
Ming Pao, 45
Minority Report (2002), 215
Mirror, 245
Misrepresentation:
    defined, 259
    of police image, 150–151

Mitchell, Mattie, 61
Mochrie, Robert, 144–145
Monster, 129
Moore, Gordon, 198
Moore, Tyria, 129
Moral majority:
    defined, 257
    moral panic model, 94
Moral panic model:
    characteristics of, 81–90
    children's image, 80–81, 82–83,
        85–86, 88–90, 92–94,
        96–97, 112–113, 115–117
    consensus for, 85, 95–97
    consensus issues, 95–97
    criminology research, 80–81, 98
    defined, 80, 257
    demonization of children, 86
    deviance issues, 90–91
    deviancy amplification spiral,
        83–85, 86, 90–91, 96
    labeling theory, 80
    media production of, 82–83
    media research, 98
    mega-cases, 80
    model legacy, 98–100
    model limitations, 90–97
    moral boundaries of, 85–87,
        96–97
    morality issues, 91–92
    moral majority impact, 94
    pedophiles, 96–97
    risk societies, 87–88, 94
    risk-society issues, 94
    role of authorities, 83–85
    signal crimes, 80
    of social media, 97
    social pathology perspective,
        80–81
    social reaction to, 85
    sociology research, 80–81, 98
    source issues, 94–95
    stigmatizing groups, 91
    study guide, 79, 100–101
    subcultures, 80–82
    youth subculture, 88–90, 92–94
    youth subculture issues, 92–94
Morley, David, 29–30
Moss, Kate, 58

Munchausen's syndrome by proxy
    (MSBP), 139, 142
Murderabilia:
    crime news production and,
        57–58
    defined, 257
Murdoch, Rupert, 161
Music-incited violence, 155
Myra: The Untold Story (2013), 58
MySpace, 5
Mythical monsters as women,
    135–138

Narey, Martin, 187
Narrative arc:
    of crime film, 173–174
    defined, 257
National Center for Missing and
    Exploited Children, 61
National Cybersecurity and
    Communications Integration
    Center, 233
National Enquirer, 28
National Organization of Women
    (NOW), 49
National Security Agency (NSA),
    198–200
National security card, 208
NCIS, 162
New Criminology, The (Taylor,
    Walton, Young), 22
Newsnight, 57
News values:
    celebrity status, 55–57, 145
    children's image, 65–66
    conflict, 62–63
    conservative ideology, 66–69, 145
    crime news production, 43, 44,
        46–69, 76
    criminals as celebrities, 57–58
    defined, 257
    graphic imagery, 63–65, 145
    high-status persons, 58
    individualism, 51–53, 145
    political diversion, 66–69
    predictability, 48–49, 83, 145
    proximity, 59–62, 145–146
    risk, 51, 53–54
    sexuality, 54–55, 145

defined, 260–261
Internet role, 227
of police image, 151, 157
See also Internet; Social media

Vampire killers, 137–138
Vanzetti, Bartolomeo, 1–2
Vedder, Eddie, 183
Venebles, Jon, 106–109
Victimization:
defined, 261
police image and, 151–158
Victimless crimes, 67–68
Vietnam War demonstrations
(1968), 48–49
Vigilante viewers:
Boston Marathon bombing
(2013), 2–3
defined, 261
Violence news value, 62–63, 83
Virgin or Vamp (Benedict), 124
VKontakte, 4
Voyeurism:
defined, 261
in surveillance culture, 213–215

Wahlberg, Mark, 2
Walk, The (2015), 180
Wall Street Journal, 45
Walters, John, 67
Walton, P., 22
War of the Worlds (Wells),
17–18, 88
Washington, Denzel, 188, 189
Watson, J. B., 15–16
Watts, Barrie, 129
Webb, Jack, 159–160
Weber, Max, 160
Weekly Standard, The, 67
Welles, Orson, 17–18
Wells, H. G., 17–18
Wells, William Floyd, 70–71
West, Fred, 125–126, 129
West, Rose, 125–126, 143
West of Memphis (2012), 183

Wetterling, Jacob, 110
WhatsApp, 5, 224–225
White-collar crime, 25–26, 52
Wigginton, Tracey, 127–128, 130,
137, 138
WikiLeaks, 198–199
Wikipedia, 224–225
Williams, Hannah, 62
Winter's Bone (2010), 178–179
Wiseman, Fred, 186
Witherspoon, Reese, 183
Women, Crime and Criminology
(Smart), 122
Women's image:
agency of women, 141
bad fathers, 144–145
bad mothers, 133–135
bad wives, 131–133
carceral feminism approach, 135
in crime film, 177, 181
crime news production, 54–55,
123–143
difference of offenders, 120–122
domestic violence, 132, 133,
144–145
drug abuse, 134–135
essentialism approach, 146–147
evil manipulators, 140–141
familicide, 144
family annihilation, 144
feminist perspectives, 120,
122–143
filicide, 123, 128, 133–135, 138
in heteropatriarchal culture,
127–128
homicide, 58, 125–126,
127–128, 129, 130, 137,
138, 140, 142–143,
145–146, 150, 251
hysteria, 139–140
infanticide, 133–134, 137, 138,
139, 142, 146
mythical monsters, 135–138
news values and, 124, 145–146
non-agents, 141–143

otherness of criminals, 120–122,
143–144
physical attractiveness, 129–131
in prison films, 181
prostitutes, 126–127
psychiatric disorders, 138–140
psychoanalytical perspectives,
120–122
psychosocial approach, 120
as rapists, 128–129
scopophilic desires, 138
sexual deviance, 124–129
sexuality news value, 54–55,
124–129
sexual orientation, 125–126,
127–128, 129
spousal homicide, 55, 130–133,
132, 247
study guide, 119, 145–148
unconscious fear of others, 121
vampire killer, 137–138
Workplace surveillance, 216–217,
218–219
World Anti-Doping Agency
(WADA), 233
World Trade Center bombing
(2001):
ethnocentric coverage, 59
postmodern perspective, 32–33
retaliatory hate crimes, 68
Wuornos, Aileen, 129, 138, 251

Xenophobia, 68

Yokou Tudou, 225
Young, Jock, 12, 22
Young, Russell, 58
Youth:
defined, 261
moral panic model, 88–90,
92–94
YouTube, 4, 224–225
Yukawa, Haruna, 6

Zuckerberg, Mark, 224

About the Authors

Yvonne Jewkes is research professor in criminology at the University of Brighton, UK, with special interests in the architecture and design of prisons, and use of media and digital technologies in corrections facilities. Yvonne started her career as a lecturer in media and cultural studies and, following successful completion of her PhD at the University of Cambridge (*Captive Audience: Media, Masculinity and Power in Prisons*), has spent much of her career working at the nexus of crime, punishment, media, and culture. In 2005 she was one of the Founding Editors of *Crime, Media, Culture: An International Journal* and now serves as an Associate Editor on the journal's board. She is author of the market-leading Sage textbook *Media and Crime* (2004/2015; now in its 3rd edition).

Travis Linnemann is assistant professor of justice studies at Eastern Kentucky University, in Richmond, Kentucky, USA. His research concerns police and state violence and the ways in which the wars on drugs and terror invade everyday life. He is the author of *Meth Wars: Police, Media, Power,* published by New York University Press (2016).